NICK DANZIGER'S
DANZIGER'S TRAVELS

The western part of the city was devastated. It was far
worse than any pictures I had seen of Dresden or London:
it called the total wreck of Nagasaki to mind. The great city
of Herat, which has stood for 2500 years and witnessed
the passage of Alexander the Great, Genghis Khan and
Tamerlane, is being reduced to rubble. I looked aghast at
the destruction. Twisted timber beams jutted from collapsed walls like arms reaching out for help from a buried
body. Embedded in walls were rockets, still unexploded,
their fuses clearly visible in their tail-sections. Everywhere
was the litter of modern warfare, and across it ranged the
mujahedeen, scavenging for reusable weaponry.

DANZIGER'S
TRAVELS

VINTAGE DEPARTURES

DANZIGER'S TRAVELS

Beyond Forbidden Frontiers

NICK DANZIGER

VINTAGE BOOKS

A DIVISION OF RANDOM HOUSE   NEW YORK

FIRST VINTAGE DEPARTURES EDITION, SEPTEMBER 1988

Copyright © 1987 by Nick Danziger

All rights reserved under International and Pan-American Copyright Conventions. Published in the United States by Random House, Inc., New York. Originally published, in hardcover, by Grafton Books, a Division of the Collins Publishing Group, London, in 1987.

Library of Congress Cataloging-in-Publication Data
Danziger, Nick, 1958–
[Travels]
Danziger's travels: beyond forbidden frontiers / Nick Danziger.—
1st Vintage departures ed.
p.   cm. — (Vintage departures)
ISBN 0-679-73994-7: $8.95
1. Asia—Description and travel—1951–   2. Danziger, Nick, 1958–
—Journeys—Asia.   I. Title. II. Title: Travels.
DS10.D36 1988
915'.0442—dc19

Author Photo copyright © by Nick Danziger
Manufactured in the United States of America
10 9 8 7 6 5 4 3 2 1

This book is dedicated to the many people along the way who showed me such overwhelming kindness, generosity and hospitality and without whom the journey would not have been possible.

CONTENTS

ACKNOWLEDGEMENTS

I have been helped by countless people in many countries, many of whom I cannot mention by name for fear of compromising them with the local authorities. I can only express my sorrow if anyone suffers as a consequence of the clandestine nature of my journey. May I never forget that for these peoples and lands the struggle still continues. As they are already at odds with the authorities I feel able to mention Ismail Khan of Herat, Abdul Sattar and the mujahedeen of Hauze Kerbas to whom I owe a great debt.

My journey would not have taken place without the Winston Churchill Memorial Trust, Sir Richard Vickers and in particular Miss Anne Seagrim. My sponsors Olympus Cameras and Barry Taylor, Fuji Film, Overseas Containers Ltd and the crew of the *Kowloon Bay* also provided valuable assistance.

I would like to acknowledge the selfless work of the doctors and nurses of Médecins sans Frontières, Aide Médicale and Médecins du Monde; Amnesty International and the International Red Cross.

I would like to thank my Mother and Terry for their support and for giving me the time and space to write the book. Charlie Gore for all our discussions, his inspiration and hard work on the final draft. In addition to the many students, teachers, diplomats and correspondents I would like to mention some of those who have helped me: Henri Adrien, Mark and Juttar Brayne and family, the Pashtu Service of the BBC, Alex Brodie and Anne Gibson, Charlotte Brodie, Anna Burland, Lisa Dalton and Bernie Kramer, Richard and Harry Danziger, Bruce Davidson, Alan, Juliet and Valerie at Encore, David Foreman, Juliette Fournot, Frederike Gaensslen, my grandmother, Mats Gundstrom, Lucy Matthews and Nigel Hadfield, Charles Haswell, Robin von Hoegen, Dave Kellogg, Tadashi Kondo, Teresa Kwa, Dan Law, Elizabeth Malischewski, Judy Marshall, Noo Mavroleon, Michael Simpson-Orlebar, Gail Ridgwell, Jean-José Puig, Richard Sly, Kathy Stubbs, Swire Shipping (David Ho),

John White, Joanne Wood, Sophia Woodman, Capt. David Wright.

Amy Loveday, Robert Fraser and Sam King were influential in my life and sadly have not lived to see publication of this book.

The Islamic Republic of Iran was the only one which blessed the journey with a visa. And I must mention my donkey in Afghanistan whose slowness will always linger in my memory.

Thanks are also due to Anton Gill who helped reduce my unwieldy tome into a more readable book. Jane Bentall for typing my journals and most of my manuscript. Richard Johnson, Deputy Editorial Director at Grafton Books, my agent, Mark Lucas, and the Art Department at Grafton, in particular Marianne Taylor, Ros Saunders, Maurice Robinson, Steve Abis, and also Maggie Usiskin in publicity.

I apologise for inevitable errors of omission.

MAP OF DANZIGER'S TRAVELS

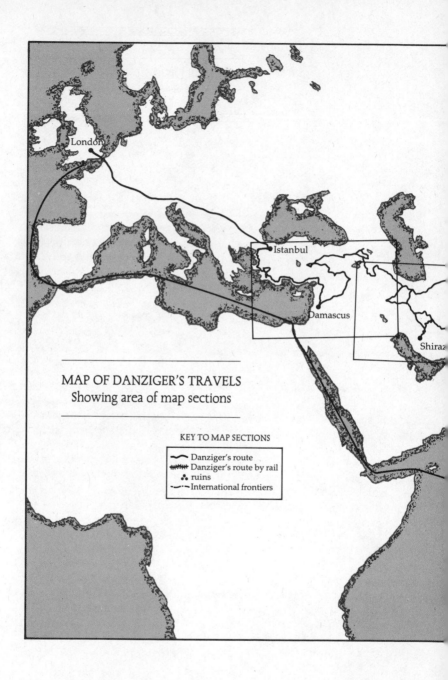

MAP OF DANZIGER'S TRAVELS
Showing area of map sections

KEY TO MAP SECTIONS

〜 Danziger's route
⌗⌗⌗ Danziger's route by rail
⁂ ruins
–·–·– International frontiers

London

Istanbul

Damascus

Shiraz

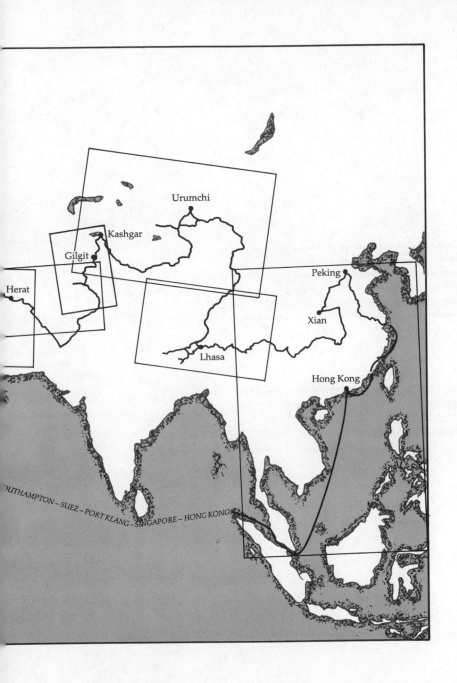

Urumchi

Kashgar

Gilgit

Herat

Peking

Xian

Lhasa

Hong Kong

SOUTHAMPTON – SUEZ – PORT KLANG – SINGAPORE – HONG KONG

So many worlds, so much to do,
So little done, such things to be.

Alfred Lord Tennyson

DANZIGER'S
TRAVELS

INTRODUCTION

'Just take a seat over there, Mr Danziger. They won't keep you long.'
I was the last to be interviewed, and although I ought to have been at least a little confident, having reached the short list, I couldn't help feeling nervous. Originally, there had been 800 applicants for the fourteen Open Category Fellowships awarded by the Winston Churchill Memorial Trust. The weeding-out process had thinned our ranks, but there was still a long way to go.

One of the secretaries handed me a slip of paper showing the seating arrangement of my interviewers, so that I'd know who was asking the question. I glanced down at the list of their names. Dame Rosemary Murray, the former President of New Hall, Cambridge, and Major-General Sir Roy Redgrave, GSOII Intelligence HQ Rhine Army headed the list. Every other name on it was just as impressive – and formidable. The minutes ticked by with agonising slowness. To stop myself fidgeting, I thought back briefly over the chain of events that had brought me to this room in London on a cold February afternoon in 1982.

I'd left Art School eighteen months before, and since then had spent a good deal of time applying for grants, fellowships and scholarships. This process had been punctuated by a successful exhibition of my work at Riverside Studios in West London, which had provided me with the means to journey to Central America. For a long time I had been fascinated by the Mayan civilisation, led there by my own art works: paintings, drawings, sculptures and constructions based on mathematics and assembled in a vast web of geometrical and architectonic patterns. From an early age I had been mesmerised by adventure and foreign travel, but it was not to the great explorers or travellers that I had looked but to Hergé's fictional hero Tintin. I sought a Central America of ancient monuments jutting out of a sea of trees and swamps, swarming with snakes, monkeys, vampire bats and hordes of insects. A continent beset by political turmoil that offered the challenges of pitting oneself against the elements, of survival, discovery and especially discovery of past and present peoples, customs, cultures and civilisations; if danger was involved it would be as a consequence rather than a prerequisite. I thought with exhilaration about the new people I would meet. For to me the essence of travel, especially to remote places, is precisely that you are on your own. There are no printed guides and maps to help you, and so the only way to see the place you are visiting is through the eyes and with the help of the people who live there. True travel doesn't just involve visiting a place, and seeing its monuments; it involves getting to know its inhabitants.

It was during my first visit to Central America that I had begun to develop the idea which formed the basis of my application to the Churchill Memorial Trust: I wanted to return to Guatemala, fell my own tree, build a dugout canoe, and in it try to retrace the trade routes of the Mayan civilisation along the rivers that cut through the jungle.

'Will you go anyway, even if you don't get a Fellowship?' the other secretary asked me, as if she'd been reading my thoughts. I was so tense that for a moment I wondered if the question might have been a ploy – a sounding-out of my resolve.

'Of course I will,' I replied, returning her smile. In truth, though, without funding my project would be impossible to realise. I put the thought to the back of my mind and tried to concentrate on what I would say to the people sitting round the table behind that polished mahogany door.

But I was too late. The door was opening.

If time passes slowly before an interview, it flies while you are being questioned. Not that it had been that unpleasant. By the end the interviewers were becoming positively friendly.

'How do you expect to obtain provisions on this river trip of yours?' Dame Rosemary asked me.

I had the answer to that one. In the best tradition of exploration, too. 'Through barter,' I said. 'I'll take a supply of beads, and buttons.'

'Then you'd better go to Woolworth's,' they advised me. 'They have a marvellous selection.'

Of course once I was out in the street again my mind, which was now racing with ideas, inevitably suggested all the answers I could have improved upon, all the opportunities for presenting my case that I had missed, and all the million and one things that I'd totally forgotten to say. The most difficult task had been convincing the Trust that my journey fulfilled the criterion that it would be of benefit to Britain. I'd explained that through documenting my journey I would hope to bring a greater richness to our society, and extend our understanding of the world – or at least, of another part of it. And I hoped that I might on my return pass on through my painting some of my impressions and experiences to others. I walked down the street wondering if that wasn't something of a long shot.

It was a month before I heard from them. I left the package on the table untouched while I ate my breakfast, looking at the WINSTON CHURCHILL MEMORIAL TRUST frankmark, and trying to prepare myself for what I was sure would be a bitter disappointment. Then it occurred to me that it was, after all, a package, not just an envelope. A 'we regret to inform you' letter wouldn't merit a *package*, surely. And I thought that after all, it's nearly always the interviews that you feel you've failed that turn out to be successes. I opened the package. I had been right. It was good news. It contained a list of the successful applicants, with their addresses and details of their projects, and a book containing all the names of past Fellows.

It was as if I had been magically transported to Central America. Although it was still the middle of winter, I dressed in my Indian light cotton outfit, put on a waistcoat, took up my machete, a relic of my last trip, and danced a victory jig.

That night I met up with some Colombian friends and we went to a Mexican restaurant to celebrate.

'Are you ready to order?' the waiter asked. He clearly didn't like the look of us.

'We'd all like beans, rice and eggs,' I said.

The dish wasn't on the menu. He pointed this out, testily. 'This is a Mexican restaurant – you must eat Mexican food.' All I could do was remind him that what we'd ordered was all most Mexicans ever ate. He couldn't deny this and went to order the food.

As this was a celebration, we managed to drink large amounts of Mezcal, the cactus-based spirit, drunk with lemon and salt, which I had come to like during my first visit to Central America. At the

3

bottom of each bottle lies a dead, pickled worm – a kind of maggot that lives in the cactus from which Mezcal is derived. Tradition has it that he who finishes the bottle must eat the worm, and tonight this dubious honour fell to me, though I could not tell you what the worm tasted like.

After the restaurant my Colombian friends dragged me off to a place they knew of in Earl's Court. I was refused entry at first, being a gringo. But my friends soon solved that problem and we danced the night away to the rattle of timbals and the pulsating rhythms of *Salsa*.

Once the hangover subsided I started to organise my journey, but as I progressed with my preparations I became aware that all was not quite as it might be. There was the American 'archaeologist' whom a contact of mine at the War Office thought might be of help to me. However he seemed less interested in the Mayas than in what I thought of Al Haig, and in the forays I had made on my last trip along the frontier between Nicaragua and Honduras. And then there was the affair of my flat.

On several occasions my flat was broken into. Whoever was responsible had rifled through everything in detail – correspondence, files, and even clothing – but nothing was ever taken. Because of this, and the lack of fingerprints, the local police quickly lost what little interest they might have had, but I was beginning to feel jumpy. I'd grown up in French Switzerland and because of my fluent French I worked part-time as an interpreter for the Metropolitan Police. Thus it was that I knew a certain three-digit number which you can use, by dialling it in conjunction with your own phone number, to check if your line is clear. It's also used by telephone engineers. When I checked my line, it wasn't clear. What *was* clear, however, was that my phone had been tapped.

I wondered who might think I was that important. After all, I was just an impoverished artist who liked to travel, and who eked out his meagre income by occasional interpreting work and by lecturing at Reading University and Chelsea School of Art. I pursued the matter through friends at Scotland Yard but finally came up against a brick wall.

'Kids looking for cigarettes,' the Deputy Assistant Commissioner told me, referring to my break-ins. 'I've had the same problem.' And the only joy I derived from my phone-tapping query was a visit from some rather irate telephone engineers, wanting to know how I knew their secret testing number. Perhaps I ought to have let the matter rest, but there was something else: I was listed in the phone book as Flat 2, but in fact I lived in Flat 4. Flat 2 had been broken into – as had all the others in the house – but after a cursory search it had been left alone. Only mine had been singled out for special treatment. And whoever was doing the break-ins was very well aware of my movements, since they knew exactly when I would be out lecturing, or engaged in my police work.

'Maybe it's some Latin American country,' suggested a counter-intelligence contact at the Yard.

'Surely not. Anyway they could hardly afford to send agents all the way over here after the likes of me.'

'Oh, no. But they could hire people over here. It's been known . . .'

If they had, I wondered what they would have made of the posters of numerous Latin American liberation movements which were affixed to my walls – for decorative rather than political reasons.

'D'you know anything about microdots?' my contact asked me.

'Not a thing.'

'I'll show you.'

I was also shown all the equipment of a recently-arrested Soviet spy – a Canadian who had posed as a western agent. I read his almost poignant final decoded message, arrested in midstream: 'Your cover has been . . .' It was of no practical use to me, for whoever had been through my flat had left no trace at all of who they might have been.

I turned for help to a friend at the Foreign Office. He promised to look into the matter for me, but when I went to see him again a week later he seemed worried. 'I'm afraid I can't tell you anything,' he said.

'You mean you haven't been able to find anything out?'

'I mean I can't comment.'

By now I was really concerned.

Meanwhile the news from Guatemala was sombre. Letters from my Indian friend Jorge were becoming increasingly pessimistic about the likelihood of my venture being successful. Guatemala was torn apart by a civil war, the consequences of which were soon to be brought home to me in a very real fashion indeed. I heard from

Miriam, another friend, that her own son had been dragged out of her house by the military and summarily executed. Then came more news, and it came at the eleventh hour. Only five days before I was due to depart Jorge informed me that the President (who was himself soon to be deposed) had rescinded the permission to travel in the interior which he had formerly granted me. Jorge added that to attempt the journey now would be suicidal.

It was the last I was to hear of Jorge.

Bitter as the disappointment was, I realised that I must change my plans. For a moment I thought I would forfeit my Fellowship, but the Trust could not have been more understanding, and gave me a year to prepare and submit an alternative plan. Various ideas presented themselves: I would go to Burma; to the South Sea islands. I thought about a journey to the Moluccas, and considered kayaking in the Falklands; but none of these quite struck the right spark with me. I knew what I wanted: something that would stretch me, mentally and physically, to the limits. I yearned for that intensity of feeling which would make each day be lived as though it was the last, full of the zest and lust for life that seem so lacking in our society. In one sense too, I needed almost to dice with death (though I have never, and would never, take an uncalculated risk), because sometimes you simply have to live on the edge to appreciate the vitality of life. People around me sometimes seek their 'highs' in other things: in fast cars, in parties, in pubbing. I find mine in my art and in travel – but I have to tell you that I also find one every other week on the terraces of Stamford Bridge. The one article of clothing that went everywhere with me on my travels was my 'You Can't Ban a Chelsea Fan' T-shirt.

It was a friend and fellow artist, Charlie Gore, who first suggested the idea of following the Marco Polo route – along the old Silk Road. I took to it at once, and the more I thought about it the better it seemed. The history of the Silk Road is fascinating, and in the Islamic art of the countries it passes through I would find many resonances with my own work – form, structure, permutations and repetitions of geometric patterns, tessellations – all worked out in a variety of materials, paint, tile, brick. The route also presented precisely the kind of challenges I was looking for. I would have to travel through countries rarely visited by westerners in recent years, and thus countries which are poorly understood by us. What's more, there was an element in it, and a large one, of my original conception for Central America: I would be tracing a trade route. The Silk Road was for centuries the great artery linking east and west, the great transporter of culture, civilisation and ideas as much as pearls and silk, cinnamon and silver. Mentally blessing Charlie for his inspiration, I started to make preparations.

I soon discovered that the name Silk Road was actually something of a misnomer, because in fact there were several roads – or, more properly, organised caravan routes. The term 'Silk Road' was only coined in the 1870s by the German geographer, Ferdinand von Richthofen. Those traders who, like Marco Polo, actually traversed its entire length were relatively few in number, and even they could never plot an exact route, for the 'Road' was infested all along its length by brigands, bandits and warlords who either preyed upon travelling merchants or taxed them heavily for crossing their territories. Some even forbade passage altogether. Despite these local irritants along the way, however, the impetus to trade stimulated merchants to seek the new markets the road opened up for them, and not only in relatively recent times. As early as the 3rd century BC the Chinese were known abroad as the Seres – Greek for 'silk people' – and in 138 BC the Emperor Wu Di sent his emissary Zhang Qian to forge trade links with the West.

The goods that were carried along the road were glass, coral, lapis lazuli, cobalt, amber, grapes, agate, wine – and also syphilis – from the west; and from the east came pomegranates, chestnuts and cotton. Animals were traded: Ferghana horses; camels; lions; peacocks; rhinoceros. Technologies were transferred: silkworm breeding, iron smelting, irrigation. European craftsmen captured in battle worked at the courts of the Mongol *khans*, and Chinese craftsmen captured by marauding Arabs set to work in Baghdad – as weavers, gold and silversmiths, and painters. The message of peace and goodwill of the Great Lord Buddha travelled along the road from Gandhara in present-day Pakistan to the Tarim Basin in China, but the art of Buddhism was influenced by the Greek soldiers who pressed far into the east following the conquests of Alexander the Great.

The routes were determined by the natural contours of the land, following rivers, picking up oases, crossing passes, skirting where possible deserts and mountain ranges. The modern traveller using them encounters barriers of a different kind. He is not stopped by sand, rock or rain, but by politics: the closed frontiers of countries which, unsure of their own internal control, wish to shut out foreign influence. Not in itself anything new, but I think in general people get on with each other if left to do so without the interference of politicians and soldiers, and for me frontiers are there to be crossed. Sadly, though, that isn't always possible, and it wasn't long before I became bogged down in political entanglements. Perhaps I should have known better than to attempt a route which crossed Soviet Central Asia to China.

At first things had looked hopeful, but the hope soon waned when officials learned that I wanted to make the whole journey overland.

'You want to cross the desert?' enquired the man at the Russian Embassy incredulously.

'Yes.'

'But you can see it from the aeroplane.'

'I'd like to take the train.' I happened to know there was a much-used line.

The man at the Russian Embassy smiled apologetically. 'There is no train,' he said. He tried to be helpful, but I had no desire to adhere to organised plans that made it impossible for me to change my itinerary or extend my stay.

Once again I had to alter my plans, but this time it wasn't a question of back to the drawing board. If I couldn't travel across Russia, then I'd take a more southerly route, through Turkey, Iran, Afghanistan and Pakistan. I could reach China that way. The conditions I set myself remained the same. I would do the journey overland, using local transport, hitching and walking. I had no desire at all to join the present trend for travelling long distances in eccentric ways, like cycling or hiking all the way. My journey would be one of discovery, and its object would be to promote greater understanding of the peoples along its route; it would not be a journey about me; it would be a journey about them.

Pakistan was the only country which showed any interest in my plans, but the tiny flame of hope which this kindled was soon extinguished by the Chinese.

'There is no point in considering your request,' they told me.
'Why?' I asked.

'Because even if you succeed in reaching Afghanistan from Iran, your chances of arriving in Pakistan alive are nil. So, you see, there is no point in considering your request.'

I knew that as far as Afghanistan was concerned there would be little to be gained from approaching the government. My best chances lay with the rebel *mujahedeen*, who controlled much of the country. With their help, I hoped to cross the mountains and deserts that make up much of the terrain there, and prove the Chinese wrong.

The Iranians rejected my proposals on several occasions, but I have long since learnt that if you want anything from officials you have to wear them out by badgering them: it's rather like a war of attrition; the trick is not to be worn out first. Finally, after numerous letters, and visits to their consulate, I was granted an audience. One of their men in London listened to me guardedly as I talked about my previous travels, about my genuine sympathy with oppressed and exploited peoples, which I understood the Iranians to have been under the Shah, about my solidarity with indigenous movements, and finally about my intention to retrace the route which had carried Islam to China.

It had been quite a speech. The official didn't say anything for some moments. He was obviously thinking things over.

'We will certainly give your request for a visa our most careful consideration, in the light of the nature of your journey,' he informed me carefully. 'But I must tell you that your stated intention to travel through to the border with Afghanistan is quite out of the question. In any case, it would be highly dangerous.'

I decided to go onto the offensive. 'But what about all your public statements of support for your Afghan Muslim brothers? Won't they ring a little hollow if you refuse to grant me access to the frontier?'

He looked uncomfortable for a moment, spreading his arms and hands in a little gesture of deprecation.

'Perhaps you are worried about possible diplomatic repercussions if I'm killed,' I said, and I saw immediately by his expression that that was indeed one of the things that was troubling him. 'If so, I'm prepared to sign a disclaimer absolving Iran from any responsibility in the event of my death.' I added, as I always do, that I would be willing to place all my photographic and written material at Iran's disposal at the end of my journey.

There was another pause for thought.

'You must write a letter,' he said at last, 'setting forth your request formally, and stating your aims.'

I breathed out in relief. 'And to whom should I address the letter?'

'To Ayatollah Khomeini.' Noticing my expression he added, 'Although of course it will actually be sent to the Ministry of Foreign Affairs.'

I left the building feeling hopeful. If only I could gain permission to enter Iran I could leave the rest to chance. With careful planning I had little doubt that I could slip across the frontier to Afghanistan without the help of another visa. Come to that, I knew it was possible to enter Iran clandestinely too, via Turkish Kurdish territory, but I'd been told that it was impossible to travel around in Iran without proper documentation. In the event, this proved to be incorrect, and I did. But that was still a long way in the future.

Concepts of time and space, and any western sense of urgency, all change radically as you progress eastwards. I hung around London, trying to keep a tight rein on my patience, as summer turned to autumn. By November 1983 I was beginning to lose hope, though my Iranian assured me when I asked him that a reply from Tehran would be forthcoming, and in all likelihood favourable. I was also encouraged by the fact that the Churchill Trust had approved my new project. However, I knew I would have to set off before too long, because by now dwindling funds had forced me to start spending the money that went with my Fellowship.

To put the time to best use I started on a regime of intensive physical training. I don't use heating and I wash habitually in cold water. But I needed to be sure that I would be able to walk or run for long distances without getting exhausted, and I needed to build up my endurance. The training started well, but was interrupted by my developing a cyst. Even this, however, brought a blessing in its wake, because the doctor friend who told me how to treat it was also able to advise me about putting together a small multi-purpose medical kit, whose contents met the approval both of the Ross Institute of Tropical Hygiene and the Hospital for Tropical Diseases.

There would be very few doctors *en route*, and although it was impossible to prepare for every eventuality, experience had taught me that certain medicines could be invaluable not only for treating oneself but also for general applications to locals who would automatically look to the western medical kit for a cure. Some of my medicines would double up to cover different maladies, and for those illnesses for which I didn't carry tablets there would be local remedies, I knew; remedies tried and tested over centuries, and usually as effective as their modern counterparts.

My preparations began to take on a momentum of their own. Equipment had to be simple, light, dependable and basic. The single most expensive item I took was a solid pair of hiking boots. These boots cost £50, and were on my feet in every imaginable terrain for most of seventeen-and-a-half months. They are still in one piece. The next item on my list was an army poncho, with a hood and made of parachute nylon. As well as being an all-over waterproof, it would double as a ground-sheet, sleeping-sack, bivouac and knapsack. *In extremis* it could even be rigged to collect rainwater. Then came a length of light, thin rope, but strong enough to tow a car, and a pair of climber's carabiners. Properly rigged I could use the rope and the carabiners for a number of purposes, from crossing a torrent to hanging my washing up to dry. A canteen came next, and a money belt made to my own design by a leatherworker friend. I am rather proud of the belt. It looks like an ordinary one, about an inch wide, but it is backed by two fine leather strips that run the length of the belt. Fastened by velcro, one strip folds over the other to form a long narrow pouch at the back, which contained my money – the last place a would-be robber would think to find it.

There were other items that also had to be carefully considered. Apart from my Swiss Army knife – the largest there is and quite indispensable – I needed another knife. Not conspicuous, and not one that could look like a weapon, but still large and strong enough to enable me to live off the land if the need arose. I needed maps, too, with enough detail to be of use, but not so much as to arouse the suspicion of the authorities if I were caught with them. Another necessary precaution was to cut the military publishing house markings off them. But I took the maps for general guidance only. The groundwork on frontiers, and where they could most easily be breached, I had already prepared in the Map Room of the Royal Geographical Society, whose map collection is the best available.

On all major journeys I always take a number of letters of recommendation with me. These are carefully worded, on headed paper, and bear as many rubber stamps and signatures as possible to give them enough weight to impress the stubbornest official and the most intractable bureaucrat. With the help of friends, and other interpreter colleagues from Scotland Yard, I was able to have these letters translated into all the major languages of the countries I would be crossing. I have to admit that I was deeply impressed by the printed Persian version, and the calligraphy of the Chinese version was a delight to the eye.

Backing up these letters was a selection of fake documents. I carried a variety of student cards, ID cards and visiting cards which conferred a variety of names and impressive professions on me. The *pièce de résistance* was a fake press card, beautifully printed, enjoining help to the bearer in five different languages, and hermetically sealed in plastic, complete with my photograph.

My preparations were complete.

There were times, of course, when I wondered what on earth I was doing all this for. I remember when I was six years old my father asked me what I wanted to be when I grew up.

'A tube train driver,' I said.

'Why?' asked my father.

'Because I want to travel.'

'Well, you won't travel far that way,' he said. 'Only from one end of the line to the other.'

Remembering this, I looked again at my projected journey. There was very little to inspire confidence in it. My friends and my family were sympathetic but doubtful. More practically, the Churchill Trust's insurance company would not insure me against death for certain sections of the journey. Gloomy as this seemed, I shrugged it off, and reflected that I had no responsibilities or dependants at home. I decided not to worry about insurance – the more so as the premium for other sections amounted to half the value of the belongings I would have with me.

There was something else which bothered me more. This was the nagging anxiety that I always felt on the brink of journeys, and it was based on superstition. I have had an inordinate amount of luck on my travels, and I was worrying that this might be the time when it would finally give out.

I was also worried that perhaps the journey wouldn't bring in the sort of adventures I anticipated, but that didn't seem very likely, given that the peoples I would be visiting had been cut off from western influence for most of their countries' histories by political, economic and political barriers. Peoples who although not nationalistic or tribal in any narrow or negative sense, nevertheless were still bound by codes of conduct so strict that the slightest deviation from them might mean exclusion from their society. I looked forward keenly to finding out how they would react to my presence among them.

One item of my equipment that I have not mentioned yet is my cameras. I am not a professional photographer, but of course as an artist I use cameras frequently. Olympus and Fuji had provided me with cameras and film, and I realised that my photographic record would form a substantial part of the story of my journey. However, I have found that a camera distances you from the people you are among, at worst singling you out as a tourist; and I feel that photographing people especially makes them into objects of curiosity and somehow robs them, and me, of dignity. The compromise I reached was never to carry my cameras openly. I hid them in a small khaki bag. And I remained wary of taking photos of people, often envying other travellers who were less fastidious.

In fact, as things turned out, keeping any kind of record at all at times became impossible. I was to experience circumstances where even sketching and making notes might have been a fatal mistake, especially when travelling in Afghanistan disguised as a *mujahed*. As for being accepted by the people of my host countries, cameras and notebook apart, I found that the secret lay less in what one had than in how one behaved.

My other responsibility was towards the friends and family I'd be leaving behind, especially my mother. My only hope was that if I died the fact that I had already led a very full life, following my own chosen paths, would be a consolation to them.

———

There was still no answer from Tehran, and so I set a departure date anyway. Come what may, I would leave in April (1984). To delay longer would have seriously affected my schedule, for I hoped to cross the high passes from Pakistan into China before winter closed them.

I'd been to the Iranian Consulate in February.

'Another month. Just wait one more month, Mr Danziger. I assure you . . .'

A month later there was still no news of my visa.

'I'm going to have to leave, with or without it,' I told my Iranian official, explaining my reasons.

'A week,' he said, hopefully. But I had made all my preparations, and the moment of no return had arrived. I had left my flat, and said most of my goodbyes. All that was left was to take my leave of my sponsors at the Churchill Trust, who had already generously granted me additional funds for my journey, although I knew that the Director-General, Sir Richard Vickers, was highly sceptical of my chances of success. The person I most wanted to say goodbye to there was Miss Seagrim, the secretary who had supported me loyally from the beginning, and without whose help within the organisation I might well never have got the extra funding I needed to make my trip a reality.

I still hadn't got my Iranian visa, but I now had just under a thousand pounds in my pocket to reach Peking.

I paid my last visit to the Iranian Consulate on Monday, 9 April. It was a pretty desperate last visit, too, for I was leaving by train from Victoria Station an hour later. As usual there was pandemonium, not helped by the interminable time it took for each visitor to pass through the security doors before being allowed to enter a minute, stiflingly hot reception room, made even more claustrophobic by the jostling crowd of nervous and impatient Iranians who irritably waited beneath the revolutionary slogans and portraits of ayatollahs.

I didn't think there would be time, but finally my turn came.

'May I speak to Mr Shad-Kam?' I asked, naming my contact.

'That's not possible.' The stock answer.

'He's expecting me,' I countered.

The man at the desk looked at me a little helplessly. 'Please wait here.'

Mr Shad-Kam approached me timidly. 'Mr Danziger, I'm sorry, but if you could just wait another weekend . . .'

'I'm leaving in an hour from Victoria.'

He sighed. 'Very well. I will issue you with a two-week transit visa. I'm afraid that's all I'm permitted to do without higher authority. If the full visa appears within the next few days I will telex Istanbul.' The decision had obviously cost him quite a lot of sweat, but I was relieved. At least it meant that the first frontier which might cause real problems wouldn't come until Afghanistan.

I made it to Victoria with a little time in hand. My mother and stepfather were waiting to see me off, and true to form Noo, my ex-girlfriend, turned up at the very last minute. I had a borrowed blue rucksack on my back and a very expensive camera bag, donated by the manufacturers, in my hand. It contained two cameras and eighty rolls of film, as well as maps, medical kit and a toothbrush, and was quite heavy. I was wearing jeans, an old pair of broken-down shoes, and a canvas bomber jacket Noo had picked up for me for £2 on a second-hand clothes stall in the Portobello Road. I always carried talismans with me on my journeys, a small superstition I did not wish to break, and now Noo gave me two more – to join the little green plastic crocodile and the very battered mini Fozzie Bear who had been all over Central and South America with me – the two newcomers were Nitty and Natty, each an inch high, a colourful South American Indian couple in traditional dress.

It was hard parting from Noo. Although we had split up, I knew that I was still in love with her, and it came as a shock to realise it afresh now, standing in the middle of Victoria Station, far too late to retreat and already worlds apart from her. I hadn't seen her for a while, and indeed in the weeks leading up to my departure I had allowed myself a flurry of brief, amorous relationships which were in part expressions of genuine affection, but were also the result of my feeling free because I was leaving soon. The fact that my partners felt this too gave our brief loving great intensity.

But now here were Noo, and my mother, the two people who mattered most to me, saying goodbye. I asked myself questions. Like most of us, there are different sides to me. There's a part which is timid, contemplative, a dreamer; and there's a part of me filled with a lust for life, with enthusiasm and anarchic energy. Still I hesitated. I was filled with trepidation, there were butterflies in my stomach. Was I leaving things unfinished, hanging in the air? I'd just had an exhibition of my work in Cork Street, and while there had been few sales a lot of interest had arisen around it; one or two public collections were considering purchases, and there had been talk of a touring exhibition. Shouldn't I have followed all that through? Then there were my students at Chelsea. It was unlikely that I'd be back for their diploma shows. My Fellowship for the journey covered three months, but I knew very well that six months to a year would be barely enough. I had a schedule mapped out but it was a safe bet that the vagaries of travel would soon make a nonsense of it.

I sneezed. On top of everything else, I had a stinking cold.

'Well . . .' I said.

'You'd better go . . .'

I'd have to hurry now, if I was going to catch my train.

PART ONE

The Beginning

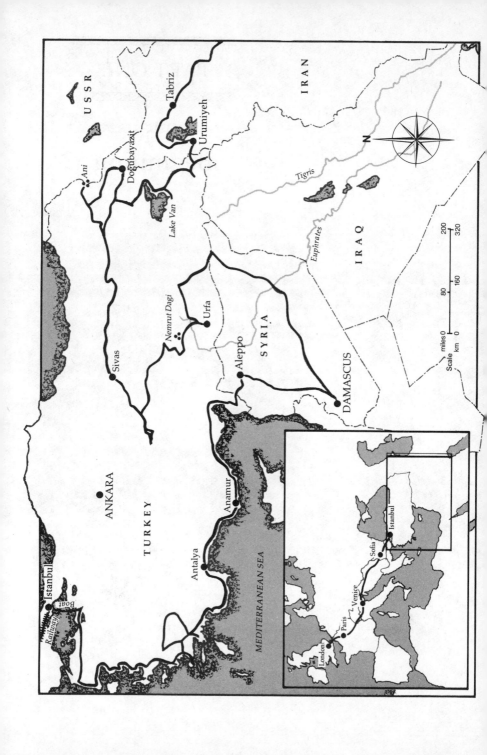

A FISHERMAN'S TALE

As we pulled out of Victoria, my fears and worries were soon replaced by the simple excitement of moving forwards towards new faces, new peoples, new meetings. I felt a surge of pleasure at simply being alone, and in control of my actions, if not of my destiny. The painter's life is a solitary one, and for me travel was to a certain extent the same. I was able to live with myself, and I knew that travelling solo had many advantages. Alone you are approachable. As for actual loneliness, that is rarely a problem. As a foreigner you are usually the object of great curiosity, and there were to be times when I longed for solitude, even for simple privacy. But you are the visitor, so you have to adapt. I was also aware of my responsibility as a traveller from Britain. At moments when I longed to be on my own, to be relieved of the duty of politely answering innumerable boring and repetitive questions, especially when the answers were simply not taken in, I had to remind myself very hard of that responsibility. Then I became an actor: patient, friendly, open-minded, even-tempered, genial, unruffled. It was one way of paying my way, of showing respect to my hosts.

As the train clattered out into Kent I looked unseeing at the suburbs giving way to fields as I considered the dangers I would have to face. Alone as I would be, the chances of dying an unrecorded death were high. I thought of my mother, of Noo, when the news from me suddenly dried up forever. But I couldn't really believe that I would die. Who can? Besides, I have always relished difficulty. It keeps you on your toes. I may take risks now and then, but I enjoy life too much to be foolhardy. I reckoned that, mentally as well as physically, I was as prepared as ever I would be. Now I looked at the green fields whisking past the dirty window of the train and tried to imagine the grey-brown barren hills of Afghanistan. It was impossible. Did such a place really exist?

My thoughts turned to a Frenchman I hoped to meet in Paris. He had travelled extensively in Afghanistan on what he called 'fishing trips', and with his help I hoped to go into the country armed with a greater knowledge of it than I had now, and possibly he would suggest contacts to me as well. Perhaps the whole thing would seem more real after I had talked to him.

The train was heading towards Paris, the part of the world where I had first started travelling. I am the product of a pretty rootless background. I was born in England, the son of an American father and an English mother, but from the age of ten I'd lived with my parents in Switzerland, spending my summers with an aunt and uncle in France. I had thus grown up well accustomed to foreign places, foreign food and foreign languages.

It was while I was at school in Switzerland that I first really became aware of my surroundings. I felt bored and frustrated, and it was in travel that I sought to discover the world about me. I resorted to schoolboy escapades to alleviate my feelings. I pretended to be holding up a perfectly ordinary tree, to prevent it from falling. I conned a passing farmer into taking over from me, and left my victim in the lurch, supporting the 'dangerous' tree while I went for help. On another occasion I raised Cain by pretending that my brother was locked in a postbox. But these goings-on were not enough to disguise how divorced I was from the real world. Amidst my comfortable surroundings, I started to plan my first journey: to a Bolivian tin mine. I complained to my mother about the privileged way we lived, but she retorted that I seemed quite happy to benefit from it. I was offered a change of school, but I didn't take up the offer. There seemed to be no point.

However, school did equip me with two very valuable skills: fluent French and an ear for other languages. The knowledge of other languages acquired at school was rather selective, though: I learnt from fellow foreign students how to swear fluently for three minutes in six or seven different languages. Not that any of that was much use to me on my present trip. I could insult someone roundly in Persian for thirty seconds, but I didn't know the Persian for 'hello'.

Paris was the destination of my very first journey. I made it there and back without money when I was thirteen years old. My worried parents couldn't imagine how I'd managed, and even had visions of me staying in a brothel. Actually doing it was relatively easy, and I never went to a brothel at all. Fairly soon I'd reduced Western Europe to a series of train rides, all of them free. I quickly learnt that to avoid showing a ticket to a guard you hid in the toilet, but I also learnt that you didn't lock the door. If you did, he'd wait outside. If another passenger tried to come in, of course you'd both be covered in confusion and embarrassment and apologise to each other. And once in the town I'd chosen to visit, I would sit sketching in the sun, and it wasn't long before I could recognise the kind of people who would be prepared to help me. There were women who even made advances to me, perhaps finding the idea of a naive adolescent attractive; but there were others who, from simple kindness, would provide me with a meal and some loose change on which to get by. In fact I never asked for money, and if it was offered I protested. If, however, they still pressed me to take it I would. It made the difference between eating and going hungry.

If school had taught me the importance of languages, my stepfather taught me something as important, if not more so. It also had to do with language, though. It was to do with how you spoke to people rather than what you said. My stepfather, I noticed, could switch accents according to whom he was talking with. I followed this lead, but for me switching accents and therefore class was a way of escaping from my own privileged upbringing. The more important side effect was that you are much more quickly accepted by a group if you speak their language exactly. I found it easy to move from one group to another but I never felt at home with anyone. I saw myself as a nomad, freed from the trials and tribulations of a constricted, conventional life. I took to scraping a living by doing menial jobs – cleaning out warehouses, for example, where the stench of rotting mould was so great that when I travelled home on the tube in the rush hour, people made space around me, making me the only passenger who travelled comfortably. As soon as I was old enough to drive I switched from casual labour to van- and truck-driving in London. But I still moved from world to world without appreciating the differences between them. Only when I began to work for the police as an interpreter did I become truly aware of the differences there could be. They were particularly evident in court, where prejudice, bigotry and bias came to the fore. No attempt was made by those prosecuting or those defending to understand the defendant's point of view, and because no one attempted to put himself in the accused's position, communication broke down completely. I noticed that the barriers still owed their existence as much to class differences as to those of race and language. Juries at Knightsbridge Crown Court would hand down decisions totally different from those which in a similar case would be given at Elephant and Castle Crown Court.

In the light of these experiences, I looked at the task which confronted me now. It was daunting. I could not expect to learn all the dialects and languages I would encounter on my journey, and I had no dictionaries to help me. But without a common language, how would I understand and come to know the people I would meet? I would have to try to break down any possible prejudice I came up against by my actions, and at times it would be to my advantage simply that I was a stranger, a foreigner, for people frequently find what is new and unusual more attractive and interesting than the familiar. In any event, travelling as I would be through countries in political turmoil, I was determined to keep an open mind, and to interpret what I saw rather than judge it. Certainly if I was to succeed, I would have to stay enthusiastic, cool and persevering. I would have to use all the guile that had stood me in good stead in my former travels, and all the audacity too.

I had outlined a route which would take me through Istanbul and down the Mediterranean coast of Turkey, and thence into Iran where I expected to visit Qom, Tehran and Mashhad before crossing into Afghanistan and travelling across it to Pakistan. I would cross into China from northern Pakistan, making my entirely illegal entry over the Karakoram mountains. It was 35 years since the area around Kashgar had seen foreigners of any description. But despite my planned route I intended to stay flexible, knowing that frequently circumstances would take matters out of my control. Two places I would avoid at all costs: the vast Soviet airbase at Shindand in western Afghanistan, and the capital of that country, Kabul. The other place I had been strongly advised to steer clear of was Lop Nur. Close to my proposed route in western China, it was also the town closest to China's nuclear testing ground.

But I was still a traveller without a cause, and sometimes I longed for one. As an adolescent I had wanted to see the great museums of the world. I had spent whole days at the Prado in Madrid, at the Uffizi in Florence. But as I travelled I became aware of other things in cities besides the museums. Of poverty. Of the *favelas* of Rio, the *barrios* of Lima. I couldn't ignore the child gangs that roamed Rio offering stolen goods, sex and drugs. I couldn't ignore the demonstrators in Peru, being shot at by the police or fleeing the choking tear gas.

My hope was to help break down the social, political and racial barriers that plagued society. Particularly in the Third World, with its festering wars and its grim insecurity, I wanted to help the ordinary, innocent mass of people who lived their entire lives in the presence of poverty and per-secution, manipulated now by the Right, now by the Left, and in certain ethnic groups, such as the Kurds, fighting an oppression that was on the brink of genocide. But with all that, I still stood detached.

The train pulled into the vast, bleak, grey, empty hall that is the Gare du Nord in Paris. My first task was to telephone my French contact, the man who had been to Afghanistan on his 'fishing trips', and learn as much as I could from him on south-eastern Afghanistan. The best journeys are those made with the pooled knowledge of fellow travellers. It was late at night and the station was all but deserted as I made my way to a row of telephone booths where three young American students were ploughing through the phone book in their search for an hotel. I offered to help but they ignored me and continued to feed the phone with francs as if playing a fruit machine. I made my way to another booth along the row and had just started on my own phone calls when I was interrupted by someone tapping on the glass door of the box. I turned slightly to see a man who looked stoned, or drunk, or possibly both. I ignored him, but the tapping grew louder, and now he was shouting that he needed to use the phone.

As soon as I was outside he grabbed me. At first I was too astonished to do anything, but I managed to parry his not very accurate blows.

'US out of the Lebanon!' he shouted. He had clearly worked himself up into a frenzy for he was completely out of control and I could see that his pupils were dilated. I am not a small man and I was able to pin him down so that he couldn't hit me any more. In this position I set about trying to explain to him that the fact that I was cleanshaven and lantern-jawed, and wore my hair very short, did not necessarily mean that I was a US marine. This didn't make much impression on him.

'*Sale flic!*' he shouted. I was about to tell him that I wasn't a 'dirty cop' either, but by now he was off on another tack.

'You're not superior, I'm not inferior,' he informed me. I agreed, and tried to tell him that I was English, but he didn't seem too convinced of anything any more. Finally he subsided and I was able to make my phone call to my fisherman contact, LeClerc. He agreed to meet me at the Montmartre Metro station and as we didn't know each other I arrived early for our appointment, thinking that I'd be able to pick him out from the crowd. He ought to look like an adventurer. Time passed and he appeared to be late, when I realised that apart from myself only one other person was obviously waiting for someone. He was a suave, slightly-built man in his late thirties, immaculately dressed in a pinstripe suit and carrying a briefcase. I approached him hesitantly.

'*Monsieur LeClerc?*'

'*Oui, bonjour,*' he replied, smiling, and switching his briefcase to his other hand in order to shake mine. 'Let's walk . . . and tell me again, who did you get my name from in London?'

Of course I'd told him on the phone – both when I'd talked to him from London, and again when we'd made this appointment the night before, but clearly he was a man who needed reassuring. Now as we walked along I didn't quite know how to open the conversation. It seemed appropriate, before launching into the mass of practical questions about Afghanistan, to make a little small talk, but M. LeClerc was not the easiest of men to talk to and in my confusion I blurted out the one question he was least likely to answer:

'What do you do when you're not in Afghanistan?'

He gave me the faintest of smiles. 'I am freelance – as you say in England.'

He suggested we go to a bistro. Once installed, he started to tell me what I wanted to know. He spoke quietly but assuredly, occasionally pausing to make a quick sketch on a paper napkin. Few foreigners had reached the parts of Afghanistan I wanted to go to since the war began in 1979, and although one man had crossed from Iran into Afghanistan, no one had made it through to Pakistan. He forbade me to take notes, so desperately I tried to cram into my memory the names he was giving me – names I had never heard spoken but only seen on maps and written in books or periodicals. He gave me information about the location of government strongholds and Soviet airbases. He gave me names of possible contacts. He also gave me essential guidance about the nature of the Afghan resistance. This was vital since the resistance is not unified against the common enemy, but different groups with different allegiances control different parts of the country and fight as much amongst themselves as against the Russian and Government troops. Knowing whom I would meet where would be necessary information when I was travelling in the interior. But M. LeClerc didn't stop there. He was a mine of information, even being able to provide me with an idea of the price of horses according to region, and the cost of hiring a guide. I was deeply impressed by M. LeClerc, who was clearly as careful as he was self-effacing, for before we left the bistro he folded the napkin on which he had been drawing and put it in his pocket. He never once spoke about the political situation, but I could sense the deep respect he felt for the country and its people.

There were others I had to see in Paris before continuing south. Aide Médicale works out of a tumbledown building in the 20th arrondissement. Their office is reached by a rickety staircase, and when you enter it and see the files strewn all over the bare floorboards you wonder how any order at all can come out of such chaos. And yet they send teams of incredibly brave French doctors and nurses to Afghanistan, Colombia, Kurdistan and Burma. When I was there they were talking of sending people to Angola. There were other agencies of a similar nature, such as Médecins du Monde, and Médecins sans Frontières who worked out of plush offices with efficient secretaries; but there was no difference in the degree of their devotion. At Médecins sans Frontières I spoke to a young woman who was in charge of sending teams to Afghanistan. She was so busy that she could only spare me a moment, and even then I don't think my presence registered. Indeed I knew it hadn't, for I was to meet her again, just over four months later, in Afghanistan, and she had no recollection then of ever having seen me before. At any event in that Paris office she quickly dismissed me and my ideas of retracing the Silk Road as that of a crank or a lunatic.

With only a few minutes to spare after a hectic day in Paris, I caught a taxi which whisked me to the Gare de Lyon just in time to catch the 23.58 to Venice and Istanbul. I slept briefly in my seat and when I woke we were crossing the Valais. The snow had not yet completely melted, and the dawn mist hung low across the valley, shrouding the mountains. It was a comfortable feeling to be travelling legitimately, ticket-in-hand, and I enjoyed not having to scurry off to the nearest loo as soon as a guard came down the corridor. As a Churchill Trust Fellow I was not about to travel illegally.

But old habits die hard. When the train reached Lake Maggiore I was tempted to get off. I didn't, and stayed aboard until Milan when the temptation became too much for me and I decided to return to Stresa and the lake. Inevitably my compartment door slid open to reveal a ticket collector.

'Istanbul?' he said, peering at my ticket.

'Yes,' I replied, confidently.

'But you're travelling in the wrong direction'; he was peering at me now.

'Oh . . . I think I must have overslept.'

He peered at me some more. Well, it wasn't the greatest excuse.

In fact, I hadn't planned to stop anywhere en route for Istanbul, but I followed Stresa with a short stopover in Venice, where at this time of year the pigeons in St Mark's Square are outnumbered by the tourists. After Venice, the train filled up with Yugoslavian shoppers. The two young men in my compartment pulled down the blind, glancing at me and smiling apologetically. They then proceeded to put on two pairs of jeans, the pair underneath tucked into the tops of their socks, an elastic cummerbundpouch filled with things like cufflinks and penknives round their waists, and over that several shirts. They looked like Tweedledum and Tweedledee and I could only hope for their sake that they would fool the customs. As we approached the border another Yugoslav poked his head into the compartment.

'You have umbrella?' he asked me.

'No,' I said.

He gave me one. In the course of the next few minutes I was showered with gifts – everything from bottles of Brut aftershave to Levi jackets, though of course once we were past the Yugoslav frontier my benefactors came streaming back into the compartment to relieve me of my booty. Suddenly everybody was tremendously relieved that the customs duties that had been levied were not greater, and all started talking at once. It seemed to me extraordinary that the customs officials, who had busied themselves holding mirrors under the carriages and knocking screwdrivers against their sides, had missed what was right under their noses, but perhaps they were looking for bigger contraband than what my friends had been carrying. At any rate the two young men could breathe out and undress.

It was after the train had left Belgrade that Turkish workers started to board the train, bringing me my first tastes and smells of the Orient. They were returning home from jobs in West Germany, Holland and Austria. The compartment seats pulled out across the aisle between them to make beds at night, but the Turks pulled them out now and sat cross-legged. On this platform they set a cloth which they proceeded to pile high with food. Like an escaped genie gorgeous spicy smells wafted from their compartments and spread around the whole carriage.

I didn't have a visa for Bulgaria and, as I had expected, my request for one at the frontier was turned down; but, as I had equally expected, this decision was miraculously reversed for a 'financial consideration' in the form of US dollars in cash. In my experience US dollars are pretty well the pass-key to the world. I was impressed by the Bulgarian ticket collectors, who looked more like five-star generals with their green uniforms, red-trimmed peak caps, and their gold buttons and epaulettes. I made a brief stop in the capital, Sofia, and noticed a crowd outside the US consulate's library. They were gazing at the images of radiant America in its windows: a space walk; modern appliances; state-of-the-art technology; an operating theatre; a skyscraper of concrete and glass, and a big sports car – a custom-painted Camaro. There was not the slightest blemish or even a speck of dust on this cosmetic rendering of a nation.

It wasn't ten days since I had left London but I suspected that in taking my time to reach Istanbul I was guilty of postponing the moment of plunging into Asia. I was reluctant to part company with the familiar, and maybe too I wanted to savour what would probably be my last chances of any kind of self-indulgence for a long time to come.

One way and another I had dawdled long enough in Europe. I caught the next train from Sofia and did not stop until I reached Istanbul.

Constantinople, Byzantium, Istanbul – crossroads of the world and capital, successively, to the Roman, Byzantine and Ottoman empires, as seen in the monuments that are the creations and expressions of those empires. The ponderous mass of Haghia Sofia served for a thousand years as the cathedral of Constantinople before it was taken over as a mosque when Mehmet III conquered the city in the fifteenth century. For another five hundred years it was one of the imperial mosques, right up to the time of its most recent manifestation as a museum. And above it the Blue Mosque, with its cascading domes and semi-domes and six slender minarets. And the other great building of the town, the Topkapi, now a museum of unimaginable treasures, but once the glorious palace of the Osmanli Sultans.

Istanbul is an extraordinary jumble of buildings. Tiny Byzantine churches, mosques with cradle-vaulted roofs, stained glass windows, attractive galleries, cool blue tilework of extraordinary luminescence, marble, woodwork inlaid with mother-of-pearl and ivory. Intricately carved doors, window-shutters and wooden balconies hanging over the streets. Everywhere the exquisite Arabic calligraphy which the

29

Turks used before Ataturk imposed the Roman alphabet earlier this century. There are still plenty of neighbourhoods which have conceded nothing to the modern age, where there are cobbled streets and ramshackle wooden houses, where children in rags play football in bare feet, and where the *çeşme*, or fountain, of which there were once over four hundred from the monumental to the humble, remains the only source of water.

My time became precious as the four days I had scheduled for Istanbul became eight. For I had to reach and cross the Karakoram range, and the Khunjerab Pass that separates Pakistan from China, before the snows made it impossible. It was still only mid-April and winter seemed a long way off, but I knew that the time was passing quickly with so much to see on the way.

Good news had come with the ratifying of my Iranian visa. No sooner had I entered the Consulate, its outer wall affixed with photographs of the victims of chemical warfare in the Gulf War, when a lady cloaked in a voluminous black *chador* hesitantly asked:

'Mr Danziger from London, I presume.'

She couldn't change the transit visa I had been issued in London but added a series of numbers, including the telex transmission that was later to confuse officials and allow me to travel wherever I pleased in Iran.

Crossing rural Turkey by way of the Mediterranean coast I quickly learned that a certain stoicism was always necessary. But at least the journey was never without incident, especially when I was hitching. Once as I waited at the side of the road some locals appeared, set up an upturned crate for a table, and brought me a lunch of tomatoes, salt and bread. Then the men sat around in the shade smoking and drinking tea while the women slaved in the fields. The women stared at me inquisitively when they thought I wasn't looking, but whenever I turned my gaze towards them they lowered their heads, so that all I could see was the screen of their headscarves. Finally a truck arrived, and the men, slowly and apathetically, started unloading crates of tomatoes from it. They were highly amused when I started to help them.

When I wasn't hitching lifts, I travelled by bus. Local buses stopped anywhere and everywhere, often just for a chat with someone at the roadside. You have quickly to forget any western sense of time or urgency and you have to become more philosophical, too, because the more agitated you become, the slower everything seems to go. In the evenings, I was entertained everywhere I stopped by song and dance, for the Turks are an effervescent and gregarious people. Music for these evenings was usually a three-man band playing fiddle, fife and dustbin-lid. Melancholic songs about loved ones were accompanied by the vibrant rhythms, the hollow rattle of the drum lid, the wavering high-pitched staccato of Ottoman Turkish music, while food was served piquant with the aromatic spices and cooled with delicious yoghurt.

In this way I covered half of the south coast of Turkey, passing through Antalya and Alanya, and reaching Anamur, with its ponderous massif of a castle built by the crusaders to protect the vegetable gardens which supplied their armies with food. In Anamur I passed one of the worst nights of my entire journey. I later thought of it as the Night of a Thousand Mosquitoes. But it wasn't just the mosquitoes. My squalid room was alive with cockroaches, and they were better left alone. Better a live roach than the slimy mess that a dead one leaves once trampled underfoot. Otherwise Anamur was a charming and romantic spot, the killing heat mitigated by the coolness of the sea.

I liked Turkey. The people were friendly and curious, and never hostile. Many, of course, had been guest-workers in western Europe. There was the ex-Peugeot factory worker from Strasbourg, and the man who had worked in Paris, who described wretched and pitiful conditions of work but who directed any criticism at the poor Cambodians who, he said, had flooded into Paris and taken all the jobs formerly held by Turks.

'But after all,' he told me, finally taking the broader view, 'they need the work. They have families of eight or nine kids. I only have four.'

Most workers who'd returned home from jobs in the west had started their own businesses. One was breeding chickens. Another ran a mini-bus company. All seemed happy to be home, living in a country where you weren't ruled by the clock.

As I travelled eastwards, I discovered the great Greco-Roman theatres of Side and Aspendos, with their perfect acoustics; the perfectly proportioned Bouleterion, or Council Chamber, at Priene; the erotic marble statues of Aphrodisias; the giddy clifftop necropolis of Hierapolis, believed to be shrouded in an atmosphere poisonous to all but the ancient priests. Perhaps the most striking fruit in this cornucopia was Aphrodisias, which was the centre of a school of sculpture and of Venus-worship.

And there is the mighty funeral sanctuary of King Antiochus I of Commagene. Built at an altitude of 2000 metres 2000 years ago, Nemrut Dagi is a gigantic artificial tumulus flanked by terraces, and surrounded by colossal stone statues of gods and kings, their toppled heads scattered on the ground together with those of stone lions and stone eagles. The biting cold wind and sleet swept across the mountains down to the spectacular views of the Mesopotamian plain below. This was a citadel built to testify forever to man's power, but earthquake, storm and the wind have taken their toll, a telling reminder of our transience.

Recent political upheavals have made Turkey very aware of her present and her future. In one village along my route I spent the night in a peasant's hut drinking raki, the local aniseed-based liquor, and listening as a group of rich Istanbulis expounded the virtues of communism to my host, Mehmet, a poor man who was much more inclined to see his salvation in Islam, still the religion of the country despite the fact that with Ataturk there ceased to be a state faith.

My own knowledge of Islam was slight. There had been Muslims at school, but then in those days half the school had claimed to belong to the True Faith in order to get off eating the insipid pork we were served at mealtimes. Either that or we claimed to be Jewish: the effect was the same. As my journey progressed, however, it would become increasingly bound up with Islam, and lead me to a greater understanding of it. In Turkey I noticed that while there were plenty of people who wouldn't dream of touching a set of prayer-beads, there were just as many who'd be glued to a television set to watch a prayer-meeting, joining in with cupped hands. And as they said goodbye to me, their parting words were always,

'May you find your way to the Truth and Islam.'

I was in Cappadocia. Its surreal landscape of elongated rock cones, capped pinnacles like giant toadstools, and craggy ravines were the result of tens of thousands of years of wind-erosion of the volcanic tuff which had been thrown out by the two great volcanoes of Erciyes Dagi and Hasan Dagi, now both extinct. The rocks have become homes; the soft stone is easy to work and hollow out, and the area once held outposts of refugee Christians. Still today you can find many rock-churches, hollowed out precisely according to the Byzantine layout, and decorated with frescoes of scenes from the New Testament. And a jumbled mass of troglodyte dwellings developed into human warrens where thousands could take refuge in interconnecting rooms on twenty different levels, descending as deep underground as 85 metres – the ultimate defence against Arab raiders. But the warrens were really cities, with rooms designated as grainstores, kitchens and stables, emergency wells, airshafts and heavy stone doors the shape of millstones which roll along slot-like grooves cut into the floor, and are so perfectly balanced that only two people are needed to move them.

This way of life continues. I saw dwellings in which everything about and in them has been hewn from the rock: not only rooms and windows, but chairs, tables and chimneys. The houses are cool in summer, and totally sheltered in winter. In one of the villages I met Ali Osman, who showed me a relief sculpture of reclining women he had carved along one wall of his newly completed house. His only furniture was a mattress on a raised platform. Even his candleholders

were carved out of the walls. Only the arched roof was not hewn from the tuff.

My own art is based on the mathematical development of established geometrical patterns, and I was already finding in the art of Islam much of the stimulation I'd discovered in Mayan work. But impressions were banking up. My mind sorted through its most recent impressions: the fine stone masonry of dressed and carved tuff of Cappadocia; and the elaborately luxurious decoration of Seljuk portals: flat ashlar interwoven with deeply-cut bands of interlocking patterns – projecting planes, and subtle reliefs: geometric *tours de force* creating exciting contrasts of light and shade. The upper part of the portal would be filled with recessed *muqarnas*, stalactite-like pendentives which formed an overhanging canopy of stone supporting and decorating the pointed-vault roof, and which became a honeycomb of reflected and refracted light, floating in a dazzling network of pure design which reminded me of the limpid fluidity of Arab calligraphy.

But I was increasingly aware that I was poorly read, and the sheer weight of my ignorance outweighed whatever chance discoveries of knowledge I might make. My aim was to look at everything with a completely fresh eye, or to try to see it from a different point of view from my own, but I remained in danger of being the victim of my own preconceptions and prejudices. I badly needed academic knowledge to back up or shoot down the conclusions I was reaching by myself.

This was something which was to plague me for much of the journey. When, for example, in western Afghanistan, I was confronted with man-made caves, with a view to converting them into a field hospital, I was unable to determine whether or not they belonged to the Kushan era. The locals were unable to enlighten me, and indeed locals very rarely knew anything about their own history in any detail. At Taiwara in central Afghanistan there is a ruined fort, but the people there could only tell me that it had been sacked once by Genghis Khan and then again by the British. They were much more interested in telling me how many Russian jets they'd shot down. I didn't have time in that war-torn country to inspect ancient buildings very closely, and I had no way of confirming even the scanty knowledge locals were able to give me. Similarly, I could only make my own tenuous connections between the Zoroastrians' Towers of Silence and the Tibetan sky burial. On the other hand I found more fertile ground in the study of languages, which didn't recognise political frontiers, and in the music and musical instruments which had found their way, in one form and another, right across from Europe to China. The European shawm (a woodwind instrument), for example, is clearly traceable in the *zurna* of Turkey and Central Asia, the *shanai* of India, the *surnai* of Afghanistan and the *sornay* of western China.

These considerations apart, my all but obsessive desire to cross new frontiers had led me by now via Iskenderun and Antakya to the Syrian border. I was in the extreme south of Turkey, an area where few tourists penetrate, despite its rich history. I could walk down the streets of Iskenderun and not have people calling out to me in a selection of western European languages. In any case the port is too busy profiting from the Gulf war, trans-shipping goods to both sides, to bother with the likes of me.

Although it wasn't on my itinerary, I couldn't resist the temptation of a quick foray into Syria. Before setting off I went to the British Consulate which was housed in the Catoni Maritime Agency. It was an imposing building that had seen better days and was now cut off from the seafront by a garden and a dual carriageway. The Turkish proconsul gave me a warm welcome and took me into her sanctum sanctorum, a room she had organised around a portrait of the Queen. She'd been proconsul for twenty years and was very proud of her garden, with its Union Jack and its coat-of-arms emblazoned on a wall. I found myself in the odd position of having to talk French to a British national from Lebanon who couldn't speak English. I had met several Lebanese in her position. Once the French mandate had ended, these people found themselves split between Syria, Turkey and Lebanon. Those I spoke to regretted the day the French had left.

The first thing I noticed as I travelled across the no-man's-land that separates Turkey and Syria was a sign in Arabic and English which warns: SLOWLY SLOWLY EXPLOSIVES. I wondered what lay ahead. Of course I had no visa but I had already decided to use the tactics which had always been so successful on other occasions. I would start by admitting my own incompetence, and I would place myself at their mercy.

The ramshackle border post was festooned with flags and pictures of President Assad. Gusts of wind had swept sand all over the inside of the customs hall and piled it up into little drifts on the floor and against the broken window panes.

The frontier guards were ramshackle, too.

'You have no visa,' one observed, life stirring in his bored eyes.

'I know. I'd like to apply for one.'

'Then you must go to Ankara,' he suggested helpfully. He was too lugubrious even to be amused.

'Is that really necessary?' I asked. I was about to be persistent.

During the ten-hour wait that followed I had ample time to get to know the frontier post intimately. I talked to some Iranians who were leaving Syria and who spoke of their stay there as people might of a prison sentence. Then there was the man who'd left his car at the border post only to find on his return from Aleppo that the official who'd forced him to do so had taken his family off on holiday in it. The complaints box had GET A BIGGER BOX scrawled across it in a despairing hand. Foreign trucks whose final destination was beyond Syria were obliged to join the nightly escorted convoy through the country.

It wasn't a promising start, but patience is a great virtue and my long wait bore fruit: a telegram had been sent to Damascus and a visa was issued. The border officials, some of whom were openly in league with the black marketeers and moneylenders who hung around the place, seemed to have taken me to their hearts. They obliged me to play endless games of backgammon with them. Then they invited me to eat with them, and furnished our table by confiscating food from wretched travellers crossing the frontier. Finally they ordered a bus-driver to take me to Aleppo free of charge, 'as a favour to them'.

My visa was only for a week, so I lost no time in discovering Aleppo. It is a wonderful city. Its bazaar seemed timeless, full of heavily-laden donkeys careering round the narrow, cobbled streets. It is roofed in a procession of domes, and light to the streets below comes from an aperture at the centre of each dome. It is a cool, twilight world. At one intersection where streets met, the roof was open to the sky. The door to a nearby caravanserai (which was once a hostel for travellers) was hung with great chunks of fresh meat, and a whole skinned sheep, hooked onto nails driven into the wood. On the cobblestones, flies clustered on the blood like iron filings on a magnet. At another caravanserai I talked to a man who was one of twenty brothers and sisters. He introduced me to his father, a bald man dressed in a long robe, with fingernails painted scarlet, and looking disquietingly like Uncle Fester of *The Addams Family*. He told me that he had four wives, and was at present building a mosque on the outskirts of Aleppo that would bear his name.

I wandered away from the caravanserai to have a look at the citadel, which is if anything even more impressive than the bazaar. Built on an enormous prehistoric man-made mound, the magnificent barbican is reached by a bridge across a moat. Its plan is haphazard, but it is a town in itself, with its own mosques, a school, a dungeon, baths, and a throne-room of impressive size, richly decorated with intricately inlaid wooden panelling and stained glass. A guide attached himself to me. He could speak French fluently, so I asked him a question. He looked at me sympathetically and repeated his last sentence, word for word. I repeated my question and received the same response. He'd obviously learnt his patter parrot-fashion, without understanding a word of it. Later, I was to pick up the same trick under very different circumstances.

And that evening I came across another example of the same strategy. An English singer in a night-club I went to sang Arab songs which she'd learnt phonetically. After I had roved the streets a little I heard the rhythms of some wild music that echoed down the dimly lit street. Mogambo's was more my kind of place. The smokefilled room resounded to vibrant, pulsating music which was matched beat for beat by a scantily clad belly-dancer with long, flowing black hair and a gold-braided bikini that would have fitted into a cigarette packet with room to spare and with tassels twirling at the nipples. She moved among the tables with her arms raised, frantically working a pair of castanets, her belly undulating like a wave, her whole body scintillatingly provocative. The men and women in the audience were squirming with delight almost in time to her movements in the dance, and they urged her on to faster and faster swirls of the hips. When she danced close enough to permit it, men happily stuffed folded banknotes into appropriate portions of her bikini.

When that excitement was over a tall, thin singer called Joseph

Sakker, a Lebanese, thin and balding with a thick moustache, round-rimmed glasses and a fez, performed to rapturous applause. The Englishwoman I mentioned sang too. Later the owner of the club introduced me to the belly-dancer, who turned out to be a Canadian who taught belly dancing at UCLA.

As in Turkey, soldiers were everywhere; but there was also quite a number of rather more sinister plainclothes men, clearly recognisable by the large guns sticking out of their belts or bulging under their jackets. Very early in the morning on 21 May I was to make their closer acquaintance.

By then I'd moved on to Damascus where I met a group of Palestinian students who'd offered me a room in their flat. I use the word 'student' in a broad sense, for one of my new friends owned a supermarket and another drove a Mercedes. The flat, however, was indeed a student flat. They'd already warned me that the police would come round to check my papers as the flat was in a block that was also home to a VIP (who this was I never discovered). Sure enough in the small hours I heard the police come into our flat, but they didn't knock on my door, so I fell asleep. Some hours later, however, I awoke with a start as several guntoting policemen charged into my room. I was off my guard, but once the initial shock was over I asked to be allowed to speak to my Embassy. Already I had visions of deportation to England – and how would I explain that to the Churchill Trust? Under the terms of my agreement with them I had no business to be in Syria at all. But the police ominously refused my request. Now my visions were replaced by new ones – of rotting away forever in some unspeakable gaol.

My Palestinian hosts were equally appalled, but there was nothing they could do, beyond offering me profuse apologies, which didn't ease my feelings. The police went through all my luggage, filled in the multitude of forms which accompany every official transaction and then escorted me down to the street. My Palestinians waved goodbye from the doorway of their flat.

Once in the street, my escort and I started to walk. We had gone several blocks before I noticed that one of the plainclothes policemen, a young man in jeans, an open-necked shirt and a brown leather bomber-jacket – very much the film cop – was looking at me curiously.

'Where are you going?' he asked quite mildly.

I was astonished. 'To the police station,' I guessed.

It was the policeman's turn to look surprised. 'But you're free to go,' he said. And that was that. I stood still, numb with incomprehension as they walked on.

Damascus is a religious city, and here for the first time on my travels I was woken daily by the chanting of the muezzin from the loudspeakers at the tops of the minarets: Allahu Akbar, Allahu Akbar, Allahu Akbar . . . Ashhadu an la ilaha illa 'llah . . . 'God is the Greatest; I bear witness that there is no God but the One God; I bear witness that Muhammad is the Messenger of God; come fast to prayer, come fast to prayer; prayer is better than sleep . . .' The bands of black-and-white pattern on the mosques were reflected in the clothing of the Iranian pilgrims here; the huge, all-enveloping black chadors of the women, the white turbans of the mullahs. The posters that were everywhere showed not only President Assad, but also Khomeini, Montazeri and other ayatollahs.

The sombre appearance of the pilgrims was actually at odds with the Great Mosque with its courtyard arcade decorated in a rich mosaic based on a complicated landscape of trees and buildings. And the peace and tranquillity of the enormous rectangular prayer hall was only disturbed by attendants who went around checking that no one had fallen asleep, outstretched on the kaleidoscopic carpets.

Much as I wanted to get away from the hot, sprawling towns in Syria, the friendliness and hospitality of the Syrians made it difficult. I found it especially interesting that people kept apologising for the repressive nature of their government, and would raise a glass to their native province without hesitation, but would not do so to Syria. How many of us spend time apologising to foreigners for our dreadful governments! But time was running out, and I had to start making my way back to Turkey. Crossing the northern desert in a decrepit bus, I took delight and relief in the splashes of colour the oases provided in the midst of the muddy gold of the sand.

I returned to a very different part of Turkey, by now accompanied by an Australian girl, Jenny. She had decided to tag along as our paths had kept crossing and recrossing from the Aegean coast, for safety, as a young blonde was prey to all and sundry, especially in this extreme eastern part of Turkey. It barely existed for western

Turks, who spoke of the Kurds in the same disparaging tones that they used for Arabs. In fact, east of a line drawn through Gaziantep, Kahramanmaras, Malatya, Elazig and Erzincan, you could truthfully say that you were in a different country.

The Kurds are forbidden to speak their own language, play their own music, or to celebrate any individual form of cultural identity. There are eight million Kurds in Turkey, but even to show sympathy for their way of life is a criminal offence. I met a Turk who had spent years documenting the Kurdish way of life. He lived in fear that his exhaustive collection of slides, tapes, interview transcripts and Kurdish artefacts – a testimony to a dying culture – might be discovered and destroyed. The Kurds are a nation unfortunate enough to have a homeland which straddles the area where Turkey, Iran, Iraq and Syria meet. For this, thousands languish in Turkish prisons; for this, they are denied the right to live as Kurds. I saw two Turkish drivers spit on a Kurdish shepherd who didn't move his flock off the road quickly enough for them.

There is Kurdish resistance, of course. It is minimal in Turkey but has strong centres in border villages in Iran and Iraq. In Iran, war is waged against them, but the Iranian army, as opposed to the revolutionary guards, is sympathetic to them. Perhaps the Turks feel obscurely threatened: against a total Turkish population of 45 to 50 million the Kurds number between 15 and 20 million, and are the fourth most numerous people of the Middle East. In Turkey their homeland covers the fine pastures and rolling downs of the south-east. The men are distinguished-looking, tall and slender. They wear trousers close-fitting to the knee but baggy from there to the waist, and with them a shirt, jacket and peaked cap. The women wear endless layers of clothing, despite the heat: baggy trousers or skirts over trousers, fine embroidered shirts and jackets, the dominant colours green and red, purple and orange, juxtaposed against one another in a way so discordant to the eye as to be almost jarring. The colour of their skin is a rich, deep brown, their black eyes piercing in lean, high-boned faces. Their hands are strong and large, and speak of hard work. They are shepherds and nomads. You can see their caravans stretched out across a plain, their few possessions tied to donkeys and oxen. Accompanying them are their dogs, called *kurt-kopegi* – a breed similar to a small St Bernard but with larger jaws and a powerful chest. They are trained as puppies not to be afraid of wolves, and their jaws can snap a wolf's neck in seconds. When used as sheepdogs they wear a heavy collar studded with iron spikes to protect them in battle with wolves.

Eastern Turkey is conservative and devout. Buses would stop by rivers and streams at prayer time so that the passengers could perform their ritual ablutions. Most mosques were packed on Fridays, but the women were always strictly segregated in side-rooms behind screens. Women indeed led a repressed and constricted life. In the town of Van, a woman whose daughter had been knocked down by a car refused to have her taken to hospital, afraid that her husband would beat her for letting her daughter out into the street. But this grotesque social organisation breeds sexual libidinousness among the men. On one occasion Jenny was so badly mauled by a passer-by that I hit him. It was the first time in my life that I had hit anybody, and I was shocked and trembling, but I had become increasingly infuriated by the freedom Muslim men allowed themselves with western women. To be so oppressive to your own, and so hypocritically free with others, and with apparently no idea of, or attempt to understand, other ways of living, seems common to mankind. I felt no remorse at all at having slammed into Jenny's attacker. In fact he was lucky that some of the other townspeople separated us, apologising for his behaviour.

We travelled north to Ani, high up above a gorge where two rivers meet. Ani is right on the frontier and I could see the Russian soldiers watching my every move from towers behind a tall fence as I visited the churches there. Legend has it that there were once 1001 churches. Now there are only a handful, and those are ruined, but you can see the glory of what once was even in a broken cupola or a faded fresco. Ani is in such a sensitive area that although you are still on Turkish soil the Russians have managed to forbid the taking of photographs, and you can only visit the site with a military escort. One of our soldiers told me rather smugly that lightning had struck one of the churches, but spared another which had been converted into a mosque. The soldiers, however, did not seem especially religious. We were now five days into Ramadan, but only one soldier at the local garrison had been able to keep the sunrise to sunset fast. After sunset, it was difficult to find a meal. Most people preferred to eat privately, it appeared, and most of the restaurants had closed for the month.

Further along the Russian border lies Igdir, said to be the place where Noah first set foot after leaving the ark on Mount Ararat. The people who live there now tune in to Russian television. We found a bar which served vodka, and a raucous evening of song and dance followed. I'd been a drummer in my teens, and once played in the West End production of *Man of La Mancha*. Tonight my drum was a metal water jug, and my drumsticks a coin between my fingers. But it was a successful evening. Even when a fight broke out and the police arrived to calm things down and remove a few of the revellers the party spirit refused to be dampened. And Jenny and I found that the party became a private one that went on for the rest of the night.

People remained charming and helpful, sometimes impossibly so, for they preferred to give wrong directions rather than no directions at all. The major drawback was the constant source of attraction that Jenny provided to the men. At one point, unable to get hold of any food (it was still Ramadan), we were invited to eat at a police canteen. After we had eaten, three of the policemen told us that they were off on a patrol and could give us a lift. We accepted, though I thought at the time that a lift of 45 kilometres was excessively generous. We went outside to the patrol car – a battered Renault 16 – and piled in.

Although the talk was friendly enough, since we shared a common interest in football, I didn't like the way they kept eyeing Jenny, or the look of the sub-machine gun between the front seats. I began to feel uneasy and started to look for a way out of the situation, but this time it seemed as if we were trapped. We had left the town of Van far behind us and were now out on a remote road. If the policemen decided to kill me and rape Jenny, nothing could stop them, and no one would find them out. As my panic grew I tried desperately to intimidate them by stretching the truth a little and telling them that I was a policeman too – from Scotland Yard. Unfortunately they had never heard of Scotland Yard and remained unimpressed. The situation was very ugly. But by pure luck a bare kilometre from our destination, the lakeside town of Gevaş, a call came through on their radio requesting their immediate assistance in Van. They dropped us apologetically and turned round. I felt lightheaded with relieved amusement as I thought of the time it would take them to cover those 44 kilometres in that old Renault, and so far from the beaten track.

Soon after this incident Jenny left me to return by bus to the safety of western Turkey and I travelled on to Hakkari, a city that has become flooded with Iranian refugees. These desperate people have been ferried over the mountains by Kurds, who charge them according to their means and according to how badly wanted they are by the Iranian authorities. The average price varies between £20 and £40, though some had paid up to £3000. The trip across the mountains can take four or five days, and the Kurds frequently introduce a side-trip to one of their own resistance centres, so that the Iranians have the Kurdish cause impressed upon them.

Most of the refugees I met were university students or men of an age to be conscripted into the army – the equivalent of draft-dodgers. The reason for their departure was obvious. However, not all were Muslims or even Iranians – there were three Iranian Jews who had come over the mountains under their own steam and had narrowly missed wandering into Iraq. I met a couple of exhausted Iraqis who'd fled from their own country's regime into Iran. There they had been interned, and now they had escaped and were seeking temporary refuge in Turkey or Pakistan.

All of them were insecure, worried about what lay ahead. None had any possessions left, and most had spent their last *rials* on a decent pair of track-shoes for the trek over the border. Those few who had money shared it out. Now they, and I, were all staying together in what had once been a decent hotel, but which had recently been converted into a refugee centre. Each room was packed with beds, as were the corridors. There were queues for the loos at all times of day, and even longer ones for the washbasins in the mornings. The stench can be imagined, though little boys were constantly at work with brushes and pails in an attempt to maintain a modicum of cleanliness. Most demoralising of all for the refugees was the inactivity. They spent their days glued to the TV which had been rigged up in one of the reception rooms that hadn't been turned over to a dormitory, but they only watched with half their attention. They were waiting, anxiously, for a telegram from friends or news of a visa, trying to keep their spirits undaunted, their hopes up as the months passed. If they didn't, they would succumb to a deadly and despairing apathy, and they knew it. They were realists. Many hoped to make it to the USA or West Germany, but they knew that without connections or money they had very little chance of success. They'd heard that Italy, Spain and Scandinavia weren't bad. They would go gratefully to whomever would have them.

There was still a handful who wanted to plan revolution against the Khomeini regime but the array of different rebel groups was so great that there was little hope of a united front. Some were training alongside the Kurds, but even the Kurdish freedom fighters are divided into a complex number of conflicting sub-groups. At least they have an umbrella name for themselves – the *Pesh Merga* (Those Who Face Death). Without some solidarity it is difficult to see how any of these would-be revolutionaries will achieve their ends, no matter how justified their cause.

It wasn't surprising in this atmosphere that many refugees remained tight-lipped, though this was probably also due to the fact that they believed Khomeini's vow to take the Islamic Revolution beyond the frontiers of Iran. Would he inexorably catch up with them? However, they all had letters they wanted delivered, and when they got wind of my plans they wanted me to take them. Of course I couldn't run such a risk, though some of the people were so sad that it hurt me to have to refuse. The Turks were nervous too, because they were keen to build up trade links with Iran; but at the same time such a powerful and proselytising neighbour worried them: what if Khomeini sent agents over to stir things up among the minority Turkish Shia population?

Because of this additional anxiety it was impossible to discuss doctrinal disputes between Sunnis and Shias. Not only that, it was equally difficult to talk about the four major schools within Sunni Islam. I found that a little odd, until I realised that it wasn't so much the subject that was making them nervous as the fact that they'd be talking to me. I was being shadowed. Obviously my repeated requests to travel into the mountains between Iran and Iraq had aroused suspicion. Partly my fault. I'd been posing as a journalist, until I discovered that that wasn't too highly regarded. I'd then produced one of my 'official' Churchill Trust letters, in Turkish, covered with 'official' stamps. That had helped, but I'd learnt that even UN officials had only visited the area twice since it had become a restricted zone. My only hope, if I was going to proceed as planned, was to leave the area, in order to allay suspicion, and return later by a different route.

I spent my last evening in Hakkari drinking tea with the local worthies – the bank manager, an engineer, the doctor, a chemist and a teacher. They were all gloomy. Turks regard postings to areas like this as something of a punishment.

The evening drew to a close and I raised my tea-glass to propose a final toast – with my fellowship in mind – to Sir Winston Churchill.

The others raised theirs. 'To Sir Winston . . .' they said in ragged unison.

Returning to Van past glorious snow-capped mountains, busy, bright streams, and terraced valley walls with houses and tents clinging to them, I went over my strategy in my mind. It was difficult to concentrate, for everywhere I looked presented a feast to the eye. What I remember best on that route is the butterflies, so gaudy that they seemed too bright for nature: they looked as if they had been printed on the landscape. I pondered my situation. It was never easy to know whether to ask for permission officially in the knowledge that refusal would be almost certain, for if I was caught having been refused permission I would not have the advantage of being able to claim that I'd travelled in ignorance of local laws. Since I intended to go whatever they said, I decided to ask permission anyway. Once it had been refused, I'd set off, and if I was caught, I'd be frightfully sorry and allow it to become clear that through my faulty Turkish I'd misunderstood. Not very subtle but at least it cut to my advantage both ways.

I stayed four days in Van and then set off for Hakkari again, this time turning south, away from the Valley of Zap. At night I slept rough, and covered my tracks carefully, laying a false trail and then retracing my steps backwards before taking the path of my actual route, when I would brush out my footprints with a branch.

At all times I decided whom I could trust and whom I couldn't by the simple and obvious method of looking at their eyes. I knew that by and large I could trust Kurds – they would dislike Turkish officialdom as much as I did. Thus it was that I accepted a lift from two truck-driver brothers. Once I was aboard, they rather alarmingly suggested that I might like to take a trip into Iraq, but as I didn't have an Iraqi visa, but did have an Iranian one, I thought it might be better not to be tempted for once. They dropped me close to the Iran–Iraq border. I'd avoided the army checkpoints en route by hiding in an empty water cistern on the back of the lorry.

Considering that this trip had in fact been nothing more than a reconnaissance I thought I was doing rather well. I had no idea how many checkpoints I'd been smuggled through in the cistern, however, and so I thought I'd better count them on my way back. The first one I came to, just outside a place called Semdinli, was positioned on the track between a rising cliff and a falling precipice. There was nothing for it but to walk through. I tried to be as nonchalant as possible. The guards stopped me, of course, but seemed more interested in offering me a cup of tea than in looking at my papers. After tea came lunch. Then I said I'd better be going, but at that moment a commander arrived, who told me to stay as a minibus would be leaving in half an hour and I could hitch a lift on that. A whole series of half-hours followed, in the course of which I realised that I was being politely but firmly retained. I tried to calm my nerves by drawing pictures of the soldiers who'd fed me. This cheered them up because they'd been reprimanded by their commander for inviting me into the barracks in the first place – which hardly seemed fair, since if they hadn't he mightn't have got his arrest – but I still felt pretty low. I remembered a story the British Consul-General in Istanbul had told me about two British bird-watchers who'd innocently strayed too near the border and were now languishing in prison. I didn't even have that excuse, but no connection seemed to be made between my trying to obtain permission, its refusal, and my being caught. In the end I was let off with a very stern reprimand from the commander. I was to be escorted out of the area in a civilian vehicle. I was pleased about that, too, for I'd been told that the Kurds rather like to take pot-shots at army jeeps. Still, I'd learnt a lesson very cheaply indeed. Never again would I travel in such areas without a trusted local to guide me.

The bus that took me back had to stop at each and every checkpoint that I'd been smuggled past on the outward journey. All my fellow travellers, mainly Kurds, had to show their IDs, and I had to show my passport. The soldiers gawped at me, but the officers seemed amused that I had passed them unobserved.

I was dropped off at Yukesekova, a one-horse town if ever there was one, but I had pleasant memories of the journey there. Once the other bus passengers knew that I'd been as far as Semdinli, where otherwise only local Kurds are allowed, I became something of a folk-hero to them. The Kurdish passengers had taken to openly provoking the soldiers at the checkpoints, playing their forbidden music at full volume, refusing to speak Turkish, and hurling insults every time the embarrassed soldiers tried to search my bags. At one point between checkpoints, the driver even turned off the road and took a side track which wound up into the mountains. We careered along it for some time before returning to the main road, and every so often the driver would turn in his seat and gleefully announce to us that 'Now we are in Iran . . . Now we are back in Turkey . . . Now we are in Iran again . . .'

I only hoped it would all be that easy.

PART TWO

Iran

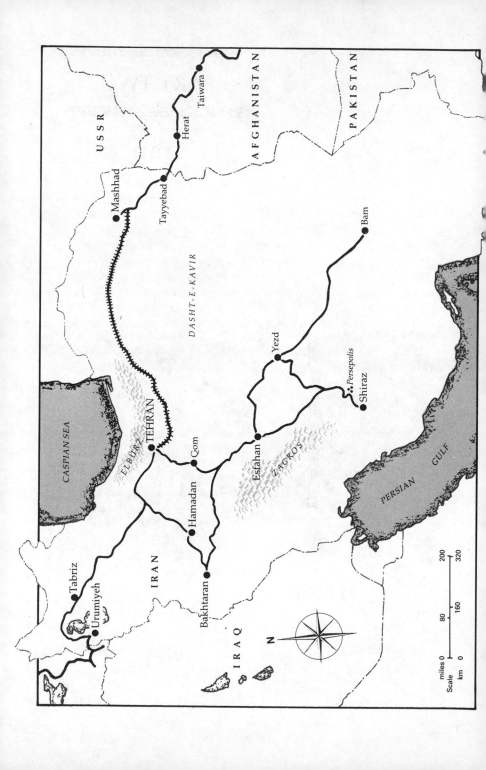

ALLAH'S WAY

The Iranian flag is a green, white and red tricolour with a composite of the Arabic characters LA ILAHA ILLA 'LLAH – there is no God but the one true God – at the centre. It seems to me to drape itself like a mysterious veil over the whole country.

When Khomeini swept the Shah away, that veil was drawn across, in January 1979. Since then, 15,000 political dissidents have been executed and half a million have been killed or wounded in the war with Iraq. Half a million more of the educated and professional middle classes are in exile abroad, and many millions are condemned to internal exile. Leadership is in the hands of the mullahs, and with the third largest oil reserves in the whole of the Middle East, Iran is well able to finance the Islamic Shia crusade, which is Khomeini's dream.

In addition, Iran burns with hatred of the West. There is even an order of hated countries. At the top of the list is the USA. The next in line, ecumenically enough, is the USSR. Thereafter come Israel, Iraq, the UK, France and, finally, West Germany. Such publicly-held enemies, however, are not inhibiting when it comes to that old leveller of ideals, trade.

Few foreigners without that excuse make it to Iran at all. The welcome is not warm, at any rate not officially. Poster art, which predominates and which is, paradoxically perhaps in such a severely Islamic country, figurative (perhaps it's just a case of no-holds-barred in political propaganda), typically depicts westerners meeting symbolic and bloody ends. One crude but powerful image remains vividly in my mind. A man dressed only in blue jeans is impaled through the chest on one of the spikes of the Statue of Liberty's diadem. Looking on like a dyspeptic Father Christmas in a black turban, is Khomeini himself, and the slogan next to him (there are slogans everywhere – even on the bandage covering the eyes of a blinded soldier) reads: AMERICA THE GREAT SATAN.

Iran is also a culturally rich country which has been the seat of great civilisations. I wanted to get to know it better, and in any case I had to cross it because the Silk Road traverses it. Also, for different reasons perhaps, I share Iran's current disgust with the intemperate and greedy West.

I was making my third attempt to enter the Islamic Republic. The Turkish customs officials didn't think this was an open border for foreigners, so before clearing me through customs I had to receive permission to enter from the Iranians. The Turks were right, of course. This southern frontier was off-limits to foreigners, but I trusted that my embellished Iranian visa would convince the Iranian frontier guards otherwise. I walked across no-man's-land having tidied myself up for the occasion.

'Asalaam Aleikum (Peace be on you),' said the guard.

'Aleikum Asalaam (On you be peace),' I replied.

He took me over to a small office where an immigration official looked at my passport. He was clearly impressed by their attaché's name on the visa, and I wondered if Mr Shad-Kam, whom I had so badly pestered in London, wasn't some sort of revolutionary hero. I didn't dare ask, however. Too many questions invite suspicion. I just stood there, relaxed and smiling, as if there couldn't possibly be anything more straightforward than getting into Iran this way.

'It's fine,' smiled the official, handing me my passport.

'Thank you.'

'Come back tomorrow. Then you can cross.'

'Tomorrow?' Doubt crept in immediately. I knew that 'tomorrow' could easily mean 'three weeks'. Or even months, come to that.

'Yes.'

The conversation was clearly over. I thought hard. There was no transport back on the Turkish side that day, and the little frontier post of Esendere comprises nothing more than the customs office and a few houses. I'd have to sleep on the border.

'Until tomorrow, then,' I said very firmly.

He appeared mildly surprised. 'Of course. Once the border is open in the morning we will come and fetch you.'

I retraced my steps and told one of the Turkish customs officials what had happened. He didn't appear at all surprised and kindly invited me to use the spare room in his flat for the night. I slept soundly and in the morning I couldn't imagine why my host was so excited.

'There was a gunfight in the night,' he said. 'Over at the Iranian frontier post. Do you mean to say you didn't hear it?'

Now I realised why I hadn't been allowed to cross the previous day. It had simply been too late. At night the road becomes unsafe for the very simple reason that the Kurds attack it.

As good as their word, at ten o'clock in the morning the Iranians came to collect me.

The Iranian post was located at a place called Sero. I had never seen a frontier post like it. The customs shed was adorned with vast murals of Khomeini, and an Islamic Revolutionary Guard lolled on a concrete bench, nursing a very big machine-gun. He was not the stuff, one would have thought, that wars were won with, since he was well over sixty, paunchy and bald, but then this was only the first of many misconceptions I had about the country and what was happening in it. The so-called Sepah Pasdaran, the true Guardians of the Islamic Revolution, are quite separate from the army, but they are well-equipped with sophisticated weapons and what they lack in military training they make up for in religious and revolutionary fervour. I was later to be struck by how many of the most ardent revolutionaries are men in their fifties and older.

Meanwhile the officials were falling over themselves to be helpful. As they whisked through the formalities they made small talk. If you could call it that.

'What do you think of Bobby Sands?' asked one, referring to a Provisional IRA man who'd starved himself to death in custody in Northern Ireland a few years earlier.

'I keep an open mind,' I said.

'In Tehran we have renamed Winston Churchill Avenue, Bobby Sands Avenue.'

'Have you?'

'And what of our Islamic Republic?'

I remained evasive. The officials chatted on, wanting to have my opinion on Mrs Thatcher (they pronounced it *tacher*), Mr Heath, Mao Tse-Tung and Deng Xiaoping. They became more businesslike when checking to see that I carried no alcohol (very strictly forbidden), and when making a note in my passport of my cameras' serial numbers – to ensure that I did not sell them on the black market. They asked about money, too, and I showed them what I had in my pocket. I didn't mention my money-belt. To be caught changing money illegally carries a mandatory death penalty.

Finally my passport was stamped: '22 Khordad 1363' – 12 June 1984 – and I was officially in Iran. A truck-driver was summoned and ordered to give me a lift. I was irritated by this treatment of the driver, who I suspected would have given me a lift anyway.

We hadn't gone a hundred yards when he pulled the massive lorry into a petrol station. I noticed that the little office building attached to it was pockmarked with bullet-scars. But the pumps were working, and petrol here is nearly a hundredth of the price it is in Turkey. My driver had calculated his tank carefully, to have just enough to cross the border.

The sun was high in the sky by now and beat down on us, melting the tarmac on the worn old road. The truck's cabin was like a furnace despite the open windows. Jeeps, ambulances and army lorries raced up and down the road, and the buildings on either side all showed signs of being battered by war. Every two hundred yards stood an Islamic Revolutionary Guard; motionless, weary sentinels, while behind them in the fields the Kurds quietly tended their crops, their clothes dimmed by the sun and fading into the colours of the land – tinged with the reds, pinks and yellows of desert and sand.

I was dropped on the edge of a little town. I didn't know where I was, I had no map and I couldn't read or speak Persian. The driver gave me some instructions, but I didn't understand them, and couldn't ask questions. I felt like an abandoned child. However I knew that it is fatal to look lost or doubtful – you immediately become a victim. I strode off purposefully. I was bound to meet someone who could help me, and indeed already people were miming the act of drinking tea. I was about to accept one such invitation when a car pulled up. It was a taxi and in it was my truck driver, who gestured me to get in. I managed to understand that it would take me to the bus station, but he would be getting out before that. Once at the bus station I took heart, but I had no idea of fares so when we reached our destination I held out a handful of coins to the taxi driver. He took about 5p's worth, which I thought was very reasonable, but later I was to discover that the entire 14-hour ride to Tehran would only cost about £3.

Finding the right ticket office wasn't easy, but I managed it with the help of locals, and fortunately 'Tehran' doesn't have to be translated. Over the bus station hung a large picture of Khomeini, soon a familiar sight as his image is everywhere. I bought my ticket and discovered that I had three hours to spare, which pleased me as it gave me a chance to wander back into the little town, which was busy and friendly.

Never once on my travels have I been the victim of theft. This may have something to do with a nature that is characteristically cautious and suspicious – some would say to the point of paranoia – but it must also be because I never carry any visible signs of wealth, such as rings or even a watch, and I keep my cameras concealed unless, of course, I'm using them. In all my time in Iran, I never once felt worried about my personal safety, and although I was constantly afraid of being singled out as a foreigner I rarely felt at all politically threatened by people filled with revolutionary zeal. I was, after all, a citizen of an 'enemy' country.

I discovered that I was in Urumiyeh. Its population is made up of Iranians, Kurds and Turks, and it is an important agricultural centre, situated as it is in the middle of a rich oasis. Produce piled high on the pavements for passing pedestrians or motorists to purchase provided a sort of ad hoc market, and it wasn't always easy to manoeuvre one's way through the mounds of melons, motor-repair shops, cars, people and buildings. The heat was stifling, but I noticed that the women all remained covered from head to foot in chadors. The few who didn't wore drab coats like mackintoshes, with a scarf over their heads. They must have been baked. I was thirsty, and without thinking I bought a melon. I was even given a stool to sit on while I ate it and watched what was going on around me. I settled down and took off my jacket. Thus in the space of a minute I had broken the Law of Islam (and therefore of Iran) twice: I had exposed my bare arms, and I was preparing to eat. I had forgotten that it was still Ramadan, and though as an infidel and a *mosafir*, or traveller, I was doubly excused for breaking my daylight fast, it was inconsiderate to others who could not. However no one batted an eyelid, and I might have never noticed my transgression myself; but suddenly an army jeep roared up and out of it bundled two or three Pasdaran. For a moment I thought my number was up, but curiously they didn't seem to notice the melon, and I hastily pulled on my jacket. They were in a hurry. They were lost, it seemed, and they were asking me for directions, thinking that I was one of them. I thought this odd, but later I realised that in the two months since I had left London my hair had lengthened and I had grown a beard. This beard, in particular, made me look very revolutionary. Still, I had been unnerved, and I returned to the bus station.

The great advantage of travelling by local transport is that you encounter local people. I was to meet many Iranians, and I found by their actions that love of a country, just like love of a people, is stimulated by the private actions of individuals far more than the broad public gestures of friendship so much loved by politicians. Iranians' ability to be subtle and cheerful, friendly and humorous, despite the fundamentalist regime they live under, was extremely touching. Everywhere I went I was greeted with nothing but kindness and help. Those who had remained in Iran were proud of their country without descending to the narrow-minded dialectic of the Revolution; and I sensed that those who were loyal to the regime had a greater loyalty to the idea of their nation, and if they went abroad to study they did so from a disinterested love of and desire to help their nation. The personal self-advancement on which the west operates has little place in their lives.

Dusk was falling as the bus pulled out of Urumiyeh, and one of the passengers jokingly called out to the driver, 'Can I eat?'

A lot of people laughed at that.

'How do you decide when it's dark enough to eat?' I asked my neighbour.

'It's supposed to be when you can't distinguish between a black thread and a white one,' he replied. 'But unfortunately the threads aren't always available.'

As the journey progressed I quickly lost count of how many times we were stopped at a checkpoint. It must have been a dozen times over 120 kilometres. There was something haphazard and halfhearted about the checks. The women were never searched or even asked for their IDs, although I was always singled out. Sometimes the guards examined my passport minutely, but upside-down. The Pasdaran were surly to a man, but at one regular army checkpoint an officer half-apologised to me, referring to the need to check for smuggled weapons, which seemed ludicrous since any of the women could have been carrying a whole arsenal either under their chadors or in their equally capacious bags.

I knew, however, that the time-consuming checks were largely due to my presence on the bus, and so I apologised as best I could to my fellow-travellers; but to my surprise they stuck up for me, reserving their anger for the Pasdaran and the military.

'He's already been searched fifteen times, why don't you leave him alone?' one said. And another: 'What sort of impression do you think you're giving of our country?' Most of the people around me had not stopped cracking jokes with me since we set off, and two passengers had swapped seats so that I could sit next to Said, who was studying medicine at Tehran University and who could speak English. Although the night was hot, the bus, a Mercedes, was comfortable compared to what I'd been used to, and one of the three drivers served iced water constantly.

I was bombarded with questions.

'Aren't you afraid of the Pasdaran?' one man asked me.

'Not specially,' I said, in as non-committal a voice as I could.

This seemed to disappoint them somehow. 'You must be, though. That's why you've grown a beard, isn't it?'

'What has my beard got to do with it?'

'Come on, you must know. They all have beards.'

'The Ayatollah Khomeini has deemed facial growth Islamic and propitious,' explained Said.

'Why?' I asked.

No one seemed to know the answer to that, although someone ventured that it might have something to do with stressing the difference between the sexes. The truth about my beard was that I had grown it partly from convenience, and partly as mild camouflage for when I was in Afghanistan.

Much of the conversation centred on Khomeini and the Pasdaran. People grew vociferous.

'Shouldn't we all be discussing this a bit more quietly?' I wondered nervously.

'No,' said Said. 'Everyone talks about the situation all the time.'
Particularly to foreigners, it seemed, since wherever I went I was
singled out for such conversation as soon as it was discovered that I
came from abroad. None of my present companions showed any
liking for the present regime, but there was equally no desire to
return to what were regarded as the bad old days of the Shah. The
consensus of opinion was that the present regime was something
that had to be endured with resignation as a stepping stone, hopefully,
to something better. No one was happy about the lack of any
organised or strong opposition parties, or that the army had been
weakened by countless purges, or that the reactionary priesthood
was so firmly in control.

'You know,' one of the passengers told me. 'If you lift Khomeini's
beard you'll find the words "Made in England" written underneath.'

There was more laughter at this. I'd already heard the joke in
Turkey, and one explanation of it was that Khomeini's grandfather
had been born in Northern India when that country was under
British rule. The family had returned subsequently to Khomein in
Iran, where the Ayatollah's father, a mullah, was murdered – some
say by friends of a man he'd had executed for breaking the fast
during Ramadan. The joke is that the British, in their desire to divide
and rule, had Khomeini planted in Iran to sow religious dissent
and general discontent. Curiously, everybody had their reasons for
blaming the current turmoil on the British. Khomeini's supporters
pointed to the British Secret Service's complicity with the CIA in
the 1953 coup that brought the Shah back to power; anti-Khomeini
factions cited British collusion with Khomeini himself: 'After all,
how come the British diplomats weren't kicked out with the Yanks?'
More seriously, there was the widely-held belief that the British had
provided the names of hundreds of communists to the regime, as the
result of the defection of a Soviet diplomat called Vladimir Kuzichkin.
Those betrayed were executed, hundreds of arrests were made, and
the communist Tudeh party was banned.

We had reached the main road linking Dogubayazit, Tabriz and
Tehran. It is the main link road between Tehran and Europe and it
is not wide enough. We joined one single uninterrupted chain of
vehicles, nearly all of them lorries. Modern heirs to the goods-train,

articulated trucks came from all over Europe to queue on this road – from both parts of Germany, from Hungary, Greece, Yugoslavia, Romania, Italy, Czechoslovakia and Bulgaria – the last country's trucking concerns covering 25 per cent of road-transported goods into Iran. Their loads were building materials, concrete pylons, rolled steel, harvesters and armaments: up to 1500 lorries a day, the majority from the Eastern bloc.

It was dark, and we pulled into a roadside café whilst the trucks rumbled past, on a road whose sides were littered with the wreckage of other trucks – the results of drivers falling asleep at the wheel, or of misjudged overtaking, which was always done at tremendous speed.

After a night of fitful sleep in the bus, we approached the outskirts of the capital the following morning. The population of Tehran doubled between 1965 and 1980, and has all but doubled again since the Revolution because of a great shift of population from the country, and especially from the war front. The city is thus surrounded by huge, sprawling and ugly suburbs. It does not make an auspicious first impression.

TEHRAN

'Revolution!' I yelled as I stood in the middle of the road in a bid to stop one of the fixed-route taxis. I was on my toes, ready to spring back to the relative safety of the pavement if the taxi wasn't ready to stop. You had no warning, either way.

The taxis, like most of the cars in Tehran, are based on an old Hillman model, still rolling off the production line and called Pak-yans. To cross town effectively, you plan a route of interconnecting taxis, which really operate on the principle of buses, having a fixed journey but stopping wherever requested, and picking up whenever there's a spare seat (or even corner) according to the driver's whim. To stop one, all you have to do is stand in the middle of the screaming traffic and flag one down. It's simple, if you're brave and strong and don't set too high a value on your life, and you have to yell out your destination, because of course the taxis don't display their route, so you have to find one by trial-and-error. My destination that day was Revolution Square. Not surprisingly, all the street names have been changed since Khomeini seized power – and all the names that bore even the remotest reference to the Pahlavi dynasty have been expunged.

Any taxi depositing a passenger was immediately surrounded. Two women normally sat in the front, to segregate them from the men, who squeezed into the back. The cars were driven with the wild abandon of dodgems and the few remaining interior parts, like the odd door-handle or window winder, were held on with Sellotape. Turnover of passengers was fast, and so conversation within the car was terse. To alight, all you do is shout 'Baleh' at the driver, who will immediately and with no regard for any other traffic swerve to the kerb and drop you in exchange for a few pence. I found the whole experience hair-raising, for I wasn't always sure where I was, and if I asked fellow passengers the issue often got further muddled because in Iran an upward nod of the head means 'no'. No matter how well you understand this rationally, you are so conditioned to taking a nod to mean 'yes' that you always get confused.

Tehran is strangled by traffic. The streets are solid with vehicles and the pavements are jammed with people. The pavements are also filled with mopeds, which are the local equivalent of the small family car and usually carry mum, dad and the kids perched precariously everywhere, and all adding to the deafening noise.

The city is covered with graffiti – slogans proclaiming the virtues and aims of the Revolution. Posters and placards too: stuck up, torn down, replaced, reaffixed. And notices of the deaths of the 'martyrs' of the Gulf War. And slogans of loathing: NEITHER WEST NOR EAST! LIBERALISM: THE BUTCHER OF COLONIALISM AND THE STEAMROLLER OF IMPERIALISM! Huge murals which are portraits of the various ayatollahs, their patrician beards filling the frames. And everywhere the super-patrician Khomeini – solemn, proud and defiant: WE DEFEND THE OPPRESSED AND FIGHT THE OPPRESSOR. Radios ceaselessly play revolutionary chants, songs and sermons. Public address systems broadcast prayers. Television news starts with martial music and shots of tanks and multiple missile launchers ranked against the arch-infidel, Saddam Hussein of Iraq. Many people have grown immune to this unending aural bludgeoning, but in Ramadan, a holy month, I noticed that vendors of cassettes of sermons were doing a roaring trade.

There were, however, small, individual signs of defiance, little gestures of individuality: women wearing chadors or raincoats which were somehow stylish, or discreetly patterned: pinstripes, buttons, slivers of gold thread. And occasionally beneath them you could glimpse signs of wealth, of taste, of the real person: a gold watch, jewellery, jeans, a smart dress. Indeed it would be a mistake to assume that women are totally condemned to the chador. It is only in public that they must wear it. Under it they can dress how they like, within reason. There are shops in Tehran that sell the latest haute couture imported from France.

But defiance must be guarded, must be kept discreet. If not, you invite the wrath of the numerous self-styled guardians of public morality, the scum on the surface of any revolution. I heard of a woman who had taken to razor-slashing other women whom she thought improperly dressed. And there are the Guards of the Mobile

Units of the Wrath of God, and the Centre for Combating Sin, and, worst of all perhaps, the Hezb-ollahis (the partisans of the Party of God, sometimes referred to as the 'club wielders'). Brooding over all these petty corps is the omnipresent Revolutionary Guard. In the view of those most fanatically converted to the views and aims of Khomeini, the Ayatollah is a divine figure, and aide to the Twelfth Imam, whose mission is to save mankind.

Martial music is permitted. Pop music is not. All music that is not martial music is deemed to be pop music.

I settled into Tehran quickly. My first visit was to the British Interests Section of the Swedish Embassy. This is in fact the old British Embassy. The Swedes have their own embassy elsewhere, and so to all intents and purposes this is a British Embassy, staffed by British diplomats. It is only officially that there is no British Embassy!* The building stands in an enormous compound, its surrounding walls covered in graffiti exposing the duplicity, etc., of the infidels within. The guard at the gate only let me enter when I showed him my passport. I had no forwarding address other than the embassies en route and the Churchill Trust had given me the names of all the First Secretaries in them.

The First Secretary here was less than encouraging about the next leg of my journey, although of course his misgivings were couched in discreet terms:

'I have been given instructions by Her Majesty's Government and the Foreign Office to dissuade you from going to Afghanistan,' he told me. Did I say discreet? In fact I knew that there was really nothing he could do to stop me, but he made me angry. No doubt the truth was that HM Government would simply be embarrassed

---

* However the Iranians cannot guarantee British diplomatic immunity. Thus it is that we are there under the aegis of Sweden. The building I was in flew the Swedish flag.

if I were arrested or killed because then without doubt I'd be labelled a counter-revolutionary British spy. I had no intention of letting my country down, but to some extent I was my own representative too, and my mission was to cross frontiers, to communicate on an individual level, and to show that it was possible, in spite of all that politicians and soldiers could do.

I collected my letters, which after several months with no news were very welcome indeed, and I would pore over them again and again, reading them each time with as much eagerness as if it were the first. The nicest thing about the letters was that they put me in touch with world affairs, although I found I had not missed much during my travels.

Usually I feel nothing but disdain for the diplomatic and expatriate way of life, which, it seems to me, can only ever arouse resentment among locals, because diplomats and expats almost never enter into the spirit of their host country, often not even bothering to learn the language. Here, however, to a certain extent they were prisoners of their own environment, and deluged with requests for visas. Long queues formed outside the French, British and German embassies where touts operated and where the police had to hold the crowds in check, many sleeping on the pavement at night. They were seeking visas for their immediate family, but the line of questioning used by the diplomats soon revealed that most individuals had no intention of returning to Iran once they had escorted their families out.

'How many of you are planning to travel to England?'

'Just my wife and children.'

'What collateral can you offer us so that we know you will return?'

'Here is a letter of access to my bank accounts. Here are the deeds to my properties.'

'We may require more than that.'

'It's all I have.'

'We may require that one child be left here as guarantor of your return.'

Then, of course, there was uproar.

There were others, equally desperate to leave, but actually with a perfect right to a visa. They spoiled their chances by being over cagey when they were questioned. So desperate were some that they travelled as far afield as Indonesia, where they had heard visas to

Britain were easier to obtain, while others joined the line of refugees who left the country via the frontier with Turkey, to join the wretched band I had met in Hakkari; still others tried to cross the southern deserts of Baluchistan, to reach Pakistan.

As for the other major embassies, the US Embassy was now a training camp for Revolutionary Guards, and the Soviet Embassy was like a fortress: no wonder no one had attempted to penetrate the compound, and so forbidding did the building look that even its outer walls bore little graffiti – a rare sight in Tehran.

The next step was to discover somewhere to live. I found the Bozestan Hotel down an obscure alley overflowing with little workshops. I came upon it by chance – nobody could have found it unless they knew it. It was central, clean, friendly and cheap, more like a boarding pension than a hotel proper. Admittedly my room was small – I had to move sideways between table and bed – but there was an electric fan, and it worked. Communication was easy too, since the Shabestaris, who owned it, were from Iranian Azerbaijan and thus spoke Turkish as their mother-tongue. My only problem was to see if the local *hamam*, which is as much a social club as a bath-house, would accept me as a customer, since I was an infidel. The hotel itself had no bathrooms. In fact there was no problem at all; the hamam staff couldn't have been more agreeable. I decided to take a little time out to wind down, and think about what I'd done and what I had to do. Funnily enough the hotel had a large print of Lake Maggiore in the reception area. It seemed like another world – indeed it was. The two months that had passed since I had been there might just as well have been ten years.

Of all the staff and fellow-guests I especially took to Sadeeq. About 35, academic and gentle, he was an Iranian Baluchi, and thus not a Shia but a Sunni Muslim. He was constantly being taken for an Indian, and it irritated him when people ignored his perfectly good Persian and tried to talk to him in broken English. He'd been sent up here by his company to order spare parts, and every morning at seven he was woken by a phone call with his shopping-list for the day: water-pumps, gaskets, piston-heads. He was short, with thinning black hair and a jet black moustache, and he was an avid reader. He spent every spare moment of the day and night reading

— and he would read on every subject imaginable. He was working his way methodically through the great writers of the world, and his room was crowded with them, in teetering piles: Persian translations of Shakespeare, Dostoevsky, Hugo, Descartes, Plato . . . one by one, they kept him company during his annual three-month sojourn in Tehran, and at the end of his stay they would be shipped home to Baluchistan. He'd had barely any formal education, but he spoke four languages fluently. His English was perfect, too, though he couldn't write it, and he said his ambition was to be able to read it.

'To read your great writers in their own language, that would indeed be a pleasure,' he would say, his eyes shining. Whenever he was confronted with an electrical fault, like a broken pump, he sought a solution in his books. Similarly, if he was ill, he would resort to self-diagnosis through his books.

'I don't trust doctors,' he said.

I felt frankly ashamed that I was so poorly read myself, the more so since he regarded me, being English, as an oracle on all matters pertaining to English literature.

'Surely you have read *Chance* — a traveller like you.'

'I'm afraid not.'

'Perhaps you do not care for Conrad.'

'That may be it.'

Sadeeq remained forever humble and modest, and therefore my ignorance mystified him, and the gaps in my knowledge of literature confused him. I was simply sorry that I could not be a more entertaining person for him to talk to. For his part, he was constantly amusing and helpful. He was also a perfect guide to Tehran, and took delight in showing me the city.

He took me up through the northern suburbs to visit the palace of the Shah. I should explain that north and south Tehran are two different worlds. The south is a noisy, vigorous jumble of poor people, jostling traffic, winding streets, noise, dust, heat, crowded humanity. The north is cooler, the streets are wide, uncluttered, quiet. Large cars glint in garages, white villas stand in lush gardens. There are small supermarkets with western goods and air-conditioning. At the highest and coolest point stands the Pahlavi Palace, only now it is a people's park, and you gain admission by paying for a ticket which includes a guided tour.

The palace is a masterpiece of craftsmanship and shows the skills of the woodcarver, the tileworker and the mosaic-designer. It is sumptuous and costly, and yet also somehow cold, and even vulgar in its blousy display of wealth. Is it that there is simply too much on display that makes it seem gross, for none of the individual items is vulgar? I wandered through its rooms with mixed feelings, for now, interspersed with the treasures, there are large photographs of how people were neglected under the Shah. Above a Sèvres tea service hovers a starving child. Behind a Louis XV settee an old woman scratches at dust with a wooden rake. The Empress Farah's walk-in wardrobe contains a hundred evening gowns: near them, a bulldozer has flattened a shanty-town. The dispossessed stand mutely by.

Back at the Bozestan Hotel I was greeted by Tarik, one of the resident guests and a street pedlar in electrical equipment. His grin was especially broad for today he'd actually made a sale: a tape recorder. The next to greet me was Abdullah, the dishevelled but always chirpy cleaner. Abdullah's English was very limited, but he aired its full extent whenever he met me:

'One-two-three-four-five-*egg*!'

Actually the counting was my fault, since I'd taught him, and the 'egg' he'd picked up by himself. Well, we quite frequently ate eggs. Perhaps he was asking me how many I wanted. But I think not.

Mr Shabestari invited me to take tea with him. This is drunk in the same way as in Turkey, filtered into the mouth through a piece of sugar held between the teeth. The only difference is that here the tea is served so boiling hot that it's poured into the saucer and drunk from there.

My first few days in Tehran had whetted my appetite for more and so I decided to set about renewing my visa. I girded up my loins for a real battle, but funnily enough in what should have been a bastion of political conformity, the police aliens' department, there was a genial atmosphere of combined humour and resignation. The place was packed with Asian students, and the offices were divided into those for Eastern Bloc citizens, Western Bloc citizens, and Others. Whilst supplicants jostled about nervously in the waiting area, the three offices, open to view, remained largely empty, the policemen behind the desks hidden behind an Everest of paperwork but pushing papers around like children toying with food.

Ultimately my turn came, but my request was greeted with disbelief.

'The Ministry of Foreign Affairs is aware of my predicament,' I pointed out, politely but firmly.

'Do you want an extension from them, or from us?' retorted the policeman in charge, curtly.

'If you are prepared to grant me an extra two weeks, I will leave matters in your hands,' I replied, magnanimously. I was handed a form and filled it in, leaving my occupation blank. It is a good idea, when given a form, to leave as much blank as possible. I hoped very much that this blank would go unnoticed as I'd been posing, up to now, as a journalist, artist, writer, student, teacher, police interpreter, truck-driver and tourist, as the occasion demanded. The corresponding space in my passport was blank, and I changed that, too, in pencil, according to circumstances.

The policeman looked up. 'Occupation?' he said sharply. He'd noticed.

'University lecturer,' I plumped.

'In what?'

'History of art.'

'History of art,' repeated the officer, with a dry laugh.

'I beg your pardon?'

'Iranian history of art . . . history of blood,' he mumbled. 'Come back in a day or two.'

I made many subsequent visits. The Everests of paper disappeared, and in one office the policeman was reduced to flicking paperclips from his desk onto the floor. No progress was made.

'Come back in a day or two,' they said.

While I was waiting I came to know the city better. The laws were harsh. It was still Ramadan, and though some people sneaked meals or glasses of water in back rooms during the day, they did so at their peril. I remember a woman getting into a fixed-route taxi in tears. Her eight menfolk had been surprised in the middle of a meal by Revolutionary Guards, arrested and taken away. Indoor games, like cards, chess and backgammon, the last two ironically almost certainly invented in Persia, were now banned, deemed to be unhealthy. The sports pages of the papers exhorted people to train their children in swimming and archery. Television films were heavily censored and I was amazed to see university students going wild over, of all things, old Norman Wisdom movies.

Sadeeq was keen on the movies, but there wasn't much choice in Tehran, apart from a profusion of war films. We opted for an Italian thriller. The cinema had all the friendly ambiance of a tube station at rush hour, people constantly coming and going irrespective of the film's progress. Of course the film had been cut to ribbons but there was one very striking moment that had escaped the scissors – a woman appeared in a sleeveless cardigan. This sent the all-male audience into a state of near-hysterical excitement.

There were great inconsistencies. Communist literature is banned, and yet English copies of Marx and Engels were freely available. At the Museum of Modern Art, I was saddened but not surprised to see that the entire priceless collection had disappeared. Only a few heavy statues, by Moore and Giacometti, remained neglected in the museum gardens, not hidden from view but emphatically not included in the exhibition. The exhibition itself was a nightmare of Iranian post-revolutionary art: a sort of debased surrealism obsessed with blood and death, and crude political propaganda. 'Martyrs' City' was vaguely reminiscent of Magritte: only his clouds were replaced here by floating, shrouded corpses. In another, a barefooted, chadored woman stands on a windswept hill holding a gun from whose muzzle a rose, the symbol of martyrdom, extends. Wrapped in the folds of her chador at her back, a baby sleeps: a mixture of belligerence and cloying sentimentality. Yet another depicts Jesus fleeing from a shirtsleeved Mr Hyde, on whose chest are tattooed a gun, a Star of David and a whisky bottle. The message of the painting is written on it, in English: 'While running away Jesus said: "An ignorant man is coming."'

Most of the paintings were figurative – unusual in Islamic art and indeed proscribed by the Koran. I asked one of the artists about this apparent anomaly.

'You will notice that the figures are not well painted,' he said. This was indeed true, although the general technical execution wasn't at all bad. 'This is deliberate. Minor faults are intentional because only God can create perfection.'

So man has to be deliberately imperfect, I wondered, but did not say.

The Revolution is certainly far from perfect. The residents at the hotel and Mr Shabestari in particular were always treating me to eggs – fried or scrambled. I decided to buy some eggs of my own and repay the hospitality, and so I went to a small grocery shop nearby and asked for a dozen. Although there were plenty of eggs, the grocer couldn't sell me any.

'Why not?' I asked.

The man shrugged apologetically: 'Essential food.'

I had forgotten that. Eggs are thus classified and so cannot be purchased without ration tickets, which are only obtainable through the mosque. But this isn't rationing as we understand it. There are no strict quotas of food, but it is dispensed according to one's standing, piety, and the level of one's donations to the mosque. Thus to buy eggs, for example, you have to be well in with your local mullah.

Everyone talked about the corruption that had existed under the Shah, but there was clearly some under the new élite. Vast sums of money could be made on import licences, and possession of a Letter of Credit for specified goods to be imported gave the holder what amounted to a licence to circumvent Iran's currency restrictions. Not very surprisingly, such Letters exchanged hands at high prices, and a new class of *nouveaux riches* is emerging, with contacts with the clergy and the Revolutionary Committees, many of whom forget about their revolutionary zeal when it comes to making money. Millions of dollars collected in fines have not found their way to the State Exchequer. By yet another irony, the black market in Iran is referred to as the 'free' market.

'Anything is possible and everything is obtainable in Iran today,' one young racketeer confided in me. Yet I was surprised to find not a few people prepared to risk execution by peddling heroin. More innocently, while pop music is banned, I went to more than one party where, behind closed doors and windows, and drawn curtains, Michael Jackson was softly played and danced to. There were no chadors at these gatherings – men and women were together, their faces a mixture of sadness and temporary relief – a kind of abashed delight. To drink, 'rocket-fuel' – a loathsome vodka made from distilled raisins, but at least, however clumsily home-made, blissfully alcoholic. These were sad occasions for me. The music was so soft that if anybody talked you couldn't hear it, and although I was made welcome I knew that my presence represented a risk for my friends. Had anyone seen them talk to me in the street? Followed us home? I didn't like keeping my distance from people who in happier circumstances would have become friends, but I didn't want to bring trouble on them either. That I went to their parties at all was because their sadness attracted me (sadness does), and I flattered myself that my presence might in some way alleviate their melancholy.

At one of these parties I ran into Majid, a young man who'd just returned from military service, and he offered to borrow his parents' car (they lived in the prosperous northern suburbs) and take me to visit Behesht-i-Zahra.

Behesht-i-Zahra means Gateway to Heaven. It is a vast cemetery on the outskirts of southern Tehran, and it is the place where Khomeini first spoke on his return from exile in 1979. It is also the location of the Fountain of Blood – which spouts red-dyed water in commemoration of the Iranian martyrs, and which provides a focus for all the conflicting factions in the Iranian government. Majid got the car without difficulty and we drove down from his elegant home (it might have been an elegant suburban home in any western city) through the teeming southern part of the town. As we approached the cemetery Majid became less and less enthusiastic about the outing which he himself had proposed.

The place was far larger than I had expected. It is unlike a western cemetery. The 'tombstones' are actually small metal and glass kiosks, each containing a photograph of the deceased and memorabilia connected with him. There are also plastic flowers in gaudy vases, and a photograph of Khomeini. Often the 'martyr' is somehow forgotten amongst the mess of propaganda that shares his memorial. Tens of thousands of people lie here, and as far as the eye can see stretch the flags – red for martyrdom, black for Shia and green for Islam – waving over the incomprehensible self-destruction of a nation's youth, casting their shadows over the fathers, mothers and wives who mourn there.

But here there is no equality in death. The sectarian lines were drawn up according to political merit. Pride of place goes to those who have died in the holy war against Iraq, and to those who died in the revolution against the Shah – provided, that is, that they were Muslim revolutionaries, and not communists. I asked to see the communist graves. Majid became worried, but he did take me to the corner where these non-Muslim revolutionaries were allowed to lie. However, when I asked to see where those who had fought for the Shah lay buried, he became almost aggressively nervous.

'Very well. I will drive you to that part. But I cannot stay with you. I will collect you after five minutes.'

He dropped me and drove off. Even in death these counter-revolutionaries were ostracised. They lay alone, without shrines, under blank concrete slabs. No one dared mourn them.

I was profoundly shocked by the wanton waste of human life represented by this obscenely large cemetery. Later, I was to see it duplicated in every Iranian city I visited.

Majid collected me as he had promised, but his attitude towards me had cooled and, like so many others, once the initial novelty of talking to a foreigner had worn off, he decided that it would be less risky not to be seen with me. No relationship could be entered into without suspicion.

This was true even with the Afghan refugees who had taken menial jobs in the city (Tehran is a cosmopolitan eastern town, with many Bengalis, Sikhs, Sri Lankans and so on, but the Afghans are definitely second-class citizens). I came into increasing contact with Afghans, from whom I hoped to learn of conditions in their country. Many were too miserable or too frightened to talk very coherently. They worked as waiters and dishwashers, bearing the brunt of much animosity and racial abuse. One waiter I met had been beaten up no less than three times by the dreaded *Baseej-i-Mustazaffin* (Mobilis-ation of the Deprived Volunteers), and on the last occasion they had actually dragged him from the restaurant where he worked to do their dirty work.

Other Afghans had been sent to Tehran to recuperate from their war wounds, but they only spoke to me of their desire to return to the war front. Once in touch with these freedom fighters it became easier to gather information, but the news was not good. A vicious Soviet offensive in the Herat area was claiming thousands of civilian casualties, and as many more were fleeing blindly into Iran as scarcely welcome refugees. Russian carpet bombing, in response to successful rebel activity, had destroyed many villages. There would be little hope of my crossing into Afghanistan under cover while fleeing refugees were causing so much border activity. I would have to wait until things simmered down.

Not being one to waste time, however, I decided to put it to good use by becoming a real tourist and exploring more of Iran. I said my goodbyes at the Bozestan, and packed my bags. To my surprise, I found a watch in one of them. At first I thought it must have slipped from the wrist of a customs man, but then I noticed that it bore traces of pink paint. I remembered decorators at a hotel back in Turkey. They'd obviously been rifling my bag. I hadn't really checked its contents since. Nervously, I did so now. Fortunately they'd taken nothing but some dysentery tablets. That seemed a fair swap for a watch, which would make a good gift for someone.

The following morning, I shouldered my pack and headed for the bus station.

OF AYATOLLAHS
AND MULLAHS

As the bus emerged from the stark and arid hills we descended towards the plateau where the golden copper dome of Fatima's shrine glinted in the sun, its baroque minarets dominating the city of Qom. It was still early, but the heat was already suffocating. We passed men lying in the shade of the trees in a state of collapse, but forbidden by the fast to take food or drink until dusk.

Immediately after we'd arrived I set off for Fatima's shrine. The tomb of the sister of the eighth Shia Imam makes Qom one of the holiest cities in the Shia Islamic world. From here, too, Khomeini first preached against the Shah. Qom is the ideological crucible of Shia Islam and no aircraft may fly over it. I followed the narrow, deserted streets past souvenir shops selling holy memorabilia, and little clay tablets made from the ground of Mecca and Medina. The salesmen were almost too listless to trade.

The city is home to over 15,000 theological students, and as their schools are grouped around the shrine I expected to see the place teeming with young men clutching piles of books. Instead I saw only turbaned men in black gowns and brown or white robes – the *rohani*, or clergy, who strode purposefully to and fro past the front of the shrine, the backs of their shoes bent flat to make them into *babouches*.

Islam is hard for westerners to understand, for it is a way of life as much as a way of worship. Everything is ordained, and life is led from a set of instructions, the *Hadith*, or sayings of the Prophet, and from the Koran. Unlike the Sunnis, however, the Shias constantly re-evaluate the sacred texts, and Qom is the spiritual epicentre of that work. Students of Islam from over 40 countries, including England, study here.

I knew better than to enter the holy place, the more so since beneath an Arabic inscription to the glory of Allah another in English forbade entry to infidels. I was left to admire the intricate tilework and calligraphy of the portals, even though the overall aesthetic impression was marred by a row of dusty Nissan ambulances parked along the wall. I followed a line of pilgrims around the walls to the main entrance, and through it I was straining for a view of the interior when I felt a hand on my shoulder.

'Papers,' said an officious unshaven man in a suit. There was no doubt about it. I was under arrest.

Actually my arrest had its advantages, for I was taken inside the mosque to the guardians' office. The reflected light from the white stone was blinding. The office was in one of the side-cells set in the walls of a courtyard. I was asked to sit down and they checked my papers in their usual laborious way.

'Who are you?' they asked. 'Why are you here? What are you doing? Where are you going?' They were courteous and pleasant. Only the man who'd arrested me nagged like a terrier.

'I'm going to Qom,' I said, politely. After all, I'd only just arrived and I was tired from the bus journey. I was in no mood for a fight. They looked at me doubtfully, and made several phonecalls, while I watched what was going on in the courtyard outside: men making their ritual ablutions before prayer at the pool at its centre, making sure that no water passed their lips for fear of breaking the fast; and women, not in the black chadors of perpetual mourning but in motley shirts and trousers – the *shalwar camise* which is one of the universal outfits of the east, and which I would soon adopt myself.

The officials finished making their phonecalls and barked orders at each other. My interrogator took me by the arm and marched me out of the mosque.

'Where are we going?' I asked him.

'Bus station,' he replied, firmly. He must have been very hot in that suit, but he kept the jacket buttoned.

Once we'd arrived at the bus station, he asked me once more, 'Where are you going?'

'Esfahan,' I said, realising that this was one fight lost from the start. However there was no disturbing the sleeping ticket clerk. There was nothing to be done but wait, in a waiting room that could have doubled as an oven, until the Esfahan bus arrived. My poor guardian not only had to stay with me, but he had to stay awake. I think by the time he saw me off he was beginning seriously to regret his zeal.

On the Esfahan bus I encountered the usual friendly atmosphere. Passengers mimed winding a turban round their head in silent sympathetic mockery of the mullahs, and I soon cheered up in the warmth of their company. Travellers gain an extra bonus during Ramadan: they are allowed to eat during the day. (I couldn't resist imagining a whole nation continuously on the move in order to avoid fasting.) The two drivers were clowning around, one exchanging the driving seat with the other while the bus travelled at full speed, Ali's foot on the accelerator and Ahmed's hands on the wheel. As we overtook a pick-up truck laden with fruit, one of them reached over and grabbed some fruit from the top of the pile, distributing it among the passengers. There was plenty of refreshment: endless cups of iced water on the bus itself, and frequent stops at roadside cafés for rice and mutton with *nan* and tea or soft drinks. The method of buying this food was curious: you actually bought plastic tokens which you then exchanged for the food. This may have been a kind of hygiene control – those who handled the food never handled money.

It was dusk by the time we reached Esfahan, though the driver did not slacken his pace one jot and took delight at charging roundabouts, scattering cyclists and pedestrians with a blare of his horn as his colleague hung out of the window and hurled abuse at them for not getting out of the way quicker. Finally he jammed on the brakes and dumped us all on the pavement. I had bought a *Guide Bleu* to Iran in Tehran so I was not at quite such a loss about where to go as I'd been in Urumiyeh. The first thing to do was find a place to sleep.

I walked the length of the Tchahar Bagh (the Four Gardens), a wide, tree-lined boulevard flanked by shops. People were promenading along it, jostling with beggars on the pavement. The air was still, heavy, and laden with dust. I tried a number of hotels but I found their prices (£1 a night) exorbitant. Finally I settled for a room without a window but with a fan in a hotel which was found for me by a young man who had inexplicably first taken me to an antique shop run by an old Jew. A small group of Jews had settled here in the fifth century, and the locals still refer to them as Israelites, or *Kalimis* (Followers of Moses). Although the Jews have not been persecuted, the old man was nervous of talking to me. I could well imagine that the mob rule prevalent in Iran must have been a constant source of fear to him in the twilight of his life.

Esfahan has no peer. The Iranians say 'Esfahan nesf-i Djahan': Esfahan is half the world. Half the world, that is, in size, beauty and richness. To my eye the city's architecture was a feast. The mosques' glazed domes breathed coolness and transparency, reflecting the sunlight in a subtle play of light and shade. Imperial Square is now called Imam Square (of course), but it is still surrounded by a regular cadence of vaulted arches, only interrupted by the royal buildings.

At one end of the square is a bazaar – a warren of covered streets the size of a London neighbourhood. As soon as I passed under its great portals I was approached by 'carpet dealers' – risking death to deal in foreign exchange. I felt sorry for these men, all by nature traders, now doomed to a kind of suspended animation by the regime. Like most businessmen, they wanted a government that would serve their principal interest in life – making money. They had no time for Khomeini's anachronistic idealism. With little to do, the merchants in the bazaar went to each other's stalls to chat. They regretted they couldn't take tea with me because of the fast, though I did see one push a rug aside to reveal a water-bottle from which he took a swig. He introduced me to Firouz, who sold repoussé work. Firouz spoke English and once he'd learnt that I was an artist asked me if I'd consider drawing a traditional Iranian female nude so that one of his artisans could translate this highly illegal drawing onto metal. He told me that he'd taken over the business from his father. In his father's day it had been so prosperous that he'd been sent away to study in the USA with a fat allowance. He'd married an American and even had a Green Card.

'Why haven't you left Iran, then?' I asked him.

'I can't renew my passport,' he sighed. 'I've avoided the draft so far, but if I renew my passport, it'll almost certainly mean I'll get called up and be sent to the Front.' He was hopelessly lost – divorced from his wife, who'd found life in Iran impossible. He invited me to his house, and played Fleetwood Mac and the Rolling Stones on his cassette player as we drove over there. But every time we slowed down he turned the volume low in case the music was overheard. At home, for lack of any other recreation, he played with a deck of cards so much used that it was barely possible to identify them individually any more.

On learning that I wanted to travel on to Shiraz, Firouz offered to drive me there at the end of the week and in the meantime he invited me to stay with him. He lived with his parents, grandmother and brother in a traditional house whose blank outer wall, facing the street, gave no hint of what lay beyond. It was a one-storey building set round a courtyard with a pool at its centre. The living rooms faced the courtyard and the workrooms were set at the rear. There was no furniture other than cushions, my room had a mattress rolled out for a bed. Meals were served on trays and placed before us on the sumptuous carpets. The food was rich and varied. They offered me a fork, but I preferred to eat as they did – using their right hand, and a piece of *nan* for a spoon.

The days and evenings were spent sitting on the shaded verandah, which was reached by several steps. Our main topic of conversation was religion. Firouz senior, who only rarely went to the bazaar, maintained that he was a good Muslim, but declared that Khomeini was not. This was fighting talk, for one of his daughters was married to a Revolutionary Guard. I was looking forward to meeting this son-in-law, and on my last day in Esfahan I did. He was a high-ranking officer and I hoped it might be possible to have a reasonable conversation with him, but he was too full of revolutionary zeal. All he could talk about was the Ordained Path and the Righteous Cause of Islam.

'You have a new baby,' I said. 'Don't you owe something to your family?'

'My duty is neither to my family, nor even to Iran,' he replied. 'It is to Islam.'

I refrained from asking him why in that case he had started a family in the first place.

'My task is to propagate the message of Islam,' he continued, in the rhythmic tones of Persian that would have sounded charming had their content been different.

'You might die,' I said.

'Martyrdom isn't death. We live for death in a holy cause. Our greatest reward is to die for Islam.'

However he did admit the possibility that Iran might not win the

Gulf War – and he was the first and only zealot I met to do so. It was a big concession.

Firouz and I left for Shiraz on a national holiday to mark the anniversary of the First Imam – Ali, the Commander of the Faithful. It was also the nineteenth day of Ramadan, and Firouz, who had yet to adhere to the fast for even one day, decided that he would do so today as a test of will. This meant that the 300-mile journey was nothing short of purgatory for him. The road lay across parched desert land, barren hills and naked mountains. The sun had burnt the landscape into every possible shade of brown. On several occasions we stopped to top up the car radiator, and each time Firouz insisted that I eat and drink. When, out of sympathetic solidarity, I refused, he became angry. He seemed determined to be a martyr today.

As we approached Pasargadae the scenery began to change: we saw herds of goats, and then nomads' tents. Children emerged from behind a hill and ran towards us like ambushers, their little bodies covered in dust, running along by the car and beseeching us for water. We had reached the province of Fars, where the two great Persian dynasties, the Achaemenid and the Sassanid, were born. Streams gave way to canals and irrigated fields, and the unrelieved browns turned to yellows and greens. The people we passed were semi-nomadic Qashqai, their language a mixture of Turkish and Persian. They are easily recognisable by their hats – brimless bowlers with an upturned flap, perched precariously on the very tops of their heads.

Finally, mercifully, dusk fell, and in the distance the flames from the Shiraz refineries were clearly visible. As soon as we reached the city, Firouz drew up at a refreshment stand, and proceeded to drink it dry. I sympathised with him, and found myself more than making up for the fast at the end of the day.

Firouz found me a hotel with some difficulty, because Shiraz is a holy city and on this day, which also happened to precede the Sabbath, it was full of pilgrims. When the time came to say goodbye, both of us looked grim. I had to face the road alone again, and Firouz would no longer have a diversion from the protracted misery his life had become. I only hope that he has managed to find some happiness by now.

The next day large rallies were held in the vicinity of the mosque, Masdjed-i-Vakil. I rose early, to quiet streets. Unusually quiet, and there was a heavy police and Pasdaran presence. I approached the mosque in trepidation, taking care to roll down my shirtsleeves. No one stopped me from entering but like everyone else I was thoroughly searched. The mosque was quite beautiful, though its courtyard was covered in scaffolding over which a rough canvas awning was spread to protect the worshippers from the sun. The colours were the deep blues and lemon yellows of Esfahan, joined by pink, white, green and gold. The roof of the prayer room was supported by five rows of barley-sugar columns. Not wanting to offend anyone I asked an official if I could take photographs. He said 'no', but to my surprise he suggested I come back at prayer-time, when I would be allowed to.

With time to kill, I wandered the streets, visiting the much-venerated mausoleum of Shah Tcheragh, and watching the life on the streets. Sitting outside the Madrasah-i-Khan, oblivious to the rubbish in the street, the graffiti and the parked cars, a mullah sat counselling a woman. She was a young woman, cradling her baby. The mullah sat cross-legged on the stained tarmac, his holy books carefully resting on a sheet next to him. Every so often he would consult the scriptures, raising his hand to add weight to his arguments. It was an intimate scene, and a timeless one. I was allowed past them into the Madrasah after only a cursory search, but I hesitated as I entered it, seeing no one in the shaded courtyard but mullahs, who were conferring in small groups as birds sang overhead. They seemed more amused than anything by my presence. I looked at them sitting in the dilapidated courtyard, a certain knowledge of power in their eyes: a contrast, perhaps, to the old mullah counselling outside. These were Khomeini's executives – the men who had helped him pull Iran back to the Middle Ages.

Hearing the muezzin summon the faithful to prayer, I hurried back through the streets to the Masdjed-i-Vakil. Machine-gun toting

79

Revolutionary Guards patrolled the streets, some even guarding the standpipes to make sure that nobody drank. I was desperate for a drink myself, but could only sprinkle water on my face and arms. There were others worse off than me. I saw a man shield his wife, who was carrying their baby, from a Pasdar's gaze, so that she could take a brief, surreptitious drink. Another group, who'd been moved away from a standpipe, caught my eye. We exchanged rueful grins – a small sign of solidarity against the oppressors. But now people's attention was drawn away.

We could hear the sound of marching feet approaching the mosque. In a moment a column of those ready for martyrdom approached – Baseej volunteers. They were raw recruits, unarmed, in new fatigues, mainly the under-18s and the over-40s, those either too young or too old for regular army service. Some looked worried, some nervous, others proud. Some cheered. 'We are the righteous army!' they shouted, and their cries were echoed by the massive crowd that had gathered to support them. They would have six weeks' training before being sent to the front.

The mosque was packed, its entrance guarded by a number of men with Kalashnikovs. I was to see many of these Russian and Chinese-made automatic rifles over the next couple of months. A young man took charge of me and ushered me past the courtyard into the prayer hall, where the mullah was in the middle of a bellicose sermon. For my benefit they switched on powerful lights and I brought out my cameras. Suddenly the congregation erupted, beating their breasts with their right hands and shouting, 'Ali! Ali! Ali! Ali!' Some were moved to tears as they lamented the martyrdom of their First Imam, fourteen centuries ago.

I thought my best method of travel was to keep moving from town to town, for there was always the danger of not having permission to roam around Iran. If I was caught and seriously questioned, I might put my chances of reaching Afghanistan in serious jeopardy. I might even be repatriated. Thus it was that I decided not to stay too long in Shiraz. I wasn't leaving, however, without visiting Persepolis, the great Achaemenid metropolis known as Takht-e-Djamchid in Persian. The journey took me back along the road to Esfahan, and as I was hitching it involved several rides and an hour-and-a-half's time. Finally I arrived at the monumental stairway which gives access to the terrace, its foundation built of immense but perfectly cut stones. Founded in the early sixth century BC by Darius the Great, it never held the political or economic importance of Suse or Babylon, but it was here that Darius' son Xerxes erected his sumptuous palaces and halls, which were destroyed by Alexander the Great when the city fell to him in the course of his great push east from Macedonia in the fourth century BC. I was especially impressed by the long bas-reliefs showing representatives of vassal peoples to Babylonia – Sogdians, Parthians, Scythians, Ethiopians and Egyptians, with gifts of animals, weapons and vases. It is quite an experience to see Persepolis in these days of the Iranian Revolution, for there are no tourists about, and in the withering heat, in the silence and isolation of the desert that now surrounds it, the city stands stark and proud against the hard blue sky. From a distance it could be any size, so perfect are its proportions: gargantuan or miniature. It is one of the world's cultural tragedies that such a work of art should now be so inaccessible.

However, a still greater tragedy was only just averted. Persepolis represents the old order, the monarchy. It was built by a king, and according to the Prophet the title of King is the most hated of all titles in the sight of God. Naturally Mahomet's words have been taken quite literally by his followers. Nearly all statues of former shahs have been toppled and smashed, and references to shahs and kings at archaeological sites have been scarred and defaced.

I was told that only a last-minute intervention had prevented a Commander of the Revolutionary Guard from having Persepolis bulldozed.

Returning to Shiraz I hitched a lift with several Afghans in a car. One of them stood apart from the rest. He was dressed in western clothes and spoke some English. I didn't immediately start talking to him about my proposed visit to Afghanistan because he was a leader of the Hesbi, one of the major Afghan resistance groups but a rival group to the Jamiat-i-Islami which I hoped to join. He told me that his name was Mahmud, and unlike his Iranian counterparts, his attitude was both open and moderate. We discussed the splendours of Persepolis and as I began to feel more at ease with him I started to edge towards talking about Afghanistan. He might be trustworthy. After all, he was a fundamentalist, and Jamiat was a fundamentalist group.

I told him first about the general aims of my journey, and when I mentioned that my route would take me through his country he beamed with delight. However, he quickly became severe again, and warned me of the almost insurmountable dangers I would have to face.

'And no one has got through to Pakistan from Iran by way of Afghanistan,' he concluded. 'No European, that is.'

'Perhaps I might be the first.'

'Perhaps. And how do you intend to cross Afghanistan?'

Hesitantly I told him that I planned to make contact with the Jamiat, and Ismail Khan, their leader in Herat.

'Wise decision,' he said immediately. 'The situation in the Herat area has become extremely grim. You couldn't possibly travel alone even if you were disguised and had safe-conduct passes from the mujahedeen. The Jamiat control most of the Herat region and I'm sure they'll do their best to help you.'

I couldn't help suspecting him for his totally disinterested standpoint, but if he did have any ulterior motive for being so open and friendly, I couldn't put my finger on it. As we arrived back in Shiraz and they dropped me, he jotted down his phone number.

'I'll be in Mashhad next week. If you need any help when you get there, give me a ring.'

If all Afghans were going to be as endearing as the ones I'd just met I shouldn't have many problems.

Back at the hotel a young man came over and introduced himself as Daoud – 'But you can call me David'. He was the desk clerk and he'd just arrived on duty. Hearing that I'd checked into the hotel, he came over to introduce himself to me as he wanted the opportunity to speak some English. Having spent fourteen years of his life in England, attending a public school and university there, he was far more English than me.

'I got home just before the revolution and I haven't had the chance to speak English since,' he told me, gesturing around the foyer, where, it was true, there were no tourists. 'Only pilgrims,' said David, a little sadly. 'That's all we get these days.'

Like many Iranians who remembered the days of the foreign

tourist boom he spoke with a mixture of nostalgia and pity about the good old/bad old days of the sixties, remembering the cannabis trail and the long-haired hippies who travelled it, camping in Iran on their way to Afghanistan and India. We chatted on into the evening and when his shift was over he took me home with him to meet his brother Yusuf.

'Wotcher, mate,' said Yusuf, who'd studied engineering at a London polytechnic.

'Is that where you got your accent?'

'Nah – New Cross.'

He went on to tell me about the way he made a living in London, picking up old bangers for £50, doing them up with a mate and then selling them for a tidy profit. 'We used to make abaht a tenner a bash.' He'd been able to live cheaply – £8 a week in a flat in a housing association that had been opened by Prince Philip. Then he had returned to Iran and the revolution.

'With the visa and the money situations the way they are, we don't have a hope in hell of getting out just now,' said David. 'All we can do is make the best of it, settle down and start a family.' He'd taken his own advice already. 'But do you know,' he continued, 'the government is actually thinking of imposing a law that says you mustn't give your kids non-Islamic names. Thank God my kid's already got one.'

'What is it?'

'Souren.'

The brothers produced some 'rocket fuel' from what looked like old Evian water bottles, and poured out generous slugs over ice.

I was by now treating my *Guide Bleu* as a kind of bible, and following its lead decided to head for Yezd in the north-east. On a long journey a lot can depend on who's sitting next to you on the bus. A boring or irritating companion can turn what might have been pleasant into purgatory. I found myself unable to avoid sitting next to a bearded Pasdar in his mid-twenties, dressed in fatigues. As I'd expected, he didn't lose much time in asking me what I thought of Khomeini. I didn't want a lecture, and the thought of being harangued for the next six hours was too much for me. I smiled politely.

'Khomeini's fine,' I said.

That wouldn't do. 'Fine? what do you mean, fine?'

I wondered if I should pretend to be feeling travel-sick. Anything to put him off. 'It seems to me that the majority of the people are behind Khomeini, and that's fine by me,' I tried.

'You can't mean that!' he replied; but his tone was incredulous rather than belligerent, and he nudged me in the side as if to say, 'you can trust me'. I didn't feel like putting this to the test, though, and I looked away, rubbing my brow as if in pain. Maybe he'd leave me alone after all.

He leant closer to me and lowered his voice: 'Khomeini has destroyed our nation – he is an enemy of the people.' Now it was my turn to be incredulous. He looked triumphant, and permitted himself a small smile. 'I am a member of the communist party,' he continued. 'I'm wanted in Tehran by the police so I've moved south to join another cell. There is a lot of work to be done.'

'Why are you dressed like a Pasdar?'

He smiled more broadly. 'It's a good disguise. It fooled you. And dressed like this, I'm not searched at checkpoints.'

By now, of course, he'd warmed to his theme: the role of the communists in the downfall of the Shah. It made me think of what would happen if Khomeini fell from power. The opposition factions seemed to be in such ideological disunity that once the throne was empty again, as it were, there would surely be another wave of bloodshed.

We arrived in Yezd in the early afternoon. It's a city born of man's ingenuity, harboured in the centre of a sandy desert but watered and irrigated by underground canals which lead from the massive Shir Kuh mountains to the west. The water is stored in underground cisterns which are cooled by patterned-brick wind-towers. These towers look a bit like elongated, partially-open matchboxes, and are designed to trap and funnel downwards every scrap of wind. A sort of super air conditioning. It's a giddying city, everything is vertical – towers, minarets, houses with high blank walls turned to the narrow streets – wide enough for a cart to pass, but narrow enough to trap the maximum amount of shade. To walk the streets there was to be suspended in time – there was nothing modern to relate to. Now and then a fleeting black shadow would disappear round a corner – a woman in her chador, escaping the eye of the outsider.

The main reason for my visit to Yezd was to see its Zoroastrian community. There are about 50,000 people here who follow the teachings of the Persian prophet Zarathustra. It is an ancient religion, founded some six centuries before the birth of Christ, and based on the dualistic nature of the universe, symbolised by their belief in the continuous struggle between the god of creation and light, Ormazd, and the god of destruction and darkness, Ahriman. My communist friend from the bus, who'd introduced himself as Ghulam, offered to show me a Zoroastrian temple. He'd never visited one himself, however, and had to stop and ask directions from some women. They were Zoroastrians, as was immediately apparent from the fact that they didn't wear the chador, nor were they veiled. Indeed, their skirts were knee-length, though they wore knickerbocker-length trousers underneath. Their faces were entirely European, and one of them looked exactly like the lady who keeps the local cornershop in any English village.

At first they appeared to be nervous of us, but when they learnt that I was a visitor, they welcomed me with broad smiles and told us how to get to their temple. When we arrived there, the custodians were no less welcoming. It was a modern building, no more than 50 years old, set in a garden with a circular pool before the steps that led up to a colonnaded verandah which was surmounted by a tile portrait of Zarathustra at the centre of an enormous span of feathered wings. Like the painting of him that hung in the reception room, executed in 1951 in Bombay and the only decoration other than a photograph of a Zoroastrian temple in Baku in the USSR, Zarathustra was depicted in a long robe with flowing hair and a beard of impressive size, making parallels with Renaissance depictions of Jesus spring inevitably to mind. Our guide did his best to explain the symbolism of the portrait of the Prophet-Priest: the large ring in his left hand meant that the world should be at one with itself; the ring around his waist meant that there are many divisions; the two cursive bands on each side of his robe symbolised the fight between good and evil which never ends and never pauses.

At the centre of the temple was a room which housed a large urn containing a flame – the focus of their worship, which, they told us, had been burning continuously for the last 1500 years.

Outside the town, in the desert, stood their burial grounds. Known as 'Towers of Silence', they are man-made structures not unlike large barrows with flattened tops surrounded by a wall. Burial consisted of laying the dead on the flattened top of the tower, their heads tenderly rested on a V-shaped wooden pillow, and leaving the bodies for the vultures to pick clean. There was a belief that you were destined for heaven or hell according to which eye the vultures plucked out first. This reasonable way of getting rid of dead bodies in desert lands was banned ten years ago by the government on the grounds of 'hygiene'. The parapet wall had been breached at one point and we climbed up to explore, but there was nothing to see other than the flat stone floor, with a pit at the centre into which presumably any small remains were swept.

The Zoroastrians, together with the Armenians, continue to retain some of their traditions in an uneasy balance under the present regime. Both, according to their customs, are permitted to drink alcohol; but for how long they will continue to enjoy this relative stability and freedom nobody can tell. Other minority sects, especially Islamic ones, have been fiercely persecuted.

I travelled in Iran by every conceivable means of motorised transport: on buses of various size and age; on motorbikes, either as a pillion rider or sandwiched between driver and pillion. And on lorries. Every time I hitched I felt the exhilaration that comes from putting your thumb out and knowing that the vehicle that picks you up may then take you halfway across the country. Hitching never presented a problem, since traffic on Iran's roads is always dense.

Close to the war front, however, transport was harder to come by, and I was lucky to get a lift on a huge articulated truck. By the time it had come to a halt I had quite a way to run to reach it. As I reached it the cabin door swung open and the driver leant across to greet me – my head was at the level of the floor of the cab.

'Hamadan?' I asked.

'Baleh,' he replied.

The truck was bright orange and its filter was a massive funnel. Steps led up to its cab, which if you took the engine into account was about the size of a shunting locomotive. I struggled aboard with my bag and already the driver was talking to me, introducing himself and asking me questions in rather careful English.

'Hello. I am Bahador. Where are you from?'

'England,' I replied, hauling myself gratefully into the cabin.

Bahador laughed. 'For a moment back there, I thought you were a Pasdar, with your beard. I nearly didn't stop.'

'What made you change your mind?'

'Pasdaran don't wear blue jeans.'

It was my turn to laugh. 'Where did you learn your English?' I asked, as he swung the massive lorry back onto the highway.

'It's a long story . . .'

I wondered if I would hear it. But it's a long drive from Bakhtaran (it used to be called Kermanshah but the Revolution has changed it) where I had come from, across to Hamadan, and even in an unladen truck the journey would take all afternoon. As we conversed about this and that I became more and more curious. Bahador was obviously an educated and well-informed man. What was he doing as a truck driver? Little by little, as his confidence in me grew, he began to tell his story.

After the revolution had turned sour, he'd tried to leave, but he'd been unable to obtain a passport. Now he saw his only chance of getting out as working as a lorry driver in the hope that eventually he'd be sent abroad. He'd learnt to drive an articulated lorry with this in mind, but no sooner had he done so than passport restrictions were lifted, and currency restrictions imposed. What's more, there were now very thorough searches at customs posts. Undaunted, Bahador had decided on another tack: he would learn Turkish. This was because a Turkish truck driver acquaintance had offered him a job once he reached Turkey. His only means of learning Turkish, however, seemed to be via an English/Turkish dictionary. This gave us an advantage in conversation since whenever we stumbled over a word there was a chance that he'd know its Turkish equivalent.

'So what are your chances of getting to Turkey?'

'Not great,' he sighed. 'At the moment I'm working for the

Revolutionary Guard – taking supplies to the war front.' He went on to tell me that he'd just spent a week waiting for an American radar system to be unloaded from his truck. It hadn't pleased him to have to spend so long within range of the Iraqi guns, while the Pasdaran cast about for the right lifting equipment.

'Did you say *American* radar?'

'I did.'

'But I thought the United States wasn't meant to be supplying Iran with war equipment.'

'Well, if that's the case, no one bothered to erase the markings on the crates.'

'But America . . . !'

He became angry, though not with me: 'If America claims not to be providing us with weapons, that's fine by me. But then everybody says things, don't they? Look at the Swedes. They say they don't supply Khomeini with weapons, but what about the road-building plant, all made in Sweden, that I took to the front last month? You tell me that isn't to build roads to drive missile-launchers along! And what about the tons of electrical equipment from all over western Europe – that isn't to improve military communications? The word "weapons" can cover a multitude of sins.' He calmed down slightly, but continued bitterly: 'Everyone seems to want this war to continue, except the poor bastards who have to fight it. I curse the Americans. They have destroyed our nation.'

His voice lacked conviction, however, and I was soon to find out why. Like so many others, Bahador, while hating America outwardly, nursed a deep ambition to get there and make money. He wanted above all to join his best friend in Utah.

TO LIBERATE
JERUSALEM

Returning to the Bozestan Hotel was like coming home, for not only was I made as welcome as ever, it seemed as if most of the residents had been learning English for my benefit. No longer did they greet one another with their customary 'Salaam', but 'Hello, Mister.'

Mr Shabestari invited me to take tea with him and tell him about my adventures, but I'd hardly begun when Abdullah the cleaner came bounding down the stairs:

'One-two-three-four-five-egg!' he shouted, grinning.

'Six . . .' I hinted.

'Nine-seven-eight-ten-egg!'

From every corner I could hear: 'One hour', 'Five-egg', 'How are you?', 'Hello Mister, water?' Tarik came in carrying an old radio he'd just acquired and greeted me warmly: 'Goodbye,' he said. 'Welcome back.'

Sadeeq must have heard the commotion because he came charging down the stairs after Abdullah.

'How are you, Mister Nicholas?' he inquired warmly. 'Are you staying here?'

Mr Shabestari looked concerned. 'We're full, I'm afraid – unless you wouldn't mind sharing with Mr Sadeeq – that's if he agrees.'

'Of course he can,' said Sadeeq.

I was pleased at this, and delighted to see Sadeeq again, because I'd expected him to have left for home in Baluchistan. I knew he'd been looking forward greatly to seeing his wife and family again.

'Why are you still here?'

He smiled apologetically, hiding his disappointment. 'They're still sending me orders, so how can I go?'

He conducted me up to his room, where I noticed that the piles of books had doubled in height. Sadeeq cleared dozens of volumes from the spare bed and invited me to sit down, asking Abdullah to bring us some tea, *nan* and eggs.

'Now you must tell me your plans, Professor,' he said. He called me professor because he was unshakably convinced that visiting Art School lecturers carried that title.

I began to tell him, which gave me the chance to order my thoughts. 'Well, first of all I must go to the airport and find someone to take my journal and some rolls of film back to England. Then I will try to extend my visa. Also I want to find out if I can see the crown jewels, and finally on Friday I want to go to the prayer meeting at Tehran University.'

Sadeeq had been listening enthusiastically to all but my last suggestion. 'But that's Qods Day,' he objected. Qods is the Persian name for Jerusalem, and the day is one of remembrance for the Zionist occupation of the town. One of Khomeini's main declared aims is to liberate the city.

'Why on earth do you want to go?' continued Sadeeq.

'The speaker of the *Majlis* is supposed to be delivering the sermon. I thought I might take some good photos.'

'But how do you expect to get permission to attend?'

'I have a *Sunday Times* press card. If you like, you could come along too, as my interpreter.'

Sadeeq agreed. I thought it best not to tell him that my press card was a fake.

I managed to have my film and journal sent back to England as air-freight. I found this always an efficient and remarkably cheap way of sending things home, and in the same way I was able to send clothing back as it ceased to be useful and have other clothing sent out to me. My trusty down jacket made the journey in this way a couple of times. Heartened by this, I went to the police immigration bureau, where my request for a further extension met with looks of astonishment: they obviously thought they'd seen the last of me, but I told them I still had much to see, much research to do.

'Not possible,' they said.

'Why?' I asked.

The officer looked up at the ceiling.

Allah's will, I thought to myself, but it was the motionless fan his eyes were raised to.

'Come back in a couple of days,' they said. I always like to think the best of people and so I took them at their word. There was my extension.

'It is positively the last time,' they told me. But I could see that I had them worried.

The crown jewels are deposited nowadays in a vault of the Central Bank, which has been converted into a special museum. I arrived at the building and, in my quest for an official of whom to ask permission to see the jewels, was sent from one office to the next in a seemingly never-ending round. What made it worse was that each office was identical: empty save for a customary secretary. Finally I tracked someone down to a dingy little room half the size of the others and bursting at the seams with old files. This, it seemed, was where the work was actually done.

'What can I do for you?' asked the ruffled banker defensively.

'I would like to see the crown jewels.'

He broke into a smile. 'I'm afraid the museum is no longer open to the public. A visit is now only the privilege of visiting heads of state, foreign dignitaries and so forth.'

I presented several of my heavily stamped and letterheaded pieces of paper. He skimmed through them. 'What a pity you weren't here this morning,' he said. 'There was a delegation here you could have gone round with. Now I will have to consult the Ministry of Foreign Affairs. Perhaps you will phone me in due course.'

I phoned him every morning. It didn't take long. A couple of days later he gave me half an hour's notice to come over and join some Dutch diplomats who were going to look round the museum. I was searched and frisked both at the bank's entrance and at the bunker-like entrance to the museum itself. From there we were escorted to the cavernous vault, where we were treated to a lecture about the Shah's corruption before our visit.

In the dimly-lit chamber the jewels shone like sprinkled stars: emeralds, rubies and diamonds from Khorassan and Turkestan; pearls from the Persian Gulf, gifts and war booty, and straight purchases. There were trays of stones piled up like boiled sweets. There was the Darya-i-Nour, the Ocean of Light – the largest diamond in the world, at 182 carats. But such was the richness around that it was just another item on our guide's list. There was a globe five feet high entirely decorated with gems: the seas encrusted with emeralds and the countries with rubies – all, that is, except England, Iran and France, which were covered in diamonds. And there was the legendary Peacock Throne. We were told that this treasure, the property not of the Crown but of the People, had been hocked as collateral for foreign loans. We were also told that the Shah had postponed his departure from Iran in order to take three crowns with him: his own, weighing two kilos; his wife's, weighing one-and-a-half, and a third, a crown of crowns, weighing five kilos and studded with over 3,300 jewels. He failed to escape with them and our guide also gleefully pointed to over a million dollars' worth of jewellery commissioned by the Empress Farah from Van Cleef and Arpels. I wondered why this museum was kept so exclusive. The Revolution would hardly find better propaganda material.

Even at this late stage in my travels through Iran I had yet to learn that customs can vary considerably according to social standing. On the eve of Qods Day I had been invited to dinner by the British Consul. An embassy car took us to a restaurant in the northern suburbs. Here, unlike the restaurants I was used to, men and women were not segregated. There was still no alcohol, though one could order non-alcoholic Islamic beer from the all-but deserted bar.

'Sometimes some of the most abandoned women take off their headscarves,' one of my fellow-diners told me as I scanned the room.

It seemed a pretty blighted existence for most of the diplomats, who lived a kind of cloistered half-life behind the walls of their compounds, and one which extra money and comfortable accommodation (to compensate for the 'hardship' posting) did little to assuage. Some of the people I talked to had resorted to brewing packets of homemade beer from Boots and making wine from kits.

I was invited to stay with the kind Consul and his charming Colombian wife, but I preferred to get back to the Bozestan. I think the chauffeur they laid on to drive me back, and who dropped me at the mouth of my dark alley, thought I was just a little bit eccentric.

At dawn the next day, Sadeeq and I had breakfast, and then took a taxi as far as was permitted along Revolution Avenue. The crowds were already streaming towards Tehran University for prayers in the heat of the midday sun. With a huge portrait of Khomeini behind them two pied pipers – a saxophonist and a clarinettist – led a group of demonstrators into the university. The road was flooded with men, and on either side of it marched black-chadored columns of the women. The procession gave the impression of being half-carnival, half-funeral, which indeed was something akin to the mood of the day. They came in groups, civilians of all ages – brothers, fathers, grandfathers, all waving their clenched fists in the air and shouting: 'Jang, jang ta piruzi!' (War, war to the death!) and 'Margh barg Amerika, margh barg Israel!' (Death to America, death to Israel!) Then followed a platoon of goose-stepping new recruits, the broad red stripes down the sides of their light khaki trousers providing a sudden splash of colour, and each with a photo of Khomeini pinned to his chest.

I was taking photographs, secure in my status as a pressman, but it wasn't long before a man from the crowd accosted me. He claimed to be a lecturer, but if he was I feel sorry for his students. Without any preamble he started to harangue me. I had heard it all before:

'You must write the truth, not Zionist-Imperialist lies.'

'We are free of censorship in Britain. The press can write what it likes.'

'Lies! Lies! The western press is all owned by Jews!' he shouted in my face, his eyes quite crazed, unfocused. 'The Jews own everything from the bazaar in Kabul to Reuters. They are like a cancer! They must be eliminated!'

I looked around for Sadeeq but he had moved away as soon as I'd started to take photographs. I was alone with this rabid neo-Nazi. All I could do was listen quietly as the venom poured out of him. Finally he ran out of things to say and rejoined the crowd – one drop of poison in a river.

The crowd was slowly working itself into a frenzy. Mullahs who had taken part in the war marched past with machine guns with red roses in their barrels. Then came another wave of civilians, chanting and beating their breasts. Then came a column of children, marching in single file. Each held a painting or a banner and a red rose of martyrdom. I saw an eight-year-old in a tin helmet with a red bandana tied round it, and dressed in army fatigues. On one side of his chest was pinned a picture of Khomeini, on the other the insignia of the Revolutionary Guard Corps – a clenched fist holding a gun. There were many children here with shaved heads, and almost all of them wore a red bandana inscribed with their willingness to die for Islam: 'We positively accept your cause and call to fight.' These children, I knew, were potential martyrs – marked down for the war in years to come.

As I watched I became aware of being watched. A crowd of middle-aged men had gathered round me and I had my back up against a closed shop. There was no escape, and I feared that in their frenzy they might set on me. Several darted forward, snarling: 'Death . . . Cursed . . . Imperialist . . .' I caught words, not sense, thinking how bizarre and how very frightening a group of middle-aged men looked. I babbled to reassure them: 'I'm here to write the truth!' Their anger did not abate, but soon they lost interest in me and drifted back into the crowd.

In the middle of the road a solitary man sat by a vast perspex box. It was a money box, and as they passed, the crowd stuffed notes into it as their contribution to the war effort. I thought of the words of the government: that the Islamic Revolution has turned Iran 'from a selfish and over-consuming social state which is the by-product of a corrupt social culture, into a society which is purified and generous; and this generosity is in giving everything from the smallest item to the most dear possession, that is, one's own son.'

There was no shortage of volunteers for the war. The Baseej marched past – cheerful youngsters and grey-bearded grandfathers, each wearing the red bandana of their commitment. Some had even volunteered for a second and third tour of duty in their eagerness for martyrdom.

I rejoined Sadeeq and together we joined the Islamic Republic's Press Corps and a British film crew, who were apparently the first to be allowed to film in Iran for four years, on a raised platform facing a vast ocean of thousands of worshippers, mullahs, government ministers, foreign dignitaries, the military, the police, the gendarmerie, the Revolutionary Guard, Iraqi PoWs, potential martyrs, children and students. They all faced a wooden, box-like dais framed in slogans from where a robed and turbaned ayatollah was speaking. He was a notable moderate, a member of The Struggling

Religious Combatants for the Freedom of Muslim Lands. He was also the former head of the Tehran Central Revolutionary Committee, and had once been Minister of the Interior and interim Prime Minister. His name was Mahdavi-Kani. Bespectacled and severe, he clutched a Kalashnikov, invisible to most of his audience but not to us from our raised position. He addressed the crowd: 'The people of the Muslim countries must unite in order to remove the Zionist tumour from the region and they should not accept aggression against their greatness . . . one billion Muslims should make a joint effort to liberate their first *Quibla*.'* Some worshippers were choking with emotion at his words, and at one point everyone linked hands. Sadeeq was becoming very nervous, but he could do nothing when his own hands were seized by fellow-Muslim journalists on the press platform, in a wave of intoxicating solidarity.

Whilst this was going on, an Iranian student who was studying for an MA at a university in Texas turned to me and said, 'Allah is with us; we can win the war against the infidel Saddam Hussein.'

I wondered if this might be the man I'd been looking for – the one with whom I could talk about the war rationally.

'Why haven't you defeated Iraq yet, if that is the case?'

'Because we don't want to win the war yet.'

'I thought all wars were fought to be won.'

'You do not understand. Khomeini has called our war a blessing. It must continue, as it is good publicity for our revolution. Through the war we can spread our message so that other peoples will come to learn of the righteous cause of Islam.'

It was more depressing than I had thought. The nation was preparing itself for further decades of war. The Baseej were seen as a limitless source of cannon-fodder. The prospect was daunting. Over 400,000 males reach conscription age every year.

These were my last days in Tehran. I hadn't told the Jamiat-i-Islami office in Tehran of my intention to reach Afghanistan since all the Afghan resistance organisations were rife with eavesdroppers and spies, and sectarian divisions even turned them against each other. One section of Mahmud's party, the Hesbi, sometimes even

---

* The direction towards which a Muslim turns his face in prayer. Whilst Mahomet was in Mecca he used to turn his face towards Jerusalem.

found it expedient to side with the Russians, which is why I had been so mistrustful of him to begin with. One thing was certain: if the reports of thousands of civilians dying in the Soviet carpet bombing of Herat were true, then the Afghan government would do their utmost to prevent a foreigner from reaching the region. The task ahead would be dangerous to say the least, and as if I needed convincing of this, one of the women at the 'British Interests Section' spent an evening and a night with me, trying to talk me out of going. 'As far as Afghanistan and Herat are concerned,' she told me finally, 'your chances of death are far greater than your chances of survival.'

DIRECTORY
ENQUIRIES

M r Shabestari and one of his sons were cooking breakfasts on a small electric ring under the stairwell. They both bade me farewell in the traditional manner, a hug with three kisses on alternate cheeks. They knew of my plan to reach Afghanistan, wished me *Insha' Allah* (Godspeed), and told me to remember that there was always a place for me in Tehran. Some of the residents gave me their addresses, and Sadeeq insisted on accompanying me to the station where, to avoid having my bags rigorously searched, he waited outside the ticket office with them while I entered. The office was a shed that resembled the entrance hall to an antiquated sports stadium, with iron barriers separating the various grille windows. I thought I knew enough letters of the Persian alphabet to make sense of place-names, but twice I found myself in the wrong queue. The only ticket window without a queue was the one under the sign MOSCOVA – written in Roman letters. I tried not to think about what a glorious journey that might be.

Despite the rather romantic tone set by the steam whistles of the old engines, the station was nondescript, packed, confusing and dirty. Families were camped on the platforms, surrounded by their belongings which were tied together with ropes. Parents struggled to stay awake in the stupefying heat, and children dodged around weary and panicky passengers who were trying to decipher destination boards.

Like Friday prayers, there was something epic about the proceedings. Hundreds of soldiers arriving from leave, or transferred from training camps, milled around piles of weapons and kitbags. All the trains destined for Dezful and Ahvaz were troop-carriers. But here there were no shouts to the glory of God. The conscripts were either half-asleep or deep in thought. Their officers hovered round them like watchful guardians.

The train to Mashhad was being readied. It was, in fact, filthy, and most of its windows were cracked or shattered. Attendants lifted great slabs of ice on board with gigantic fish-hooks. The melting blocks were heaved onto the carriages' floors where they were broken up to be fitted into huge metal dustbins to be used for cooling the drinking water. The carriages had been made in East Germany to Iranian specifications and thus the loos were of the squat, rather than the pedestal, type.

I found that a family of four had already installed itself in my compartment and that the mother was sitting in my window seat, but it seemed churlish to complain, as there were other seats, and the window was so badly shattered that you couldn't see out of it. I dumped my bags on the rack and went back to say goodbye to Sadeeq. I hated that moment. I was lost for words, and 'thank you' seemed hopelessly inadequate. I'd bought him a Persian translation of a Zola novel and I gave him one of the six Churchill commemorative coins that Fellows are given to distribute on their journeys. The parting was made worse by the fact that the friendship had been too brief, that it had been lopsided in that he had done far more for me than I for him, and that in all likelihood we would never meet again.

In the end, 'goodbye' had to say it all. 'Khoda hafeez!' I shouted to him as the train drew out of the station.

I returned to my compartment to find that we had been joined by a mother with her young daughter and yet another passenger, who fortunately soon left to try his luck for a seat further along the train. The compartment was very crowded, and I could only think that the parents had adopted the policy that children don't take up much room and therefore don't need reserved seats. An attendant distributed brightly-coloured plastic water jugs which were immediately filled with water and ice, and the father of the first family set about slicing melons, which he shared out to everybody.

The train left the pollution of industrial south Tehran for the arid wastes of the desert. To the north, the mountains tapered off to an uninterrupted straight horizon. After the melons, the father disappeared, and to my relief soon returned with the news that he'd found the single parent and her daughter seats in a less crowded compartment. I was about to stretch out in the welcome extra space, but he returned for me, grabbing my bags and setting off to find me a seat elsewhere, where I'd be 'more comfortable'. In fact I think he simply wanted to be alone with his family so that his wife could remove her chador. I was grateful to him, because he found me a seat in a compartment otherwise occupied by Baseej volunteers.

Three were middle-aged peasants, one was a school-leaver. They had just completed a three-month tour of duty on the Kurdish war front. They were tired and obviously in need of rest. The youngest, Farhad, could speak some English, and through him we were all able to converse. They were all unstinting in their support for the *jihad*, or Holy War, and prepared to fight and die for the Revolution.

They were equally totally devoted and unwavering in their support for Khomeini.

'Would you return for another tour of duty?' I asked.

One would, it appeared, after twenty days' leave. The other two peasants were returning to farming, and they remained curiously quiet about their own personal involvement in the holy war, although their reticence may only have been due to tiredness. Farhad was about to enter a theological school, and his motives for joining the Baseej in the first place had clearly been purely religious. He was, however, at pains to assure me that he would have been quite prepared to die if he had been called upon to do so. He spoke quietly, not with the recklessness of youth but with the calculated precision of a kamikaze pilot.

'But what about the minefields?' I asked, feeling that the question was rather feeble in the face of his conviction. Not to say superfluous. He would clearly have had no hesitation in launching himself into a minefield armed with nothing more than shouts to Allahu Akbar. I only hoped that the Afghans didn't share the same willingness to die. But I looked at Farhad with a kind of respect. Out of uniform he would look like any scrawny schoolkid. He didn't seem tough enough to stand up to an attacker on his own. What moved me was that he had a temperate side, and showed an interest in other religions, countries and customs.

Mashhad is one of the holiest cities in Iran because it contains the shrine of the eighth Imam, Imam Reza. It is also the hottest city in all Iran. It emerged out of the desert to greet the train, encroaching upon the ochres and yellows with urban greys. At the station the Baseej hugged and kissed each other goodbye.

'Will you come and be the guest of my parents?' Farhad asked me.

'How will they react?'

'They will be delighted.'

Farhad's parents were Azeri-speaking Turks from Tabriz. They met at the American University in Beirut. His father was a convinced supporter of Khomeini, and entirely upheld what his son was doing. I did try to broaden our inevitable discussion about politics and religion, but I was talking to a man who was in the grip of an embittered rage against the west. His wife silently served us tea and biscuits as we sat under a large portrait of Khomeini. Nor did Farhad take part in our conversation. In fact, he soon disappeared into the depths of the house and I hardly saw him again. I suspected his father had decided to keep him at arm's length from possibly dangerous foreign influences. Farhad only emerged when he was told to find me a hotel room.

The father immediately assumed I would want to stay at the local Hyatt, now renamed the Qods; but I quickly explained that I wanted far more modest accommodation. Farhad couldn't book a room by phone so I was driven into town by his father who tried several hotels personally, announcing loudly everywhere we went that I had come to write the truth about Muslims. This did not have a great effect on the managements, and I suspected that several hotels suddenly became 'full' because of it. Finally we found a cheap place near the station. It was the sort I was used to.

I was anxious to contact the local Jamiat office, so after I'd been dropped at the hotel I headed for it straight away. It hadn't been too hard to track the office down: someone at the hotel traced it for me through directory enquiries.

Afghanistan is a conglomerate of peoples, and the tribes that make up its population have conflicting loyalties. Since 1979, Russian intervention has wrought great and terrible changes. A nation once known for its hashish, camel's wool, goat's hair, sheepskin and bandits is now engulfed in an impossible war.

Both sides are violently opposed to one another, and the fight for control of the country is ruthless. At stake is Afghanistan's very identity. Five million Afghans, over a third of the country's population, are now refugees in Iran and Pakistan. A million more have been killed in the war, and a million more have been made homeless, refugees in their own land. A civil war existed eighteen months before the main Soviet invasion. The few main roads across the country had been closed for days at a time, and ambushes were frequent. Civilian demonstrations and army mutinies culminated in the Herat insurrection as early as March 1979. During it, communists and Soviet advisers and their families were tortured and hacked to death, the victims' decapitated heads paraded through the streets. Soon after, the rebellion was mercilessly crushed by the Afghan Army which remained loyal to the government, with the support of Soviet bombers.

It is simplistic to see the war in terms of the Russians supporting a puppet regime against 'freedom fighters'. The communist Afghan government had introduced land reforms, had curbed the power of the feudal mullahs, and had introduced literacy programmes for women (which admittedly were enforced ones). The anti-communist and especially the anti-Soviet opposition within the country opposed such programmes violently. The issues are far too complex to discuss in detail here, but essentially the nationalist resistance to the Soviet presence is conservative.

Jamiat-i-Islami is one of the fundamentalist groups which have a strong hold of the Tajik-dominated north of the country. Their fight against the foreign invasion force and the government troops has as its inspiration the idea of the *jihad*. The followers of Jamiat look upon Allah as the ultimate legislator. Their leader in Herat is a former artillery officer called Ismail Khan. They are as dedicated to the Islamic revival as the Iranians are, only the Iranians are Shia Muslims; the majority of Afghans are Sunni.

I found their headquarters in a rundown neighbourhood on the outskirts of town. Amongst the disused workshops and derelict buildings the shell of a narrow, drab, four-storey concrete office block was immediately recognisable due to the large number of Afghans outside it. I made my way upstairs, picking my way through the wounded men who were sitting on the steps – mujahedeen who had been brought to Iran for treatment. As soon as they recognised me as a foreigner they smiled curiously.

Dr Aziz was the head of the Mashhad office. I left my shoes on the pile outside his door, knocked and entered. He was sitting behind a small desk in the corner of the room, facing the partisans who sat cross-legged on the carpeted floor. Dr Aziz wore a suit in contrast to the others, who all wore the shalwar camise. He greeted me warmly, though his manner remained mild and reserved, and he introduced me to the others. Each man took it in turn to stand up and greet me, clasping my hand in theirs and uttering the universal greeting of the Muslims, 'Asalaam Aleikum'. I replied to each greeting. It was a lengthy process.

I could see that Dr Aziz was looking at me expectantly and so I briefly explained the object of my journey and the purpose of my visit.

'Are you a journalist?' he inquired.

'No,' I replied.

'A photographer?'

'Not exactly.'

His puzzlement increased. 'Are you working for anyone?'

'No, I'm not.'

Dr Aziz exchanged a look with his assistant, who had started to scratch himself thoughtfully. 'You say you want to enter Afghanistan from Iran,' he said. 'I'm afraid that's not possible.'

'Then what do you suggest?'

Dr Aziz spread his hands and suggested I do what every other foreigner who wants to enter Afghanistan is advised to do: 'Try through Pakistan.'

'But that's ridiculous,' I protested. 'I'm on my way to China.'

Dr Aziz looked up sharply. I hadn't told him about China before. Perhaps I had played a trump card. Many Afghans are very ignorant of geography outside their own immediate area, but later I was to discover that China has a very special and mysterious connotation for them.

I repeated my belief that it was important to follow exactly one of the routes that had taken Islam to China, and I explained that the Iranians knew I was hoping to leave Iran for Afghanistan. Dr Aziz told me that only one foreigner had made the crossing I proposed, a German who had been given the name Ali Qapou. I too would be given a Muslim name later, though it was closer to my own than

Ali Qapou's could have been to his. All the Afghans assumed that I must know him.

'However, things have tightened up since then,' Dr Aziz was saying. 'This is all but a sealed border now, and even the mujahedeen have difficulty crossing into Afghanistan.' This was a clear hint at the animosity that existed between the Afghans and the Iranians, in particular the Revolutionary Guard. The Sunni Afghan groups had great difficulty in obtaining permission to ship arms through Iran. On the other hand, Jamiat had been bullied into providing safe-conduct through their region for Hazaras, the large Shia minority of central Afghanistan, as they headed from Iran into Afghanistan to fight the Russians – at least, ostensibly.

I wondered what choices were left open to me. I could try crossing the border alone, but with the Russians and the Afghan army patrolling it on one side, and the Pasdaran on the other I stood very little chance. Even if I succeeded, I would then have to run the gauntlet of mujahedeen forces before I could make contact with any of the people M. LeClerc had suggested to me in Paris. Assuming that I could even find them. Then I remembered Mahmud. I wondered how I could contact him without offending Dr Aziz. I asked his advice. To my surprise he was perfectly amenable, seeing no conflict of interests, and phoned the Hesbi leader there and then, inviting him over to the Jamiat office.

Mahmud came immediately and a three-way conversation ensued between us. I pleaded my case again, and they countered by telling me of their concerns: what if I were caught by the Iranians? How would something like that affect them? Finally they decided to call the other resistance groups together. The risk, if it were taken, would be a collective one, as would the decision.

I spent my days waiting at the Jamiat office, and soon became on friendly nodding terms with most of the mujahedeen there, always warmly greeted by their proud, defiant faces. Their physical features and their languages were widely different – a testimony to the great variety of peoples who had invaded, crossed, and settled in Afghanistan in the course of the centuries: the Greeks under Alexander; the Mongols under Genghis Khan; the Timurids under Tamerlane; the Moghuls; the Safavids; the British. I was introduced to their commanders, and I was shown photographs of the toll they had taken on the enemy. Their snapshots were stuck to pieces of display-card as if they were part of a school project: photos of mujahedeen triumphantly standing on their trophies. Two brothers on an overturned personnel carrier. A group on a crippled tank, holding their guns aloft victoriously.

But the price they paid for their victories was a heavy one, as I could see from the wounded who lay pathetically in makeshift wards and dormitories all over the Jamiat HQ. The beds were made of wood, some with a mattress the thickness of a cigarette packet on them, others with just a sheet. They were crammed into tiny offices on the top floor – six to a room. The rooms were poorly ventilated and the stench was appalling. The wounds the injured had sustained were grim: men had lost limbs, been crippled, and suffered terrible disfigurement. A former judge lay paralysed by a bullet wound in the neck. Old men, rendered incontinent by their injuries, lay motionless on their beds. Despite the muslin sheets stretched over the windows, flies still flew in to torment the broken men. They bore it all stoically. I was told that sometimes the Afghans were told to remove their wounded from the hospital only hours after they had been operated on. I felt honoured to be among these proud, brave and devoted people. They gave me strength and courage, and I tried to reassure them that their suffering and their fight was at least being witnessed by an outsider, who would carry news of it to the world.

I had steeled myself for a long stay in Mashhad but a decision on what to do with me had obviously been quickly reached for one day as I stood by the bed of one of the wounded a mujahed came up to me and said simply, 'You will leave here for a place near the border at two o'clock tomorrow afternoon.' My stomach felt hollow. As I had done every day on returning to the hotel, I exchanged a few words with a middle-aged man who spent most of his life mooching about the lobby. His was a tragic and pathetic story. He was an alcoholic, but of course the Revolution had meant that alcohol ceased to be available. He had turned to smoking heroin. The penalty for dealing in or possessing heroin carried the death sentence, but many former alcoholics were in the same predicament. According to many people I talked to, the incidence of heroin use in Khorassan province was extremely high.

He was a forlorn figure, talking to me of the days when he'd owned a couple of trucks and trailers, occasionally driving them to Europe himself. Now he was on skid row and he would never come up again. But he dreamt desperately of escape. 'Which country do you think I should emigrate to?' he would ask me. He had it all worked out, too. How what was left of his money could be smuggled out of the country, and how it should be invested. He spoke with absolute certainty, and deceptive clarity.

'Who is he?' I asked the proprietor of the hotel.

'He used to live at my father's hotel, but he couldn't pay the bills. As he's a friend of the family we let him stay here for nothing. It's all we can do for him, now.'

On the last night a friend of the proprietor called Karim, who had also become a friend of mine, invited me to join him at his house for dinner. Karim was a sophisticated and wealthy man and his house was a large one, modern and filled with all the comforts of the west. There was a woman present there, dressed in western clothes. The sight of a beautiful pair of legs and a summer blouse made me feel weak at the knees. I tried to remain unruffled but I was afraid that my eyes would betray me, since they were glued to her and there was nothing I could do about it. I was mesmerised by her deep, piercing blue eyes and her flowing black hair. Karim served me rocket-fuel on the rocks. My hostess Mandana apologised that all she had been able to prepare was chicken and chips – she ought to have cooked me a traditional Iranian dish. She didn't speak English, and I found it a little difficult to explain to her that after so long on little other than *nan*, rice and mutton, the thought of chicken and chips was heaven.

Conversation was fitful but good-natured. Karim plied me with rocket-fuel, and we defied the Revolution some more by playing backgammon.

'What do you think of my friend?' he asked, smiling. I replied in as restrained a way as I was able, afraid to offend him by showing too great enthusiasm. We ate the delicious food, and the evening passed quickly. Then Karim suggested that I might like to stay the night. This offer I gladly accepted. The comfort of a double bed in an airy, modern room would be blissful after my cockroach-infested hotel room.

As I lay sleepily in the glorious double-bed I wondered what I would dream of. The dinner and the drink had relaxed me, and I thought less of the journey that faced me tomorrow than of the comforts of home, and, as one thought drifted into another in that hopeless, unconnected way when sleep beckons, I imagined undressing veiled women . . .

I must have fallen asleep, but when I woke I thought I must still be dreaming. My arm had been pulled behind me and someone was guiding my hand over a soft, warm, curvaceous land. I felt a sudden surge of emotion that was curiously akin to panic. Was this a parting present or a trap? I was like a schoolboy, unsure and frightened, not in control of the situation. I was still half-asleep. I could hear her breath quicken behind me. Desire overwhelmed me and flooded out all other thoughts. The room was dark; one could just distinguish the shadows of depressions and the silhouettes of promontories. And apart from our breathing, caught-at, abandoned, nothing but silence. Our language wasn't needed any more. Our bodies spoke for us. Iran had offered me all the ingredients of a love-affair: passion, language, beauty and poetry.

Where was I? On the threshold of another journey, or simply in the middle of a honeymoon?

TAKEN HOSTAGE?

I awoke the next morning as from a dream, and so I was not surprised to find that Mandana had long gone. Only the imprint of her head on the other pillow proved that she had been with me at all.

Full of enthusiasm for my onward journey, and fired by the lovemaking of the night before, I prepared myself for the journey ahead. My blue rucksack would attract far too much attention so I exchanged it for a small khaki Japanese duffel-bag. I hung on to my tough canvas camera bag, and kept my medicine kit, a roll of loo paper, a toothbrush, a bar of soap, my lightweight rope, my carabiners, my waterproof poncho and my sleeping bag. The only clothing I kept apart from what I had on was an extra pair of socks and underpants and my 'You Can't Ban a Chelsea Fan' T-shirt. By now those around me, the hotel proprietor and his Afghan workers, knew I would be leaving for Afghanistan, and they became infected by my enthusiasm. I needed some toothpaste, and the Herati cleaner insisted on treating me to a tube of Ipanema. No sooner had I packed my new duffel-bag than the zip became unstitched and the two straps broke loose. Two doors away, a car upholsterer restitched the whole thing for me and absolutely refused to be paid for his work. Everybody chipped in to help speed me on my way.

However when I went over to the Jamiat office I found my departure had been delayed. It was a disappointment, but now I was more used to the ways of the east and knew that a clandestine border-crossing could not be scheduled like a train-timetable. The important thing was that I would be going. I only hoped that the delay would be short, since it was difficult not to stay keyed up.

As night descended so Mandana beckoned me once more. With another invitation to dine at Karim's the evening was a re-run of the previous one – like a repeated dream. Except that this time I lay in bed awaiting her. She did not disappoint me.

I bade farewell to her in the morning and set off once again for Jamiat HQ. It was a sad parting, for we both knew we would not meet again. I am sorry that I have to disguise her, to give her a name in this book that is not her real name. But, like so many people I mention, if I told you their true names I would be putting them in jeopardy.

Jamiat had promised me that I would be leaving 'some time today', but I was unprepared for the abruptness of my departure. A 20-year-old mujahed called Fraim was already waiting for me, and he was impatient to be off. He charged down the stairs as soon as we had been introduced, and I tumbled after him, clambering aboard the back of a waiting pick-up jeep, sharing the space with two enormous oil drums.

As we bucked along the streets Fraim started to explain things to me. From what I could gather, I would be crossing the border on the back of a motorbike, but the when and where of it escaped me because I had to attune myself to a new language – Dari, related to Persian but far enough from it to give me pause for the moment. Fraim also threw in the fact that he worked as a male nurse.* Other than that he wasn't terribly communicative. It wasn't just a question of the language. He obviously felt that I was a bit of a burden, and also quite possibly a liability. He was proud of the fact that he'd run this border twenty times; but at the same time he must have known that he couldn't go on getting away with it forever.

The jeep pulled into a tumbledown yard where a bus was waiting. Fraim shoved me to the back of it where I sat and waited while he and the driver transferred the two oil drums.

The three-hour journey to the frontier town of Tayyebad was something of an ordeal for Fraim. He sat next to me like a minder, or maybe a detective in charge of a convict. Of course as soon as the bus had cleared Mashhad the other Afghan passengers all turned to stare at me.

'Is he going to Afghanistan?' one of them finally asked Fraim.

* All the nurses I met were male. Fraim also fought alongside the mujahedeen, as did some of the doctors. The distinction between civilian and mujahed could be a shadowy one at all levels in this confused and confusing struggle. Even the term 'nurse' is misleading, for none of them were trained.

'No,' answered Fraim, but so diffidently that I was sure no one could have believed him.

We arrived at Tayyebad at dusk as the sky and desert merged into one at the horizon. The bus pulled up on the main street, and all the passengers climbed down. I was immediately 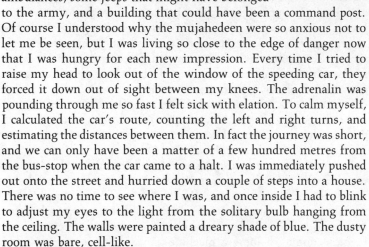 bundled into a waiting car, like a pop-star avoiding the press, unable to catch more than a glimpse of the desert that surrounded and invaded the town. Was that the road that led to Afghanistan, now only some 25 kilometres away? I saw a line of ambulances, some jeeps that might have belonged to the army, and a building that could have been a command post. Of course I understood why the mujahedeen were so anxious not to let me be seen, but I was living so close to the edge of danger now that I was hungry for each new impression. Every time I tried to raise my head to look out of the window of the speeding car, they forced it down out of sight between my knees. The adrenalin was pounding through me so fast I felt sick with elation. To calm myself, I calculated the car's route, counting the left and right turns, and estimating the distances between them. In fact the journey was short, and we can only have been a matter of a few hundred metres from the bus-stop when the car came to a halt. I was immediately pushed out onto the street and hurried down a couple of steps into a house. There was no time to see where I was, and once inside I had to blink to adjust my eyes to the light from the solitary bulb hanging from the ceiling. The walls were painted a dreary shade of blue. The dusty room was bare, cell-like.

I waited tensely alone with Fraim, expecting at any moment to hear the engines of the motorbikes that would ferry us across the border. But nothing happened. Instead, another mujahed, who introduced himself as Muhlavi, arrived with dinner. The meal was eaten in near-silence, and then, as the evening wore on, other mujahedeen started to arrive. The room filled up with these silent figures. I lost count of time, but I was worried that precious hours of darkness were slipping by. Surely we would make our move soon? No action was taken, however, and gradually I succumbed to exhaustion, both nervous and physical, and, stretching myself out, fell asleep on the floor. I awoke in the middle of the night, to find myself surrounded by sleeping bodies, each man enveloped in his *patou* – a multi-purpose sheet which they always carry with them.

Tonight was to be the beginning of a long ordeal.

There had been a change of plan. I was to join a convoy of three trucks carrying ammunition, medical supplies and returning mujahedeen. The trucks were, like much of the rebels' equipment, captured from the Russians and from the Afghan army. I didn't like the idea of the convoy. Three large vehicles would be terribly noticeable and terribly vulnerable. I trembled at the thought of how easily they could be picked out by Soviet infra-red viewfinders.

But still nothing happened. During the whole of the following day I wasn't allowed out of the room. A Pasdar lived opposite the house on the other side of the lane, and so I was not even permitted to speak in anything but a low tone. With nothing to do I became restless. In the unpleasant and uncomfortable heat I became acutely aware of the bleakness of my surroundings, devoid as they were of objects and furniture. With no architectural features either, beyond two recessed windows, each of which was shuttered, I started to feel distinctly claustrophobic. I consoled myself that it was only for a day.

Breakfast was *nan* and tea as usual, and the rest of the day was punctuated with endless glasses of tea, served, as were the meals, by two of the householder's sons, Abdulghani and Mohammed Sadiq. Abdulghani was only fourteen, but he had been a mujahedeen for two years already. Like a child playing soldiers, he reenacted his heroics, miming holding a machine-gun, aiming it, firing it, and killing the enemy. Only of course this wasn't play. This he had actually done.

Both boys were avid Bruce Lee fans and delighted in punching their legs outwards to deliver karate kicks, and in slicing the air with the edges of their hands. Unfortunately for me, they also used me as a human punch-bag, and although I was a good deal bigger than either of them, they didn't pull their punches. In fact they were little bullies, although they did at least alternate their attacks with welcome glasses of tea! They also gave me my new name: Nick Mohammed, to which was later added the honorific Khan. I learnt very little about them. There was a younger brother, and an older one had been killed in the fighting. A month later in Herat province I met their father, a mullah.

My second night in the house was fast approaching. All the mujahedeen who'd been there the night before had left after first prayers at dawn, and now some were filtering back, in the company of others I had not met before. One of them was clearly anxious about my looks – would I get past the Pasdaran at the frontier? However, most of the others were unworried. Afghans are very mixed racially, and properly dressed in a turban and shalwar camise I would look more like a native than many of them.

'Your beard alone would be the envy of most ayatollahs,' one of them joked.

'But supposing they question him? He can't speak our language,' another one pointed out anxiously. This gave them pause for thought for a moment but they quickly came up with a solution. If I was asked a question the others would raise a shout of Allahu Akbar, and I would join in. This seemed to satisfy them, but I hoped it wouldn't be put to the test.

They disliked the Pasdaran intensely, not least because they were often subjected to very thorough searches and any money found on them was confiscated. They'd found a way round that by tying money and messages up in the folds of their turban. It was quite a sight to see them arranging this long piece of cloth. First of all, a small cap called a *colar* is placed on the head, and then the nine-foot length of material is wound around it, often with the assistance of a friend. The end of the strip is tucked into the top of the turban but left sticking up like a plume. In some cases the cloth bore a pattern, and this was a clue to the tribe or homeland of the wearer.

Finally Fraim returned with Muhlavi. They were in a hurry. It seemed that at long last we were to be off. They grabbed my bags, and I started to follow them out of the house, but Fraim stopped me.

'What's up?' I asked.

'You leave in ten minutes.'

'Then my bags stay with me,' I countered, immediately worried.

Fraim was clearly exasperated: 'Do you want to go to Afghanistan or not?' he asked impatiently.

I was loath to be parted from my bags but there was nothing I could do, and I was wasting time. To prove good faith, Fraim took me to the door of the house and pointed to a jeep at the end of the lane, picked out by the streetlamps.

'But where are the trucks?' I asked.

'We're going to meet them. You will be joining us at the border.'

I grabbed my passport from my camera bag, and watched them dash off towards the jeep. Reluctantly I returned to the house, but I couldn't relax. I couldn't even sit down. Ten minutes, Fraim had said. But of course ten minutes came and went, became an hour, two hours, and still no one came to collect me. Half an hour later Mohammed Sadiq came into the room, which I was already beginning to regard as a prison cell.

'When am I leaving?' I asked him, more in desperation than in anger. I felt a fool. Had I been duped out of my bags? It is always an uncomfortable feeling to have control of one's next move slip out of one's hands.

'There has been a change of plan,' he told me.

'Again?'

But I got no more out of him, as it was time to listen to the BBC Persian Service – a ritual adhered to as religiously as prayer-time. I half-listened, understanding the barest minimum. Once I recognised Helmut Kohl's name, but I had no idea whether he'd been murdered, signed a treaty, or called an election. Inactivity and tension had made me tired. I ate dinner listlessly, and soon afterwards fell asleep.

I awoke at 4.30 the following morning, but enjoyed a lie-in while my room-mates left for the mosque. Some returned for breakfast. I was bitterly disappointed that I hadn't left, and angry that I had been so easily fooled into parting with my bags. In all probability I had lost everything except what I had on me: my Swiss army knife, my passport, some US dollars, a few Iranian rials and my collection of talismans. I had nothing to read, nothing to write with, and nothing to draw with. I felt naked. I looked at the front and back pages of my passport. I derived a certain amount of cynical amusement out of 'Her Britannic Majesty's Principal Secretary of State . . . to allow the bearer to pass freely . . . to afford . . . such assistance as may be necessary.' If only things were still that easy. But after rereading my passport a few times the amusement palled.

So in sheer boredom I started to use it to swat flies. In fact I wanted to start scratching sketches on the walls, but the flies distracted me.

With no other sound in the suffocating heat, their incessant buzzing grew louder and louder until it filled my mind.

And so the next couple of dismal days and nights passed. Each night the room was filled with a different group of people, and some even stayed two nights, but I seemed to be the only permanent fixture. I wondered if I would ever get away. One mujahed, Aminullah, had festering boils and carbuncles. He amused himself by lancing them with a needle.

The only pattern imposed on the day was that provided by the five prayer times. I took to learning the prayers by rote, and in this I was encouraged by Abdulghani and Sadiq. It made a change from hitting me, I suppose. The first thing I learnt was the *kalimeh*: Bismillahi'r-Rahmani'r-Rahim. La ilaha illa 'llah Muhammadu rasulu'llah – 'In the name of God who is the most benevolent and the most merciful. There is no God but the one true God and Mahomet is his messenger'. Knowledge of this proved very useful later, as to know it distinguishes the believer from the infidel. To begin with I had no idea what it meant, learning it as I do all foreign languages, parrot-fashion, imitating inflection and tone exactly. I soon knew many prayers by heart in this way, without having a clue as to what I was saying.

In the evenings I asked as many of the transient guests as I could if they knew when I might be leaving. They gave me soothing and vague answers, like 'Soon', 'Today', 'Tonight', 'Tomorrow' – words plucked at random to keep me quiet. Even though I knew their assurances were of no value I went on asking. Perhaps the act of asking reassured me. But I was not entirely wasting my time. I might have been learning the prayers parrot-fashion, but with every day I was adding to my store of individual words. Helped along by the two brothers, it was a black-and-white vocabulary: *dushman* – enemy; *dust* – friend; *Shuravi* – Soviet, which was synonymous with *sac* – dog. The two boys would test me in the same way as the mujahedeen would converse with me. It went like this:

'What do you think of the Russians?'

'*Dushman*,' I would answer to wild applause.

'And the mujahedeen?'

'*Dust*,' I said.

When I wanted to use the toilet I had to be escorted and the women had to be first cleared from the courtyard where the toilet stood, my exercise being limited only to these walks. Then the women would return and I'd look at them through the cracks in the door.

To alleviate the tedium I took to teaching English to whoever wanted to learn, and I also taught the little brother, Abdullah, Persian numerals. I found that time was beginning to lose any real proportion, and as a consequence of this I was losing my sense of perspective. I complained bitterly to Sadiq but he was unsympathetic:

'You have food,' he reminded me indignantly.

In the evenings, when the room was crowded, I didn't feel so bad. The Afghans have a rough and ready sense of humour and although jokes were hard to transmit because of the language barrier I was able to act some out and it pleased me to be able to bring ready laughs to their tired faces. They were fascinated by England, which they entirely identified with the BBC.

'Are the English Muslims?'

'Do you have mosques in England?'

These were constant questions, and if they were disappointed that the answer to the first one was 'no', they were mollified to hear that the answer to the second was 'yes'. Their picture of the outside world was altogether a strange one. They knew the names of nations and peoples, but could not relate them either geographically or even to each other.

'Do the English speak English?' Abdulghani once asked me. But the question is not so bizarre, for in Afghanistan there are many discrete tribes, with their own 'nationalities', and, to some extent, languages. It is a heterogenous country which only through the present war is making steps towards a national identity.

The daily 'wash' didn't clean me at all, and the dirtier I got, the more depressed I became. Finally I asked if I could have a proper wash. A theatrical scene ensued. Little Abdullah and his younger sister ushered me into a room on the other side of the corridor that led to the courtyard. It was a storeroom, almost the twin of the room I was staying in, except that no light entered from the blocked window facing the lane. Only the window onto the courtyard offered a little indirect sunlight. I was left with two buckets: one full, the other empty. I decided that my best course of action would be to pour water from one over me, catching as much as possible of it in the other, in order to recycle it. In fact I was brought another full bucket by one of the women, who went to enormous lengths not to see me or be seen. The door opened outwards and nearly swung away from her. I had a glimpse of a brown arm flailing to grab it after she had shoved the bucket into the room.

Once I was clean, I felt a lot better, and to improve matters further, I was given a clean set of *toman penard,* as they call the shalwar camise. The baggy pants could have fitted three people at the waist, and even folded in half I could still wrap them around with plenty of room to spare. The reason for their bagginess up top is to provide maximum ventilation, and they are enormously comfortable. The shirt is not so baggy but it has tails that reach to the knees, and is worn over the trousers. The cut of the tails can provide a clue to the wearer's tribe. Accompanying them is the other essential item of clothing, a tough eight-pocketed waistcoat (four outer and four inner) in which all a man's personal possessions are carried. And then there is the patou, about the size of a single bedsheet and carried over the shoulder. At least I now looked the part.

On the evening of the fourth night, Fraim returned.

'I thought you were meant to be in Afghanistan,' I said, a little cuttingly.

'Don't worry about your bags,' he said, reading my thoughts. 'We were crossing the desert when we were ambushed by tanks. They opened fire. We fought for half an hour. They captured one truck and blew up another. One dead and quite a few wounded. Maybe they took prisoners too. I managed to get the truck with the medical supplies back into Iran.'

'I see,' I said.

'Your bags have been saved. They will take them to Ismail Khan. I saw one of our men pull them from the munitions truck before it was blown up.'

That did seem improbable. Surely they would have tried to save badly-needed arms before my bags. I said nothing. Besides, I now had something else to worry about. My Iranian visa had expired. If I was caught by the authorities I would have quite a lot of explaining to do. I was seriously beginning to wonder if anyone had any intention of smuggling me into Afghanistan. Perhaps those who had cared originally about my plans had forgotten them: they had plenty else to occupy their minds. And still the only answer I ever got to my question, 'When?' was '*Farda*' – tomorrow.

Perhaps I was being held hostage for some reason? After all, for the past two days I hadn't been left alone for an instant – one mujahed had taken to staying with me even during prayer-time, using his patou as a prayer mat in the room. I wanted to telephone Dr Aziz in Mashhad but there was no phone in the house. Then I was told that he had gone south to Zahedan.

But I never really thought of turning back, even though the loss of my equipment would henceforward make it hard if not impossible to record my journey. And who knew? Perhaps my bags might turn up if I went on; but I'd certainly never see them again if I turned back. Something in Fraim's eyes told me he was not lying about the ambush – so perhaps he was not lying at all.

I decided to remain hopeful.

After a week in my 'cell' I decided that I must start taking some exercise, despite the cramped space. However, rescue was closer at hand than I'd dared hope, for shortly afterwards a certain Dr Sajad arrived. Dr Sajad had stayed at the house a week earlier, and was horrified to see me still there. He set himself to work on my behalf and as a result of his endeavours a mujahedeen leader called Agi Khan arrived within an hour, accompanied by a truly broad, grizzled colleague bearing a fresh set of *toman penard*. For good measure, his companion also gave me his scarf – a black and white check cloth which is worn folded into a triangle and tied around one's head. It

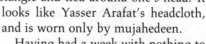

looks like Yasser Arafat's headcloth, and is worn only by mujahedeen.

Having had a week with nothing to do, I now didn't even have time to tie my new turban, but I was very happy indeed at the promise of fresh air, movement and excitement after so much enforced inactivity. There was only one cloud on the horizon: supposing they were merely moving me from

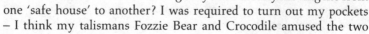

one 'safe house' to another? I was required to turn out my pockets – I think my talismans Fozzie Bear and Crocodile amused the two mujahedeen gripping their deadly Kalashnikovs. Then I was escorted out to the new Japanese pickup they had arrived in, and asked to sit between them. They told me neither to move nor speak should we be stopped.

Our drive was uneventful and after only a short while we arrived at one of the many adobe villages that have sprung up since the mass exodus of refugees from Afghanistan. There I was left in the hands of two brothers who, it transpired, were to be my guides across the frontier. They immediately asked me the usual questions about Khomeini and as usual I hedged, wary as always of the political allegiances of total strangers. The brothers soon reassured me: they not only hated the ayatollah but referred to him as a friend of the Russians!

One of them disappeared soon after but returned in the early afternoon with a massive Russian motorbike, captured from the enemy. They explained that this would be our transport to the border, but that every so often I would have to dismount and hide while they scouted for Pasdaran patrols. With these brief instructions, we set off as the sombre shadows of late afternoon lengthened into the cracked, umber shingle of the plain ahead.

We hadn't gone far into the desert when they slowed the bike and indicated that I should dismount. At first this was welcome, because events had started to happen so fast that I had barely had time to collect my thoughts.

'Watch out for spotter planes. Bury yourself in the sand if you hear one,' they warned as they roared off.

I hadn't been alone long before relief gave way to doubt. What if they couldn't find me again? The desert was wide and crisscrossed with millions of tracks. I waited for what seemed like hours, straining my ears for the sound of the returning bike. But none came. Instead, one of the brothers returned alone, and on foot.

'Come on,' said Abdul Aziz, with no explanation of why we would now have to continue under our own steam.

We continued into the early evening, caked in sand and parched with thirst. The few nomads we passed were in a similar state to ours, and had no water to spare. There was no shelter as even the humblest hut had been razed to the ground – though some refuge was to be found in the remains of crumbling adobe walls. Abdul left me crouching under one of these while he went off to forage. In due

117

course he returned with the smallest watermelon I have ever set eyes on.

I began to be grateful for the enforced inertia and myriad cups of tea I'd had over the preceding week. As the sun set, Abdul nudged me.

'Let's go,' he said.

We set off at a run, a crouching run to avoid being spotted. We were approaching the site of the Pasdaran control post which we had to pass, and in the darkness we could see the lights of Iranian patrol cars as they roved the desert. We rested here until it was pitch dark, and then Abdul gave me one of two branches of shrub he had collected. It was time to make the final dash across the frontier.

I soon discovered what the shrub was for. You held it in front as you dashed at headlong pace through the black night over the featureless terrain, and it gave you warning of depressions and hollows or rises in the land. However you were travelling so fast that there was no time to respond to such warnings. It was a bit like skiing at night. Our turbans wrapped across our faces for protection from the sand, we would scamper a few hundred yards, then stop, fixed to the ground like lizards, before scampering on, keeping an ever watchful eye out for the patrol cars of the Pasdaran, which were fortunately easy to detect because of their bright headlights and red taillights.

Finally we came to a big ditch with steep banks on either side. This was a manmade demarcation line – the physical frontier between the two countries. No sooner had we climbed the opposite bank and caught our breath than Abdul stood up fully, stretched himself, and grinned.

'Welcome to Afghanistan,' he said with obvious relief, throwing aside the branches. 'It's OK now – have no worries!'

From now on our crouching sprint was replaced by a brisk walk. We knew we were approaching a village long before we could see it because of the noise of barking dogs. At length we arrived at the foot of a high mud wall, and then proceeded to follow it round, searching for an opening. We found one and clambered over it into a farmyard, stumbling within feet of one of the watching dogs, a ferocious-looking beast whose bark would have struck fear into the heart of a Goliath. We continued into the village until we caught sight of a glimmer of white – a turban. Abdul called out and within minutes several men with guns appeared on top of the walls of the buildings as others came down the street to greet us. They were mujahedeen. We were ushered into their command post, and offered tea, bread and sweets. I looked around the ten bearded faces illuminated in the dim lamplight as their fierce expressions changed from suspicion to delight when they learnt I was from England. Their ages and that of their guns covered a similar timespan. The oldest man must have been as old as his 1917 Enfield; the youngest mujahedeen carried Kalashnikovs and were still well in their teens.

The village itself was a fortress with guards posted everywhere. I was conducted to a roof and despite my protests two sleeping mujahedeen were moved on so that I would have a place to rest. I lay down to sleep under the starlit sky, surrounded by heavily bearded, turbaned men standing guard, and could have imagined myself in North Africa during the campaigns of a century ago. I was in Afghanistan! But as I drifted off to sleep, I spared a thought for Abdul, already speeding through the darkness back to Iran.

The village seemed to sleep until one the following afternoon, and I was glad of the chance to rest my legs, still aching from the efforts of the preceding day. But we were all galvanised into activity by the threatening sound of an approaching Russian helicopter. I looked up to see that it was in fact a pair of them, one hovering directly over the village while the other patrolled the perimeter. I watched the village children staring at the machines through the heat haze, shielding their eyes from the sun. Would the Russians attack? Would they spot the partially concealed old Russian truck under a tree? Would they see the hiding mujahedeen? Or would our side open fire and shoot the helicopters down? The last, I guessed, was unlikely, for fear of retaliation. It is one of the tragedies of this war that even when the resistance has a chance to launch a successful attack it sometimes dares not for fear of heavy retribution dealt out to the innocent. Last year, fields had been burned and livestock destroyed.

After a time the choppers flew away to the north. They had been on a routine patrol and mercifully had seen nothing suspicious.

Later that day I went on patrol myself with a mujahed called Bismillah.

'How far are we from the frontier?' I asked.

'One kilometre,' he replied, pointing out a border post.

I felt sick inside. I had assumed we were much further into the country. I tried another question.

'Where is the toilet?'

Bismillah smiled, and with a sweep of his arm, indicated the vast space of desert around us.

'Choose your spot,' he said.

I did so, remembering to squat, even though all I wanted to do was urinate. To stand and do so is considered unseemly. I was later to commit another faux-pas: that of eating with my left hand – the hand which is reserved for dealing with bodily hygiene. The fact that I am left-handed made life very difficult for me thereafter, especially as my new-found friends would not touch food from the common dish after I had mistakenly dipped into it with the wrong hand.

Religion and tradition play a large part in their lives. On my first day I saw a sight which became a typical, almost a representative one: at dusk a lone mujahed placing his weapon down in front of him and then praying towards Mecca, bowing and kneeling with the material of his *toman* billowing in the wind, a solitary figure in the burnt, open fields with the dwindling light as his backdrop: one of Allah's armed fighters, whose continuing faith gives them the conviction and the sustenance to battle against overwhelming odds.

PART THREE

Afghanistan

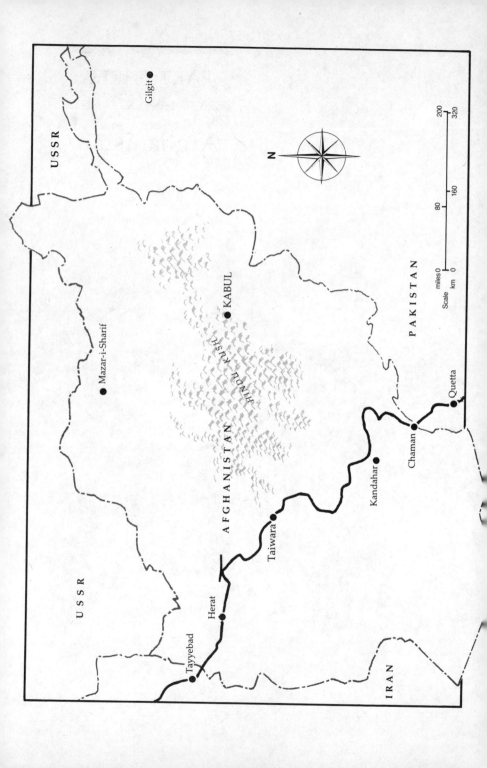

HERAT, THE
MARTYRS' CITY

They moved me across the country in stages. I never knew when I was about to travel, and I doubt whether those in charge knew either. But it always seemed to be contrary to my anticipations. The same applied to modes of travel: if I was expecting to walk, they arrived in a jeep. If I longed to be driven, I'd have to walk.

And so it was in the evening that I had to leave my first village. I had just finished my after-dinner tea when a mujahed stomped up the stairs to tell me that I was to go immediately. I was taken by bike to the edge of the village where dozens of mujahedeen had gathered in the dark. We were a small convoy of a captured Russian truck, a Mercedes minibus in which I was to ride, and a motorcycle outrider. We were given the all-clear to move out by a series of torch signals from scouts posted just outside the village, but once past them we were on our own. We drove along at a fast pace. It was impossible to keep our bearings, since we were driving around the edges of dunes, skirting crests and troughs, and then skimming across flat desert. There were no villages or any other landmarks in this limitless sea – and no hope of avoiding ambushes or landmines. Still, the journey would have been great publicity for Mercedes, for never have I seen a vehicle take such a pounding so well. Every time we lurched up a gradient we switched off our headlights so as not to reveal our position, but suddenly while driving along the top of a ridge we saw a light flicker in the distance.

'*Dushman! Dushman!*' shouted my companions in panic. I thought of the ambush that had befallen Fraim not a fortnight earlier and my blood ran cold. It was perfect ground for an ambush. The truck ahead of us made a U-turn and headed back towards us as we made a desperate attempt at a three-point turn in the sand. The mujahedeen were baling out onto the ground and gathering in small groups.

I heard my name called out: 'Nick Mohammed!' and saw two of

my companions beckoning from behind a dune. I went to hide with them. Someone was sent up ahead to reconnoitre. We waited tensely, fully expecting the sound of gunfire, but instead the scout returned to signal the all-clear. He was followed by a motorbike, the source of the light that had panicked us. We climbed back on board the minibus, but our nerves were thoroughly shaken and despite the odd nervous joke, most banter quickly degenerated into argument as we all scanned the horizons for danger signs. Finally the desert flattened out and we turned onto the asphalt road that leads from Tayyebad to Herat. We travelled along it for a couple of kilometres before heading off into the dunes again, but there was no sign of the truck that had accompanied us. We were truly on our own now.

We stopped in the middle of nowhere and everyone proceeded to argue for a good hour about what to do next. Eventually we returned to the metalled road and drove along it at breakneck speed for some time. I was beginning to feel a little weary but just as I was dozing off the sound of a shot ringing out brought me round with a start.

'Nah Shuravi! – Not Soviets!' yelled my companions as one. We had arrived at a village, and were soon surrounded by the local mujahedeen.

As we got off the bus I was astonished to see that someone was actually paying the driver our fare.

The first watery gleams of light the following morning saw my companions already at prayer. This village bore little resemblance to the previous one as it was badly damaged and had clearly suffered repeated attack. Houses had been reduced to piles of rubble, perhaps entombing their occupants, and gardens were filled with stones. Few walls remained standing, and rooms of buildings stood open to the creeping dust of the plains.

The womenfolk did not dress in the sombre chador of Iran. Instead, they wore a kind of tartan blanket over their heads, with which they all veiled their faces. Children played in the irrigation canals, which had been reduced to muddy bogs by the war. Little seemed to have dampened their spirits, at least.

After an hour's rest and some tea and bread, we moved on. I remember the groups of heavily-armed men at their posts, bracing themselves for the next, inevitable attack.

———

So we continued, from one village to another. As we waited on the outskirts of each to be greeted by the elders, we could hear the calls of the women being shooed into hiding from the strangers. Without the blessing of the elders we could enter no village. I learnt that each mujahedeen 'cell' is known as a 'komiteh'. One looked at me anxiously as I was introduced: twenty proud, weather-stained faces creased with anxiety as they asked:

'BBC London?'

It was as if they were pronouncing a magic spell. I told them that I was from London, though I couldn't claim to represent the BBC, but that didn't worry them unduly, and although it was early morning they brought in a great potful of boiling offal, which we proceeded to eat – by now I was careful always to use only my right hand.

This same 'komiteh' provided us with a donkey and a young muleteer to keep the beast moving, so that my three travelling companions of the moment – for we had long since parted company with the minibus and the remainder of its occupants – could be relieved of their baggage. I, of course, had none, since there was still no trace or mention of my bags, nor indeed did I seriously expect to see them again. We also needed to keep moving as fast as possible, to reduce the risk of attack as we crossed a particularly exposed stretch of desert. Only one of us carried a Kalashnikov, and he hid it under his patou. As we hurried along, one of them pointed to a distant building.

'Russian post,' he said.

'Russian?'

'Maybe Afghan army. But tanks, helicopters.'

We dashed on – if dash is the word, for the donkey, far from helping us, slowed us down, and we decided to leave him and his muleteer to catch us up later. This they did with ease for my three companions were constantly halting anyway to have long discussions about what direction to go in next – which was disconcerting, to say the least, as we stood in the middle of the desert.

In the opposite direction to us, towards the Iranian frontier and safety, passed a pathetic procession of refugees – an old man with his camel, the sole survivor of a bombing raid that left two generations of his family dead; three orphans from different parts of the country;

women with babies on their backs. The men's glazed stares told all the story we needed to know. I wondered what would become of them. If they made it to the frontier, they would have to get past the Russian patrols, and then if they were expecting a welcome in Iran the Pasdaran would quickly disabuse them.

Finally we reached the other side of the desert and our muleteer returned home. Now we were passing through small villages we followed a small river which provided us with constant water – most welcome to me, at least, since our punishing pace never slackened. I noticed few buildings left unscarred by war, but at one point not far away I saw the untouched silos of a Russian cement factory – evidently left unscathed for fear of reprisals. However I learnt that the arrangement wasn't quite that simple; it was a kind of tit for tat: the Afghan rebels left the factory alone, and the Russians left the neighbouring village alone.

My trek seemed endless, and despite the relief offered by the stream and the trees that provided shade along it, I was disheartened at the sight of the road stretching into apparent infinity ahead. I was, however, lucky enough to hitch the occasional lift – once from a local 'taxi' – actually a gaily decorated horsedrawn cart, and once from a motorbike. It was while waiting for my companions to catch me up after one of these that the MiGs struck. It was broad daylight, and their target was a small, insignificant hamlet.

There were six of the aircraft, descending like deadly needles from the clear blue sky. They followed what I was to come to recognise as a standard attack pattern. First they dropped flares which were used to attract heat-seeking missiles. Then the bombs sent huge columns of smoke and dust spiralling skywards. I was riveted, with fear and excitement, since this was my first sight of action. If such a brutally unfair attack could be called action: the rebels have no means of retaliation, and no ground-to-air missiles. The Russians know this, and their attacks were not especially hurried. The jets attacked two by two, releasing their bombs and then circling up and around to join the back of the 'queue' for a second run. I hadn't realised this at first, but when I did I thanked God that I hadn't followed my first instinct to run to the help of the injured immediately. I looked up. So sudden had been the attack that I hadn't even taken in the two helicopters that had accompanied the jets. They hovered parallel to each other, like floating goalposts, marking the attack zone. As long as they stayed there the attack would continue. I grew to hate those Russian helicopters on every occasion that I saw them.

On the ground there had been moments of frenzied activity. The Japanese motorbike on which I'd had my lift was immediately hidden, for if it had been spotted the entire surrounding area would have been blitzed. I remained rooted to the spot long after the planes and the helicopters had flown off. This was no game. I really was in a war zone. The British Interests Section of the Swedish Embassy hadn't been exaggerating. Death was commonplace here and yet it was too late to back out now. I'd have to go on and take my chances with everyone else.

I looked around me. Incredibly the raid seemed to have made little or no impact on the pattern of life. Turbaned men continued to walk by with their donkeys laden with produce, cyclists rode by, peasants working in the fields had apparently hardly bothered to look up. Even the animals seemed to have paid no attention to the bombing.

From here to Herat the war was to be brought home to me in its full and vivid horror. The dirt road was littered with tangled debris from the repeated attacks, and pockmarked with craters from bombs that had missed their targets. Graves of the few that had been retrieved from the rubble stood forlorn, green flags placed on the mounds of stones raised over individual or mass graves.

I wondered how the ancient city of Herat would look. I had seen photographs of it, dominated by its great, soaring mosque, but I knew that what it was now would bear little resemblance to how it had been before the invasion.

The western part of the city was devastated. It was far worse than any pictures I had seen of Dresden or London: it called the total wreck of Nagasaki to mind. The great city of Herat, which has stood for 2500 years and witnessed the passage of Alexander the Great, Genghis Khan and Tamerlane, is being reduced to rubble. I looked aghast at the destruction. Twisted timber beams jutted from collapsed walls like arms reaching out for help from a buried body. Embedded in walls were rockets, still unexploded, their fuses clearly visible in their tail-sections. Everywhere was the litter of modern warfare, and across it ranged the mujahedeen, scavenging for reusable weaponry.

The bombing here had been more than intense. In some places there were craters three metres deep, which now contained pools of stagnant water. Herat had been so hard hit because the government troops and their Russian allies had decided to starve the mujahedeen of any support, and to deprive them of any cover for attacks on army installations. But the mujahedeen lived on in the shells of the buildings, behind splintered doorways at the ends of blasted gardens. Their rooms were bare save for a few cushions on the floor, and the Kalashnikovs and ammunition pouches that hung on the walls from bits of wood driven into the mortar between the mud bricks. Many of their guns were decorated with gaily-coloured Islamic decals and invocations; others, for good luck and protection, had small chains attached to the gun-barrels, or a small triangular pouch with a Koranic scroll inside. These last were also often worn around the neck or upper arm, like a garter.

The kitchen of the 'komiteh' with which I was to stay in western Herat consisted of two ironware pots set on stones for a stove. Cooking, which meant serving and washing up as well, was done or a rota-basis. The 'komiteh' consisted of twenty men, which seemed to be about the usual size. It was a large number to cook for, and the job was made more arduous by the fact that one of the cooks' other duties was to draw water from the well. Bread for our 'komiteh' was provided by a man called Gholalam, a partisan who was also a conscientious objector. Despite his refusal to bear arms, the tough fighting mujahedeen admired him, since they knew that the task of collecting bread from the town centre and delivering it to the 'komiteh' was as hazardous as going into battle. Every morning shortly after dawn prayers Gholalam would arrive with the bread wrapped in his patou and spread it on the floor of our room. Breakfast never varied: the bread was torn into strips and eaten with either *tchai saps* (green tea) or *tchai sia* (black tea), of which there was always a plentiful supply.

The mujahedeen's military operations were conducted at night, and during the day one took what respite one could, while keeping an ear open for the distinctive, cutting, chopping sound of rotor blades. The sound of approaching helicopters was the signal for frenzied activity as everyone slipped on their sandals, grabbed their guns, and headed outside for the cover provided by a crumbling dried-out, tree-lined irrigation canal. I found myself frantically trying to tie my shoelaces (for shoes and sandals were not worn indoors), but it always took so long that I abandoned my shoes in favour of the slip-on sandals my companions wore.

When an attack came – and the arrival of the helicopters nearly always heralded the approach of MiGs – we would spread ourselves along the length of the canal. I tried to make myself as small as possible, huddled up against the edge of the bank, tucked as far as possible under trees for maximum protection. I have never been so terrified as I was during those attacks: the noise of the jets' engines and the whining crash of the bombs as they hit isolate you – deafen and blind you – and you become unaware of anything but the flashing, banging, hammering scream of the jets. You are totally alone. There were moments in this inchoate hell when I prayed that if I were hit at all, I should die outright – but mostly I was determined to live – to survive – for to die would be to disappear without trace And so one crouched there, until the final sounds abated, the pitter-patter of the helicopters returning to base gradually dwindling to silence.

Once an attack was over, we would greet each other with relief – at first cautious, and then delighted, leaping and punching the air in joy, just as if we'd scored spectacular goals. In fact I found the easiest way to keep a grip on myself was to imagine that I had done just that – in front of an enthusiastic crowd at Stamford Bridge. However, my relief at surviving the onslaught was tempered by the knowledge that every day, two or three mujahedeen I had come to know from the different 'komitehs' which had sheltered me in Herat had been killed – paying the martyr's price. But there were days when the bombardment was so unremitting that there was no time at all to relax. Once the jets had gone, the artillery would start up, and the two forms of attack would continue inexorably throughout the day, taking turns, as it were, to try and kill us. However, one came to recognise a regular pattern to their attacks. The most dangerous moments of the day were at prayer- and meal-times, when the government forces knew that we would be gathered together. It was impossible to shoot back, because the DhSKs, the heavy, Chinese machine-guns which were the only artillery they had remotely capable of shooting at the jets, had run out of ammunition. The other alarming thing is how desperately inexperienced the Afghan guerrillas are when faced with the technology of modern war.

Very little could dampen their spirits, however, and their delight when one of their sparingly-used land-mines blew up a tank was unbounded. And they did have one very effective weapon apart from the Kalashnikov. This was the RPG, or rocket-propelled grenade, which was ideal for use against tanks and armoured personnel carriers, as well as buildings. My group had two shoulder-launched surface-to-air missiles as well, and they spoke gleefully of the day they had brought down one of the hated helicopters. They might have hit both helicopters in that particular attack, but their second missile failed to launch, owing to the fact that its battery had gone dead – a misfortune that would not have occurred if the Afghans had been properly instructed in the missile's use.

'Where does all your equipment come from?' I asked one of the commanders.

'Mostly from China, now – or we capture it from the Russians,' he informed me. 'We got the Soviet-made missiles and some of the Kalashnikovs from the US who bought them from the Egyptians.'

The rebels are dependent on outside sources for all supplies, and nowhere is this more pathetically evident than in their field hospitals. I visited such places in Herat where there was no running water – the water was drawn from a ditch and boiled before use. The male nurses were untrained, the beds had no linen. In one hospital I fainted. It was suffocatingly hot, and the room was unventilated and stinking. I had watched a doctor remove the dressing from a suppurating wound in order to clean it, but that was all I saw. I woke up surrounded by the hospital staff, anxious for my welfare. Later, I told myself that I would not have fainted had it not been for the heat, but in honesty, it also had much to do with the sight of the wounds: one man's whole mouth had been cut away by shrapnel, a sight imprinted for ever in my mind.

Basic sanitation is not the least of the problems that beset these field hospitals. No sooner do the government forces learn of their whereabouts than they become targets. Thus it was that on one visit the sound of MiGs sent us scrambling away from the hospital, which was moved every four to five weeks. I cannot personally imagine what leads the Russians to bomb hospitals. I can only think that it is because the doctors and nurses occasionally carry arms themselves.

To the west of Herat few villages have been spared the carpet bombing. In one, where five hundred families had lived formerly, there were only twenty people now. In another, three old men remained. The rest of the population had either been killed or had fled to Iran. I hadn't believed them in Mashhad when they had told me a story about a hundred and fifty villagers being burnt alive after taking refuge in a Karez well (a subterranean channel). Now I saw how easily such an atrocity could have occurred. In the only village that I visited to have largely escaped the bombing I ate my meal underneath a gaping hole in the ceiling where a helicopter's bomb had exploded. And yet life went on, and there was even an administration of sorts, in a building which doubled as courtroom and mosque; and in another village they had set up a Banda printing machine in a ruined building to produce a fortnightly newsletter.

The fact that an administrative infrastructure survived was of crucial importance. Even in the heart of Herat itself, the mujahedeen could still obtain spare parts for captured Russian vehicles and petrol – their collaborators being referred to always as 'Muslims'. My US dollars could even be exchanged on the black market – but not before someone had been to the bank to check the official rate. The man who organised this for me was Ahmad – a former teacher, and now a mujahed. He was the deputy commander of a 'komiteh', who had been driven to smuggling heroin in order to raise the money to support his imprisoned son who depended on him. He was a courteous, homely man in his late forties, and his hatred of the Russians is better imagined than described.

With the money he obtained for me I was able to purchase a splendid tailor-made Afghan waistcoat, with eight pockets – four on the outside and four zippered ones on the inside, and a length of Japanese-woven polyester-and-cotton material which would serve as my patou. My waistcoat was brownish-red and of exactly the same pattern as Ismail Khan's, except that his was grey.

Ismail Khan, the supreme commander of 13,000 Jamiat partisans in the province of Herat, called on our 'komiteh' several times. He made an immediate and profound impression on me. A temperate and pleasant man in his late thirties, his eyes reflective, his face sad behind his large, untidy black beard, he bore his responsibilities with a military professionalism which explained his high rank. One of many brothers, his home lay in the province of Farah at Shindand, a town which is now host to the largest Soviet airbase outside Kabul. There were two marks of rank: one was a small, modern radio of the Sony Walkman type, on which he would listen religiously to the World Service. The other was a gold tablet which he wore round his neck, and which bore an inscription from the Koran in impossibly fine writing. His voice was soft, tender, but determined, and I never once heard it raised in anger. He spoke good English in a clear and deliberate way. His movements were like his speech: considered, unhurried. He was worn with work. In the last seven years he had only once been out of Afghanistan – for one night, to meet Professor Rabbani, the Jamiat leader, in Tayyebad. He often used the expression 'Oh God' – but '*Ai Khoda*' really means something in Dari. It isn't a meaningless oath. It is an appeal. He is a man who personifies the Afghan guerrilla movement: deeply religious, and deeply in love with his country.

His visits to us were always brief and unannounced. He travelled in a jeep with another one as an escort, and both vehicles were bristling with mujahedeen armed to the teeth. If he stayed for a meal, it was eaten at top speed, for he was high on the government's wanted list and had to be constantly on the alert and on the move. As soon as he learnt that my bags had disappeared, he sent word to the border, and within a day a Japanese camera arrived with some Russian film. Sadly the two were not compatible, but I was already impressed at the speed and efficiency with which he could produce results. As I came to know him better over the following weeks, so the first impression deepened into great regard.

Herat's tradesmen acted as go-betweens for government soldiers who wanted to defect to the mujahedeen. Such defectors were carefully vetted, however, because infiltrators in the pay of the KGB or KHAD, the Afghan secret police, sometimes masqueraded as defecting soldiers too. I remember that early one morning a 14-year-old boy came to offer his services. His credentials were inspected – letters of reference from a member of his family known to a commander of the mujahedeen. At first everything seemed straightforward, but then, after some three hours of questioning, holes began to appear in the boy's story. Far from breaking down under the interrogation, however, he seemed proud of his task. With the feckless amorality of a true vagabond, he explained his true mission: he had been enlisted by KHAD to eliminate the commander and to poison the 'komiteh's' food.

Once unmasked, he was only too happy to illustrate the devious skills he had been so splendidly taught. They timed him as he broke down and reassembled a Kalashnikov, and applauded his skill, which he acknowledged with a grin. He told them that he'd been paid 10,000 *Afghanis* (about £65) a month, all duly paid into a bank account, but his immediate repentance seemed to me due more to fear than (as he said) to suddenly seeing the error of his ways as a true Muslim. He obliged the extempore court further by betraying two adult collaborators, and because of his relatively tender age he was not executed, but sentenced instead to be educated under the Koran. This seemed to me extraordinarily humane, given the task he would undoubtedly have carried out if he had not been detected. The two men were executed.

Under the constant constraint of having to conceal my real identity, of having to treat every stranger as a potential enemy, and always disguised as a mujahed, I was also obliged, against my will (for I had sworn never to do so), to carry a Kalashnikov and a chest pouch containing four spare magazines – 120 bullets in all – and a clip of grenades. I succumbed to this because I wanted to visit the centre of Herat, and to go there unarmed would have brought me to the attention of government spies. So we set out with me armed to the teeth and with the loose end of my turban wrapped round my face so as to reveal only my eyes.

The streets were like a scene from some futuristic movie, with us the only survivors of a nuclear holocaust. We were five armed men – I say men, though I, at 26, was the oldest by three years and Nasser, their leader, was several years older than the rest – walking spread out across the street. Everywhere there was the debris of war – a Russian tank with its turret torn off its body and slung a hundred yards from it; the wreck of a veterinary hospital; razed walls; cratered roads. Desolation everywhere, and no sign of life beyond the dust blown by the wind – if that could be called life. At least it was movement. I thought of the ruins of Persepolis in Iran, and reflected on how little we learn from history.

We were walking towards the tenth-century citadel, now an Afghan government garrison, when the shooting started. I had already become edgy and now I turned to Nasser in anger and panic.

'I thought you said there wouldn't be any shooting?' I knew I was useless with a rifle – and even modern ones are extremely heavy to handle.

Nasser looked at me and smiled reassuringly: 'Don't worry,' he said. 'It's just the government troops firing into the air to make the Russians think they are fighting the mujahedeen.'

We continued our walk under the shadows of the towering minarets of the great mosque, Medresse Sultan Husain-e Baiqara. I was lost in admiration of the splendid building, at that time still undamaged, but not so lost as not to notice that my companions were becoming more cautious. They sent an unarmed scout ahead – unarmed to look like an ordinary Herati. Now, when we crossed one of the wide avenues, we did so at a sprint, one after another, while the others covered for us. I ran as fast as my legs would carry me, but I was beginning to be weighed down by my weapons, the tension and the heat, and the whole thing took on a slightly ludicrous air when children scuttled up to play at being mujahedeen like us. We promptly shooed them away, remaining on our guard until our scout returned with a local policeman. He greeted me warmly.

'Welcome to Afghanistan and Herat,' he said in perfect English.

Under the circumstances I found his greeting more than a little bizarre.

That particular outing ended safely, but there were others. I remember particularly Wednesday, 1 August 1984. I had been in Herat one week but it seemed like a lifetime. It was 5.20 am, and I was standing in the middle of the street, when all of a sudden I was aware, not two hundred metres above my head, of a MiG dropping its deadly load of bombs. For a long moment I was rooted to the spot, but then I ran like hell, along with the others who'd been caught out like me. Running was terrible, because you couldn't actually move: fear had turned me numb, and I was transfixed in the best tradition of bad dreams. Movement came when the shockwave from the third bomb, which exploded with an earsplitting bang just behind me, picked me up and hurled me to the ground in an excited flurry of sand and dust which whirled into my eyes and mouth. Now I was galvanised into desperate activity, as I picked myself up and ran for real. I had time to see that all of us who were running were actually doing so in true disarray – in every direction that was generally away from the road where the MiG hovered: like a herd of wildebeest running from a lion. Now the MiGs seemed to be everywhere in the sky above us. There had been no helicopters to herald them. That was why they had taken us all by surprise.

We spent some time sheltering amongst the trees, from where we could see the jets circling overhead. One of my companions, Ahmad, or 'Eustase' (teacher) as he was affectionately known, squatted next to me, as badly shaken as myself.

'Did you see it?' he asked me sombrely. 'While I was running across the field I saw a goat's leg fly over my head.'

'Where did it land?'

'Somewhere over there – in that scrub.'

Once the jets had flown off we went to search for it, but found instead a man's arm, already covered with ants and flies, diligently gorging themselves on the remains.

I was certain that our 'komiteh' must have been destroyed, but on returning to the building I found that the MiGs had missed it by about a hundred metres. All around, however, was devastation, and against one wall I saw where the headless torso of a man had been flung. It was splattered against the dried brick, its legs torn away, its clothes burnt off, no more than food now for the myriad insects descending upon it. My reactions are difficult to describe. On the one hand, I reflected very practically that if only I had had my camera, I could have taken the war picture to end all war pictures. On the other hand, if I had had a camera, I might have been tempted to photograph the MiGs, instead of fleeing from them – in which case they would almost certainly have killed me. And after all, this man was dead. Maybe my practical reaction came to save me from a more emotional one. I spent the rest of that day deep in thought. It was unlikely that I would have a closer brush with death, and come out alive again. I wondered whether I should continue with my journey – but I was in so deep now that there really was no turning back.

I spent the afternoon with the 'komiteh', holed up in a barn some way from the street. For my own safety, the mujahedeen had adopted a policy of moving me from group to group, and I hadn't yet found out where this one was based – the name of this little village so close to Herat.

'What is this place called?' I asked Ahmad.

'Hauze Karbas,' he replied. It was a name I will never forget.

We inspected our wounds. My only injuries were to my feet, since I had lost my shoes running and my ankles and toes had been slashed by the thorny undergrowth. At night we returned to the scene of the attack, and placed the torso, already rotting, into a jute bag. The body was neither cleaned nor prepared in any way.

'Those who fall in the cause of Islam are buried as they fell, in their bloodstained war-garments,' explained Ahmad. 'In the eyes of the Afghan, no death is more glorious.' Later I discovered thousands lost their lives in this summer's Soviet offensive.

The ceremony over, we made for base. The acrid smell of the dead animals' rotting flesh strewn around the all but obliterated fields assailed our nostrils, and if we passed too close to a body, the flies rose up in an irritable black cloud. It is interesting that one wasn't aware of the flies at all until death struck, when they rose and hung round the corpses and the severed limbs like a living pall.

After the near miss, our routine changed somewhat. No sooner had we risen in the mornings than prayers were said and we would leave for the barn where we had spent the day after the attack. Only two mujahedeen remained behind to prepare the meals.

I was keen to join in their activities, rather than merely be their guest, and offered to help. Above all I didn't want to give the impression of freeloading. But even when I tried so much as to pour the tea they would seize the pot from me and tell me to sit down. Finally I was detailed to do cooking and washing-up with Abdul Sattar, the second-in-command; but when our turn came, all was not well. The others were clearly displeased at the arrangement, though a little embarrassed as well. I pressed them for reasons.

'You are an infidel,' they said.

I felt like a child that has been told by others that he can't play with them. An infidel – and therefore unclean. It hurt, I decided, because I had flattered myself that they had accepted me. Now I found that there was a barrier between us that would always be there – unless I converted to Islam.

But it wasn't at all that they didn't trust me – rather the contrary, for the job they gave me as a kind of consolation prize was to look after their funds. They came to me for money when they needed it and asked for it with the touching naïveté of little children asking their father for pocket-money. The job delighted me, for it gave me some idea of their cost of living. It wasn't high. A kilo of tomatoes cost five pence or so; a kilo of yogurt about the same. However, their funds were not extensive either.

Evenings in this group were always spent huddled around the garish light of a Tilley lamp. There were moments of sputtering light, a mujahed resuscitating the flame by frantically pumping away at the primitive contraption to build up the pressure and a steady flow of gas. The two sets of evening prayers were in close proximity to each other. The mujahedeen ran about gathering up their patous, which they had left dotted about the house, and if they couldn't find their own they would pick up the nearest in their anxiety not to be late.

Depending on the size of the prayer gathering, they would either line up in a long row, or in two shorter ones behind the commander, who led them in prayers as well as battle. Barefoot and standing on their patous they alternately bent forward, knelt, bending over with hands and elbows touching the ground, foreheads pressed against it, and then stood upright again. The fifth and final prayer session of the day was the longest, save for the elaborate Sabbath midday prayer.

Once the prayers were over, there was a time for reflection, the faces of the men exhibiting a mixture of quiet resolve – the strength that Allah gives them – and sadness – at the wreckage of their country.

I heard endless stories of despair from them, and it truly seemed that not one family, at least in Herat province, had been left un-scarred. There was one man whose sixteen-year-old son had been overheard expressing subversive comments at school. The boy hasn't been seen since his imprisonment, and that is just one story typical of many. Indeed, it is far from being the worst. For relief from the agony of his thoughts, one of them smoked hashish, but only secretly. I was offered some and when I refused he immediately became panic-stricken that I would tell the others. Drugs of all descriptions are not only forbidden by Islam, but are reserved for use as barter by the mujahedeen. Russian conscripts will exchange cash, food and cigarettes, even ammunition and weapons for drugs. And to my amusement I discovered that the other much valued commodity among the Russians is nailclippers – which are apparently almost impossible to obtain in the USSR.

However much the Russians earned the anger and contempt of the mujahedeen, the West came in for its fair share too.

'Why aren't you helping us in our struggle?' was a frequent question, and one which I was at a loss to answer in terms that they could begin to understand, because the ramifications of modern politics would seem so absurd to these men, who still retain simple concepts of honour and friendship. Their anger was intercut with pleas for aid, and their need is desperate, for both medical supplies and weaponry.

For much of the time, too, they were fighting in the dark, for their only source of news was the BBC's Persian Service. They would also listen to Radio Kabul, but only for the traditional Afghan music that it plays. If the BBC was ever jammed, they could tune in to the Voice of America, but their trust and regard was reserved for the BBC. This was despite the fact that Herat province was rarely if ever mentioned.

'Why do they never talk about our struggle?' Ahmad asked me. 'Why do they always speak of what's going on in Panjshir?'

Recognising the hurt in his voice, I attempted to explain: 'It's because Panjshir isn't so far from the Pakistan border. It's easy for Western journalists to travel to that part of the country.'

'At least they seem to be giving the Russians a good thrashing over there,' he said, mollified. And it was true that news of any victories against the loyalist troops and the Russians cheered them no end. Numbers of enemy casualties and lists of destroyed equipment would be repeated for days afterwards. News of defeats, on the other hand, was greeted with stony silence – more sulky than stoical. Once there was an uproar when my companions learnt that two Soviet

PoWs who had been shipped to Switzerland by the Red Cross had opted to return to the USSR. I dreaded to think what action might be taken as a result of this news.

'What happens to soldiers you take prisoner?' I asked my second-in-command nervously.

Abdul Sattar stroked his beard. 'We keep them safe,' he said laconically. 'Sometimes we try to exchange them for our own men, but the *Shuravi* [Soviets] don't like that.'

Since the beginning of the civil war and the subsequent invasion of Afghanistan by the Soviet Union, it is surprising that the fight has continued so long at such odds which must partly be due to many of the mujahedeen commanders being, like Ismail Khan himself, ex-army officers who can impose at least a fashion of military discipline on their men and who are trained in strategy. Add to this that they are fighting for their home on territory that they know and love, and you have a very strong fuelling of morale. There is also a successful network of men who have remained apparently loyal to the Afghan army, and have retained their commands within it, but who in fact are on the side of the Muslim forces, and leak information about convoys and outposts which are vulnerable to attack.

On the other hand the mujahedeen are split and splitting into various factions which not only fight each other, but may on occasion fight on the side of the Russians and the Afghan loyalists. My group, the Jamiat, is almost exclusively Sunni, and dislikes and distrusts factions of both Khomeini and his Shia followers. The Jamiat have even clashed with Pasdaran border patrols. In one exchange, the Pasdaran killed three mujahedeen, upon which the guerrillas seized many more Pasdaran, releasing all but three, who were duly executed: a simple demonstration of tit for tat.

Then there were the groups with whom the Jamiat sometimes formed uneasy alliances: the Hesbi and the Harakat. These groups themselves were, however, further subdivided, and it was possible to encounter both friendly and unfriendly factions, both calling themselves Harakat, for example. On the other side, the communist government is itself divided into two rival parties: the Parcham (Red Flag) and the Halq (People's). Most frightening to the mujahedeen are the government militia, who dress like them and employ the same military tactics. Stirred into this already complex imbroglio are the bandits, who inhabit the border regions in organised groups, loyal to no one but themselves.

Further, due to the shortage of weapons, allegiance to a particular group can sometimes depend on its ability to acquire them. I have seen individual mujahedeen change groups for the sake of better guns – or for the sake of getting a better chance at having a crack at the enemy. There is also a standing offer from the Iranians that anyone joining a pro-Iranian group will automatically get a 'free gift' of a Kalashnikov.

Temporary arrangements were reached between rival factions when it came to making an attack. This was very evident in Herat, where not a few times a group of mujahedeen would stroll into our 'komiteh' to give us advance warning of their launching an attack against a government post. The east of the city was 'off limits' and has remained largely intact, as many of the mujahedeen's families have moved there, causing the price of property to rocket in the east as it has tumbled in the west, where you just had to squat somewhere and hope for the best. I remember one mujahed returning from a two-week holiday with his family in the east of the city.

It was harvest-time, and Ismail Khan had given a general directive not to launch any attacks against the government troops for fear of retaliation in the form of crop-burning before the wheat could be garnered. Nevertheless a programme of spasmodic harassment continued. One trick was to set off for a government-held building and fire one rocket-propelled grenade at it. You would then offer the soldiers inside the chance of joining their Muslim brothers. As the alternative was to suffer an attack, and they knew that the second and third RPGs would be more deliberately aimed than the first had been, the wretched soldiers would often surrender – indeed, nearly always the only people who objected were the officers. The actual Russian command posts were so placed as to make attacks on them extremely difficult, and when an offensive was launched, the Afghan troops always made up the vanguard. The Russians brought up the rear.

'The Russians are hard to get at,' I was told.

'What if you took their uniforms – dressed up like them? You could surprise them that way.'

'It has been done; but we would not.'

'Why not?'

'It would be against the Will of Allah.'

The nights were punctuated with bursts of machine-gun fire; mortars and rockets pumped into the darkness; incandescent flares created great leaping shadows across the sky like the ghosts of ruined buildings. Now and then the more ominous, constant beam of a searchlight mounted on a tank would pierce the blackness. I would lie down to sleep in great irritation, for not only were these night-time forays against Ismail Khan's orders, but those who went out on them were egged on by their fellows in the most foolish way possible: they stood on the rooftops and fired their guns in the air. The red and green tracer lines of their bullets scratched the black surface of the sky, adding to the already impressive firework display, but revealing their position, and above all wasting precious ammunition.

I was often ill at ease during my time in Herat, and I think that quite frequently I could not really believe that I was actually where I was, and doing what I was doing. It all seemed so bizarre. Though I was tired at night, I would sometimes use the powerful radio available at my committee HQ to tune in to the Olympic Games which were taking place on the other side of the world in Los Angeles at the time. While I listened to the commentary on a race run by Sebastian Coe or Steve Ovett the shells burst outside my window.

The civilians of the city were badly hit. They still came into town to sell their produce, but they looked like a funeral cortège as they made their way to the pathetic remains of a market, never raising their eyes from the ground as they walked, oblivious sometimes even if their donkey wandered off. Their faces barely concealed their deep anguish, but they were clearly numbed by the incessant bludgeoning they had received over the years. Most of the men were old, and like their animals there was nothing they could do but carry on with their lives. One old man in particular I remember with admiration. He was one of the few who still cultivated his fields. He went about his daily tasks and tended his animals as if nothing had happened to his life, but he distributed what little he had to the mujahedeen, giving the younger guerrilla fighters tangible strength through his jovial, quiet resolve.

I thought sadly of the day when I would have to leave my companions and continue on my way. For I always had the possibility of escape – of simply walking away when I had had enough. These people were condemned to see their fate through. As if they sensed this and distanced me from them because of it, I was always given the safest place – under a lintel – during shelling. If they wanted me to be spared as a witness, then I had served them ill, for I had been unable to collect the photographic evidence which would have been so valuable to show the outside world.

I am certain that no army of repression will ever conquer their resolve. It will have to kill them all first. Against the MiGs that fly in so fast you only hear them *after* they have made their run and dropped their bombs, there are teenagers with Enfields. But spiritual strength can move mountains; and if the 80-year-old men I met were anything to go by, with rifles as old as themselves, their white-bearded faces like walnuts, determined to kill one Russian before they die, then mountains will be moved.

WITH ISMAIL KHAN

I had talked a lot about buying or hiring a horse to continue my journey. In fact I didn't know how to ride, but an opportunity unexpectedly came my way. One day while I was sitting on the roof of an ammunition depot in a village west of the city I saw two beautiful horses being led into the square below me. I asked my companion, a former army officer who had joined the mujahedeen after a period as a prisoner-of-war, whose horses they were.

'One is for you,' he told me. 'The other is for Ismail Khan.' I looked at him in disbelief. He was a strange man, embittered by his experiences, but as if in confirmation of his words I saw Ismail Khan appear, as suddenly and as unannounced as ever, and go over to where the horses were standing.

Excited at the prospect of riding, I clambered down and greeted Ismail Khan respectfully. He returned my greeting and indicated that we should go for a ride together. Watching him closely, I was able to copy his movements successfully enough to mount, and to my delight my horse moved off when I nudged him. In fact I later discovered that the horse I had been given was worth 1500 dollars – a king's ransom to the mujahedeen. And yet such was Ismail Khan's generosity of spirit that he had seen fit to let me ride the horse, although I was an inexperienced horseman.

We rode off alone together, and if Ismail Khan set a cracking pace, my horse was up to it. I kept my head low to avoid the branches overhead and with one hand gripped my turban firmly to my head. Now and then we were challenged by other mujahedeen, but Ismail Khan had only to lower the bottom half of his turban from his face for them to fall back with muttered apologies. He was known everywhere.

After that first ride I was to improve, but not every foray into the countryside was made on horseback. I was spending more time in Ismail Khan's company now, and as I got to know him better I came to feel that I had passed a test of some unspoken kind, or a period of probation, and in the days ahead we shared an anteroom when it became time to rest, for now began the tour of inspection.

Travelling by vehicle was always a hazard, not least because of the primitive roads and bridges. The scream of a jet engine would send us scrambling for our jeep; but it wasn't only jets we had to fear for there were plenty of Russian tanks on the prowl which were difficult to avoid in the open countryside. This could be very frightening. One day we were driving over the tenth-century Pol-e-Malan bridge across the Hari Roud when Ismail Khan calmly pointed out a line of tanks positioned along a modern bridge a kilometre away. I tried to appear calm but the whole situation left me bewildered. There was, it seemed, a stand-off: the Russians wouldn't attack if they themselves were left alone. Somehow the mujahedeen always seemed to know when and how they would be attacked, and conversely when it was safe to travel. On this occasion we passed by the Russians unmolested, but I wasn't only frightened of them: our jeep was packed to the gunnels with ammunition – there was even a crate of World War II bullets – and the road was extremely bumpy. Finally, however, we arrived in the husk of a deserted village where we waited until nightfall to cross the Herat–Kandahar road. As we crossed I could see the lights of Herat airport not far off, and an Afghan army post from where the soldiers must have been able to see us. However, no action was taken against us as we went over, men, mules and horses together.

It was quite a sight to see a hundred men, a couple of dozen riders, donkeys with muleteers, all stretched across a wide area, fanned out, or at other times travelling in single file through a village in the moonlight. We looked like an army of phantoms. It was vital to cross empty stretches of desert at night so as not to be caught in the open. The vehicles carried us as far as they could go, but where the terrain became impassable for them we would switch to travelling on foot or by horse.

The mujahedeen travel on foot at great speeds, but I was usually put on a horse when we had to forgo our jeeps because otherwise I could not keep up. Some of my companions, when travelling on foot, found it easier to do so without their sandals or plimsolls. As they charged on past me they never failed to ask how I was – 'Khob hasti,

Nick Mohammed?' – and at times I was ashamed of my tiredness. Such journeys were always made as fast as possible, with only two or three short breaks and no refreshment other than a little water. Occasionally a packhorse or a donkey would shed its load. It would then have to be chased, caught, and reloaded. Reluctant animals would have to be tugged, pushed and otherwise encouraged up some of the steep slopes.

However we travelled, the sight of approaching helicopters was the signal to move on, and there was never any escape from the claustrophobic feeling of being hunted. I grew to admire Ismail Khan. He was unlike many of the other prominent commanders, who had gained their positions because of their wealth rather than through any fighting ability. But in one especial respect Ismail Khan was different: most other commanders allowed their followers to stoop and kiss their hands. Ismail Khan would not only attempt to drag his hand away if this happened but in so doing would stoop lower than the man who greeted him.

He was deeply concerned about the recent turn of events in the war: the indiscriminate bombing of villages and the resultant toll on human life. It was frustrating for the mujahedeen, who had little or no comforts in the form of food, shelter, clothes and medicines to offer the civilians who were suffering so wretchedly as a result of the remorseless Russian attacks. Thus the mujahedeen, who see their own friends and families cut down, are slowly losing some of the great moral strength which has sustained them for so long. Increasing numbers of them ask permission to go to Iran, either for a break or to earn some money for their families; increasingly they do not return. Added to this is their awareness that they are not being helped by other apparently friendly countries.

'What are they frightened of if your people gain power?' I asked Ismail Khan.

He smiled a little wearily. 'I suppose they fear that a free Afghanistan will be another Islamic Republic, and they think that there are already too many such republics in the world.'

'You mean like Iran.'

'Exactly so. That's why it's so ironic that Khomeini refuses to authorise the free passage of arms into Afghanistan. The world fears a united Islamic front.'

'But haven't the people who have been here to see what your fight is about been able to tell the outside world something of the truth?'

'I don't know. I am not impressed by the people who come here, with their cameras and their notebooks, tongues lapping for a sensational story. But not for our benefit. For their own.'

'Journalists, you mean?' I asked, somewhat relieved that my own equipment had been lost. Or might he be withholding it from me? That didn't seem like him.

'And adventurers,' he said.

Luckily I knew that by now this could not be a barbed remark for my benefit. He had accepted me because I had stood the test I now realised he had prepared for me in sending me to the severely embattled village of Hauze Karbas. The mujahedeen of Herat city were held in high esteem, and every other mujahed I met would ask me how it had been there. The conversation was always the same – Hauze Karbas was bad, the place (wherever it was) that I was now in was very good:

'Inja kheli khob, Hauze Karbas kheli bad,' I would say – this place is very nice, Hauze Karbas is very bad.

'Kheli bad?' they enquired.

'Kheli, kheli bad,' I answered.

'Kheli, kheli bad?' they asked.

'Kheli, kheli, kheli bad!'

And so it went on.

As time passed I began to feel more comfortable again. True, I had lost my possessions and my cameras, but I was still alive. And lack of a camera made me more like one of them. Only my Swiss army knife, the object of much admiration, set me apart. That and my good boots, which would be needed for a good many miles more yet. They had bought me a Russian maths exercise book to write in, and I drew small portraits of the mujahedeen to give them as presents: these turned out to be a great success.

I would constantly ply Ismail Khan with questions:

'I notice that when a person is sick, your doctors will give him an assortment of pills, and sometimes the pills they give are counter-effective. Why do they do it?' I asked him one day.

'They can't diagnose the illness and so they prescribe many drugs in the hope that one will be effective,' he replied with his usual gentle calm.

He had his questions for me, too, and asked me what I thought of communism. It is a pity, looking back, that I was not sure enough of my ground to give him more than polite answers. I would have liked to tackle many topics with him: to tell him about the benefits of education, as I had learned to my own cost; about birth control, the emancipation of women, and so on. Perhaps such subjects would not have been welcome. Perhaps Ismail Khan felt that the first job was to win the war. He did mention a Frenchman who had lectured him on socialism once, but he referred neither to the Frenchman nor his theme with warmth.

In mid-August Ismail Khan, myself, and 25 hardy mujahedeen set off to the mountains of Qasa Murg. If Herat had been Purgatory, then the mountains were Paradise. The moonlight softly lit the jagged peaks ahead of us as we climbed, and we were greeted long before we reached the first village by locals who had walked a couple of miles down from their homes to welcome us. With great ceremony we were escorted up and treated to a sumptuous dinner, even though it was long past midnight. I was ravenous after the long climb and ate very heartily before stretching myself out to sleep.

The following day horses were made ready. There were not enough to go round but by doubling up every man got a mount. My first horse had been left at our base, but I was still the object of special treatment and was given a horse to myself here. We followed a river sandwiched between two towering, sheer rockfaces, the cliffs so deep and high that sunshine rarely penetrated the gorge. At several points the river water was up to our knees even though we were mounted. The horses felt their way forwards cautiously, but for all their caution they sometimes stumbled, hurling their riders into the water to everyone else's amusement. In a bid not to be laughed at myself, I kept my feet firmly in my stirrups, thinking that that way I could not be toppled off, but as soon as Ismail Khan noticed this he brought his horse up to mine.

'You must take your feet out of the stirrups,' he said quietly. I am sure he wanted no one else to notice my lack of riding experience.

'Why?' I said, obeying nevertheless.

'If you fall off and your foot is entangled in a stirrup, it may be that the horse will drag you under.'

He continued to ride beside me and, as we continued to converse, gradually revealed a little more about himself.

'I was an artillery officer when the Herat uprising took place,' he said. 'But I could not turn against my Muslim brothers. I was able to take over an AA installation and shoot down Russian aircraft that were bombing my people.'

'How do you come to know these mountains so well?'

'I fled here after the insurrection failed. But this is the first time I have been back.'

'So what are we doing here now?'

'Well, we are not on holiday, Nick Mohammed. I want to see if we can locate some good places for secret ammunition dumps, for one thing, and possibly for a field hospital. It is cooler up here, and water is plentiful, and there will be less chance of attack . . .' Indeed there were a large number of man-made caves in this region, often constructed with interconnecting rooms. Totally invisible from the air, cool and secure. An ideal site for a hospital, if the wounded could be carried up here and no one found out about it.

The days passed idyllically. Each village treated us like heroes and everywhere feasts were prepared. One I remember especially well. A large sheep was slaughtered, hung upside down from a tree, and 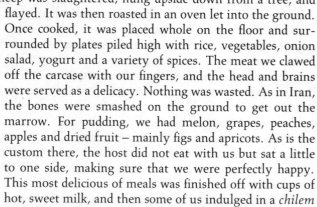 flayed. It was then roasted in an oven let into the ground. Once cooked, it was placed whole on the floor and surrounded by plates piled high with rice, vegetables, onion salad, yogurt and a variety of spices. The meat we clawed off the carcase with our fingers, and the head and brains were served as a delicacy. Nothing was wasted. As in Iran, the bones were smashed on the ground to get out the marrow. For pudding, we had melon, grapes, peaches, apples and dried fruit – mainly figs and apricots. As is the custom there, the host did not eat with us but sat a little to one side, making sure that we were perfectly happy. This most delicious of meals was finished off with cups of hot, sweet milk, and then some of us indulged in a *chilem* – a water bubble pipe. I nicknamed one of our commanders Chilem, for he never failed to smoke one when time permitted, the tobacco being crushed by a manservant in the palms of his hands. Cigarettes were held upwards between two fingers and puffed through the fist. I was accorded special treatment: whenever possible I had my own bowl of food (probably because I was an infidel); at night my clothes were taken away to be washed, and I was always given a mat, an extra cushion and a blanket. I also shared the commanders' distinction of having a man to look after me at all times.

There were unsavoury moments too. The lavatory at this particular village was simply a small hill, the path to its summit littered with excrement. You had to find a vacant spot to squat in. But in the clear air that didn't seem to matter too much, and I began to relax. There was no holiday for Ismail Khan though. He worked from dawn till dusk every day, and his work principally involved him in that bane of all leaders – paperwork. He would reply personally to a vast number of letters which were brought at all times of day from all over his province – letters asking advice, offering support, and reporting atrocities. One such report told of three Russian soldiers who had tried to rape two women in a village. Two of the troops had been stabbed to death by two elderly villagers, but the third soldier had then shot them in turn. This particular story gave me pause because I had been considering the possibility of travelling disguised as a woman, although I had hesitated so far because of my height and size. Now I saw that the scheme would have to be abandoned, for it depended upon Russian soldiers respecting the veil of purdah.

Ismail Khan's replies to all these letters bore his official stamp – an outline map of Afghanistan inside which the Koran stood open above a pair of crossed swords. The stamp was always made in green ink, and countersigned. Each commander had his own stamp – his seal of authority. The mujahedeen run a very efficient postal service, and although letters usually arrived opened, I was able to send a letter to England with some confidence that it would get there – and it did.

Our work done, it was time to return from the mountains to the arid reality of the plain, and I for one was reluctant to do so. Our journey back, however, was some compensation. I cannot adequately describe the keenness and the clearness of the air in Afghanistan, and the intensity of the light, which bathes the scenery in a rich glow. The mountains opened up vista after vista as we travelled, and made me forget my hunger, for I had no food other than the berries I was able to pluck from the trees my horse passed under. I wondered if I would ever have the endurance of our guide, an old man who always appeared on the next ridge ahead of us, a lone figure who travelled on foot over some of the ruggedest terrain on earth, and yet who clearly had to slow his pace to allow us, on horseback, to keep up.

The food problem was solved for me by the nomads whom we encountered. They were so generous with their presents of dried fruit that I tried to cover my waistcoat pockets to prevent them from trying to cram even more in. But there was no stemming the tide, and in the end not only were my pockets filled, but my hands and arms as well. As a final gesture, they looped strings of nuts over my head – all this in gratitude that I had come to visit them. At first I felt encumbered by the food, but I was grateful for it in the days to come, when it provided my sole nourishment apart from tea and *nan*. Tea was offered everywhere I went. I always thanked my hosts for the tea.

'No, no,' they would reply. 'We thank you.'

'But you have given me refreshment. It is I who should thank you.'

'No. We thank you.'

I might have drowned in tea, I suppose, if Ismail Khan had not come to my rescue.

'Drink tea in the morning and in the evening,' he advised me. 'But not in the middle of the day. Then, it will make you tired.' He never seemed to tire himself. His very few moments of leisure were spent in prayer, during which, if you looked at his meditating eyes, you could sense that he was asking himself whether or not the struggle was really worth while. So devastating was the war that there would soon be nothing left for the victors to inherit. In other moments he would clean his Kalashnikov – a weapon which singled him out, for most of the other chief commanders now had the more modern and powerful Kalakov rifle – which of course carried greater status.

As we gradually descended so my own sense of sadness rose. But there was little time to indulge it. Our final descent was a headlong race down a broad slope, with a village at its foot. Hardly had we arrived than we heard a sound which even in a few short days had become blissfully unfamiliar, but which now returned to torment us; the sound of a MiG. We left immediately, and continued for some time, moving from village to village. I noticed that they were relatively unscathed, and asked the commander of one how frequently he was attacked.

'Once a week,' he told me.

I still needed reassurance and asked him when the last bombing had been.

'A week ago,' he said, placidly. I was sent into an immediate panic, but of course the raids were not made on a precisely regular schedule, and no attack came during the time that we were there.

We were now out on the plain to the east of Herat. Ismail Khan had decided to convene a major meeting in a village, and hundreds of men began to arrive there from all directions: from the south across the Hari Roud by horse and on foot, from the east and west by motorbike, bus and truck, and from the north by horse. They were all gathering for Friday prayers, five regional commanders each with one to two thousand men at their command, 120 commanders of towns and individual committees, and two mullahs. The stream that ran through the village was lined with them, performing ablutions; patous were draped over the squatting men so that they could lower their *toman* to wash their private parts. Once clean, they filtered into the mosque.

They took up their positions there in two long rows facing each other. Every new arrival made his way down the centre, greeting each commander in turn, who had to rise on each occasion. I was embarrassed but also honoured to find myself seated next to Ismail Khan and one of the mullahs. Hundreds of mujahedeen crowded into the mosque's forecourt, squatting on the walls and in the trees. Still others stood in groups outside the overflowing building, straining their ears to hear the service and the speeches that would go with it.

The mullah sitting next to me made the first speech. His points were succinct: 'Let us rid all Muslim countries of communists and infidels . . . destroy Israel . . . liberate Syria . . . free the Palestinians . . .' but instead of the rapturous applause and enthusiastic reactions he (and I) might have expected, all he received was a few desultory shouts of 'Allah O' Akbar!' I noticed plenty of people yawning and scratching, and some even dozed off. I knew that the mujahedeen felt little sympathy for the Palestinians, but that hardly explained their totally apathetic reaction to this admittedly predictable call to arms. Perhaps they had had enough of bloodthirsty priests.

Ismail Khan's speech, when it came, was an impassioned one, full of anguish and anger. He talked about the Russian atrocities, of their attempts to subjugate the people. He said that he would continue the fight regardless of the odds, that it was his duty, and the duty of every man there. He ended by calling for victory, and the destruction of the Russian army. The speech, which had been made in a level, considered tone, and was not at all rabble-rousing, gained the reception the mullah's failed to win.

When the meeting was over, I had the opportunity to meet one or two other commanders. There was the almost legendary commander of Karuch, Khaje Wazir, the killer of a hundred Russians – some said with his bare hands. He looked capable of it. He was a huge man, ferocious in appearance, with a thick, black beard and wild flowing hair, a wry smile, and piercing brown eyes. If I'd been the average Russian conscript I'd have dropped my rifle and run if he'd come within a hundred yards of me. But there were less threatening characters too – one old man looked exactly like some retired major from Surrey, with his perfectly groomed moustache and his immaculate Afghan army uniform. He liked to parade up and down in front of his 'komiteh' swinging his bolt-action gun at his side, for all the world as if he was on guard at Buckingham Palace. Guns and ammunition – the latter especially – are worn decoratively; not so much in bandoliers as in body-harnesses, with rows of individual bullets arranged in geometrical shapes which sometimes extend to strips strapped round the biceps.

Ismail Khan was preparing to send men to Pakistan to collect weaponry. They would therefore be travelling unarmed, and it was decided that I would accompany them, and enter Pakistan as one of their number. The exhilaration of continuing my journey was tempered by sadness at parting company with the friends I had made in the Herat region, and in particular with their commander. There were inducements for me to stay. One commander offered me a beautiful wife; another a gift of land; a third, a house; a fourth, a couple of oxen and a motorbike – though he added that the bike wasn't in great working order. I struggled not to hurt their feelings by refusing their offers, and told them that I would be of best use to them by reaching Pakistan, and in the end returning to my own country to write a book in which I would tell the outside world of their plight. This they accepted, but I was still deluged with offers of gifts from the ordinary mujahedeen, who offered me fine embroidered shirts and caps. I was tempted by these gifts too, but could not accept them. Most people here no longer had the money to buy clothes.

As the time for my departure drew closer, I learnt their greetings properly, in preparation for the time when I would be travelling through territory held by rival groups, perhaps not as friendly as the Jamiat. Up to now I had simply aped their salutations, mumbling instead of using proper words, and this had been accepted, probably because they had only half listened to me, assuming that I was saying what they expected to hear.

'But you know our greetings,' they said in astonishment when I asked to be instructed in them.

I explained what I'd been doing and they fell about laughing.

'OK,' they said. 'This is what you should be saying: *Chitouri* means "How are you?" *Monda nabashi* is "May you not be tired"; *Khair Khairyat* means "All's well?" *Jon jorast* is "You're in good health?" and lastly *Al Hamdulillah* is "Praise be to God."'

I thanked them but they asked me to continue my old routine towards those not in on the secret. I did so, and they watched as their friends were taken in by my mumblings. Shaking with laughter, they then shared the joke.

There was little I could do to show my gratitude to them all for what they had done for me, but I was asked to make a speech. As usual the room in the village where this took place was packed, the doorway jammed with people, and the window a mass of faces. I spoke as honestly as circumstances permitted and as much as my Dari would allow. My speech had actually taken me a week to prepare. The vast majority of the mujahedeen were illiterate and politically uneducated. They had no idea of what precisely they were fighting for, although many nursed a vague resentment of the West. I spoke of the solidarity of the people of Europe, the Americans and of many other nations with Afghanistan's plight, even if our governments showed little concrete interest. Since they had always been curious about why China, a communist country, was their chief supplier of arms against Russia, I tried to explain a little of the balance of power between those two giants, and the importance of Afghanistan, which shares frontiers with both, in that balance. I told them that even in communist-controlled countries there were people who believed in God, although their God might be Jewish or Christian rather than Muslim. I ended by reciting their prayers, and the sight of their faces as I did so, so trusting and so sad, made me cry. Tears breed tears, and some of my audience started to cry too. Typically, it was Ismail Khan who restored order and dignity to the proceedings by formally thanking me for my speech. In this he was seconded by several of his commanders.

We were right on the eastern frontiers of Ismail Khan's domain now and I fully expected to be leaving the morning after my speech, but it appeared that much still remained to be done. A mass of letters had to be made ready to facilitate our passage to Pakistan, and others were addressed to contacts across the frontier. These were stuffed into my travelling-companions' waistcoat pockets. Money was also being collected: 65,000 *Afghanis* (about £440) were bundled up into wads of ten and twenty denomination notes and wrapped in a patou. During all this another banquet was organised and for it Ismail Khan asked me to make another speech.

'I can't,' I said. 'I've said all I can, and I've used up all my Dari on my first speech.'

'It doesn't matter,' he said. 'They love it when you speak in our language. Just repeat the speech you made the other night. In any case,' he added, grinning, 'I won't let you go unless you promise to speak for at least two minutes.'

It was after I had delivered this final speech that I was made one final offer: that of becoming a commander of one of their mountain villages. This really tore at my heartstrings. But then I thought about it. The village concerned had only come under attack once during the whole war. If I became commander of it word would surely get around, and because my presence would be such a morale-booster for the mujahedeen, the Russians would surely make every effort to obliterate me, and my command. This consideration tempered my romantic visions with something much more down-to-earth: fear. But there was something else: my own motivation would not be right. It would be all too easy to become involved with these people for romantic or sentimental reasons, but if I had no absolute commitment, then such an undertaking would be pointless. Also, I had a deadline to meet, if I was going to get across the Karakoram before winter set in. It was already September. On the other hand, I said to myself, I could stay until the spring, and then resume my journey . . . No. No, it was an unrealistic dream. I am not a warrior, and it is in the nature of such dreams that wanting them is somehow more attractive than having them. With a full heart I told them that I was unworthy of such a position. In the end they induced me to accept a talisman; a bullet mounted in silver, on a leather thong. The bullet had lodged in a man's muscle, wounding but not killing him. Such bullets are considered very powerful charms.

The time finally came to depart. At least two hundred mujahedeen gathered to bid me farewell. For the first time in my life I felt as if I had shared contact with a lot of people, but the pleasure this gave me was touched by sadness and even guilt. The westerner's disease of visiting, doing one's bit and then leaving.

'When will you come back?' they asked me.

What could I tell them?

ENEMY
TERRITORY

Although there were supposed to be sixty of us, my much smaller group set off alone, with the intention of joining up with the others somewhere later *en route*. This kind of strategy was nearly always achieved with what appeared to be perfect precision; but I was never sure how.

After only a couple of hours on the road, our guide, a balding, jovial man called Abdul Mohmy with a tough and stubborn streak, announced in his rather unusual high-pitched voice that we were lost. I wondered what the reaction of the others would be? Maybe they would lynch him. Instead they all laughed merrily. I didn't see the funny side myself as we roamed about the hillside in the darkness, losing some of our party in the process. So dark was the night that our search for the little village of Torkaq which was our goal ended only when we suddenly saw walls loom out of the blackness, and a tiny point of light from a hurricane lamp told us that we must have arrived. A barking dog announced us, and within minutes the place was alive with villagers scrambling out of houses and over walls to come and have a look at us.

All's well that ends well, I consoled myself. But we had been lost, and Abdul Mohmy was supposed to be Ismail Khan's best guide. I was not filled with optimism for the rest of the journey, especially later when I knew that there would be days in the desert when one canteen of water, containing about a litre, would have to suffice for sixty men.

In fact very soon life became more grim. We were up and off before dawn each day, and worst of all, we didn't even get a cup of *chai* to wake up with. Never mind, I thought; at least we are making progress. Now all we have to do is join up with the others and all will be well. And at this rate I'll be in Pakistan in no time. The thought of being away from the MiGs and the helicopters was beginning to be very attractive. But just as I started to put my faith in the idea of progress, Abdul Mohmy and our leader, Abdul Rahman, disappeared on their own – conceivably to gather some more of the sixty together. I was sent to a village to await their return, which I was assured would be within 24 hours. I wondered about this, but couldn't help living in expectation – which is nearly always a mistake.

The village, Chashma Azizan, was a small place, its buildings blending into the grey-brown mountains behind it. Threshing was in progress, and I watched the yoked oxen turning round in a tight circle, their hooves trampling the wheat. It was a biblical scene, but circumstances were far from idyllic. Food was scarce, and dung was the only fuel available for cooking. The villagers' clothes were in tatters; their hands were scarred by years of toil, and their faces tanned and wrinkled like old leather. After a lifetime spent in bondage to their landlords, I should have thought these people would have welcomed communism, but they were too deeply bound by the feudal and archaic life of their forebears with its Muslim touchstone of sacrosanct honour for the men and segregated subservience for the women.

They had put me up at the mosque, a modest structure built of mud and timber. The first day passed, and then another, and then another, and there was no sign of my travelling companions. I found that I was grateful for the rest, especially as I had developed a stomach ailment which was taking a turn for the worse. They had prescribed 'Afghani novalgin' for it – a plant crushed into powder – but it had had no effect at all. Nor did the rock-hard, sour goat's cheese that I ate, and I refused the tablets that I was offered because there was no indication at all of what they were. In their solicitude for my welfare the villagers summoned a 'doctor', who gave me a rather dubious examination and then produced a small bottle of milk of magnesia for me – the very last thing I wanted.

With my rebellious stomach I felt at a low ebb as I rested and wrote up my journal. I was not personally very pleasant, either, as I was both sweaty and grimy. At the back of my mind, too, was the old fear that I was not master of my fate, and another source of irritation was the villagers themselves. Of course they meant well, but they had no conception of my need for occasional privacy. It is not unusual for a mosque to double as the village inn and community hall, and so I had visitors every hour of the day. I would fall asleep under the curious, unwavering gaze of silent villagers, and wake up to find them still there, still staring.

And then one day something happened which was so odd that at first I was convinced I was dreaming. Two strangers arrived in the village with a green rucksack and a canvas camera bag: six weeks to the day since I had last seen them, I was reunited with my luggage. That this should have happened was a miracle, for the two men hadn't come to the village because I was there – they were merely stopping there for a moment in their pursuit of me; for several weeks my bags had been travelling around the country in relays so that they might be reunited with me. Despite the fact that I had learned to do without most of the contents, I was delighted at the thought of such luxuries as clean underwear. The arrival of the bags raised my spirits.

Although everything in the bags was covered in dust, nothing was missing except for a couple of biros, a torch, a compass and some batteries. My cameras were intact, my rolls of film (I'd brought 80 with me out of England), my pocket radio, and even my loo paper. This spoke volumes for the Afghans' sense of honour, but as I sifted through my stuff I also reflected on how materialistic we are in the West. In fact before long the bags became a burden to me not only physically, but also because they were the objects of intense curiosity. The villagers were especially puzzled by the toilet roll, and, as I couldn't ignore it, and as an explanation of its real use would have been embarrassing all round, I told them that it was a kind of bandage. In fact I didn't need loo paper any more – over the past few weeks I'd got used to using sand, as the Afghans did. As for my sleeping-bag, though I longed to use it on cold nights, I didn't allow myself the luxury while my companions only had their patous to sleep in. I continued to sleep in mine, like them.

I had resigned myself to a long stay in Chashma Azizan when suddenly a message arrived informing the local commander that Abdul Rahman and most of our group of sixty had gathered at Al Paihissar. I was to join them there. We set off at once, and as soon as I arrived Rahman proceeded to introduce me to his men. Here there was no problem about their accepting me as there had been with Fraim when I first entered Afghanistan. None of these men had ever seen me before, and yet they knew all about me. They quoted parts of the speech I had made, and they even knew the names of some of the mujahedeen of whom I had made little portraits. However these men, unlike the previous mujahedeen I had met, didn't fill me with confidence. Most were peasants from the mountains who had never done battle. Few had ever travelled outside the province, and most had never left the mountains before. Now they were to cross Afghanistan on foot, in a bid to reach a foreign country and bring back weapons from it. I hoped they would be up to it; clearly Ismail Khan could not spare more experienced men for the job. But even Abdul Rahman, though he was young and sturdily built, was not a great commander. He never showed any capacity for leadership and I concluded that he must have been given the position because he was good at leading prayers.

At the end of our first day's travel from Al Paihissar, we arrived at a bazaar, where we were to meet Abdul Mohmy and the few remaining members of our group. The bazaar was really a series of tents and a large open yard around which were stores. Most sold rice, tea, sugar, salt and sweets, but there were various Chinese trinkets on offer too, and pocket torches and scissors. One store even had a bar of Imperial Leather soap for sale. Few of our mujahedeen could afford any of these items – though one or two were singularly better off than the rest. For most of them, their families had clubbed together to give them some money for their great excursion. The lucky ones had about 400 *Afghanis* each (about £3); others had as little as 200. I was grateful for my good boots, and I noticed that a couple of the mujahedeen had decided to invest in a pair of socks. The others were barefoot in their primitive shoes, though some wrapped their feet in leaves before putting on their shoes. By evening this packing would have disintegrated, and their feet would be stained an orange-iodine colour. I had noticed tyre tracks in seemingly impossible places in the desert – places where no vehicle could possibly get – and now I found out the reason for the mystery: one of the stores had sandals on sale that were made out of old tyres.

We settled down to wait for Abdul Mohmy, and Abdul Rahman bought two sheep at 1000 *Afghanis* each for our dinner. It was the last proper meal for ten days.

It was late at night when Abdul Mohmy arrived with the rest of our band. He was rather excited, explaining that the delay had been caused by a battle.

'I didn't know there were army units in this area,' I said.

'No – it wasn't a battle with the Russians,' Mohmy explained. 'It was with some Hesbi who were taking pot shots at us.'

I thought that it was ironic that the Jamiat should have been fighting the Hesbi only two days after a radio announcement that the two mujahedeen groups had decided to join forces against the common foe.

The following morning we were on our way again. For one mujahed to carry one of my bags would have slowed him – and the rest of us – down, and so my belongings were parcelled out to others and wrapped up in the versatile patous. We were meant to split up into smaller groups so as to be more difficult for the enemy to spot, but in practice we stayed together in one large knot. The pace set was that of a very fast walk – all but a run – and if you had to stop to urinate you'd have to run for five minutes to catch up again. Whatever the terrain, whether over rock and stone, sand or scree, up hill or mountain, the mujahedeen maintained a flowing, gliding, bouncing step, and rarely ran out of breath. All maintained the pace effortlessly, and many had reserves of energy that had them overtaking one another, or running off the track up a slope after birds, flinging stones at them as they flew overhead. They always accelerated down the last bit of a hill to give them added momentum for the uphill slope.

It took me some time to get into the swing of their pace. At an early stage in the journey one of the local 'komitehs' we stayed with gave me a donkey, but barely able to trot, he was more of a hindrance than a help. I called him Khomeini, to everyone's delight.

'Khomeini khosh – Gee-up, Khomeini,' I would say, amidst great hilarity, but he never would gee-up, and we finally left him with another 'komiteh', no doubt to his great relief. News of him had, however, travelled ahead of us, and for days after we'd left him behind we'd arrive at a committee and immediately be asked for news of 'Khomeini'. However weary, the mujahedeen were never too tired for an argument or a joke, and once they made a joke, they would work it to death. This particular joke fortunately succumbed long before we reached the territory of Shia mujahedeen, who would not have been amused.

The days passed and still we travelled on. I had attached myself to a tall, gangling, older man with an enchanting gap-toothed smile, whose steady lope I found easy to swing along with. But I had no sense of distance travelled or progress made.

'How far is the next village?' I would ask.

'Nazdig – close,' they would reply.

Or,

'How long will it take to reach the mountain?'

'Three hours.'

Three hours later, the mountain would look just as far away, and I'd repeat my question.

'Three hours,' they would answer, smiling.

Although I gradually learnt to cope with the crippling pace – and it really was a case of march or die – I never could get used to the achingly steep gradients that frequently confronted us. These nearly always stretched ahead for miles in a depressing series of ridges: no sooner had you topped one than another rose ahead. However, near the top of these gradients there was usually a natural spring, and it provided a strong incentive to try to keep up with the leaders of the group. The mere scent of water was enough to send my companions sprinting forward, and when they arrived at the source they would throw themselves to the ground and hurl water into their mouths with cupped hands. Those not able to find room in the first assault would have to wait patiently, so as not to waste valuable energy, but those last to arrive would often find nothing but wet mud with which to quench their thirst – the pool having been all but drunk dry. Real thirst is an indescribable thing.

All this time my stomach was still giving me trouble, and I frequently had to resist the temptation to rest, especially on the bigger climbs. At first I had relished the thought of reaching the top and the subsequent 'reward' of the downhill slope, but I soon learnt that going down could be just as hard – harder – than climbing up. Some of the mujahedeen didn't bother to negotiate the down-hill paths. They just aimed themselves straight down the mountain-side, their descent gaining in momentum like a snowball in an avalanche bounding down and all the while screaming like reckless maniacs. Why no necks, let alone legs and ankles, were broken, is beyond me.

The only respite from the pace was provided by prayer-time, but even in their praying this group seemed to expend more energy than I had seen others do. At rest, they would groom their beards and moustaches, or cut their hair as short as they could with scissors. Possession of a pair of scissors was considered a great luxury. Most mujahedeen's sole property was a comb, and although many took *nazwar*, few owned the shiny tin snuffboxes it came in, and which doubled as mirrors. None of my group was without a beard or a moustache, and it was rare to meet a cleanshaven Afghan anywhere. Facial hair is a great source of male pride, to judge from the hours of attention spent on it.

Our direction – south-east – wavered only when we had to skirt a main road or a large town. The scenery we passed through was unrelievedly bleak and open – a greyish beige wasteland of serried ranks of mountains stretching to more distant, barren mountains. The pale blue sky was unremittingly cloudless, the sand seeping into every cavity of our bodies, and the dust covering every surface and every inch of exposed skin. If there was a wind, it was invariably suffocating and hot.

Whenever we paused at a village, babies were brought out for me to examine and cure. Most of these poor little creatures were not taking fluid; their tiny bodies were caked with dry excreta, and there was nothing I could do. They would die of dehydration. Seeing them, I thought without surprise of the passage in a book I'd read which had informed me that Afghanistan has one of the highest infant mortality rates in the world. I had few medicines, fewer that would be of any real help, and I knew that my little lectures on basic hygiene weren't being taken in, just as my attempts to teach one or two simple herbal remedies, using what few plants they could grow, were greeted with scepticism. I did manage to impress upon them the importance of making sure water was boiled properly, but fuel was in such short supply that I doubted if they would 'waste' it on what might seem a senseless exercise.

Even my more sophisticated travelling companions looked on with astonishment as I burnt my bread to make charcoal to eat in an attempt to cure my stomach. I was getting increasingly desperate, as every day my stomach was more and more bloated with wind, and our staple diet of bread and tea did not help. I'd long since exhausted my supply of dried apricots, having shared them with my companions as hunger had overcome their bashfulness and they had responded to my offers. Now, I wasn't the only one to be ill. Abdul Mohmy had become very seriously unwell and there were doubts about our being able to continue. Luckily we had recently been joined by a stray mujahed who had brought his horse with him, so we were able to put Mohmy on it. For a time he was able to guide us, but late one day he lapsed into semi-consciousness and we were forced to stop. We could do nothing but wait and pray that he would recover. Without our guide we would have to return – a prospect which I dreaded.

We made camp close to an enormous ruined fort called Taiwara, apparently little known outside Afghanistan, but which is of some historical interest, having been sacked both by Genghis Khan and the British. It now houses a 'komiteh' of mujahedeen, who at first made extravagant claims to us about the number of aeroplanes they had shot down. There was, indeed, plenty of wreckage strewn about, but when I pressed them with questions, they admitted that the pilots of the planes had brought about their own destruction, by flying into the mighty cliff-walls of the nearby mountains. From a distance these same mountains seemed to form an impenetrable, unbroken chain, but now we were close we could see that there was a gap between two chains. I wanted to explore alone, but of course it was a hopeless ambition. I had a minder, and he escorted me everywhere – even to the loo; even if he hadn't been around I would have had no solitude, for the mujahedeen are preternaturally curious and would certainly have followed me wherever I went for no other reason than to see where I was going.

Abdul Mohmy only made a partial recovery, but as soon as he was fit enough to travel, we headed off again. The further we strayed from Herat, the more tense everyone became. Our reception at villages became less predictable: in some, they refused to give us bread. We had the same experience when we encountered communities of nomads. Those who would not help us had insults hurled at them by my companions:

'Call yourselves Muslims?' they'd say with heavy sarcasm; or they would just say the word, 'Muslim', with a lip-curling sneer.

The nature of the bread (when we were given it) had changed too. It resembled and tasted like *crêpes*. It was delicious, and above all it was different. I would never have imagined that so small a thing as a change in the type of bread could have such a morale-boosting effect.

We needed all the morale we could get, too, for we were now moving into enemy territory. Jamiat control was giving way to that of the Harakat-I-Engelab-I-Islami – a moderate, traditionalist (as opposed to fundamentalist) Sunni faction holding sway adjacent to an area known as the Hazarajat. As we were unarmed, we would require their protection in their province, so we left our route to reach one of their strongholds. I decided to keep a low profile, unsure about how they would respond to me, and indeed Abdul Rahman, our leader, told me to do so.

It was therefore with some trepidation that I entered the Harakat camp. In appearance, the men were Mongolian-looking – only the posters on the walls describing different political goals indicated that we were no longer in Jamiat company.

At first conversation seemed tentative, but pretty soon an agreement must have been reached for there were smiles all round and I was proudly brought forward into the limelight and introduced to our hosts.

'These Harakat are great mujahedeen,' Abdul Rahman told me flatteringly. 'They have fought many battles with the Russians, and like us they are at war with the Hesbi.'

'You are welcome here,' their commander said. 'You are all welcome. There is plenty of food.' That was good news indeed, and could only mean one of two things: no aerial bombardment, or a military stand-off. 'This is a free area,' continued the commander, proudly. I received this news with only partial enthusiasm, because 'free' is a very relative term in Afghanistan. My travelling companions were always keen to point out 'free' areas, and the guerrillas are always pushing the claim that they control 90 per cent of the country; the sad thing was that the 90 per cent they spoke of was all desert and barren land: areas which the Russians and the loyalists probably wouldn't even want – unless it was to extirpate the mujahedeen.

Food and rest we had, and my stomach let up a little, but there were new stresses. Because we were out of our own territory, I had to become one of the crowd – it might have been very dangerous if my true identity was found out. I looked every inch an Afghan, but my cameras were taken away and hidden, my good boots and socks were replaced by local sandals, and I was forbidden to write – an activity that would have aroused immediate suspicion. Most worrying of all to my companions was how I would behave during prayers – though I knew the words and actions perfectly well – and it was decided that I should have to pretend to be too ill to participate.

This subterfuge became increasingly important as we left the friendly Harakat and moved into more dubious Hesbi territory. Although there was not a permanent state of war between Jamiat and Hesbi, relations were strained, and Hesbi had been known on several occasions to have joined forces with the Russians.

Not unexpectedly, the first Hesbi village we came to refused us food, but we found shelter with a group of nomads who provided us with bread (the delicious pancake variety) and tea. It was a cold and uncomfortable night, for we were camping on the steep slope of a hill, huddled together under our patous for warmth. Every muscle in my body ached, I remember, but I was too tired to care and gave myself up to welcoming oblivion.

The night was all too short. We set off again at four in the morning, in a cold so intense that it took your breath away. Through the darkness we stumbled, occasionally jumping back at the ferocious barking of one of the nomads' dogs as we made our way past their encampment. At first light we halted for prayers, and gathered brushwood for a fire. Movement had warmed us too, to some extent, but within two hours the cold had given way to the usual baking heat of full day. Up and down hills we raced, on one occasion scaling a mountain which I cursed and cursed as the rocks cut my hands and the sweat ran into my eyes and stung them, but which rewarded me when I reached the top with one of the most stupendous views I have ever seen.

Descending the other side, we were met by nomads who mistook us for Hesbis. We had crossed a language frontier on our journey, and were now in Pashtu-speaking territory. Thus it was that communication was difficult. I think the nomads realised that we weren't Hesbi, but I don't think they ever found out who we were exactly.

For the first time that night, we split up into two groups, and sought shelter in two different villages. My group received a very unfriendly reception, but eventually the villagers agreed to put us up in their small, but beautifully decorated mosque. These Hesbi were Shia Muslims, so there was quite a bit of tension at prayer-time, when the two different sects took it in turn to pray; but the tension didn't express itself in violence, as I feared it might.

Although it was still only early September, the cold at night was cruel, and that night seemed especially bad. I tried every position in a bid to keep warm. I huddled myself up like an embryo, arms wrapped round myself, fists clenched, and lying on my arms, using them like skater's irons, to achieve minimum contact with the ground. I was sorely tempted to use my sleeping bag, but it would have been so unfair that I simply couldn't do so.

Somehow we got through that night, and another, and then, just after sunrise on 7 September 1984, we reached the market town of Nouzad. It was in the full flood of harvest time when we arrived. The flour mill spluttered and roared with its primitive machinery; tractors loaded with wheat trundled by. In the central square men were winnowing, tossing the grain high into the air with shovels. Also in the square were three jeeps, one with an AA machine-gun mounted on it – these belonged to the Hesbi. Abdul Rahman and Abdul Mohmy (now happily better) went in search of the Jamiat committee (being a town of some importance, Nouzad is host to all factions of the mujahedeen), while the rest of us waited patiently, squatting in a line along a wall. Everyone was visibly relieved to be among real friends again, though there were communication problems as all but a few commanders could only speak Pashtu or Dari. I finally had my stomach seen to by a mujahedeen doctor, who gave me Vitamin B12 and charcoal tablets.

The language and attire were different, but I was sorry to see that the Dari-speakers' habit of spitting under carpets or against walls during the taking of *nazwar* was just as prevalent among the Pashtu-speaking locals.

But at last we had arrived somewhere. At last our journey was marked by a milepost of a kind. And Pakistan seemed suddenly a good deal nearer.

AN UNSEEN GUIDE

We weren't in Nouzad long, and left it in the middle of one afternoon by truck – it was bliss not to have to walk any more. Half of us sat on the floor and the other half sat on the wooden slats fitted between the iron framework of the truck's 'hold'. From this raised position we were able to pluck pomegranates from trees overhanging the road that wound out of the town and into the desert. The truck soon began to reel under the weight of its load. It strained at every incline, and often needed to make several attempts, its tired iron and wood frame creaking, its radiator leaking and its engine wheezing. Every time we stopped, or slid backwards down a hill, we disappeared in a cloud of dust. What with the sticky effects of steam and sweat, within three hours the truck, our clothes, our skins were all the same desert colour.

The truck took us to the Helmand river, which flowed in several beds although only the central one ran deep. Here, it was spanned by a rickety bridge, made of log pylons and hole-worn woven matting. This we negotiated one at a time, and the only way not to lose balance as it flapped and sawed in the flurries and gusts of wind was to dash across at great speed. Cheers went up as each of us cleared this hazard.

Darkness had descended by the time we had all reached the far side. We were soaked from the crossing, and pretty soon we were lost, too. The cold came creeping up with the darkness, and I wondered how much more of this I could bear. However, when all seemed lost, we chanced upon a man and a woman eating supper on a carpet outside their house. The woman immediately fled. The man gave us directions to Sangin – our next port of call. Mercifully not far.

But the walk into Sangin was sinister. Unlike Nouzad, it had been badly hit by the enemy, and recently, too. What met my eyes was the aftermath of an orgy of destruction – wrecked buildings, doors hanging crazily, the charred remains of burnt-out lorries, metal twisted into abstract shapes. Life had reestablished itself despite the punishment the town had taken, but we were to learn that the already overflowing cemetery now had fifty new tombs.

It was a while before we were challenged. A mujahed flashed a torch into our faces and ordered us to stop. This was at a road junction and, just as in the movies, several more mujahedeen suddenly materialised to surround us. Abdul Rhaman presented our papers, and after a quick inspection of them the mood relaxed, and we were escorted to the mosque to be fed sour milk and bread.

'In two nights, Pakistan,' Abdul Mohmy told me with a triumphant smile. I knew enough by now not to take this optimistic assessment at its face value, but perhaps the worst was behind us. And here at least I could use my cameras to record the destruction.

But as the following day wore on the situation became progressively worse. First of all, though, I was told that I wouldn't be allowed to take photos.

'Why not?' I protested. 'The Harakat are our friends.'

'It is different here. These Harakat are only Pashtu-speakers.'

'Should that make a difference?'

'There are also political differences,' Abdul Rahman said, and went on to explain them. It turned out that these Harakat in Sangin, and the ones we had encountered earlier, were as distinct from each other as either would be from Jamiat. I let myself be convinced, and concealed my disappointment.

'OK,' I said. 'I'll take a stroll round the bazaar.'

'The bazaar is closed,' I was told firmly.

'What?' I said, with rising scepticism.

'It is *Id-e-Qorban* – the feast of the servant of God,' they replied. This popular feast celebrates Abraham's willingness to sacrifice Isaac, but instinct told me that that couldn't be the only reason for the bazaar's closure. Probing some more I found that there was a much more serious reason: the road from Sangin to Pakistan had been sealed by government troops. I listened to the rumours with a sinking heart: it had been 15 days since a vehicle had reached Sangin from Pakistan; and various other vehicles which had tried had been blown to bits. I watched my dreams of a shower and a cocktail in a plush Pakistani hotel fade.

How to reach Pakistan? To go south-west across the desert wastes of Registan would take six nights by truck. Even the most optimistic of our party viewed the idea with gloom. Relations with the local Harakat were strained, which did nothing for our sense of security, and an enforced stay whittled away our funds needlessly. Surely something would happen? We couldn't stay in this limbo forever. At times it was a difficult thing to believe.

But redemption was near at hand. Somehow the road passed into mujahedeen control. Suddenly one morning vehicles started to flow into Sangin again, and the town awoke from its torpor. Three large, Iranian-assembled Cherokee pickup jeeps were found – two belonging to Harakat, and one to Jamiat – to provide us with transport down the road. The jeeps, which are called Symorghs, do not 'belong' in a formal sense to any one mujahedeen group, but are owned by their drivers, who alone determine who they work for. The group selected by the driver then provides him with an armed mujahed or two to ride shotgun, and then the driver and his jeep will perform the risky ferry trip in and out of Pakistan. For this they charge 60,000 *Afghanis* (£420) a trip – which I thought outrageous. That was before I knew the risks involved.

Each Symorgh carried 20 of us, plus the driver, an armed mujahed and an armed mechanic. There were also two little boys, sons of a couple of the drivers, and three locals who were hitching a lift part of the way. The driver, mechanic and 'shotgun' rode in the front. The rest of us fought for what little space remained in the back, sharing it with a mighty oildrum, since petrol for the return journey had to be bought in from Pakistan. There was also an RPG launcher, and several grenades. We were squashed in far worse than sardines, which at least don't get crushed in their tin, and cries and screams went up in profusion as hands were trodden on, backs kicked or legs squashed. Outside the jeep, the bystanders who were seeing us off gaily squeezed and pushed more and more of us in. Two sat on top of the oildrum. It was like squeezing too many clothes into an already over-full suitcase. Straining for a view over my companions, I noticed with envy that one of the other jeeps had had the novel idea of having the passengers sitting around the side of the vehicle with their legs dangling out, the people on the inside sitting with them back-to-back to keep them sufficiently propped up.

We set off. It was unnerving to travel in broad daylight across wide open spaces. I comforted myself with the thought that the drivers wouldn't take unnecessary risks as they had their little sons aboard. We encountered other vehicles on the road, and one Symorgh loaded with ammunition, and with a couple of mujahedeen sitting on top, stopped to talk to us. Their faces were grim with terror: theirs was the only jeep left out of a convoy of three. The first one had been destroyed by a land-mine on the asphalt road that runs between Kabul and Kandahar; the second, in a rocket attack the previous night. Somehow in this open wasteland – we were heading due east on a dirt track in the desert to the north of Kandahar – the other Symorgh managed to scrape ours, carrying away our rear bumper. This didn't please our driver, though the mechanic told him that he'd be able to patch it up. I suspect that he was a good mechanic. He certainly needed to be, to judge by the number of running repairs he had to make on the jeep. These repairs were never done with any sense of urgency, and were punctuated with frequent tea-breaks, taken lying in the shade of a tree.

We appeared to have lost the other two jeeps in our convoy, but I discovered that this was not the case. Each driver seemed to know exactly where the other two were at any time, and whether they had stopped, and we always kept a strict line order as we drove along – probably to ensure regular turns to be line-leader, to share the risk of being first to hit a mine equally. I ceased to be surprised that every time our jeep started up, my companions automatically invoked Allah and ritually wiped their beards.

I was under instructions to avoid prayer-time in case I gave myself away, and my excuse was illness. Only it wasn't an excuse any more, for my stomach pains had returned with a vengeance. On the second evening one of the drivers noticed my absence. All three drivers were particularly devout, but this man was a positive Calvin. He came to rouse me from where I lay doubled up in the back of my jeep.

'*Namaz! Namaz!*' he shouted, calling me to prayer. When I didn't answer, he leant over and shook me violently. I began to think that he would hit me. Indeed he may have done so; the pain in my stomach blacked out all other sensations.

'*Meriz*,' I groaned, thinking that if I looked as ill as I sounded he must surely have mercy on me.

Not a bit of it. *'Namaz!'* he bellowed again.

Luckily at that moment some of my own group came up and restrained him, explaining that I was, indeed, very ill. They led him away grumbling, and in future I tended to avoid him whenever I could.

Prayers over, we set off again. The journey, as we bucked and bumped our way across the desert, was quite backbreaking, but I felt that I could take it pretty uncomplainingly, for after all it would only be another couple of nights, and then . . . Then, goodbye helicopters, MiGs, RPGs and barren desert. Why, in 72 hours' time I would be relaxing in the swimming pool of a sumptuous hotel.

My daydreams were abruptly overwhelmed by the sight of another burnt-out Symorgh. It was the fifth wreck we had passed. How many dead, I wondered, just in this little struggle for control of the road. Clearly it was not firmly back in mujahedeen hands.

We were going to have to travel for a short stretch along the main road that links Kabul and Kandahar, and we had sent scouts ahead to check if it was clear. Now, we pulled over to await their return. It was a tense time, and I found myself having to breathe deeply and regularly to contain my excitement. I did not think I could bear it if they were to return and say *'Ra band'* – the way is closed.

'When can we expect them?' I asked one of my companions – a rather better-off young man, who had feigned sickness off and on in the hope of getting me to give him some pills, which I think he took to be like sweets.

'Two hours,' he said promptly. I decided to expect them in four. In fact, they returned in precisely two hours, and you could tell by their faces what they were going to say.

'Ra band.'

We spent the rest of that night and the whole of the next day holed up tensely at an oasis, marking time under the shadow of the trees, while the scouts were dispatched yet again to keep an eye on the situation. Restlessly, we once again discussed alternative possibilities. As we did so, Abdul Mohmy, his usual tireless self, went to bake bread for us at a nearby hamlet.

'Could we walk?' I asked.

'It would take five days – if we could get through.'

'No water,' said Abdul Rahman. He was more restless than anyone else, and clearly couldn't relax.

'What's the matter with him? Is he ill?' I asked Zahir, my minder.

'I think he must be afraid,' replied Zahir.

With two hours of daylight left the scouts returned, this time with the heartening but almost unbelievable news that the road was once again '*ra azad*'. I hoped it would still be so by the time we reached it. We headed off at once.

We had only just cleared the first hill and begun to travel along a dry river bed when someone near me began to scream,

'*Tiare!*'

The panicky word caught on, and soon they were all yelling it, craning for a sight of the sky from the packed jeep. They had spotted a plane.

The jeep slowed violently, and we struggled to bail out, but there were many unable to jump when the jeep decided to take off at full speed. We were the middle jeep. The leader had carried on apparently unaware; the last one had seen the panic ahead and reversed up a hill. Ours had come to a halt some way off and the driver and the mechanic were throwing a tarpaulin over it. We had all rushed up a steep incline and now crouched huddled together, taking refuge in whatever crevice we could find – all, that is, except for one man who had taken off in the other direction – into the open – where, to my total disbelief, he now knelt and proceeded to pray. We strained our ears for the noise of the returning jet, but we must have been just in time to get out of its way, for the sound of its engine faded and finally died.

Once the danger was over, the whole group settled down to pray – I have to say that I found this vexing, given how urgent our situation was. Our driver seemed to pray for an inordinately long time.

We caught up with the first jeep. They, too, had heard the plane, and had rounded a bend and pulled up close to the cliff-wall of the valley we had been passing through.

'Thank God for that valley,' the mechanic said.

'Thank God we weren't five minutes further along the track,' said the driver. 'Then we would have been in open desert.'

During the long days of marching before Nouzad, I had learned to tell the time by measuring the length of my shadow cast by the sun. Now I tried to teach myself how to get my bearings by the stars. I always kept an eye on where the nearest mountains were, and remembered the location of the last oasis we had visited. This wasn't easy. We never took a direct route, but were forever weaving around the desert. I was most impressed by our drivers' uncanny sense of direction, but perhaps the close brush with the aeroplane had disconcerted them more than somewhat, for all at once the three jeeps pulled up together and the drivers announced that they were lost. It was by now dark, and to go on without a guide would have been foolhardy. Luckily, and as always happens in the Afghan desert, other life appeared within a matter of moments, in the form of a tractor and its driver.

Immediately our drivers started to argue with our commanders about who was going to pay this guide for his services. Each side was trying to outdo the other, of course, and there was lot of lip-curling and 'Call yourselves Muslims?' going on. Meantime valuable minutes ticked by, and my nerves were becoming frayed.

'How much are you arguing about?' I asked.

'He wants 1000 *Afghanis*.'

About £7! I was about to pull out the money in *Afghanis*, thinking, to hell with this, I'll pay, but then I stopped. I knew that such a gesture would be hopeless. It would also betray me and endanger my companions. So I sat and seethed until the argument was resolved, trying to calm myself with the thought that for an Afghan, £7 is a considerable sum.

The tractor-driver guided us down a dirt track to a village where dozens and dozens of children milled about, despite the fact that by now it was the middle of the night. We stopped for the mechanics to overhaul the jeeps as far as they could, and for our drivers to find out how far we were still from the Kabul–Kandahar road.

'Three hours,' came the inevitable reply. Gloomily, we refuelled the jeeps from the oildrums they carried and set off again – but at snail's pace, for the track ahead was full of pitfalls, and we had to send two mujahedeen ahead of each vehicle to guide us. However, at length we reached the road. Our tractor-driving guide left us, and I was about to breathe a sigh of relief. Then one of the jeeps broke down. It took half an hour to repair it, by which time I estimated that we had a bare hour of darkness left to travel in. But now, instead of taking to the road, our drivers took off along a track to the left of it.

The track led us to a bowl-shaped area surrounded on three sides by precipitous mountains.

'What are we doing here?' I asked Abdul Rahman as calmly as I could.

Abdul Rahman had recovered quite a lot of his composure. 'We will camp here tonight, and then in the morning we will climb to the guerrilla stronghold at the top of that hill,' he said.

During all my time in Afghanistan, I tried to place my faith in the people in whose hands my safety lay. I had had no difficulty in doing this with Ismail Khan, but I felt doubtful about Abdul Rahman. I decided that I would try to panic him. Fortuitously, high overhead, a large plane flew by. It was still dark enough to see its red landing light flashing clearly.

'Do you see that?' I asked him.

'Yes.'

'That light is a camera. The Russians are taking photographs of us every time it flashes.'

I had hoped that he would order an immediate evacuation. Instead he looked rather pleased and wandered off. I was nonplussed but a few minutes later I was surrounded by delighted mujahedeen.

'Did you see that plane?' they chorused.

'Yes.'

'It was taking pictures of us. Isn't that something?' they announced proudly. 'Abdul Rahman told us. Truly, he is a great commander, to know such things.'

I did discover that the mujahedeen stronghold we had invited ourselves to belonged to a group called Jabhe. In the freezing dawn of 13 September we threw tarpaulins over the jeeps, parked, as I now saw, among several other similarly shrouded vehicles. Then, wrapped in our patous, we climbed the path uphill. We hadn't gone far when,

'Halt! Who goes there?' demanded a young mujahed, popping up from behind a rock, complete with Kalashnikov, which he proceeded to fire, once, into the air. We were frisked and disarmed, and only then allowed to proceed. We were told not to stray from the path, which was clearly marked with black flags, and on either side of which drivers and passengers lay sleeping in niches and crevices in the rocks. We came to a halt at the top of an improvised waiting area-cum-mosque. The holy *mirhab* of the mosque was simply marked out in a semi-circle of stones. Here, Abdul Mohmy spent several hours in prayer – an action which gave me serious and grave concern. Mohmy was highly intelligent and genuinely tough. He would not pray so long and so earnestly without good reason. I noticed too that high morale and good humour had somehow evaporated overnight. To my horror, it looked as though the trip to Pakistan had finally been abandoned, though I could not fathom why.

Later the reason became clear. There had been a report on the BBC the night before that the Russians intended to seal the border once and for all. Most of the day was spent brooding, or in *sotto voce* discussion, but by late afternoon a decision appeared to have been reached, and we all trooped down to the jeeps. Hope rose in me before I could suppress it.

'What's happening?' I asked Aminullah, a brazen commander who had joined us on the road.

'Tonight we will try for the border,' he said. 'Tonight it will be make or break.'

Our party was joined by eight heavily armed Jabhe mujahedeen in their own Symorgh. They were mean-looking characters, and one of them still sported his sunglasses, though the light had long since faded; but any demonstration of extra support was reassuring, as we would have to join the main road at a junction by a village where a Russian garrison was situated. We left after a lengthy prayer meeting, but finally the engines roared, beards were wiped, Allah was invoked, and off we went.

The extra Symorgh carrying the eight guerrillas took up the rear. We never saw them again.

On reaching the Kabul–Kandahar road we were confronted by a tumult. Our headlights caught a crowd of mujahedeen running hither and thither, brandishing their guns and shouting frantically. Not far beyond them loomed the sinister shapes of buildings. The first jeep roared off down the road, and the second jeep and ours followed closely, while we passengers either kept a look-out for mines or bent our heads in prayer. We could in fact have been travelling faster, but we dared not, for fear of not being able to brake in time to avoid a pothole or a mine. I wondered if we could have avoided a mine anyway, but then I realised that the local mujahedeen had sent scouts up ahead and these had lit signal flares to tell us that a particular stretch of road was clear. Proceeding like this, from signal to signal, we travelled some way. After a time, we braked hard and swerved off the road down a steep bank to the right. Lights ablaze, we headed for the foothills, but we paused briefly with a group of mujahedeen who proudly showed us the mines they had collected. Mines are simply placed on the tarmac by the army, and the same technique is employed by the mujahedeen when they manage to collect them, rather than being blown up by them. But I hadn't got time to try to make sense out of this, for I was worrying now about why we still had our lights on as we headed across country. What if the Russians had landed heli-borne troops ahead to ambush us? Sometimes I wished I hadn't such a vivid imagination.

Soon the track we were following petered out, and several mujahedeen with torches were dispatched to find it again in the darkness ahead. This was done amid several arguments about the relative correctness of the route we'd chosen. We made slow progress, but soon it became evident that the route was impassable.

But impassable or not, there was no turning back now. We all left the vehicles to walk. Maybe with no load, the drivers could coax the jeeps through the slippery uphill scree. This they did, but we had to gather rocks to build some kind of grippable surface for the tyres ahead, and progress became agonisingly slow. Sometimes a jeep would get stuck and we would have to construct a winch to haul it forwards – a process that took several hours. Our hands and feet were bleeding from the rocks, and we were covered with dust.

This went on for two despairing days, but just as our water was running out, the terrain eased. We made a relatively trouble-free descent to a dry river bed, gratefully climbed into the jeeps again and roared off. The river bed was as good as a motorway after what we'd been through, but still better was to come: a village had been sighted ahead.

'Afghanistan! Afghanistan!' my companions all shouted in relieved triumph.

The only obligatory halts were those made for prayers, though even then only a few people descended – most of us were too impatient. Our driver took ages, and grated on everyone's nerves.

'Do it later,' people shouted at him. 'We're nearly there!'

Placidly, he completed his prayers. Then and not before did we head off again. We were the last jeep. The others had already disappeared from view and we were on our way at speed to catch up. It was dawn, and soon we could be easily spotted by enemy aircraft.

'Never mind – we'll be in Pakistan in an hour,' someone said confidently.

I was still doubtful, but the mujahedeen could hardly contain their jubilation. Another village had appeared on the horizon. Could it be that that village was in Pakistan? It seemed likely, people thought. Closer and closer we came to it. Then our engine seized.

The order was quickly given to make a run for the village, while the driver and mechanic stayed with the vehicle to see what was wrong. The village was soon reached. No, this wasn't Pakistan, they told us. Pakistan was an hour away.

At least we were sheltered and reunited with the other two vehicles. Ours limped into the village soon after, and all three were covered to prevent them from being spotted from the air. There was nothing to do now but kill time until nightfall, so we spent the day either in prayer or eating pomegranates. I'd never eaten one in my life before I travelled to Afghanistan. Now I was developing quite a taste for them. Kandahar airport was to our west, and we could see in the distance the ominous roving of helicopters and MiGs. The area we were in, however, seemed to have been untouched by the violence of the war. This may have been due to the policies of the local Russian commander.

As usual, estimates varied about how long it would actually take us to reach the border. One hour was the most optimistic, six hours the most pessimistic, but the general consensus was that we would have to spend an hour and a half driving through a narrow gorge, mined by the Russians, and here an additional danger existed. Here indeed the Russians sometimes landed heli-borne troops to ambush those entering or leaving the country by the strip of road that threaded it.

A village scout had been sent ahead to spy out the land but by late afternoon he still hadn't returned.

'He'll be back,' Abdul Rahman said.

'I hope so. If he doesn't return, it'll mean he's been either killed or captured – and both those things mean the enemy is around,' I said. I thought about what Rahman had said to me when I'd broached the possibility of walking across – 'They'll either catch you in the open or you'll die of thirst' – he was probably right. I had better stick with the jeep, come what may, I thought.

We were all exhausted by now, after all the struggles and dashed hopes, but we still felt anxious and everyone prayed vigorously. Dusk fell, and there was still no sign of the scout. They decided to leave it in God's hands – 'Insha' Allah' – and piled into the jeeps.

Our jeep hadn't gone a hundred yards before the engine stalled again. They'd obviously made a botched job of the repair – what was needed was a new starter motor, of which we carried a spare – and now – when we had least time – they would have to do the job properly.

As they worked I watched them in exasperation. Then an old man appeared wraith-like out of the darkness.

'The tanks are coming,' he announced.

My heart stopped. But he had spoken Pashtu, of which I only understood a little, and perhaps I had misheard him.

'Did he say the tanks are coming?' I asked Abdul Rahman.

'No,' replied Rahman. 'He said the tanks *aren't* coming.' But it seemed to me unlikely that the old man would have gone to the effort of following us out into the darkness to impart such non-news. Besides, one of the drivers' little boys had started to wail bitterly.

'How's the starter-motor going?'

'Nearly there,' came a muffled and frantic reply, which might have meant anything.

I looked around desperately. I couldn't believe our bad luck. Everyone was crowding round the open bonnet to conceal as far as possible the torchlight which was illuminating the mechanic's work. Our armed escort, bringing his rifle to the ready, ordered some of our men to prime the grenades for the RPG, but then it transpired that no one knew how to. What a way to perish, I thought bitterly. By now we could hear the ominous rumble of tanks quite clearly. The little boy whimpered. The rest of us were silent, gazing fearfully into the night behind us.

And then the engine fired. I think that the noise of that engine will remain the sweetest sound I shall ever hear. We piled in before you could say 'Allah' and, praying that nothing else would go wrong, bolted down the road after our companion jeeps.

Incredibly, the other jeeps had waited for us. Irrespective of danger and the possibility of escaping, I noticed that no one was ever abandoned. A frenzied search now began among the other mechanics to find the requisite nuts and bolts from their own toolkits to bolt our new starter motor securely into place. We were in open desert, and a kilometre away we could see the faint glimmer of the lights of the tanks. Oh, God, I thought . . . so near and yet so far . . . please don't let them get us now . . . All at once I found myself repeating the *kalimeh*, and it comforted me.

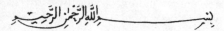

The two little boys clung to each other and wept, while the mujahedeen awkwardly tried to comfort them. I watched the tanks. Surely they could see us with their nightsights?

And then I realised that they were not heading towards us, but away from us. The patrol hadn't seen us. All of a sudden a red tracer bullet soared high into the air to the south. We couldn't make out what was going on, but one thing was certain: the Russians' attention was focused elsewhere.

An hour later we reached the mouth of the gorge. We switched our headlights off, and the jeeps filled with the murmur of prayers. I, too, cupped my hands and repeated *'Bismillah Rahman-i-Rahim . . .'* once again. The tension was overpowering as we gazed up at the looming sides of the gorge, soon lost in the thick darkness.

Allah must have been with us. This last part of the journey was a kind of summation of all that was Afghanistan for me: whether the scout had actually come this far, whether he had returned or gone off somewhere else, I would never know. We had allies though: the goats and sheep gently foraging for food, and with them – a shepherd. Where the terrain was so rough that apart from this strip of road the only access troops could find to it was by helicopter, a shepherd stood alone somewhere above us on the walls of the gorge. We could not see him – indeed, we never saw him – but his voice drifted down to us like a god's – and it provided, as all Afghans do, information. After the usual formal exchange of greetings, he told us that another vehicle had passed safely through not two hours earlier. There had been no activity since. Therefore there were probably no mines, and there could be no ambush. Our hearts leapt.

Further on there was a grim reminder that others had not been so lucky. The wreck of a burnt-out jeep lay by the side of the road.

We emerged from the gorge feeling that truly nothing could stop us now. And as if to confirm our confidence, there on the horizon we could see the twinkling electric lights of Chaman, just inside the Pakistan border. It had been two months since I had seen electric light, and even at this distance it seemed strangely miraculous, and bright.

'Only an hour to go,' someone said in the dim hold of the jeep, and I found myself grinning broadly. This time the estimate was surely about right. However, infuriatingly we stopped at a lonely house, and the mechanic and driver got out to have a leisurely chat with its occupants. I calmed down again as soon as the jeep was once more in motion, but then we arrived at another house . . .

This continued for some time.

After about the fifth social call, we still didn't seem to be any closer to Chaman. Meanwhile the dirt track was getting worse and the progress was ever slower. For some reason we now turned east, away from the lights. I became despondent. I knew, I told myself, that I shouldn't have raised my hopes, shouldn't have become confident about reaching Pakistan. We were now heading for the mountains. Chaman, I thought gloomily, must now be two hours away.

We headed east for an hour, leaving Chaman to the south. Its lights had disappeared.

'Where are we going?' I finally asked Abdul Rahman, unable to bear it any longer.

'To Pakistan,' he replied, surprised. 'The road to the south was bad, so we took a detour east. But as soon as we cross the next dry river bed we'll be there.'

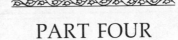

PART FOUR

Pakistan

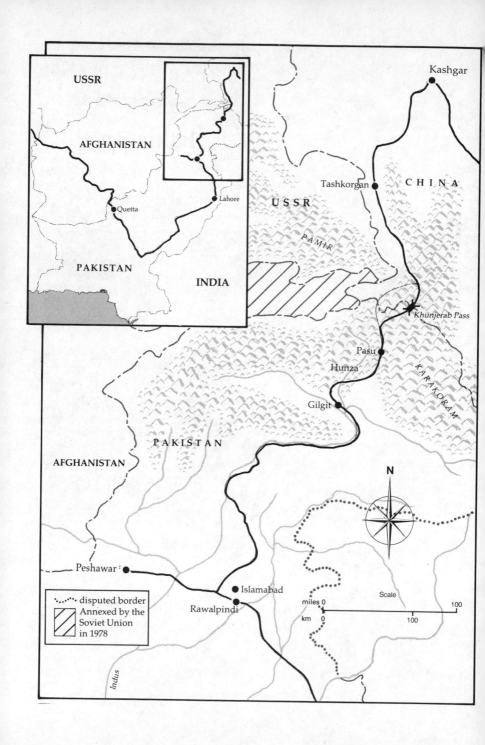

DOUBLE
DEALINGS

We were taken to the dismal town of Chaman on a lorry. Once there, Abdul Rahman contacted the local Jamiat office and they managed to hire a bus to take all sixty of us to Quetta. I felt a vague sense of anticlimax. Now that the danger was over, the mind and the body were – against all reason – disappointed. But despite this I still felt keyed up.

The bus was the most ornately decorated I had come across. Every square inch of wall panelling, including the floor, was covered in bright, luminous designs – arabesques and floral patterns. Mauve, pink and yellow felt flowers adorned the dashboard, and there were pictures of mosques, landscapes, and a portrait of the driver. The original sat in state on a bench, rather than a mere driver's seat. The fact that the bus was a Bedford made the vehicle even more incongruous. It was hot and most of my companions elected to ride on the roof. This suited the driver fine, because although the bus was rented by us exclusively, he was not about to refuse other paying passengers who wanted to make the same journey. Indeed, he stopped at every village and blew his horn in the hope of drumming up further custom.

The landscape we passed through could have been an Afghan one: the barren hills, the parched and dusty land, and the dry river beds were the same. Only, here, the roadsides were littered not with war debris or the black tents of the Afghan nomads, but with the white tents of relief agencies, and those donated by 'The Government of Saudi Arabia' – as they proclaimed in bold, stencilled letters. The tents housed the three million refugees from Afghanistan and their livestock. Some way along the road to Quetta we encountered our first checkpoint. Even though I had entered the country illegally I was not unduly worried, for unlike Iran the mujahedeen have free access here. I was, however, concerned about what would happen if the officials discovered my bags. They climbed aboard and nosed around, but luckily they didn't search the roof, where my bags were. Further down the road we were stopped by traffic police, decked out for all the world like the kind of US Highway Patrol cops you see on television – right down to the sunglasses. They were going to give us a ticket for carrying too many people on the roof, but as soon as they realised that we were mujahedeen they waved us on with a raised-fist gesture of solidarity. It was obvious that Afghan freedom fighters enjoyed a good deal of kudos here.

The bus dropped us on the outskirts of Quetta and we marched through the streets feeling like heroes, enjoying the admiring glances of the townspeople as they made way for us. The thoughts at the forefront of my mind concerned the best hotel in town. I could, I felt, afford it, since in the whole of my two months in Afghanistan I had spent only £8. I fondly imagined finding a Hilton or a Marriott, and then spending two hours in the shower, followed by an afternoon lounging about the comfortable, neutral lobby, listening to muzak. An orgy of western familiarity. I thought of such untold luxuries as sheets, chairs and cutlery.

Even Abdul Rahman had taken on a martial air which had never been his as he strutted up to the door of Jamiat HQ and knocked. We waited for a moment – rather too long a moment for heroes, we thought. Finally a small door in the main gate opened and a short disgruntled man emerged.

'What do you want? We're closed,' he snapped.

Despite this temporary setback, we were herded through a sports stadium complex, past dusty arid fields and then through endless back streets to the Jamiat Residence. This was a medium-sized family house which was at present home to 200 mujahedeen. Despite the cramped circumstances, we received a warm welcome from our comrades, who came from all over Afghanistan. They had heard from Ismail Khan of our impending arrival, but because we were long overdue they feared us dead. They were here for the same reason as ourselves – to collect arms, but there was a shortage of supply. In order to comply with his commanders' wishes, it appeared that Professor Rabbani, the leader of Jamiat, had issued a number of letters authorising the release of a given amount of weaponry from the Jamiat depot here. However, the Professor had written so many letters that they were worth only 10 per cent of their face value. So there was a backlog, a waiting-list. One group from Ghurion had already been here for five months, and I could see my companions suffering the same fate, and then there was the problem of waiting for permission to arrive from Iran for shipment of weapons through that country. Ismail Khan had sent his group directly into Pakistan in the hope of avoiding such delays, but even if my companions were able to return in two weeks, and encountered no delays on the home run, the round trip would have taken them two months. If Ismail Khan could have had free access through Iran to an arms supply, his men could have collected and returned within two weeks.

The worst time had come – the time to say goodbye. It was especially difficult, for we had been through so much together, but now that the dangers we had faced were behind us, and now that they were with more of their own companions, the gulf that had really always been between us widened, and it was pointless to ignore it. Besides, I had my own journey to accomplish, my own promises to keep, and above all, I suddenly wanted nothing more than some time to myself. I bade farewell and went in search of the best hotel.

What I found was not the imposing but impersonal brass-and-glass number I had had in mind, but a rather dowdy, single-storey colonial affair complete with bungalows in the grounds, lightweight flapping doors which rebounded against their frames and mosquito nets.

No matter. I asked for a room.

'We are full, sir,' said the receptionist, eyeing me with disfavour.

'Really? But it isn't eight o'clock in the morning yet. Surely somebody's checking out.'

'I'm sorry, but no rooms are available until the 21st September.'

That was five days away. You can't do this to me, I thought. 'I'd be quite happy with a double room, if there are no singles.'

'I regret, sir . . .'

'A triple room?'

'Every room has been taken,' he said, beginning to weary of me.

'Money is no problem,' I said, pulling a handful of dollars out, but for once they failed to have the desired effect. His disdain turned to suspicion. Perhaps I was a drug dealer, he may have thought.

For once I was defeated, and I beat a retreat. So high had my imagination set my goals that I dreaded to think, now, what the second-best hotel would be like. I decided to lower my sights a little and told myself I'd be content with a room, plain and simple, but there would have to be a shower. My taxi driver couldn't have been kinder: I was mujahedeen.

The next hotel seemed to have all I required, and the people were welcoming. Then I went in search of soap, shampoo and a comb. Reaching a nearby shop my entry was blocked by a European couple. I indicated to them that I wanted to enter the shop, but they merely scowled at me.

'Get lost,' they snarled at me in English.

I realised from their accents that these were no Europeans, but Australians or New Zealanders.

'I only want to get into the shop,' I said, also in English.

As if by magic, their attitude changed. 'Oh. Sorry. We thought you were an Afghan beggar.'

'I'm sorry, too,' I said, sorry that my first encounter with representatives of my own culture should have to be so unpleasant. Nevertheless it was good to talk English, and I invited them to have a drink with me – albeit a non-alcoholic one, for Pakistan was my third 'dry' country.

I found a cake-shop and ate half a dozen pastries and a box of chocolate biscuits. Next on the agenda was a shower. I undressed expectantly and, confidently turning on the taps, was hit by a jet of the coldest water this side of a glacier. Philosophically I dried myself, dressed again, and went in search of the management. They apologised and sent me back to my room with someone helpful, but when he tried the taps no water came out at all.

'Wait one minute,' said the helpful person uncertainly.

Half an hour later I confronted the manager again. 'It's not our fault,' he apologised feebly. 'The system's broken down. In five minutes there will be hot water.'

Glumly I went back to my room again. Five minutes later – glory of glories! – there was boiling hot water in profusion. The only problem was that there was now no cold.

Finally I managed a shower of sorts, but it wasn't the pleasant experience I'd promised myself, for I was in constant dread of the water turning scalding or glacial, which it threatened to do at a moment's notice.

———

I spent some time unwinding, and exploring Quetta. The town has all the appearance of an old, colonial, tropical city, with bustling, colourful streets, brightly painted trucks and buses, horses, donkeys, camels and scooters – all overflowing in a nonstop cacophony amongst the low, pastel-coloured buildings. Over it all a lazy sense of peace, and a sweltering heat that lulled one into a languid slothful torpor. However, time has not stopped here, as in Afghanistan. Most of the women went about unveiled, and those who didn't were probably Afghan refugees. The presence of the refugees (there are Iranians here too, who've come across the deserts of Baluchistan to escape the Ayatollah's yoke) has caused a good deal of friction in Quetta. For example, the price of property has risen faster than anywhere else in Pakistan, and locals find themselves unable to compete in the property market with rich Afghans. At the other end of the spectrum, there are the cripples and the war-wounded. For these victims treatment is many days away, and most have made the journey from Afghanistan under punishing conditions. The miracle is that any survive it, but help in Quetta consists of only two surgeons and an anaesthetist at the Red Cross Hospital who cannot cope with the flood. The head of the mission, Rudi Durer, told me that he'd seen cases of people who had travelled for days with an arm shot away and the wound wholly untreated. In lieu of bandages, a dead bird is tied across the stump of the limb to staunch the wound.

Four mujahedeen that I had met in Quetta were planning to travel by train to Peshawar, and as that was in my direction I decided to accompany them, but they returned from the station with the disappointing news that no seats were available. I thought this highly unlikely as there were always several wagons allocated to unreserved seats. Because of the refugee problem, the hero-worship of the mujahedeen is tempered in some quarters by an animosity towards Afghans in general. Certainly that was why I'd got such a hostile reception at my first hotel. I decided to investigate and explore the station.

It was a hive of activity, but immaculately clean, with railway attendants of every description dressed in gleaming white jackets with brass buttons. These people, I thought, can't be all bad. There were two hours to go before the train to Peshawar was due to depart, but the train was already at the platform, and bursting with passengers. It was a delightful little train, painted cream and green, and made of wood. It was like an Alpine train from a picture-book, or at least it would have been were it not for the swarming mass of humanity inside it – on seats, in aisles, and even in luggage racks. The only carriages which still appeared to have seats available were those reserved for women only, and the front and rear ones, which were for our escort of armed policemen – a facility I have not seen before or since provided by a railways board.

Obviously my companions had been told no more than the truth. Nevertheless I tracked down some officials and explained to them how urgent it was that I reach Peshawar.

'We regret,' said the officials. 'All reserved seats have been sold for today and for the next four days. You could try for unreserved seats tomorrow but you must come early.'

I looked suitably impressed and regretful, and then produced one of my 'official' documents. They gazed as if hypnotised at the seals, stamps and signatures. Wheels were set in motion. I was passed from one office to another like a football at the feet of expert dribblers. My ruse had worked.

Actually it had worked too well, for the document had looked so important that everyone naturally assumed that I would be travelling first class. This was a disappointment to me but I reflected that I could use this to my advantage – and to that of my companions. As the ticket was being issued I said casually, 'There is the question of my assistants.'

'Assistants?' they said, looking up sharply.

'Yes.'

'Well, er, how many of them have you?'

'Four.'

'Four?'

Four was clearly going too far. We compromised. I could take one assistant. But there were no first-class seats left. We would have to travel in the corridor.

I hurried back to my companions with the news, and we quickly agreed that Hanif would come with me by train while the others found a lift on a Peshawar-bound truck. Fortunately the first-class corridors were more spacious than the second-class ones, and so there

was room for us to spread our patous out on the floor and lie down
– which was far more comfort than we deserved. For most of the
first part of the journey, the view reminded me of
the barren mountains of Afghanistan, punctuated
by small oasis settlements. Unlike Iran, the train
didn't stop at prayer times. Instead, the faithful
swivelled round in their seats in the general direction of Mecca and conducted the rite from there.

Despite the crush, I enjoyed the journey. The Pakistan railway
still retains its original character, with stations that have hardly
changed over the years, and are beautifully kept. The railway is
probably as efficient as it ever was under the British, the only
drawback perhaps being for hawkers, who find it difficult to make
their way up and down the carriages selling their wares because of
the press of people. Some hawkers have found a solution to this:
they cling to the outside of the train and sell through the
windows.

Most of the passengers had brought their own food, and were
generous in sharing it with others around them, but you could also
buy dinner from people on the platforms of stations where the train
stopped. For a few rupees a large tray containing several courses was
passed through the window. When you had finished, you gave your
tray up to someone on another station further down the line.
Everywhere, the railway attendants had on their spotless white
jackets with the brass buttons.

The train travelled south-east to Sukkur, then north-east by way
of Multan to Lahore, and finally north-west to Rawalpindi. Because
of all this meandering I had an opportunity to see how diverse the
nation is, with different races speaking different languages boarding
the train from time to time as we passed through widely varying
geographical landscapes, from the arid deserts of Baluchistan to the
tropical Punjab. And however built-up a town had become, it never
seemed to have lost its rural roots. Even in Lahore I kept seeing the
massive, beautiful and entirely ubiquitous water buffalo – either
wallowing in mud or deliciously submerged up to the nostrils in
sluggish water.

The train all but emptied in Lahore, but the fact that only a handful
of passengers remained on board thereafter, stretching luxuriously

in the unaccustomed space, didn't deter the dozens of mobile kiosks, and the hawkers of samosas, ice-creams, soft drinks, apples and bananas, from descending upon us.

Finally I fell into a slumber so profound that I do not know when we left Rawalpindi. I awoke to the train chugging through fantastic scenery: high, ragged, tree-covered hills showing off every shade of brilliant green under the sun. We crossed streams and rivers, brown and silt-laden, finally reaching the muddy expanse of the Kabul River which churned and tumbled like rippling muscle between its banks.

We had reached the North-West Frontier Province.

The train, as if aware of the long distance it had come, crawled wearily into Peshawar. Like Quetta the city has been colonised by Afghans, and whole neighbourhoods have been taken over by refugees and mujahedeen. With them have come intrigue, murder and political assassination. Peshawar is now commonly referred to as a city populated by spies, mujahedeen, drug dealers, journalists and relief agency workers.

My second day in Peshawar doubly confirmed my suspicions about the city. In the morning I was about to leave the foyer of my hotel when a soft-spoken middle-aged couple stopped to ask me if I was Mr Danziger. I was on the point of replying, 'Yes, I am Nick Mohammed', when I remembered that I had left Afghanistan behind and was with two Americans. They proved to be representatives of Helsinki Watch and had already heard of my journey through Herat on the grapevine. I spent the morning answering their questions about human rights violations.

Later on that day of coincidences I heard that M. LeClerc was in town preparing to go on a 'fishing expedition' to war-torn Afghanistan. I decided to pay him a visit. I called on his hotel and greeted him warmly. We had a pleasant evening comparing notes. Now he treated me as an equal, as one who had been brutally initiated into the barbarities of the war. He had changed since Paris; he appeared less diffident and there was a note of urgency about his attempts to gain more up-to-date information. He told me that, for the first time, he felt nervous about travelling into Afghanistan; maybe this time he would not return. All I could do was to wish him good luck and good fishing. I never was to find out what exactly he was fishing for.

In the welter of Peshawar the Afghans engage in internecine struggles, which have resulted in a recent spate of bombings. The Pakistan government has told the various mujahedeen groups to move their headquarters out of the city. Not only Afghans have been the victims of attacks. A grenade exploded only a short time before my arrival in the town in a Frenchman's house, and killed him. This action was interpreted as a warning to French doctors working for one of the three French medical relief agencies to stop sending teams to Afghanistan, but this interpretation was easily refuted as the dead man wasn't a doctor. Indeed the French medics claimed that the killing was the result of an *'histoire d'amour'*. Even if the man had been a doctor, they added, and even if his murder had been a warning, it wouldn't have stopped them from working; indeed, it would have encouraged them, for it would have provided a kind of proof that their work was effective.

Once inside Afghanistan these French doctors and nurses have to live and work in appalling conditions; their supplies scarce, their acceptance dubious. Unlike many relief workers I met, who tended to sentimentalise their duties, these people saw their work simply and straightforwardly as a job that had to be done. They were not all young, either. One of Ismail Khan's chief wishes was for a team to be sent to the Herat area, and to this end I visited the offices of Médecins sans Frontières. There I had quite a shock, for the first person I met was the young female doctor-administrator I had spoken to briefly an age away in Paris.

Her name was Juliette, but the Afghans affectionately called her Jamila. She had spent the last six years setting up field hospitals and coordinating the teams of MSF. Like so many of her colleagues, she had been bitten by the bug of Afghanistan, with its cheerful, helpless, struggling people, and could not now break loose from its spell. Of course she did not remember me from Paris. She had been far too busy there to be more than vaguely aware of me. Now she was busy too, but there was time for a little conversation, and we became friends.

She was a tireless worker: soothing the nerves of colleagues on the verge of departure to the war-zones, organising mule-trains of medical supplies to Badakhsan, and acknowledging the expressions of gratitude that were heaped on her by mujahedeen wherever we went in the town. Of course she could not remember them all, but none of them had forgotten her:

'Eh, Jamila, do you remember – I brought my friend to you and you pulled his tooth – but he fainted before you did so?'

I could not help being drawn to her tired, sad eyes, to her intoxicating good looks, her infectious compassion and strength. She had given her all to her work, and it had all but drained her of her youth. I worked alongside her, caught up in her spirit. In the early hours of one morning, when we could no longer press the pills for transport from their packaging, I drew her spontaneously into my arms. Brought together by the common bond of horrors she had experienced, and of which I had some inkling, we were driven to temporarily escape their memories. I hugged her with all the love I thought had left me for good, and so we buried ourselves in each other; but no amount of love could dam the flood of the all too vivid cruelty that had passed before our eyes. Here with Jamila, thoughts crossed my mind of Mandana in Mashhad, and of Jenny at the foot of Mount Ararat; but those times were an eternity away from now.

'What will you do next?' I asked her, much later. 'Can you not rest?'

She smiled. 'Rest? Not yet. I have to go on a reconnaissance mission to Lowgar first.'

I closed my eyes. Lowgar is one of the most desperately war-torn areas of Afghanistan.

But Jamila survived. She has not forgotten the horror, though; nor will she ever forget. Not long ago, I had a postcard from her from the West Indies, where she was scuba-diving. 'Even here, even amidst all this beauty, and diving to 25 metres,' she wrote, 'I still see their eyes before me.'

My work in Peshawar also involved speaking with various mujahedeen leaders, some of whom lay great store by the opinions and reports of foreigners. This was evident by the vast number of posters of Ahmed Shah Massoud, the commander of the Panjshir Valley, who receives regular visits from the western press. Through them he has been built up into a kind of demi-god, though his deeds in the war are no greater than those of other commanders of less accessible areas. However, his role as a focus and figurehead in Afghanistan's struggle for freedom is a very useful one. With the glamour it also brings danger, for Massoud is at the top of the Russians' hit-list.

The mujahedeen leaders I met wanted me to meet members of the so-called 'Alliance', an organisation which attempts to act as a unifying force between the seven major factions of the mujahedeen. My most important contact, it appeared, would be the man who controlled the purse-strings. Apparently he had received large sums from the Arab states, and financial and humanitarian aid – or at least, the money to purchase them – lay in his gift.

He was surrounded by a tight security cordon, but finally my companions and I were shown into a small room with chairs along three walls and a desk at one end, behind which sat a balding man in his fifties. My little group (the four mujahedeen from Quetta) sat in silence, holding their breath and urging me on with unspoken prayers. I knew what I had to say, and what appeals I had to make for arms and clothing and medical supplies on behalf of Ismail Khan – I had made them already to many other leaders-in-exile. I knew also that this man was very powerful, and that he was despised by those Afghans who had stayed behind to fight, for it was common knowledge that he channelled most of the funds that came his way to the refugee population of his own tribe, with him in Pakistan. Jokes in Afghanistan abounded about how, when it rained, the mud of the 'mud huts' his refugees lived in was washed away – revealing brick houses beneath the disguise.

Nevertheless I made my plea.

'I know, I know,' he said. 'Everybody needs something.'

'And you have the power to give it.'

'How do you want me to help?'

'In any way you can. They need warm clothing, bandages, quinine . . .'

He ran a hand over his bald head and sighed, shaking his head. 'Always the same story,' he said.

'Don't you care?'

He shrugged his shoulders. 'What difference does it make? We will lose the war.'

'Have you been back? Have you seen how hard they are fighting?'

'I do not need to go back. My men tell me all I need to know.'

I left the man in disgust, understanding better the frustration felt by those Afghans who have stayed behind to fight. The bazaars of Peshawar filled me with anger, for they were stocked with goods destined by rights for the 'freedom fighters', but diverted here and sold for profit. Here, one could buy dozens of Kalashnikovs a day if one had the means. My companions shared my anger as we walked away from the meeting through this shameful cornucopia.

'If I had a gun like one of these I would go straight back and shoot the bastard,' one of my friends muttered.

'Win or lose, some of us will come back here and put an end to him,' promised Hanif.

I grieved for the work of the conciliatory 'Alliance'. With men like the one I had just come from hiding like maggots in the apple of Afghan resistance, their job was a labour of Hercules indeed.

Internecine wrangling, however, isn't the sole preserve of the various Afghan parties. I counted 28 relief agencies in Peshawar, not including those of the United Nations, and there is little or no coordination between them. Not only that, they are on occasion appallingly ill-informed. There was, for example, a British medical team that seriously expected to be able to reach Herat to carry out 'a feasibility study into setting up a centre for preventive medicine' – not curative, note, and ignoring totally the fact that the area they hoped to go to was one of the most war-torn in the country. The biggest joke of all was that they had allowed three weeks for the entire operation. Then there was the young French couple who planned to go in and distribute money to the populace. They talked of building schools in an area where schools are prime targets for both sides. I suggested that they give the money to a commander of my acquaintance who is trying to create the organisational infrastructure without which any ultimate victory will be meaningless.

'Impossible,' they said.

'Why?'

'Because we need photographs of what has been achieved with the money.'

'What on earth for?'

'So that the people who contributed the money will feel that it was well spent.'

This left me speechless. In the event, they left for Afghanistan with the equivalent of £13,000 in cash. They got as far as Spin Buldak – just across the frontier – where they were promptly ambushed, and where all the money went up in smoke.

The International Committee of the Red Cross not only have a hospital in Peshawar where they operate on war wounded, but also training facilities where they run first-aid courses. They also publish illustrated first-aid books in Pashtu and Dari, which include homilies about humane treatment of the captured enemy. I had heard of this type of book when I was in Afghanistan, but although people had spoken widely in praise of them there I had only actually seen one – and that was near the frontier. Jamila suggested that I might encourage some of the mujahedeen I knew to sign up for first-aid courses. I did my best, but half of them were automatically disqualified because they were illiterate, and there was one man who told me proudly,

'I have no need of training. All I need are my tools.'

'Tools?'

'Yes, you know – saw, scalpel, that kind of thing.'

I looked at him. He didn't look like a qualified surgeon. I asked him if he was.

'No,' he replied earnestly, 'but I have helped in many such operations in the field. Amputations are no big problem for me.'

In the face of all this I became more and more determined to try to organise some tangible relief and support for the friends I had left behind in Afghanistan, deserted as they had been by so many of their countrymen. And I had come to a conclusion: while there were many brave individual efforts by Afghans and westerners to make the world aware of the war there, most practical work was humanitarian. The bulk of the population of Afghanistan who had stayed there supported the resistance. While it was true that the mujahedeen needed moral and medical support, they needed guns more.

I decided to take my quest on to Islamabad.

I learnt that there is a trickle of arms and money to the mujahedeen, who often obtain Russian equipment for the struggle. This is but one of the countless ironies of the war: the Russians use Kamaz lorries built with western funds, export gas to Europe yet import it from Afghanistan for themselves at half the cost. The trade imperative is irresistible. I heard that some Russian soldiers volunteer for third and fourth tours of duty in Kabul because there they can purchase electronic equipment, like videorecorders, which are unavailable at home. There are even stories of Russian soldiers siphoning off petrol from their military vehicles to sell to Kabuli taxi-drivers.

The more I talked to diplomats, observers and the press, the more they confirmed my opinion that the situation benefited the West. As long as the Russians were tied down in Afghanistan the West could use the fact to score diplomatic points off Moscow; and the Russian military commitment allowed other neighbours of the Bear to breathe more easily. Thus it made sense to supply the resistance with just enough to keep it going, but not enough to let it drive the Russians out. Thus war is used as a container. In a similar way, the Gulf War has effectively neutralised Iran.

Foreign governments in the West have shown a tendency to bestow favour on Jamiat, as one of the more moderate fundamentalist groups, but favour is all they've bestowed. There has been no attempt to help provide any of the training which Jamiat would need if after a victory they were called upon to form an effective government. There is a profusion of agreements and mutual benefits concerning countries outside Afghanistan which suits everyone except the Afghans. It is not therefore surprising that the mujahedeen are sceptical about who their real friends are – if, indeed, they believe they have any. Each 'friend' seems only too keen to exert, if not actually impose, his own influence on that unhappy country.

In this atmosphere it's hardly surprising that a good deal of spying goes on – that activity covered by the ironically disarming expression 'intelligence' – so that communications, not easy at the best of times in Pakistan, were, quite literally, bugged. I eventually got through from Islamabad to speak to Jamila in Peshawar on the phone, only to be cut off after just a few words. When I redialled, the phone had gone completely dead. I asked the advice of the English journalist whose phone it was.

'Oh,' he said, not at all surprised, 'I know what it is. You were speaking French. The man listening in wasn't able to understand, so he's cut the line off and gone to find a colleague who can. Give him a few minutes to do so and you'll get through with no trouble.'

I followed his advice and he was perfectly right.

My attempts to provide some positive help for my friends seemed doomed to disaster at every turn, but at least I was spreading the message of their predicament. On several occasions I was invited to dinner by wealthy Afghan refugees, but these evenings always made me despondent, for I had to endure the burden of my hosts' guilt at having abandoned their country.

'Your shoes are better than us,' they would say. 'They have seen more.'

However that was as far as their pity extended – to themselves. Elsewhere, a diplomat had offered me 'the chance to travel and make reports for his country', which seemed to me a dubious privilege, so I turned him down; and a highly respected journalist drew me aside and offered me a job as an arms dealer. He even had lists of available weaponry and told me that I'd be working on a percentage basis.

In the middle of all this I was trying to find ways of continuing my own journey. This was far from easy. I had heard from my mother that the Churchill Trust was no longer willing to provide me with a letter of recommendation to the Chinese government, since they were now firmly under the impression that I was working for MI6. In Islamabad, the local British diplomatic community wouldn't help me either. Their reasons were unclear. Sometimes the excuse was that protocol didn't permit it, and sometimes it was that a diplomatic approach might 'prejudice' my case. I could understand their lack of enthusiasm to embroil themselves in what might well have been hard work. No non-Pakistani had been granted a visa for entering China via the Khunjerab Pass since the communists took power in 1949. Many have tried since then, but each time someone has tried to cross clandestinely they have been caught and gently but firmly returned to the Pakistani authorities. My own plans would thus have to be completely watertight. In fact, I had already laid some foundations, since before leaving England I had arranged for some assistance in China.

I couldn't risk the slightest mistake. I borrowed a shirt, tie, jacket and trousers, shoes and a briefcase from a friendly BBC correspondent and his wife, who, with an assortment of belts, safety-pins and grooming, did her best to transform an Afghan beggar into a respectable businessman. I came out somewhere in between: a colonial cricket-player, perhaps, with white trousers, an old school tie and a blazer. Still, it wasn't bad. I rang Pakistan Airlines, booked myself on a flight to Peking, and then went to the Chinese Embassy. I presented myself as an executive from an international company, changing the occupation entry in my passport for the purpose. I told them I had come to collect my visa. Consternation. The consular section hadn't received any authority from Peking.

I frowned, friendly but concerned. 'There must be some mistake,' I said. I invited them to phone PIA to confirm that I had a flight booked to Peking – they could even call my company's offices there, I bluffed. Luckily the staff who were dealing with me were juniors who had no wish to disturb their seniors on such a matter – for I had clearly convinced them of my probity. The girl who looked after me, furthermore, was obviously unaccustomed to the proper procedure, and took forever to fill in the requisite forms, which was not entirely her fault, for I was not helpful, hoping, as I always do, to leave as many questions as possible unanswered. Finally everything seemed to be in order. All that was needed was the consul's counter-signature.

'There's only one thing,' said Mrs Liu. 'Do you mind if the visa doesn't commence for a few days? It's on account of our 35th Anniversary of the Revolution celebrations – everyone's away on holiday.'

'Leave it later, if you wish,' I said, glad to be getting a visa at all. But she took my expression to mean, 'make it longer', and so when I received the visa, I found that it was valid for a longer period than I anticipated. True, this was not a visa for the Khunjerab – it was a visa permitting entry by air to Peking – but it was a visa.

I had not finished with the Chinese Embassy yet. I left post-haste, and quickly changed out of my businessman's outfit and back into my Afghan clothes. In them, and my turban, I was indistinguishable from a native. In fact, though, I was going back as myself, flying my true colours. I made an appointment by telephone with the Chinese cultural attaché. Then I went to see him. Not surprisingly, the

Pakistani guard at the gate was mistrustful of me and wouldn't let me in until he'd had proof of my appointment.

The attaché was most cordial, but when I asked him for permission to cross the Khunjerab, he clammed up.

'Unfortunately, the Sino-Pakistani Treaty forbids the passage of foreigners across that frontier,' he explained.

I told him some more about my book, and about my journey.

'Your project sounds most interesting, and I am very sympathetic to it, but . . .' he spread his hands in a gesture I knew all too well. 'May I make a suggestion?'

'Please do.'

'Why don't you write two books? One could cover your journey right up to the Pakistan border – say, up to Gilgit. Then you can return here, fly to Peking, and possibly we can arrange for you to travel overland to the Chinese side of the same border – let's say to Kashi.'

'But that would mean a 6,500 mile detour, wouldn't it?'

He smiled, and spread his hands. He had, in any case, neatly sidestepped the fact that the area I was heading for was one of the hottest spots in the world – the borders of the USSR, China, Afghanistan and Pakistan meet there, and the Pakistani territory is disputed by India. Not a place to wander for a stroll.

Anyway, it was clear to me that nothing was to be gained by staying in Islamabad. I decided to head north for Gilgit at once, and take it from there.

BORDER
MANOEUVRES

The month of the landslides was over, and the all too frequent mishaps on the road were no longer due to rockfalls but to driver exhaustion. The 'wagons' by which we travelled – Ford Transits – and the buses take 12 to 15 hours to reach Gilgit, crouching under the shadow of Nanga Parbat, along the new road which has been described as the eighth wonder of the world – the Karakoram Highway. It is the means by which unsuspecting people will be exposed to tourism, Coca Cola, and the videorecorder. It is already happening.

Our wagon was behind schedule. The driver didn't exactly inspire confidence either. Within the first hour his eyelids began to droop. In a bid to combat the onset of fatigue he opened his window, letting in a freezing draught. Fortunately I was sitting next to him, and every time he began to nod I nudged him sharply, always prepared to grab the steering wheel in case I startled him in the process. I wondered how long I could keep this up for I too was exhausted, having spent the last few days in Islamabad in a frantic search for trinkets in case I should have to bribe my way into China. Money was going to be a problem too, as it was impossible to obtain Chinese currency outside the People's Republic.

The first section of the highway was along the Rawalpindi–Peshawar trunk road, which was full of traffic. Motor vehicles swerved and bobbed around the buffalo-carts, and a variety of bicycles and three-wheeled Vespas cluttered the rest of the remaining tarmac. As we headed north, the villages became more widely spaced out, and verdant pastures gave way to rolling hills, and then towering, snow-capped mountains. The more we travelled into the hinterland, the more colourful became the attire of the local women, traditional apparel becoming the rule rather than the exception. From the windows of the wagon I saw clusters too of neatly-dressed school-children in grey shalwar camise, and wearing navy blue berets. As the road wound and climbed amongst ever higher hills, so the greens of the fields took on an ever more intense sheen. Once across the foothills the mountains jutted out either side of the valley, obscuring the land beyond, like a series of theatre curtains opening up one by one as we passed them. Clinging precariously to the sides of the mountains were rice-fields of brilliant emerald.

The road and its bridges had been built with Chinese collaboration. The toll on human life had been great, since one Chinese had died for every two kilometres of its length. Mountainsides had been blasted away, and from them hundreds of men had hung from ropes, hacking away at the rock. What they left behind when they finished was a pencil line of road carved out of an all but sheer rockface. The huge chasms, gorges and precipices that form obstacles to the road's course are negotiated by a series of sharp bends clinging to the sides of the mountain wall or the overhanging gorge. For those lucky enough not to suffer from vertigo, you can look up at several hundred feet of overhanging grey and brown rock, and you can look down several hundred more at a steely ribbon which is the River Indus.

Sections of the road are more prone to landslides than others, and although warned in advance by a roadsign one can only hold one's breath – there is nothing else to do – until another sign tells you that you are clear. It can take days and even weeks to remove a landslide, and so vehicles often have to bump their way over layers of rock and scree. Villages became few and far between, and the driver never failed to stop at them for the obligatory *chai*, and to carry out repairs. On such long trips, I had noticed, the passengers often became one big family, as every event is a shared experience.

I continued to marvel at the driver's ability to stay awake – although he was never far from sleep. He drove as fast as he could and the only time he was forced to slow and stop against his will was at the various police checkpoints. These were run on a very informal basis. The policemen inside had to be woken up, and they drowsily passed the register for everyone in the wagon to sign. Any official in Pakistan who wishes to look up the entries for 11 and 12 October 1984, will see that HRH the Prince of Wales, Passport Number: 1, Occupation: Royal; and Donald Duck, Occupation: Husband to Daffy, passed that way *en route* to Gilgit then. The policeman just outside Gilgit had the best solution to the problem of sleep *vs.* duty. He'd conveniently placed his bed beside his barrier, and by pulling a rope at his side could raise it without stirring.

We arrived at Gilgit at 2.30 in the morning, and whereas everyone else headed for town, I left the wagon and, ignoring dire warnings about the Arctic conditions, found a smooth bit of ground under a tree, wrapped myself in my patou and went to sleep.

I was awoken by the sounds of prayer. Conditions were glacial but the fine, fairy-like frosty dawn soon made me forget how profoundly cold I was. I braced myself and waited an hour for the sun to rise and thaw me, when I would go in search of tea and bread.

The sun rose unexpectedly late as it lay hidden behind the towering mountains. However, when it made its appearance and rolled back the shadows of the hills with a sudden, imperious gesture, the rush of colour which greeted the eye was like a burst of applause: the leaves of the trees brought forth a sudden rush of yellows, oranges, and greens, and the sharp, crisp air and the keen clear sky provided a dramatic backdrop. At the turn of the century it was the British Empire trying to outwit Imperial Russia. Earlier in time the Greeks under Alexander, the Kushans, the Scythians, the Parthians, the Ancient Persians, the Seljuks, the Turks, the Mongols, the Arabs and the Huns – all these have tried to impose their authority over this strategically vital region where three great mountain ranges meet to provide natural barriers between men: the Pamirs (Roof of the World), the Karakoram (Black Massif), and the Hindu Kush (Killer of Hindus) – their very names a reminder to would-be invaders of the obstacles that earlier attempts had met. The area has always been a major crossroads for civilisations, cultures and religions, with armies, missionaries and, above all, traders, using the narrow roads and passes which have come to be known collectively as the Silk Road.

The latest influx of foreigners, including many Punjabis, who excel in administration, has turned Gilgit into something of a boom town – doubling its population inside the last four years. The outsiders have brought their own tastes and their own foods, and what was considered to be one of the world's healthiest diets – wholemeal bread, *baterine dowdo* (a dried apricot and wheatflour soup), and many other wheat-, grape- and apricot-based foods – is now suffering as the influence of a more international selection of foods makes itself felt. Before they disappear forever, let me testify to the efficacy of *karne dowdo* – fried wheatflour – which helps to cure, among other ailments, colds, coughs and sore throats – and dried apricots with a nut sandwiched between them: these provide warmth and cure dizziness. Something else which I found really delicious was *kilau* – hazel nuts surrounded with thick, dried grape.

Although the British tried to impose rules on it, pure polo is still played here in its original and undiluted form – with no rules. Riding on very handsome, solidly-built little horses with colourful saddle-cloths, the players wear bright shirts, and the occasional jaunty white cap may also be seen. The 'field' is a wide expanse of impacted earth between a row of houses set behind walls on either side. The spectators – a dedicated bunch of fans, with no room for women, except for a few young girls – squatted on a low wall which defined the playing area. They were sent diving for cover when the teams charged towards them, flailing their polo sticks wildly. I didn't know what to watch more – the game, or the intent faces following it in the crowd. If English polo could be described as a slightly violent form of croquet on horseback, then this was wrestling or rugger on horseback. The players grabbed each other quite readily, and once I saw a man ride up by his opponent and lean right over him and his horse to get at the ball with his stick.

'What's the strategy?' I asked someone.

'To crash into each other,' he replied enthusiastically.

'They might kill each other.'

He looked at me with contempt. 'Killing is an art, not a crime.'

The ground was appalling. It was totally uneven, and the little horses stumbled so often that I was sure one would break a leg, though none did. The players didn't wear team-coloured shirts, and sometimes there seemed to be actual confusion about who was on whose side. Then there were the assorted cows, sheep and children wandering out onto the pitch, as they wander everywhere and into everything. There were no tactics, since every man on the field chased after the ball directly and furiously. During the game one of the small Suzuki vans from the town drove out onto the pitch and twirled around in some confusion before its panicky driver managed to get it out of the way. There were no pauses in play, and no changes of horse.

'You only change horses if your mount dies,' my informant told me sternly. But this was not true, for one horse, whose rider had accidentally knocked it over the head with his stick and bloodied it, was promptly taken off the field and replaced.

The most impressive moment came after a goal had been scored. A player from the side who'd lost the goal took possession of the ball. He then rode up to his team's end of the field, turned, and charged back down towards the middle. At about the halfway line he threw the ball forwards in front of him, and then whacked it with his stick before it could hit the ground – a difficult thing to do, requiring enormous experience, coordination and skill. More prosaically, they sometimes scored directly from the kick-off, but no one seemed unduly worried by any restriction the scoreline may have been supposed to impose.

Polo was followed with much enthusiasm. As I learnt during my stay in Gilgit, on polo days most shops closed, the spectators dressed in thick woollen sweaters against the cold, put on *chogas* (coats with very long sleeves), or down jackets, and made their way to the polo ground past Uighur kebab sellers. And the start of the polo championships had a carnival atmosphere, with a band consisting of drummers and pipers playing highpitched, jovial tunes while the horsemen showed off prior to the matches, displaying their skills by spearing a series of small pieces of wood from the ground as they galloped past, or more flamboyantly charging past a cluster of balloons and attempting to shoot down as many as possible with a shotgun as they flashed by. During the championship I attended, the little local band burst into frenzied music whenever the home team scored a goal, and one rider was carried off on a stretcher after being accidentally hit over the head with a stick. However, by the semi-final stage, discipline was showing its true worth, for only the army and the police teams remained in contention.

I had found myself a modest hotel, and before addressing myself to the problem of how to cross the frontier decided to relax and find out what I could about the people who were now my hosts. Again, I found that religion dominated the community, though the three main Islamic sects coexist peacefully here. The area is mainly composed of Shias, and I was shown photographs of their recently-completed festival, that of the Tenth of Muharram, which commemorates the martyrdom of Hussein, son of Ali. During this the faithful take to the streets in an orgy of self-flagellation, which is very far from symbolic, since they use knives attached to chains and some of the wounds result in death. The other two sects are the Sunnis and the Ismailis. The Shias I talked to were in two minds about whether they would fight against Iraq if Khomeini demanded it; and they were doubtful about Iran's claims to Pakistani Baluchistan.

'I am a Pakistani first, and a Shia second,' one man decided after I'd asked him what he'd do if Khomeini called upon him to rise against his own fatherland to 'liberate' Baluchistan. It was deeply pleasing, too, to see that not only did they all live in harmony, but also that they expressed a genuine solidarity with their Afghan brothers.

'But how do you feel about the three million Afghan refugees in your country?' I asked them.

They thought about it. 'It is like something caught in the throat,' they said. 'We can't swallow it, and we can't throw it up.'

All things being equal, the most promising course to take in my quest to reach China was to play on the religious aspect of the journey, for whatever the local people's affiliation, they claimed that their Chinese counterparts belonged to the same sect as themselves. I thus spent my time slowly and carefully building up contacts amongst the business and military communities, all the time gathering information and names that might at some time prove useful. I was struck by the number of plots and side-deals that everyone seemed to be hatching with everyone else. Maybe this was a result of living in such a paranoid part of the world. One night I felt confident enough to mention my real motives for being in Gilgit to a businessman called Sa'id, but no sooner was our discussion under way than it was interrupted by the arrival of a customs official. I feared that all was lost but Sa'id carried on talking just as if the official hadn't been there. Sure enough it later transpired that he and the official already had a scheme going whereby they would import contraband through Islamabad. Sa'id appeared sympathetic to my plans, but I could see that he was a man who played his cards close to his chest. It would be a while yet before I trusted him completely. But as the days passed and I knew that he hadn't betrayed me to the authorities, I began to relax a little.

Against this piebald atmosphere of intrigue and rumours, nearly everybody tuned in nightly to the Urdu service of the BBC, presumably to find out what was really happening. Here, unlike in Afghanistan, the least educated person had a working knowledge of world events that would put most westerners to shame. I wondered at their mental discipline, to be so interested in the affairs of men when living in surroundings of such heartstopping natural beauty.

I decided to make one final attempt to obtain official permission to cross the Khunjerab, even though I knew it would be a fruitless quest. In making this decision I had to weigh the pros and cons very precisely. If I were caught having sought official permission, I would no longer be able to plead ignorance as a defence – and here, where English is spoken fluently, I could not use linguistic difficulties as an excuse as I might have done in Turkey or Iran. I knew enough about the Deputy Commissioner in Gilgit, too, to know that no amount of my official-looking documents would move him: the Khunjerab frontier was closed to foreigners, and that was that. There was another consideration: rumours abounded about the fate of those who had tried to cross and failed. Years ago, it appeared, Red Guards had seized an Italian traveller on Pakistani soil, taken him across to their side, and there summarily shot him dead. Others who'd tried were now mouldering in Pakistani gaols, and would be for years; or they'd been fined heavily.

I always plan carefully. The first task was to check on what kind of threat the Pakistani checkpoints and other installations along the border would pose. To this end I found a cargo-jeep that agreed to take me to Pasu. Pasu was 120 km from the border, but it was as far as foreigners were allowed to travel.

Sitting on top of the cargo I had an unobstructed view of the most magnificent scenery. What I saw was desolate mountain-desert, giddy precipices, clinging fields – and through it all, like a thread of silk indeed, slender but tough, ran the old Silk Road, a path barely wide enough for animals at times, crossing ravines by means of fragile bridges, and sometimes lost in landslides. There are still many communities that can only be reached by these tiny paths that crisscross the mountainsides.

Gradually the barren mountains gave way to the fertile valleys of Hunza and Nagar, two communities usually at loggerheads for centuries because of their religious differences. The 600-year-old fort of the Mir of Hunza dominates the first valley, which in autumn is a riot of colour, the trees shaking heads of bronze, yellow and red gold in the wind and the cold sun, the grey stone houses gaudy with drying fruit. Surrounding the splash of colour along the valley floor, the mountains rise grey to their snowy peaks, scarred by glaciers from which the water comes to irrigate the crops below.

We reached Pasu, and then, to my astonishment and delight, the jeep continued on. I couldn't believe my luck – was it possible that it would take me all the way to the frontier? We approached the checkpoint on the far side of town. The barrier was up, and the post was unmanned. This was too good to be true.

Unfortunately, it *was* too good to be true. The jeep drew up. To my fury, the driver started to sound his horn – about the only thing that worked on his tiresome jeep – and we waited. There was nothing I could do. A full five minutes passed before the checkpoint officials unhurriedly arrived. Bit by bit I produced my documents, but the officials remained unconvinced.

'I'd like to speak to Captain Sabdar,' I said, mentioning the name of one of the soldiers I knew was posted here from listening in to conversations in Gilgit.

'He's not here,' they replied, though my mentioning his name had clearly made an impression.

I took my courage in both hands. 'Would you mind getting him? He knows that I have permission to travel on to the frontier.'

'I'm sorry. The captain left for Gilgit this morning.'

In other circumstances this might have worked to my advantage, but this time it seemed that the guards' fear of not going by the book was greater than the fear of mistakenly turning me back. I was asked to leave the jeep, and pointed in the direction of Pasu.

There was some consolation. I now knew the precise location of the checkpoint, and weaving one's way around it did not look like being a problem. I decided to do a little reconnaissance trip to see how I might circumvent the authorities, though I could see that one thing I'd really have to contend with would be the cold.

I returned to the town and found somewhere to stay for the night, where I fell in with three other foreigners who were hiking in the area, and who said they'd be very happy to accompany me. I did not, of course, tell them my real reasons for this exploratory walk. We set off early the next morning, and I was glad of their company, not only because they provided perfect cover for me if we were caught, but also because the terrain proved to be a lot tougher than I'd expected. For one thing, we could not find any definable track, and more often than not would find ourselves climbing and scrambling over the harsh rocks. We were climbing towards a glacier, and the closer we drew to it the greater the hazard of loose rocks and scree became. It was difficult to get a foothold, and when the ground did give way underfoot, you had to move rapidly forward so that the forward motion counteracted the downward one. But we managed the ascent in the end and finally pulled ourselves up past the last few boulders to reach a ridge of the glacier. It resembled an army – only all you could see of the serried ranks of soldiers was their cone-shaped, greyish white hats. These ice-hats were, however, several metres high. Here we located a path – though it was no more than a shelf in a vertical cliff a couple of hundred feet high, and to reach it we still had to pick our way across a moraine of boulders, each the size of a small house.

After a couple of hours' scrambling, we attained a whaleback which rose out of the glacier and split it into two. On the one hand we now had the Pasu Glacier, which we had first seen, and on the other lay the Batura Glacier. This stretches for some 55 kilometres, and is one of the longest and most dramatic in the world. Elatedly, we slid down the slope of scree to the Batura Glacier itself.

It was alive – truly an ice river, emitting deep groans as the ice plates moved against each other, and cracks and thuds as enormous chunks of ice and boulders were dislodged and sent crashing onto further rocks, before bouncing down to the fast-flowing water that rushed along a rift in the centre of the glacier, sweeping the debris it collected impatiently down to the Hunza River.

We returned by an easier route, regaining the Karakoram Highway and walking back past the checkpoint – which was again unmanned. My companions were elated by the outing, but I was considering the possibilities it had opened for me. Or perhaps closed would be a better word. The checkpoint obviously wouldn't be an obstacle, but if I used the highway I would have to walk at night to avoid being seen by any of the traffic on it – for although it was very irregular this late in the year, it was almost all military. There was no way I could manage on my own across country, that much was clear, and without really warm clothes I doubted very much whether I could make it on foot. It was now late October, and conditions were Arctic. I would have to devise an alternative plan.

It was difficult to obtain information without attracting suspicion. Few foreigners were evident, and they only stayed a day or two. Above all I didn't want to compromise the friendly locals with the authorities. As in Gilgit, I was able to make myself understood by speaking Persian, to which some of the local dialects sounded remarkably similar. Persian used to be taught in Gilgit, but nowadays there were only a few old people who could speak it. The people here were even more European of feature than those I had already encountered in the lowland valleys. Their noses were bigger and their beards were heavier. They told me folk-tales, some of which were beyond me, but one recounted a story of treasure buried at the time of Alexander and still undiscovered. A village elder sang me a song in Persian, and seeing that I had no coat, he offered me his own: it was beautiful, hand-made of wool, covered with delicate embroidery along the cuffs and hems, and it had sleeves so long that they extended down past one's knees. I decided however that his need of it was greater than mine, for I did have my battered down jacket, which my mother had sent back out to me. Later on, I sometimes regretted not taking that coat; it was made precisely to withstand the temperatures I was about to encounter.

Although by now the road was officially closed owing to the extreme cold and the treacherous conditions, the occasional vehicle was still trundling across the border, and the second of the bi-annual trade caravans had yet to make the journey. I decided that whilst vehicles were still crossing, I could live in hope. I didn't much relish the thought of turning back, or of spending six months or so inactive here. In the middle of one night, a bus stopped at the inn where I had taken lodgings. It was taking Muslim pilgrims back to China.

The pilgrims were Uighurs, and they had just performed the hajj to Mecca. Uighurs are tall and European-looking, with nothing in common with the dominant Han Chinese, either culturally or linguistically. They are one of the many minority cultural groups that have been trapped inside modern political boundaries – and their own ancestral homelands have been divided. They were a friendly people, and like many good Muslims, they had combined religious devotion with business on their hajj. They had not been allowed to leave China with any currency, so they had taken silks, rugs and cloths with them to sell in Pakistan, and with the money thus earned they had bought more goods to sell in Saudi Arabia. Once there, the round of selling and buying had taken place again. They were now filtering back to their homeland in the west of China – going, indeed, to the very area I hoped to reach. Their bus was overloaded with goods, its roof a mountain of merchandise and half the interior stuffed with sacks, bags and suitcases. There was only a small amount of room left for the passengers. I entertained hopes of joining them, but it was impossible to think of a way of doing so – I would be stopped at the first checkpoint that demanded to see papers, and I would end up with a heavy fine, or even a gaol sentence. Regretfully, I waved them on their way. So near, and yet so far, I thought bitterly. I was so close that I felt I could smell China.

My hiking friends had long since left Pasu, and with the departure of the Uighurs I began to feel not only isolated but that I was wasting time here. And time was running out fast. If I didn't get across very soon, I wouldn't be able to move until the spring. I wasn't sure I could hold out that long. The time had come to return to Gilgit, where there would be a greater chance of finding someone who might, perhaps, be prepared to help me.

There was still some fight left in me, but I was beginning to feel pretty low, and in fact I'd all but given up hope of reaching China. Everything seemed stacked against me: without obtaining a lift close to the border (a vain hope, it seemed), it would be impossible for me to carry enough supplies to make it across alone and then on to the first 'open' city, Kashgar, which was some way inside China. Pack animals were available for sale, but I could hardly buy one without arousing suspicion. On the other hand, the contacts I had made in Gilgit had not gone cold, and on my return they began to pay dividends. Through them I heard about the sites and manning of the Chinese checkpoints. As I had little in the way of financial reward to offer anyone in return for help, I had to resort to wheeling and dealing, becoming a kind of unofficial agent for all sorts of trade. For example, I knew a man with a motorbike for sale, and managed in return for information to put him in touch with a man who wanted to buy one. Through all this web I finally came to meet Amjad. A stocky man, he was a flamboyant character who was more often than not drunk. (Pakistan is a 'dry' country, but there are local remedies for this: in Gilgit and points north it is 'Hunza Water', which is quite as dreadful as Iranian 'Rocket Fuel'.)

I outlined my plan to Amjad, rather dubious about taking him into my confidence, but having no time to be choosy.

'I will help you,' he decided. 'But you will have to wait until I have sobered up and thought things over.'

I rather liked the degree of self-knowledge this statement revealed, but I wasn't confident that I would, in fact, see him again.

He did return, however, perfectly sober, and having clearly given my journey some thought.

'It will take me a while to gather all the information we need to bring the thing off without a hitch,' he said. 'I mean, we'll need to know exactly where the guards are stationed, about troop movements, vehicles on the road – all that sort of thing. You've already got a good deal of information, but we need it to be as up-to-date as possible.'

'Do you really think we can do it?' I asked, fired by his enthusiasm and his workmanlike approach, but still wondering on how solid a basis they were built. Amjad was a great one for bravado.

He looked at me severely. 'I have a reputation to consider,' he informed me. 'I have never failed in a single exploit which I have undertaken.' He went on to recount several, some hair-raising, some funny, all with himself as hero.

'I have had just as much success with foreign women,' he added, matter-of-factly. Then he sighed.

'What is it?' I asked him.

'Well, that's the problem. My success. What you ask of me is difficult, very difficult. If I fail to get you across, what will happen to my reputation?'

'Oh, don't worry about that,' I reassured him hastily, afraid that he would decide to back out after all. 'You don't look to me like a man who could resist a challenge, and think of how much greater your reputation will be if you bring off this difficult task.'

'That is true,' he agreed more brightly. 'But we must not be hasty. And now we will drink.'

He produced, not a mere bottle of Hunza Water, but a plastic jerry-can full. It is a cross between a wine and a spirit, and is distilled from mulberries.

As we drank, Amjad outlined his plan to me. It was most ingenious, and would enable me to pass under the very noses of both border guards and government officials. However the first step was for me to fly immediately to Islamabad, for through my desperate eagerness to reach China, too many people had come to know of my plans, and it was certain that Pakistani Intelligence was on to me. Unless I disappeared for a time to allay suspicion, my arrest would follow as surely as night follows day. I jibbed a little at the idea of flying, for I had so far kept to my original intention of covering the whole distance overland; but this flight didn't constitute a true part of the journey, and not to have taken it would have placed my entire project in jeopardy, so the final decision was not hard to take. It was an odd sensation to fly again after so long: the orderliness, the numbered seats, the lack of frenzied rushing – it all seemed so alien.

I had little to do with the diplomatic community on my return to Islamabad. Those I saw took great pleasure, not in my apparent failure, but in the fact that they had been proved right: it was impossible to get past the Chinese at Khunjerab. One diplomat tried to console me with a business proposition: the captain of one of his nation's ships had offered him 13,000 cans of beer – would I come in with him and help distribute them? The financial rewards were tempting, but they were counterbalanced by the severity of the punishment if we were caught. Public floggings are not uncommon: the daily papers carry lists of the names of the unfortunate victims, their crimes, and the number of lashes they will be given.

A Pakistani friend did arrange a meeting with a member of the Chinese consular staff for me, as I had nothing to lose by making another attempt at a legal crossing. We spoke through an interpreter, but I was left in no doubt:

'There are bears in the Karakoram which can kill you with one swipe of their paw,' I was politely informed.

'I'll take the chance,' I said.

The man became a shade frosty. 'If the bears don't get you, the eagles will.'

'Let them try,' I remarked.

He became more urgent. The conditions were rigorous. I would need oxygen.

'Not at 5,000 metres,' I said.

'Maybe not for you. You look in good shape physically – at the moment. But do you know that you'll need special vehicles for the crossing?'

'I didn't know that,' I said.

They began to smile. 'Ah,' they said, shaking their heads. 'Too bad. You see, you do need special vehicles.'

'But people are still making the crossing in perfectly ordinary vehicles.'

'Once in a blue moon,' they said.

'What about the Chinese Uighurs returning from the hajj?' I parried.

'What Chinese Uighurs?'

'The ones I've just met up in Pasu.'

'Impossible. There is one official delegation that makes the crossing once a year. And that is all. Anything else would be most irregular.'

'When does this official delegation leave?'

'As it happens, it is returning to China soon. But there can be no question of your joining it.'

I grinned to myself. It was on precisely this official convoy that Amjad hoped to stow me away – aboard one of the trucks.

I had no intention of sitting around in Islamabad and set about seeing if I could acquire a fake Chinese immigration stamp, and/or a Pakistani passport. The first was quite impossible to obtain, but the second seemed hopeful when I fell in with some corrupt Afghans. who were making a mint from the United Nations High Commission for Refugees on the one hand and war profiteering on the other. These men were highly impressed that I had been with Ismail Khan, and even more so when I showed them the safe-conduct, stamped and signed, that Ismail Khan had written in my passport. But when they turned up with the promised passport, it turned out to be an

Italian one. In desperation I considered taking a Pakistani bride, in the hope that this would confer her nationality on me. Finally I resigned myself to trusting in Amjad.

I required two items before I returned to Gilgit. The first was a liquor licence. It took half a day to obtain. I filled in the form in the office, entering my name as John Frederick Forsyth Galsworthy Kerry Dixon Danziger. The lazy clerk didn't bat an eyelid at this piece of cheek – which was fortunate, or I might have been refused the licence. However, he pushed the form to one side and proceeded to do nothing. I produced my fake *Sunday Times* press card and waved it about, telling him that I would write a story exposing his idle recalcitrance. He then started to hurry, telling me apologetically about his impossible workload, and how he was overworked, underpaid, suffering from stress, etc., etc. 'Liquor Licence No 91' was stamped into my passport, entitling me to purchase up to 1 litre of alcohol per month in the State of Punjab. I bought a bottle of rum for Amjad.

The other thing I needed was a pair of blue jeans, so that when I emerged from the truck in China there would be no mistaking me for anything other than a westerner with no connection with Pakistan. I found some easily and bought them for 15 rupees, which I thought a bargain. True, the zip needed replacing, and the repair cost half as much as the jeans had. Never mind.

'How much do you suppose I paid for these jeans?' I asked the tailor bombastically as he sewed in my new zip.

He gave them a tired glance. 'Ten rupees, top,' he said.

Before I left, my corrupt Afghans tracked me down with a present: they wanted to give me a hand-embroidered shalwar camise, but I thought it too extravagant, and accepted instead a wallet embroidered with bronze thread.

KHUNJERAB PASS

I returned to Gilgit with an appointment to meet Amjad by a deserted farmhouse on the edge of town. The plan was still on, but there would now be a five-day delay. I returned to 'The Tourist Cottage' – the inn I'd stayed at before, and settled down uneasily to wait.

Seven days later I felt tense. I had had no further news from Amjad and equally there was no news about when the convoy on which I hoped to stow away would be leaving. Worse, the weather was closing in. It had been over a week since the last plane had been able to reach Gilgit; the crisp air was now bitingly cold, and I fought off its effects by eating steaming hot soup. Everywhere were the delicious smells of apricots and grapes. To pass the time and to keep the circulation going, I used to go for long walks, taking care to avoid the town, where I might be noticed, and visiting obscure historic sites: a lonely Buddha carved in a rock; one of the world's longest suspension bridges; the tomb of Shah Wali; the cemetery for the Chinese roadbuilders.

Finally Amjad brought news of the convoy's departure date, but by the time he did so it was already common knowledge. My feelings towards him had cooled very slightly, though at the time I hardly dared to admit this to myself, for he was my only hope. Although my intentions were supposed to be secret, some locals suspected my plan. One recounted a similar scenario in detail, which was alarming. Another scoffed at it, saying that it was far too dangerous. His idea was for me to work as a Northern Areas Transport Company cleaner – every truck and bus has a driver and a cleaner – and within a year I might have a chance to accompany a vehicle into China. I rather disliked this plan, for obvious reasons. However, news of the convoy's departure couldn't have come at a worse moment, for my landlord, a charming man called Abdul Karim, who was rather ashamed of his un-Islamic skill at draughts, had just left for Skardhu, and had left me in charge of the inn. Nevertheless I started to prepare myself for the rigorous journey ahead. With every passing day the cold bit deeper; even in Gilgit, 4,000 metres below the Khunjerab, the temperature now rarely rose above freezing. I would have to wear every piece of clothing I had, and I would be able to take only the bare minimum of equipment – maybe just a small bag with some dried fruit, medicines, and my cameras.

Finally I was prepared. I handed over care of the hotel to one of the other guests, left a bag with much of my stuff and a note for Karim, and tried to suppress the anxiety that welled up in me. On the very eve of departure Amjad turned up, looking apologetic. He could, he explained, no longer help me. He had succumbed to what the locals call 'hot potato' and we call 'cold feet'. He did not leave me entirely in the lurch, however, as he was able to tell me all he knew about the government compound across town where the convoy was converging, and the number of trucks and personnel.

I didn't feel too bad. After all, I had half expected this turn of events, and in fact I now had as much information as I needed. I dressed in all my clothes, thermal long johns, and thermal longsleeved T-shirt, three pairs of socks, blue jeans under my shalwar, my down jacket, my patou and my mujahedeen scarf. Then I wrapped my light coil of rope round my shoulder and under my arm, attached my two carabiners, pocketed my Swiss army knife, a torch and a notebook for my journal, and put on my gloves. I must have looked like a cross between Reinhold Messner and a cat burglar.

Once the convoy arrived at Kashgar, I would have one night to leave the truck and the compound. I had memorised a plan of the city, and I had managed to acquire some Chinese currency, which would help me put some distance between myself and the town without arousing suspicion. All I could hope was that those I left behind in Gilgit and who were in on the secret would keep silent for at least 24 hours.

By 9.30 pm that evening it was pitch dark and I made my way down the hill from 'The Tourist Cottage' to the centre of town. A jeep passed me travelling in the opposite direction, but with my patou wrapped over my head, around my shoulders and down my back concealing my bag, it was impossible to distinguish me from a local. I slipped unnoticed into town. There were only a few people left in the streets, and the only light came from under the closed shop doors, in hard yellow bars. I stuck to the shadows by the side of the streets, crossing areas lit by streetlamps swiftly, watching my shadow lengthen and then recede under the hard cold light. I froze at footsteps. Was I being followed? I continued on, not daring to turn round, forcing myself to keep my pace slow. A man's shadow slowly crept up behind me, and then passed me by. As I approached the turning to the compound I was forced to continue up Jamat Khana Bazaar instead, as three figures had appeared behind me. Again I slowed, and they passed me, but just then, to my horror, a cinema unleashed its audience. They came towards me like a pack of wolves, pedestrians and cyclists flashing torches and lights as they came down Jamat Khana. I was forced to retrace my steps back along the main road as fast as I could. I hid in the dark recess between two shops, and only reemerged long after the last group had passed.

According to Amjad, where the side-turning to the compound ended a path led along the compound's outer wall. I found it all right, but it wasn't here I was to breach the wall – there was a door to a little alleyway at the back of the compound, between it and a house. I found the door and worked the lock with my knife. Once inside the alleyway I quickly closed the door and blocked it with several stones, so that I should have plenty of warning if anyone tried to come through it. I tried to scale the wall which was all that now separated me from the compound but loose stones and mortar came away in my hands, making what seemed to me a deafening row. I walked along the wall, feeling its surface for handholds, but there were none. I would have to use my rope. I weighted one end of it with a stone and threw it into the branches of a tree the other side of the wall. The rope caught there successfully. I cut a short length off my end of the rope and tied it to my ankle and to my bag. I then shimmied up to the top of the wall, using the rope that had caught in the tree. Then I untied the rope round my ankle and hauled up my bag after me, lowering it onto the other side. Then I descended. I was unable to detach the rope from the tree, but I flicked it behind the trunk where it was barely visible.

I found that I was able to roam freely amongst four of the six trucks, their drivers and cleaners fast asleep in tents some way off. To have reached the fifth and sixth trucks might have meant creating a disturbance as they were parked somewhat closer to the tents.

There seemed to be no obvious way into the trucks, so I climbed to the top of one by means of its ladder to try and find a gap in the canvas tarpaulin that covered the load inside. I soon found that the only way to enter would mean loosening the ropes which held the canvas taut; and once inside there would be no way of tightening them again. As if this didn't present a great enough difficulty, some of the fastenings had customs seals on them.

One possibility remained. The goods in the trucks were prevented from falling out of the back not by a folding door but by a series of planks. One truck had gaps between the planks and by the light of my torch I could see that the load inside was not so tightly packed as not to leave room for me. If only I could somehow remove one plank I could then climb in. I had plenty of time, so I started sawing through the end of one plank with the sawblade of my knife, but the noise proved too loud – it set off a dog barking wildly outside the main gates. Suddenly I noticed a figure by the gate, his shadow cast across the forecourt. I rolled under the truck, my heart in my mouth, unable to stifle my noisy, scared breathing. He made no movement. He was probably waiting for guards to arrive. I wondered what I could say in my defence. Most likely they'd simply think I'd been trying to steal from the trucks. I wondered what sort of sentence they would give me. But the dog's barking died away, and the figure remained motionless. Too motionless. In my nervousness, I had mistaken a concrete pillar for a man.

I returned to my sawing, wrapping my patou round the plank to reduce the noise, but already I could see that my efforts were in vain: the thing was more likely to break than free itself from its runners – and they'd be sure to notice a broken plank.

I tried another truck, and suffered a sudden shock, for as I approached the cabin, I heard the sounds of loud snoring. Short of actually cutting through the canvas tarpaulins, there seemed to be no way of getting into a truck. I had to face the bitter fact that if there was a way into China, this was not it. Wearily, I climbed back over the wall and started for home. I looked back once before I dropped into the alleyway. The engine of one of the trucks had been switched on, and the driver was sitting up in his cabin, eating. I had been just in time.

The most frightening part of the night's adventure, apart from my encounter with the pillar, was the walk home. Stray dogs darted forwards and backwards across my path, sometimes following me, sometimes remaining motionless, blocking my path. I shooed them away, but one large dog refused to move. With great trepidation I approached him, still frantically trying to shoo him away. He wouldn't budge. I was only a few metres away from him when I saw that he was an oildrum. This was a night for ghosts, and no mistake.

I reached my hotel without further incident, but I was tired and frustrated. I had been so sure of the success of my plan that I hadn't formulated an alternative, and now I had virtually no time in which to do so. The only thing I could do, having nothing to lose, would be to take the authorities by storm. Thus it was that first thing in the morning I called at Mr Yussuf's office in the compound. Mr Yussuf was the man responsible for the convoy on the Pakistan side of the border.

'I hear your trucks are leaving for China today,' I said. 'Would it be possible to give me a lift? I have all the necessary documents.'

Mr Yussuf, busy filling in endless forms, didn't bother to look up. 'No one has ever been given permission to cross,' he replied. 'You'll have to go and see the authorities.' Then he did look at me, and something must have made him relent, for he picked up his phone and dialled the number of one of the many government agencies, repeating my request, and adding that I'd told him my documents were in order. Then he hung up, having said 'Yes' rather earnestly several times.

'You'll have to take your documents over to the emigration bureau,' he told me. 'Hurry. We leave at 2 pm.'

Most of the morning had in fact already elapsed in abortive attempts to see Mr Yussuf, but I still had two hours. As I left the compound, looking so very different in daylight, I hesitated. I was risking everything. I was going to the very authorities who'd previously been prepared to arrest me. In a bid to have my visa altered to read: 'Point of Entry: Khunjerab Pass', I hurried to 'The Kashgar', one of the two Uighur restaurants in town, in the hope of finding a Uighur who would fill in what I needed in Chinese. But I would have to wait half an hour for the restaurant to open, and I knew that they were already expecting me at the bureau.

I entered the bureau where I was greeted politely.

I returned the greetings, and showed the officer in charge my documents. He looked at the visa Mrs Liu had given me in Islamabad.

'This doesn't specify point of entry,' he said.

My heart leapt. I pulled out an official-looking document written in Chinese on the Churchill Trust letterhead, complete with the usual stamps and signatures.

'Don't you have a copy in English?'

'I'm afraid not, sir.'

'Well, we don't have anyone who can speak or read Chinese.'

'Surely there must be someone.'

In the event someone was found, and the letter, which conveyed the purpose of my journey in the promotion of greater friendship and understanding between nations, seemed to pass muster. Most important was the mention in the letter of my need to follow the old Silk Road. My hands were sweating freely now. I had been handed over to an officer of the bureau who was doing a lot of telephoning, but now that he had a translation of my letter, he appeared to be satisfied. A clerk was dispatched with my passport, and we waited. I wondered if someone would scrutinise it and notice that not only were there no entry stamps in it for Pakistan, but that the stamps that were there showed me still to be officially in Iran. But within minutes the clerk was back, and my passport bore a brand

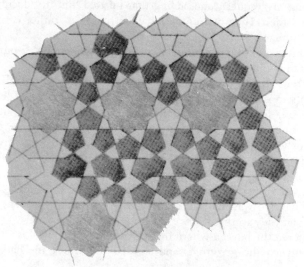

new stamp: EXIT STAMP NO. 1: KHUNJERAB PASS. It bore the following day's date as the convoy would not reach the border until then.

It was as if an electric charge had passed through my body. The impossible really had been achieved, and it had all been so quick – so simple! All I had to do now was keep a very low profile until I was off. I made my way back to Mr Yussuf's 'China Trade' office, unwisely – for whom should I see there but Mr Sa'id again. News of my visa had preceded me, for he congratulated me on it, and then drew me aside, his voice becoming confidential.

'Of course you realise that you got your visa largely through my influence?'

'I do, and I'm very grateful.'

'Perhaps you would like to show your gratitude? After all, visas can be revoked at very short notice . . .'

I sighed. 'What would you like?'

'A bottle of Chivas Regal. Or, failing that, VAT 69.'

'I may only be able to get Johnnie Walker.'

'That will do nicely.' He smiled. Mr Sa'id was the kind of small-town big fish who would go far, I thought, as I went off to collect my bag from the hotel and purchase a bottle of Scotch from one of the other foreigners staying there. Fortunately I achieved this without difficulty, and I bought a carton of Benson & Hedges cigarettes for good measure.

Mr Sa'id was waiting for me when I got back.

'Do you have the Scotch?'

'Yes.'

He gave me a wry smile, and to my astonishment began to inform me that by the powers invested in him by the Islamic Republic of Pakistan, he was arresting me for possession of alcohol.

'Hang on,' I said. 'I don't have it on me.'

'Where is it, then?'

'It's safe.'

'You do realise that I am accompanying the convoy to China?'

This was not welcome news, but I weathered it. 'Then as soon as we reach the border, I will see to it that the Scotch is given to you.'

For some reason he was happy with this arrangement – maybe it satisfied his taste for intrigue. I guessed that the threat to arrest me was just a none-too-gentle reminder of his power. Meanwhile, I had to work out a way of transferring the bottle from my bag to the truck I was travelling in without his seeing it. But in the event I managed this easily enough with the help of one of the drivers.

Finally we were off. The drive was the usual hair-raising adventure. The cold was intense, but the cabins were heated by open gas fires. I wondered how I would die: by being frozen to death or burnt alive. Our cargo was dried fruit, nuts, cigarettes and medicines, and the trucks would return to Pakistan laden with cotton prints, silk, quilts, agricultural implements and crockery. Past Pasu there were Mor Khun and Sost, and a more spartan and bleaker existence than these villages endure I cannot imagine. Already the yak was putting in an appearance, as almost the only animal apart from man that can really endure such high and remote areas. At Sost we stopped to carry out repairs to the trucks and to refuel the engines from oildrums carried above the cabins. I tried to keep to myself but I was summoned to join the customs officials, in full uniform for the occasion, and Mr Sa'id. They kept on about how lucky I was to be the first foreigner to be allowed to cross into China, and I tried to turn the conversation towards yaks and Marco Polo sheep in vain. By the time we left we were running late and in the drivers' haste to be off one of them drove over his own tool-box, crushing it. Gradually, the plain we were crossing narrowed to a gorge, over whose precipitous cliffs towering, snow-topped mountains were just visible. Dhee, the last and what must rank as the loneliest outpost of civilisation in these parts, was manned by a demented creature whose only companion was his scraggy dog. He was jubilant at the prospect of having something to do, and eagerly noted down all our number plates. When the drivers started to honk their horns in impatience, he reluctantly raised his barrier, but he let us through with a cheerful wave.

We were now approaching the border. We were climbing higher and higher, travelling more and more slowly, the road a series of hairpin bends through scenery so awesome and so forbidding that one wondered at the magnificent arrogance of the engineers who'd dared to plan a way through. And I had ceased to worry about the open gas heater. Outside the cabin of the truck, it was colder than the inside of most refrigerators.

When the road levelled out the trucks found only a little extra power in the rarefied air, and there was the added danger of skidding on the snow that covered the road in a fine blanket, though the drivers did their best to follow the tracks of the jeeps that had long since overtaken us but which would be waiting for us close to 'The Top', as Khunjerab Pass was affectionately known.

When we arrived it was not as I expected. It is not a narrow pass, but a wide open plain. There were numerous signs marking the international frontier, and two telephone pylons separated by a frontier stone. The Pakistani pylon was smart, new and metal. The Chinese one was a cumbersome wooden pole. A sign in English informed us that we were on the Chinese-Pakistan Friendship Highway. Contrary to what I'd been told by the consular official in Islamabad, there weren't any bears or eagles, and the road on the Chinese side was metalled and descended gently. To either side of it, hundreds of yaks grazed peacefully in the wide open spaces. Their shepherds, Tajiks or Kirghiz, rode among them on dark brown Bactrian camels. Because the men were wrapped in such enormous coats it looked as if the camels had three humps instead of just two.

I was in China! But I could not breathe easily yet, for there was still the question of checkpoints. The first one was manned by two cheerful young Chinese soldiers whose hands I shook with the enthusiasm of a groupie, though I remained in the cab of the truck in order not to draw too much attention to myself. Then to my dismay I saw a Toyota Land Cruiser drive up out of nowhere and disgorge half a dozen Chinese officials, who'd obviously come to greet the Pakistani officials travelling in the jeeps. They all went into the little red, orange and white checkpoint building, which looked as if it had been made out of children's building bricks, and we were summoned to join them.

The officials hugged each other and shook hands a lot, and then we all partook of a small banquet of cakes, tea, biscuits, fruit and sweets. The tea, I noticed, was not China tea, but 'tea with milk and sugar'. I continued to keep a low profile, but it was no use. I was summoned to the customs hall, where I was asked in stilted English to fill in a customs form printed on delicate, flimsy paper; the Chinese characters looked beautiful, but the questions were prosaic: how many cameras? TVs? radios? how much currency? point of entry?

point of departure? But they didn't bother to ask to see my bag, and returned the completed form to me adorned with an official stamp. I asked for one in my passport, too, but they said the scrap of paper was all I needed. Once the Customs had finished with me, it was the turn of Immigration, but they, too, couldn't have been friendlier, first sitting me down on a chair, then bringing me an armchair instead, and finally, still not satisfied, sending for a sofa. They took away my passport and my heart turned over.

'Do you know you are the very first foreigner to cross Khunjerab Pass?'

I adopted an air of incredulity. 'Really? Surely not.' Trying to give the impression that this was nothing out of the ordinary for me.

'You are, you know,' they said, filling out a form for me and bringing me tea and cakes.

I wanted to jump for joy but my whole body ached from the journey and from tension. When I returned to the vehicles I saw that one or two of the Chinese officials were looking at me askance, but the Pakistanis assured them that my journey had the full backing of their respective governments. News of that letter I'd shown the official in Gilgit must have made an impression.

'How about my Scotch?' said Mr Sa'id.

'Of course,' I said. 'It's up by the petrol tank above the cabin of the truck.'

He smiled, and sent a minion up a ladder to fetch it. No attempt to arrest me now. I was in China. Nothing could stop me now.

But as we started our engines and slowly moved out, I saw one of the Chinese officials walking towards our truck, flagging us down.

PART FIVE

Xinjiang

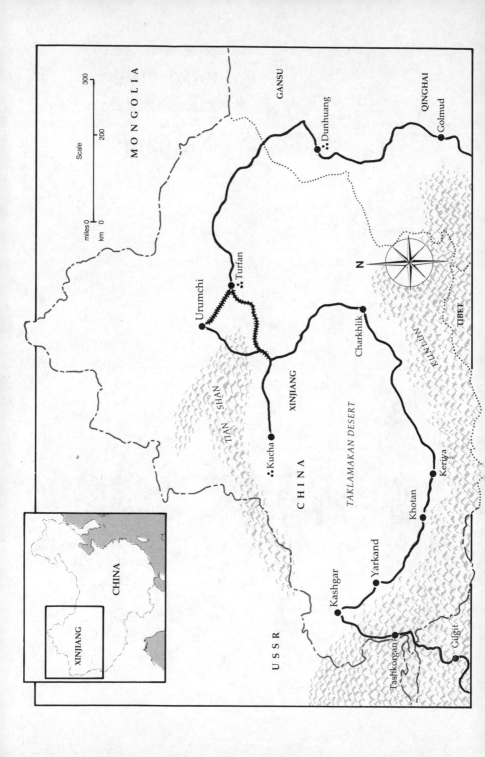

UNDER ARREST

The first truck had already started to roll forward. My driver, Abdul, had noticed the official but the truck behind ours was hooting for him to move on, and everywhere we could hear the infectious shouts of 'Chalo! chalo! – let's go! let's go!' I took up the cry, and Abdul decided to put the truck into gear, and we rolled off. I dared not look at the Chinese official, but nothing happened to halt our progress. Maybe he'd had second thoughts. Maybe he wasn't really flagging us down. Or maybe he simply wanted to ask Abdul some unimportant question about the weather in Gilgit. It had been a bad moment, and it was over. That was the main thing. We drove on and on. Darkness fell, and it was in complete darkness that we reached the town of Tashkorgan.

The hotel there was modest but clean. Each room had a coalburning stove, a table with a bowl of apples, sweets and a pot of tea; above all there was the luxury of a personal attendant, who saw to it that the stove remained fed, and who filled terra-cotta washbowls with hot water from a kettle heated on the stove.

I drifted from room to room unsure of what to do next, and indeed unsure if a room would be provided for me at all, for I was not part of the Pakistan trade mission, at least not officially, and I was not expected.

Finally an interpreter came up and explained to me with a little embarrassment that whereas 'the Pakistanis were friends', and therefore had their bills taken care of by the Chinese government, I would have to pay for my board and lodging.

'Not that you aren't a friend too,' the interpreter added, suddenly realising his *faux pas*.

I was to share a room with Mr Asharaf, the managing director of the trade mission. He was feeling the effects of the high altitude, and an oxygen bag had done little to alleviate the symptoms of altitude sickness. A local doctor had been sent for, who duly arrived and efficiently and unceremoniously injected the managing director in the bottom; but Mr Asharaf wasn't the only casualty of our journey from the border. Truck Number 8 had overturned. Fortunately no one had been hurt, except for the driver, who was dazed and badly bruised.

My own introduction to China could not have been more charming. For a start there were the beautiful and unexpected Tajik women, who, with their soft skin and their exquisitely proportioned features, combined the best of Persian and western looks. Their long hair (which they never cut) was braided into several plaits which reach lower down their backs than their buttocks, and the plaits are threaded with buttons and jewellery, and linked together by jewelled chains. All the women wear intricately embroidered hats which are tied to their heads with vivid scarves, and their clothes are an explosion of colour. Beneath their skirts they wear trousers tucked into boots. The menfolk, in marked contrast, are the image of sobriety in black, dark brown or blue; but their hats were no less colourful than the women's: most wore sheepskin hats with woollen rims, some sported canvas Chairman Mao caps, and others had wild ragged sheepskin headgear. None of this bore any relation to the China I'd imagined and I desperately wanted to stay on, but all too soon the trucks were readied for the onward journey. Repairs were carried out, for once too quickly, blow-torches were directed at the engines' frozen lubricants, and we were on the road again. There was, of course, no question of my separating from the convoy – yet.

As we approached each settlement or individual house, its inhabitants would come out and race towards us: mothers clutching babies, old men leaning on sticks, and always and everywhere, children. Some were too puzzled or too shy to wave to us, others just stood and watched us as if stupefied by the sight of us. I don't know whether it was by a conscious decision or not, but Abdul, our driver, had pulled ahead of and away from the main convoy, and we were alone when he suddenly drew up at a hamlet bordering the road. Of course the villagers had surrounded us in a flash. They gaped at our bright red truck as if it were something from outer space. A child started to decipher the Arabic script on its side:

'Pa . . . Pa . . . Paki . . . Pakis . . . Pakistan!'

The children, here as elsewhere, were a merry, motley crew, caked in dirt and dressed in rags. One thing that struck me was that there was no seam around the groin joining the two legs of the trousers they wore. At first I thought they were torn, but they all had it, and finally I realised that for lack of nappies the little ones are simply held with their legs open when they want to urinate or crap. This not only avoids the tedious business of pulling their trousers down every time, but it means that they are free to 'go' at any time by themselves without soiling themselves. But as the temperatures in these parts are sub-zero during the winter, they must have been very hardy children!

Our arrival created an immediate carnival atmosphere. The children showed off their toys – objects displaying an ingenious use of the materials they had to hand, and mostly made of bits of wire and scraps of tin, though for me the best of the lot was an origami goat whose horns and legs moved when you pulled its tail. I set about making a paper plane for them, and to my surprise not only did it fly rather well, but they recognised it and gave vent to delighted shouts of 'Aeroplan! Aeroplan!' While the children gambolled, the parents and grandparents stood at a respectful distance. Like the children, they were very poorly dressed, though their faces were open and friendly. Gradually we overcame shyness and did our best to communicate with each other, mainly through gestures.

I felt that the time had come to use the Polaroid I had purchased in Pakistan. It took some doing to get everyone lined up in a kind of family group, but I managed it at last. They gaped at the camera and jumped slightly at the little noise of the shutter release, but the immediate emergence of the photo from the front of the camera took them all totally aback. In fact my camera must have had a very vigorous ejection mechanism, for it shot the photo right out of the camera and onto the dirt road, where it lay as the villagers gathered round it. But no sooner had someone reached down for it than everyone else wanted to grasp hold of it. It was then snatched rapidly out of a succession of hands, and the scene very quickly came to look like a rugby match as the one in possession ran away from the rest. Then there was a hiatus: the picture had begun to emerge, and they all clustered round in wonder, trying to pick out who was who. However, the moment of peace didn't last long, and we were soon into the 'second half', which turned out to be even more frantic than the first, as pushing and snatching gave way to kicking and punching. I was very grateful that most of them were so well padded against the cold that they couldn't do each other much harm. In any case it was an uneven contest, dominated by a large woman who eventually gained permanent and undisputed possession of the photo, a victory which she clearly accepted as of right. I felt sorry, though, that I didn't have enough film to give everyone a photograph.

Abdul nudged me, and pointed to where a cloud of dust a kilometre away indicated the approach of the rest of the convoy. He was clearly anxious to be off before it could catch us up, and so we clambered back aboard after hasty goodbyes and left.

We remained well ahead of the rest of our group for the whole of that morning, which allowed me a wholly unexpected and completely informal introduction to the people. I was also being stuffed with food, for at two of Abdul's unscheduled stops we were invited to eat – rice and vegetables, eaten, as in Afghanistan, with one's right hand. Finally, however, we reached our official 'lunch stop', where we had to wait for the others to catch us up. No one said anything to Abdul, and I forced myself to eat the lunch, full as I was, to avoid arousing suspicion. At the lunch-stop the Chinese took the same semi-apologetic stance that they had adopted in the hotel: 'of course you are a friend too, but . . .' I paid them in dollars, which they could hardly wait to get their hands on, as I couldn't use my Chinese money because I had brought it into the country illegally.

It was not until late afternoon that we started to wind our way out of the Pamirs and out towards the desert through narrow gorges which descended to a wide, dry river bed. Darkness fell, hiding the mountains from view, but the truck's headlights picked out an unending row of poplars lining our route. Every so often we would suddenly have to swerve into the middle of the road to avoid a donkey or a cart, travelling silently along and totally unlit – a ghostly reminder of what to a westerner were bygone times. Finally, tired, travel-stained, and battered by the endless bumping of the truck, we arrived in Kashgar (to use its Uighur name – the Han Chinese call it Kashi) in the evening.

Progress through Kashgar was slow, as the streets were thronged with people returning from work in the factories. We pulled into a

large yard and were met with a reception similar to that we'd had at
the first checkpoint. After a warm welcome, we were seated around
an enormous table on which were placed biscuits, cakes, fruit and a
variety of drinks. My bones seemed to ache permanently these days,
and it was some time before the droning sound of the truck's engine
ceased to ring in my ears. I looked around at my companions, and
they all looked as weary as me. We could barely raise a smile for
our Chinese hosts. Only our drivers still looked relatively alert. I
wondered how this could be.

'They take opium. How else do you think they stay awake?' one
of the Pakistani officials informed me. I wasn't sure how true this
was, but if they were taking anything to keep them alert, it wasn't
all that effective, for just then news was brought in that another of
our trucks had come to grief – by driving off a mountainside. I hoped
for more news of this, but my attention was taken up with a more
urgent problem. The Chinese officials here were clearly beginning
to eye me with suspicion. This deepened when they asked the official
interpreter for an explanation of my presence, and he was unable to
give one. Finally one of them approached me.

'We have arranged accommodation for you at the New Hotel,' he
said. There was no reading any expression into either his face or his
voice. He merely sounded impersonally polite. But I knew that I was
being separated from my Pakistani companions, and felt that no good
could come of this.

'He can stay at our hotel for the first night, can't he?' the official
who'd told me about the drivers' drug-taking asked the Chinese
through the interpreter. 'He wants to find cheaper accommodation
of his own after that anyway.'

'I am afraid not,' smiled the Chinese official who'd told me about
the New Hotel. I became increasingly uneasy. But all I could do was
make the Chinese think that my travelling companions would be
concerned if they didn't see me again. I bade each of them goodbye
personally, taking my time over it, making our relations out to be
much friendlier than they in fact were, and telling them not to worry
about me, and that I'd be back to see them tomorrow without fail.

'If I may, I'd like to come with you to see the Commissioner of
Kashgar,' I added.

The Chinese had been watching all this fairly impassively so far, but now one interjected irritably: 'No, you won't be able to do that. What's more, tomorrow is a holiday.'

'But I have urgent business with the Commissioner myself.'

'Just come with us.'

I was all but herded out into a waiting minibus. Things didn't look too good. I had three escorts, and the situation seemed hopeless. We travelled without stopping right through the centre of town, where one would expect to find a concentration of hotels, and headed for the outskirts. I had already begun to suspect that 'New Hotel' was merely a euphemism for prison, and now I knew that my suspicions were well-founded. At least I had done everything openly: I had official sanction for my entry into China and could fall back on innocent ignorance. The worst they could do was deport me – hopefully back to England, for I don't think the Pakistanis would have been very sympathetic to me. By now we were on a dirt road. Well, I thought, at least I got as far as Kashgar, and I'm the first outsider to enter China over the Karakoram for 35 years. But it was hard to cheer myself up. We'd arrived at some high, locked, iron gates. Our driver sounded his horn.

The compound consisted of three two-storey grey buildings. At the first block one of my escorts descended from the vehicle and returned with a woman. This was a little surprising, in a prison. She boarded the van, smiled at me, and we drove onto another block. Here we stopped again and they indicated that I should get out. The woman accompanied me into the building through broad swing doors, led me down a corridor and into a room. I looked around in astonishment. I wasn't in prison, that at least was for sure, for the room I'd been admitted to was a regular hotel room, complete with all facilities, including a private bathroom, a large thermos of hot water and even a pair of slippers. I hadn't seen such luxury since leaving London eight months earlier.

The woman asked me by gestures if there was anything else I needed. I indicated 'no', and with a little bow she left me to myself. I sat on the bed to ponder my present circumstances. Was I still free? Or was I under surveillance? Maybe the bedroom door had been locked? Maybe they'd posted a guard? I approached the door silently and then opened it fast. Well, obviously it was unlocked, and outside the corridor was deserted.

I lay down on the bed and looked at the ceiling. Should I make a run for it, I wondered? Maybe I could even reach Peking and the safety of my own embassy? I considered the long, cold journey, through unknown territory for which I didn't even have a map. It was the cold that decided me. And no one was threatening me at the moment. And I was tired. And this bed was . . .

So comfortable. I fell asleep.

I was awoken by the arrival of breakfast. Rarely have I had such a feast. There was a variety of bread, honey, sliced meat, spiced vegetables, eggs and nuts; and coffee, tea or hot milk to drink. After breakfast I decided to go for a walk in the town, wrapping myself up well against the bitter cold. Nobody stopped me.

The road into Kashgar was one long uninterrupted stream of carts drawn by donkeys, little horses and a handful of camels. Some of the carts were loaded with farm produce, others carried people. They all creaked and squealed as their springless wooden frames rocked over the uneven surface of the road. Not knowing quite where to go I followed this procession, and came at last to a magical sight spread out over a stretch of open wasteland the size of several football pitches: I had come to the Sunday Bazaar. One could hardly move for the traffic, and there must have been thousands and thousands of people milling and shoving while avoiding the flow of carts. Drivers stood up and constantly shouted: 'Posh! Posh! – get out of the way!' as they nudged their carts forward to the river bank where the 'car park' was – hundreds of carts in ordered rows, their shafts all pointing heavenwards like the barrels of field-guns.

Never have I seen such an explosion of business, and as I watched I began to see order in the apparent chaos. The market was divided by section into various trade areas. In one, beautiful, brightly coloured felt Kirghiz carpets, with their bold patterns, were being sold. In another, you could buy enormous and all-enveloping sheep-skin coats. There were the hatters, the clothiers, the bakers and the snack-sellers. The bakers bake their bread in large earthenware ovens sunk into raised platforms. Beneath the platforms are charcoal fires. The baker will reach into the oven through an aperture in the top and slap an oval slab of dough against the inside, where it will stick because of the heat. When it has risen, he peels it off with a long fork and skilfully manipulates it through the small mouth of the oven. The bread is then crimped using either the fingers or with a wooden, comb-like implement. The smell of this fresh bread was delicious, but outmatched by the smell of the snacks for sale: baked dumplings stuffed with meat; noodles; cooked offal; braised goat's meat; and melons kept fresh by burying them in the cold sand: as one ate a slice, the juice would melt and run down one's beard to freeze there again, while the flesh of the melon was so cold it was like eating sorbet. Afterwards, one could warm one's hands over the kebab-sellers' hot coals.

Then there were stove-sellers, blacksmiths and carpenters, as well as saddlers – though everyone I saw rode bareback. Animals were for sale here too – camels, horses and donkeys. I was tempted to test-drive a camel, but the price was too steep for me: just over £100 each. Horses were even dearer at £200, but a donkey could fetch anything between £25 and £1.50.

For the most part people here were too busy going about their daily lives to pay much attention to me. They looked far more like Afghans than Chinese, and of course culturally they are far closer to the former. Their faces were like old leather, tanned and wrinkled and hardened by the great extremes of temperature they have to endure. The faces of the men were proud and dignified, though it was impossible to differentiate between ages unless they were very old or very young. Most of the men wore a long (or sometimes half-length) coat of black corduroy, both collarless and buttonless, and fastened at the waist with a scarf, folded in two to make a triangle and always with the apex of this triangle precisely at their back. Many wore tattered shirts open at the chest despite the freezing cold, but without exception they all had hats, and high black leather boots on their feet. Trousers were also of corduroy, and were tucked into the boots and tied at the waist with string. The old men had thin white beards, the merchants affable smiles. Although the crowd was dense, it was a friendly, companionable one.

Within earshot of the muezzin, merchants surreptitiously approached me, eager to change roubles, dollars, rupees or Foreign Exchange Certificates. The transactions were carried out in Turkish and, although I could speak neither Turkish nor Farsi well, I could just about make myself understood. Everywhere I walked I was showered with gifts of food. Just as potential buyers would take a farmer to one side of the street to feel and squeeze his sheep or goats, so people took to feeling me, stroking my beard and then holding it out for others to marvel at. Women, many of them veiled, started to feel my legs and arms. Whether or not they were satisfied with the merchandise, this practice caught on like wildfire. If I had set up a stall I could have realised a small fortune. Never in all my travels have I so enjoyed my first day in a new country. Indeed, in my exhilaration I forgot all about my predicament: I had no internal travel permits for China. However, I thought, the authorities seemed to have lost interest in me, and for the moment I had no desire at all to move on from Kashgar. Besides, the next nearest city 'open' to foreigners was Urumchi – four days' drive away. I have heard that since I was in Kashgar the Chinese have opened the town up for tourism. It will have several international hotels, and maybe even become a tax-free 'port'. At the time I was there, in 1984, I was, as far as I knew, the only foreigner, apart from a Chinese-American lady journalist, and she was only on an escorted two-day visit.

Sooner or later officialdom in the form of the local Foreign Affairs Bureau was bound to catch up with me, and it did so in the form of a fifties type of limousine, brand new and painted orange, called a Red Flag, which drew up at the New Hotel to collect me and take me to the office of Mr Chen. Despite the plethora of minority groups in Xinjiang, of which the Uighurs are the dominant one, with 45 per cent of the population, all the officials I had met so far had been Han Chinese like Mr Chen, and only one of them could speak Uighur fluently. I exchanged greetings with him, and then we settled down to business. I thought I was being summoned to explain myself, so I was pleasantly taken aback when he asked me quite mildly what my plans were. Diffidently, I introduced the idea of crossing the great central desert, the TaklaMakan.

'By camel,' I added, hoping I wasn't pushing my luck, but at the same time not wanting to pass up a golden opportunity (and here seemed to be one) of bearing an official imprimatur on all my travels in China.

'You know that "TaklaMakan" means: "He who enters shall not exit"?' asked Mr Chen.

'Yes, I've read that.'

'Crossing it will be no easy task. Nobody has ever crossed its length, in any case.' Mr Chen clearly didn't know how seriously he was meant to take my proposal.

'I wasn't thinking of crossing from west to east, but from south to north. That route would take in the desert communities I would like to visit.'

'But why do you want to cross by camel?'

'Because it will soon be impossible to do so. I know that you have a very advanced road-building programme, and soon there will be no camel drivers left.'

I produced a very simple general map of China and spread it out. I had had much more detailed maps, but had committed them as far as I could to memory, since officials in such places as China who find out that a foreigner has detailed maps of their country are apt to draw the worst conclusions. I pointed out where I wanted to go, and he showed me where tarmac roads would soon crisscross the great desert and bring the remote communities into the grasp of the rest of China.

'You will be taking a very great risk,' he said.

'That is true, but I am prepared to sign a disclaimer relieving the People's Republic of any possible responsibility for my death, should such a thing occur,' I said.

For a moment it was touch and go, and then he seemed to come to a decision and gave me a broad smile. We discussed matters further, and I was delighted to find someone to talk to who shared my enthusiasm for the venture.

'The only thing is, I will have to seek clearance for all this from Urumchi.'

'I see. Will that take long?'

'Not necessarily. But you had better have some contingency plans, in case they're less sympathetic than I am.'

'I already have contingency plans. If I'm not allowed to cross the desert, I'd like to take the road that skirts it from west to east on its southern edge.'

Mr Chen chuckled: 'You know, of course, that all of this area is closed to foreigners?'

'Yes. But the purpose of my journey is to try to encourage a gradual lifting of such restrictions,' I said cautiously.

He chuckled again. 'I will ring Urumchi this afternoon, and give you an answer tomorrow – or if you wish, you can speak to them direct.'

I couldn't believe his efficiency, politeness, and enthusiasm. It was almost as unreal as his immaculate English. This was a breath of fresh air.

Just as I was leaving he said, 'Have you visited the old British Consulate here?'

'But I thought –' I started, and then stopped, thinking it unwise to tell him I'd been told that it was now a building site.

'I'd like to do that.'

'Good. It's called the Chini Bagh.'

'What does Chini Bagh mean?'

'The Chinese Garden.'

The consulate was a mere shadow of what it must once have been. It resembled a mock-Tudor fort, with two minute towers either side of an archway that gave into a courtyard which was flanked by the main building. It has been converted into a boarding house used mainly by truck-drivers. The main building itself is no longer used, and the guestrooms are in two or three long, barracks-like huts once used by a British expeditionary force. A similar hut houses the dining hall, which is vast and austere, and dominated by enormous, sombre paintings of the heroes of communism, Marx, Engels, Lenin, Stalin and Mao, who stare down at you uncompromisingly as you eat. The lavatories were communal pits some 200 yards from the rooms. The place was good enough for me, and it only cost a fraction of what I was paying at the New Hotel. My small room at the Chini Bagh had a washbowl on a wooden stand, a thermos flask of hot water, a bed and a stove. I thought it was a room of some character.

I also went to change some money at the Bank of China. This turned out to be a room in a semi-derelict building whose front door had lost some of its glass panes. Exchange rates were chalked up on a blackboard, most of the money seemed to be stored in a small office cashbox, and the transactions were calculated on an abacus. Foreigners receive Chinese Foreign Exchange Certificates (FECs) in return for their currency. Locals use Renminbi (1 yuan = 10 mao = 100 fen). In theory, foreigners may only use FECs, but they are much in demand by locals who go to black market moneychangers for them. The moneychangers acquire their supply from foreigners who can almost double the value of their FECs in Renminbi.

Once I had transacted all my business, it was time to go and see Mr Chen to discover what Urumchi had thought of my proposals. It appeared that I would not be allowed to cross the desert, but I would be allowed to travel to four closed cities, two, Yarkand and Khotan, along the southern Silk Road, and two, Aksu and Kucha, along the northern route. The only proviso was that I should be escorted. I argued vehemently against this and eventually they gave in. We reached a compromise: they'd let me travel alone by local bus to Yarkand and Khotan, provided that I then flew from Khotan to Aksu. Flying wasn't on my schedule but I wasn't about to disagree. No foreigner had visited the places I was about to see, let alone unsupervised, since before the revolution. For the moment I let things pass: I would deal with the problem of how to reach Aksu when I came to it. In the meantime I decided to become more familiar with Kashgar, which was rapidly beginning to rival Aleppo in my affections.

The town was once a major international commercial centre on the famed trade routes of antiquity and the Middle Ages. Goods converged on Kashgar from the Mediterranean, Persia, India and Greater China, and it stood at the zenith of its fortunes from about 200 BC to AD 900. The Uighurs themselves are descended from different clans known collectively as Koek Turk (Blue Turks), who lived to the north of China and south of Lake Baikal. Harassed by the Kirghiz, they were forced to move to what is the present-day province of Xinjiang, where they were assimilated with other tribes, notably the Sak, of Indo-European descent. The Chinese (the Han Chinese, that is) have made little impact here, and the Uighurs' lives and customs are as different from theirs as those of the English are from the Indians. In the main square stands a statue of Chairman Mao, a lonely, forlorn figure covered in bird droppings. He looks out over a maze of busy streets. On every corner there is an artisan's shop of one kind or another: there are carpenters turning wood into intricate shapes on primitive lathes – the wood rotated by an instrument like a bow, the string of which is wrapped round the wood, which turns as the bow is pushed forward and pulled backwards. Then there are blacksmiths who were still making delicate repoussé *abduvars* (water jugs) identical to the ones I had seen in Afghanistan – though sadly the advent of plastic jugs will soon make this a lost art. Along the walls of the Id Kah Mosque several generations of families work side by side at a variety of trades: hatters; cobblers; cabinetmakers and saddlers; but the dominant craft in a city that depends for its transport on beasts of burden is blacksmithry. I noticed that the cobblers even fit miniature horseshoes to the heels of boots. On the steps of the post office numerous scribes sat, waiting to take down letters for the illiterate.

Medicine used to be in the hands of the mullahs, but today the local *tiwip*, or folk physician, has a rival in the *dohtur*, one trained in western medicine. Dentistry is not a developed art by our standards. They operate on the street, using pedal-operated drills, and they store extracted teeth in large glass jars. These teeth are made into dentures.

The cold makes you hungry and I was glad of the internal and external warmth provided by the Kashgari restaurants. Lunching in one of them one day I got into conversation with Adji and Ibrahim. Ibrahim was a truck-driver who told me that he took home about 120 yuan (£23) a month. He was thus a rich man, for that is double the average income. Adji was a dentist, and he wouldn't tell me what he made, though he did confess to charging 2 yuan for an extraction, and 1 yuan for a filling. After a certain amount of small talk, during which Ibrahim talked with pride about his 8-ton Russian-built lorry, the conversation turned to politics.

'Are you a dialectical materialist?' asked Adji.

'I don't think so,' I replied.

'I thought all Englishmen were . . .'

'No. We're a mixed bunch. Like you.'

'How many political parties do you have at home?'

I told them about the three main ones. They asked about the communist party in England.

'How many members does it have?'

'About 25,000.'

'And how many people in UK?'

'About 55 million.'

Their reaction to this was to look at each other merrily and then burst out laughing. So far, the conversation had been a mixture of Persian and Turkish and what few words of Uighur I had so far managed to pick up. Suddenly Ibrahim's face took on a grave expression – though his eyes still grinned – and he said, in English:

'Long live Chairman Mao!'

Then he added:

'Long live the People's Republic of China!'

That, it turned out, was the extent of his English. I asked them if they were communists, but they both answered fiercely and proudly, 'We are Muslims!'

By this time a crowd had gathered round our table, listening to our conversation with bated breath. As Ibrahim had paid me the compliment of talking to me in English, I decided to recite the one bit of the Koran I could do faultlessly: the *kalimeh*. They received this with great delight.

Food was always a good idea – at any time of day – and it was always available: kebabs, boiled offal, and mutton-filled pancakes could be had from little mobile stalls everywhere. At night, the steam from the restaurants in the main square was caught in the light of the bare bulbs hanging from the awnings. Frequently in these places I found it difficult to get the proprietors to accept money for the meal. One evening I returned to the place where I'd met Adji and Ibrahim to find it closed, but the owner's daughter recognised me and the family asked me in, insisting that I should not be sent away hungry. They greeted me like a long-lost friend, and sat me down with tea while they prepared the food – which was always made fresh before one's eyes. The dough for the noodles was rolled out on a board, and then bounced up and down in the hands, and gradually pulled out, stretched to arms' length. It's not easy to do this, as you then have to wave your arms about to encourage the elastic dough to stretch further. I saw a boy of 13 or so who wasn't tall enough to get the length right, so he had to stand on a tree stump. When they have attained the correct length, the two ends are brought together, which causes them to twist around each other. This process is repeated several times until the dough has been transformed into dozens of strips of spaghetti, when it is briefly dipped into a huge vat of boiling water, and so cooked. Finely diced meat, vegetables, white carrots which are unique to this area, and spices are added to the noodles to make a traditional local dish called *laghman*. The water in which the noodles have been cooked – *achksu* – is drunk with the frequency of tea, and like tea, it is offered 'on the house'.

I had just begun to relax properly when circumstances took a turn for the worse. I suppose I might have known it. I ought to have set off on the Silk Road again as soon as permission had been granted, but I'd been seduced by the charms of Kashgar, and now it looked as though I would have to pay for it. The border guards at Pir Ali had realised that they had been in error in granting me entry stamps and they had alerted the police here (they are called the Public Security Bureau) to apprehend me. Once I was in custody, phonecalls flew between Kashgar, Urumchi and Peking – and the upshot of them all was that I was to be deported to Pakistan. That was the very last thing I wanted, and my mind raced to find a solution to the problem, as I gave the vaguest possible answers to their questions about the circumstances in which I'd obtained permission to enter China via Khunjerab. I knew that I would have to stall the police until the Pakistani trade mission had returned, since the only practical way I could be deported would be by accompanying them. I offered to go to Urumchi, to Peking even. I considered telling them that I suffered from air-sickness in order to avoid travelling by plane. Thus I hoped to travel to Peking overland and achieve the goal of my journey in spite of it all. The worst aspect of this upset was that I was now pitted against my former ally, Mr Chen, who was not pleased to have been so roundly duped, as he saw it.

He had the British Embassy on the line.

'Who d'you want to speak to?' he said irritably.

'No one,' I replied.

'You must have a contact there.'

'No, I don't. Not every Englishman who travels abroad has a contact in each of his country's embassies.'

Mr Chen let it go at that. As he seemed to have simmered down, and as I had nothing to lose, I decided to ask whether it might not still be possible to get hold of some camels for the first part of the original journey I had outlined to him.

'Camels?' he snapped. 'You must be mad: you're being deported, and that's an end of it!'

But he was wrong. As fast as the wind had blown against me, so once again it turned in my favour. By some mysterious process my special permission to travel in the interior was restored to me. I was to learn that such a *volte face* in fortunes is nothing unusual in China, where the wind changes direction sometimes with alarming frequency. For example, one day there was an announcement on the radio that the Politburo of the People's Republic had declared the theories of Marx obsolete. Three days later, the statement was just as baldly retracted.

I continued with my preparations and in the meantime enjoyed Kashgar. I was finding out more and more about its inhabitants. Despite the fact that they live in a formally atheist country, Islam is dominant here, and even the children have a strong sense of its teachings. I was playing with some children one day, drawing cartoons for them in chalk on the top of a wooden table. When I drew a typical Kashgari man the oldest girl among the children frowned, and immediately rubbed him out. I had broken a cardinal rule in Islam – there shall be no representations of man. In other areas of their religion they were less severe. I noticed that there was more than a limited amount of alcohol consumption.

I had been here just over two weeks, and the place had whetted my appetite for more of this country. By now my preparations were complete, and, not being able to organise camels, I had bought a bus ticket for Yarkand. But the temptation to visit the Sunday Bazaar for a third time proved too much for me, and I decided to delay my departure a fraction. This meant reselling my bus ticket. Two hours before dawn I set off to the bus station to do so. I had seen the peasants arriving from the countryside around the night before: folk dressed in huge sheepskin coats and hats, with enormous felt boots. They huddled around little fires brewing tea, each member of the group contributing his share of wood. By this time most of them were sleeping, their little fires long out. With nothing but their thick clothes to protect them, the sleepers now lay under two inches of snow – curious white hillocks surrounding the ugly bus terminus. I sold my ticket back without difficulty, as there is always a large number of people travelling, and returned to town. If the country people had shown how hardy they were by sleeping in the snow, so the townsfolk, too, demonstrated a contempt for the freezing weather by going to the open-air barber shops. I stood and watched one man having his face and head shaved with deft strokes by a barber wielding a cut-throat razor. Their method was such that in the process of shaving a client they cut unusual geometric shapes in the hair which would have been the delight of a punk rocker. What were not shaved, but religiously left alone, were the white beards of the elders. These beards are a mark of dignity, and their owners are referred to with affectionate respect as *ak-sackal* – literally, whitebeards.

My decision to postpone my departure by a day was not only influenced by the thought of a third Sunday Bazaar, but also by news of an evening of song and dance at the local theatre. There was, and possibly still is, a custom among the local rich ladies to pay for a dancer to perform for them. The dancer is usually a man dressed in the costume of a woman. I heard one or two locals arguing vigorously about whether Sultan Hamid, one of the best dancers in Kashgar, was a man or a hermaphrodite, but I think I may have confused the words for 'hermaphrodite' and 'homosexual'. The ones who put forward the former argument pointed out that Hamid had a son. The others denied this vociferously. Both sides seemed to love Hamid dearly. In any case I arrived at the theatre in good time, and found that apart from myself the audience was exclusively Uighur. The lofty wooden theatre was unheated and so people took their seats on the hard wooden benches in the 'stalls' without removing a stitch of clothing, which made us a very bulky audience. I provided rather a star attraction, or perhaps I should say, a star distraction, for people milled about staring at me, and some still refused to take their seats even after an usher had remonstrated with them. However, no sooner had the curtains opened than they took their seats like eager, obedient schoolchildren. The auditorium was packed, and I found it difficult to know whether to watch the audience, whose faces lived every moment of the evening's entertainment, or the magnificently dressed cast, dancing to music which to my ears seemed exuberant and fresh.

The female members of the dance troupe were dressed in the finest silks. The brightness of their costumes matched the redness of their cheeks – which was due no doubt to the cold. Their long black plaits flew up as they gyrated and swung round their heads in a horizontal plane, their movements becoming one with the movements of the dancers' arms and legs. The dancing was reminiscent of certain forms of Indian dance, and I wondered if it found its roots in the days when this region had been Buddhist. With the more recent influence of Islam, too effusive body-movement has been suppressed, and I was told that belly-dancing (which is known) is very strictly frowned upon. It is not considered absolutely correct for a girl to choose dance as a career, though it is tolerated.

The men were dressed similarly to the women – in embroidered waistcoats and hats – but instead of skirts they wore baggy trousers tucked into boots and tied round the waist with scarves. Their shirts were baggy and loose, and their dances reminded me of those of the Cossacks. The dancing was interspersed with songs, the orchestra providing the music for all this sitting on stage with the other performers. The musicians were formally attired in suits and ties, but they also wore the traditional Uighur pyramidal embroidered cap. The instruments they played were the *rajik*, like a violin but held between the knees like a small viol da gamba; the *rawap*, held at shoulder level and strummed like a guitar; a *kanun*, like a harp, but played flat, like a zither; a *dap*, similar to a tambourine; the woodwind *sornay* and the *dutar*, a slim lute with a very long neck. The dancers occasionally played small percussion instruments themselves. The singer – clearly the local diva – was in sharp contrast to the graceful dancers. She was short and badly overweight, but her voice resounded through the hall, aided and sometimes distorted by an idiosyncratic loudspeaker system. It wasn't the only thing that was faulty; halfway through the performance, two spotlights crashed onto the stage. But whatever the show lacked in polish it made up for in the atmosphere it created. In fact, so enthusiastic did the audience become that at one point the theatre manager climbed onto the stage and ordered them to stop whistling. I wasn't sure whether he was referring to the friendly but derisory whistles that accompanied the fairly frequently missed steps, or to the ones of admiration that were given to a most beautiful girl soloist. She proved the high point of the evening for me, and I was glad to leave Kashgar with the thought of her imprinted on my mind as the last memory of the town.

THE
TAKLAMAKAN,
DESERT OF
EXTREMES

As the dawn light filtered into the spartan bus station hall, so the two mouse-hole sized kiosks opened to sell tickets underneath an enormous map of the province, showing the bus-routes crossing it. Xinjiang, the size of Iran, represents a sixth of the total land area of China, and yet it contains only one per cent of the total population. At its centre lies the TaklaMakan, one of the world's largest deserts, 900 kilometres in length and nearly 500 kilometres wide. Surrounded to the north, west and south by high mountains, and to the east by the marshy salt wastes of Lop Nur, China's nuclear testing ground, the TaklaMakan is still one of the remotest areas on earth. Xinjiang boasts some of the world's tallest mountains, including K2, and the world's second lowest basin – the Turfan Depression 154 metres below sea level. Similar to the extremes of height and depth in its topography are the extremes of its temperature. Winter lows can descend to -30 degrees Celsius, and summer highs can reach 50 degrees. As if this wasn't forbidding enough, the desert is swept by the *boran* sand and pebble storm which has been known to bury whole caravans, and which can reach speeds of 180 kph. The TaklaMakan presented the kind of challenge I simply can't resist.

There was the usual scramble to get onto the small, antique, cigar-shaped buses, but it was brought to a halt by the drivers, who called out the ticket numbers and only allowed people on in order. Latecomers had to be content with sitting in the aisles. The driver's cab, separated from the rest of the bus by a sliding door, was equally jammed with passengers, but I soon discovered that these were the chosen few, since they benefited most from the bus's only source of heat – the engine, whose hood was left slightly open to warm the driver and his favourites.

It is barely 200 km south-east to Yarkand from Kashgar, and the journey, although slow and cold, was otherwise without incident. When we arrived at Yarkand I wondered if I had done the right thing in coming. The main street was lined with drab, nondescript concrete blockhouses, whilst the avenues leading off it showed sad vistas of crumbling mud structures lining dirt tracks. No sooner had I descended from the bus than crowds gathered around me and proceeded to dog my every step. This crowd had no inhibitions at all. On my travels so far I had used my camera to photograph people only with the greatest discretion, but here I could stop, turn, and virtually hold my lens in front of people's faces without their batting an eyelid. At one point two compassionate brothers offered me refuge from the throng in their clothes stall. I could have entered their shop, but the crowd would have followed, and so I stood against their outside wall like an animal at bay. I decided to try to outstare them, but they stood six deep and the calm gaze of all those eyes was unnerving. The only jostling was from adults shooing children away in order to get a better view themselves. As the pressure increased I moved on – my presence was bad for custom as those few people who seemed genuinely to have purchases in mind couldn't enter the shop for the people around it. I walked out into the street and the crowd followed – always behind and to either side, for there seemed to be an imaginary line to my immediate right and left that only the children dared cross. They asked me now and then if I was Pakistani or Russian. I replied, 'English', but whenever a newcomer joined the throng he was told that I was Pakistani or Russian. It was apparently inconceivable that I should be English.

Most of the people were Uighurs, but there was a sprinkling of Han Chinese, and this seemed to be the pattern for the next few days' travel. I did not stay long at Yarkand, but during my time there and during the time that followed I noticed that the two communities lived profoundly separate lives. On one bus journey we pulled into a modern caravanserai and a Uighur told me that this was a lunch-stop. Then a Chinese man offered to show me the way to the restaurant and I expected the Uighur to follow us, but he didn't. I presumed he would join us later – that is, until I entered the restaurant and saw that it was exclusively patronised by Han Chinese. None of them – staff or diners – spoke a word of Uighur, so, not having any Chinese, I had to point to other people's dishes to order food.

In a matter of days I arrived at Khotan, another 300 kilometres or so as the crow flies along the southern TaklaMakan route. Here my brief honeymoon with the authorities ended. I found a hostel and checked in, but the old Chinese woman in charge was clearly troubled by my presence. One of her worries was that I would have to share a room, but I told her I had no objections. However, I'd hardly had a chance to settle in than there was a knock at the door, and a young Chinese woman who spoke English walked into the room. For a moment I thought she'd just come for some English practice, but I was soon disabused.

'I'm from the Foreign Affairs Bureau, and we have our own place for you to stay,' she told me.

'That's very kind of you, but I'm quite happy where I am.'

'No, this won't do. We have a car waiting for you.' She spoke in the firm, rather condescending and abstractedly polite manner of an air-hostess. I had immediate visions of my first night in Kashgar – a palatial room and a price to match – so I quickly pointed out that all I wanted was a simple room, nothing fancy, but she was perturbed by my presence and unused to dealing with remote foreigners like myself, and so my arguments merely confused her. She stuck to her guns and asked me to accompany her.

'We only have one type of room available,' they told me at the hotel – Khotan's equivalent of the New Hotel.

'All right, but I can only pay the price of a simple room.'

'Well, we have such rooms available, but you'll have to pay double as they are double rooms.'

'But I am prepared to share.'

'That likelihood will not arise.'

'Nevertheless . . .'

I was reminded of an incident in Argentina once when I was asked if I wanted a room for 6,000, 4,000, or 2,000 pesos. I chose the last only to discover a day later that all the rooms were identical anyway. As for tonight, my night's lodgings cost me almost double the previous day's total outgoings – 50 pence – and *that* included three meals and a bed.

It wasn't until the following day that they asked to see my travel permit, and by then I had been on several escorted tours of Khotan with Miss Chu, the official from the night before, as my guide. Our first visit was to the silk factory. Much of the silk was still produced manually here, and I asked if this was because superior quality cocoons were being used to produce superior quality silk. In fact the answer was disarmingly simple:

'The workshops haven't been fully transformed to automation,' Miss Chu explained defensively.

Khotan is also famous for its carpets and jade. The carpets we saw were of every conceivable size, and woven to traditional Persian designs, though those adhering most closely to local traditions were easy to distinguish by their free use of primary colours. The jade workshop was equally interesting. Green and black jade are found in the Kunlun Mountains to the south, and people can make a fortune prospecting for it, though it is not a secure existence as pockets of jade are difficult to strike. After the workshop, I was taken to a mosque, but Miss Chu wouldn't come in with me.

'You speak English brilliantly,' I told her.

'Thank you,' she said.

'How long have you lived here?'

'All my life – my parents moved here in 1950 – eight years before I was born.'

'So you must speak Uighur fluently too.'

'No –' with some embarrassment – 'No, I don't speak Uighur.'

I was surprised at this but soon found out that for many Han Chinese officials it is considered demeaning to speak Uighur, the language, as it were, of the natives. In fact from various little clues I became sure that Miss Chu spoke more than a little Uighur – she certainly understood it. What she was frightened of was that I might look down on her.

I was accompanied all the time. Even at mealtimes I was not free to do as I pleased. I was taken to an enormous restaurant with large tables seating eight to ten people each, but I was given a solitary table and chair behind a screen which cut me off from my fellow diners – thus eighty people filled three-quarters of the room, while I sat in solitary state in the other quarter, with only the screen and the ceiling to look at – and the waitress, of course, who was my only link with the outside world.

From here I had been told that I would have to fly to Aksu on the northern side of the desert, but neither Miss Chu nor anyone else here made any reference to this and so I started trying to find a camel driver. What I was after was someone who was prepared to make a reconnaissance with me so that I could form an impression of the conditions I might encounter. No one raised any objection to this. I explained that this would be a rare and unrepeatable opportunity for me because camel-drivers are a dying breed, as, sadly, is the Bactrian camel, whose natural habitat is slowly being eroded by man.

After some searching I was introduced to Imin Tohte. He was a proud, elderly man with an immaculate goatee and a crescent-shaped moustache. His face is permanently wreathed in smiles, and it may be that the smile has broadened since I met him, for I have heard that he now does tourist excursions into the desert.

He asked me how many camels would be required, and I explained that as all I was aiming at to begin with was a reconnaissance, I would need only one camel for myself and one for whoever might join us and maybe another for supplies. He, after all, was the expert.

He nodded. 'Meet me here early tomorrow morning,' he said.

I did as I was told and found Imin waiting for me with his son and daughter and twenty camels!

'How many of us are going?' I asked faintly.

'We four,' said Imin, and added reassuringly, 'Don't worry. Most of these beasts are young camels who'll enjoy the exercise – besides, they'd be lonely without their parents.' I think we must have made a pretty striking procession. For the first time I understood why the camel is called the 'ship of the desert'. I felt as if I were aboard a vessel bobbing up and down on the sea, and as the climate was reminiscent of the North Sea in winter it was in some ways more like crossing from Harwich to the Hook of Holland in December than riding out into one of the world's unfriendliest deserts.

On our way we had to cross several frozen streams, and at each of these Imin would get off his camel and test the ice cautiously. Once on the other side he would brush the layer of snow off the sand and then gather sand on his jacket to strew on the ice, to make the walk across safer for the camels. When we reached the last settlement before the desert proper, he sent his children back with the smaller camels. The settlement was tiny and the four camels that remained with us took up most of the track between the houses. Their bells clanked and clonked like those of Alpine cattle, and the villagers heard them and came out to greet us. Their houses were made of mud-brick strengthened with straw, just like the ones in the Bible, and their flat roofs were made of whole poplar logs. They all invited us in, and although I was pleased, I was even more pleased that it was Imin who chose whose invitation to accept, as I didn't want to give offence by refusing anyone. Everyone was terribly friendly, each man pointing to his own house and beckoning with broad smiles.

We passed through a fenced-off courtyard into a house which appeared to have many rooms. The ones we were ushered through were all small and dark. Then we entered the eating-area, which had a western type of fireplace, made of mud and decorated with a stucco of geometrical and floral patterns. Dotted around the room were sticks protruding from the walls on which a variety of hats, prayer-caps and cooking utensils hung. We didn't sit on the floor, but knelt there, our heels supporting our backs. A cloth was laid out in front of us, and bread and grapes were brought. They were the most forlorn grapes I have ever set eyes on. It looked as if a million microbes had already sunk their teeth into them. But it is impossible to refuse hospitality so humbly offered. Fortunately those grapes never did me any harm, and the rest of the meal, typical of what I'd been eating for so long, was delicious.

Finally it was time to leave, though the highly suspicious Bactrians had no desire to and we had a hard time of it driving them forward into the desert. At this point we were rejoined by one of the baby camels, who appeared suddenly on a distant hill and then scampered towards us. Clearly separation from its mum had proved too much. It was minus 20, and the snow-covered dunes with their broad, sandy crests exactly resembled huge waves. In places the dunes parted to give way to flat desert, and the snow-covered ground and white sky fused together to become one vast expanse. I would never have imagined that such uninterrupted nothingness and unceasing bleakness could be so spectacular.

Our return to civilisation was no less memorable. Knowing that they were on the home stretch, the camels regained their zest for life, stomping and chewing at the leaves and brush that protected the houses as we passed back through the villages on the desert's fringe. The baby camel, which had attached itself to the one I was riding, was full of the joy and bounce of a puppy, and its movements were so delightfully awkward and rubbery that, with its head bobbing around on the end of its neck, it seemed more like a cartoon character than a real creature. It too had a penchant for anything edible, and at times would dash off in search of something, but it would never stray too far, and would always quickly come darting back.

Once again the sound of our camels' bells announced our arrival to a village. As we passed through the village, the locals ran behind and beside us, knocking on their neighbours' doors and shouting 'An'glyalik adam! An'glyalik adam! – Englishman! Englishman!' By the time we reached the village hall in the central square, most of the inhabitants were in attendance.

Inside the building, bowls of raisins, dates, grapes, pomegranates and melons were brought. We were served hot water to drink and the woman attending me was so zealous that each time my cup was half-drunk she threw the rest away and refilled it afresh to make sure that it was always piping hot. Then the elders arrived, and took it in turn to sit next to me, their hands and faces pink from the cold, and their beards iced. Most just sat and smiled, but one spoke haltingly of a visit to Delhi he had once made, crossing the Karakoram in the days when Britain still ruled India. One or two people looked slightly askance at my beard – by their understanding I was still a bit too young to have earned the right to wear one, but this didn't lead to any unfriendliness. On the contrary, they regretted that I was visiting them so late in the year, and asked me to come back in the summer when there would be an abundance of fresh fruit. And they wouldn't hear of our leaving until we had had dinner with them.

My secret intention had always been to continue along the southern arm of the Silk Road despite what the authorities in Urumchi and Kashgar had decreed. There was little to lose in asking the authorities in Khotan if I could continue eastwards to Keriya. By now they were used to me. 'Why not?' was the almost unhoped-for answer to my request, but they wouldn't let me travel by camel, for some reason, nor did they see any reason to write Keriya into my travel permit, as I would have liked them to.

I was sorry about the camels for the bus journeys were nothing short of purgatory. So bad was the relatively short stretch on to Keriya that I almost wished I had decided to cross the desert by camel from Khotan after all. The buses' radiators were emptied for the night, and the water formed large pools of ice by morning. The radiators were refilled, but it was still necessary to warm up the motors with blow torches to get them started. During the journey, you had to move your fingers and toes all the time and at all costs, to avoid frostbite, and this took quite an effort. We traversed vast expanses of desolate terrain alternating between flat plain and rolling dune – sometimes calm as a millpond and at other times stormy as the sea. It never ceased to be beautiful, but there were moments when I was simply too cold to appreciate it.

I tottered off the bus at Keriya and immediately my luggage was grabbed by a man who ran up to me.

'Who are you?' I said, running to keep up with him as he bustled away.

'Tudi,' he replied, as if that explained everything.

He had Caucasian features, a healthy stubble on his chin, a heavy sheepskin hat that smelt strongly of lanolin crammed down over his ears, the Uighur black corduroy *chapan*, and high boots. He was sturdily built, but looked cold – I assumed that he'd been waiting for the bus for some time. I was completely mystified by his welcome.

'Are you taking me to the *mihmankhana*?'

'Guesthouse. Yes. But not first.'

'Where then?'

'Follow me.'

I had no choice, if I was not to lose sight of my luggage. Apparently word of my arrival had been sent ahead of me by Miss Chu, for Tudi led me straight to the local County Headquarters. I stood in the hallway of the bunker-like building whilst my escort went into one of the rooms that led off it. Then there was a sudden flurry of activity not unlike the kind of scene you find in old farces, with doors opening and shutting and people scurrying in and out of them like mice. This was followed by a short period of total calm. Then the door which Tudi had gone in through first opened, and he beckoned me in. All the county leaders had assembled there in a long line. They greeted me warmly as I passed from one to the other, shaking hands. My visit was clearly a great event for them and they had thought of everything to make my stay pleasant. They had reserved the best room at the guesthouse for me, and they had asked the English teacher at Yutien County Number Two Middle School to act as my interpreter.

Li Shaoming was in his early forties, and like many Han Chinese he seemed ill-suited to the local conditions. For a start it was a constant battle to stay warm, and he wore at least six layers of clothing: T-shirts, shirts, a couple of sweaters under a jacket, and several pairs of long johns under his trousers. He told me that he was from Wuhan in Hubei Province, and, like many of his colleagues, he had been lured to this remote area by the higher wages which are paid to those willing to endure the climate and the isolation. Thus it was that Li Shaoming was paid 60 yuan a month (about £12) – double what he would have earned in Wuhan. On the other hand, such Chinese basic foods as pork were more expensive here than there.

'How did you get this job?'

'I answered an ad in the local paper. It's a three-year stint, and it's a chance to save some money. There's nothing much to spend it on here.'

'But what made you come?'

'Well, I am divorced, and the only family I had after that was my mother. She died shortly after I came out here, but I couldn't afford to return for the funeral.' He shook his head sadly. Many Chinese who come to these remote parts are unmarried, although conversely in the farthest-flung territories they tend again to be married couples or families. Through talking with Li Shaoming and others I discovered that China is suffering from one of the west's major sicknesses – that of unemployment. Jobs are hard to come by, and many men's wives are unable to find work. They are resigned to the fact that it may take them up to two years to get a job, but since there is no social security in China they have to rely entirely on their family. The Han Chinese in the outer provinces live lives hermetically sealed from the 'natives' – rather as the British did formerly in their colonies; one teacher I met had been in Keriya for six months and still did not know the town was called by that name in Uighur. All he knew was the Chinese name for it – Yutien. Education was segregated too. The Han are taught in Number Two schools, and the Uighurs in Number One and Number Three schools.

I was taken to see the local sights. They had hoped to show me the hydro-electric plant, which was the town's pride and joy, but unfortunately the river had frozen over and so my visit had to be postponed.

'Is there anything you'd like to see?' Tudi asked me.

'Well, I've heard that there are the sites of some ancient Buddhist cities not far from here. Would it be possible to visit them?'

'But they are in ruins.'

'Yes, but even so –'

'And they are in the desert.'

'I know, but –'

'Look. They aren't like the hydro-electric plant, you know. They are just a collection of old buildings. You don't want to bother with them.'

And that was that.

During the evenings my room at the guesthouse resembled a doctor's surgery. A constant stream of locals (all Uighurs and nearly all men) kept on arriving, generally in groups of four or five. They came to stare and to talk to me, each group waiting patiently outside until it was their turn for an audience with the Englishman. When they came in they entered the room humbly, taking their seats still swathed in their coats, though some removed their sheepskin hats to reveal plain skullcaps underneath. Then they introduced themselves and the other members of their group: 'This is my son, my cousin, my nephew, my brother's sister-in-law's father' – all offered endless greetings. I offered tea in return, in the Uighur fashion, first pouring hot water into a cup, then swilling it around, and emptying it onto the floor before filling it with tea. But few accepted, and at first they would remain silent, taken aback, not knowing what to do with me. My beard was a great source of fascination, since it grew much thicker than theirs. A man in one group stared at it for a long time, frowning in a 'where have I seen that before' kind of way. Finally his face cleared and he pointed, exclaiming,

'Marx! Karl Marx!'

The ice being thereby broken, I quickly acquired the nickname of Marx. Then came the questions. In a rush. I had come to learn Uighur quickly not because of any skill on my part but because I heard it spoken day in and day out. Also, I was learning just a slice of their vocabulary – enough to get by and to answer the questions I was always asked, but by no means enough to start conversations of my own. It was the same with the Turkish, Persian and Dari I had learnt – all of which languages were now giving way to Uighur, with which they had linguistic connections.

'How much do you earn?'

Before telling them what I thought the average British income was I explained carefully that the cost of living was far greater than theirs. They nodded sagely, but when they learnt that the average Briton earns fifty times what the average Uighur does, they forgot all about my careful preface and immediately started to enthuse enviously about this fabulous Eldorado to the west.

'No, no,' I would say. 'It seems much, but remember that bread costs about 60 pence a loaf.'

Again they would fail to make the connection.

'Nobody could afford that,' they would say. 'You poor people. You must all be starving.'

Sometimes this could be frustrating.

When I spoke to them about the war in Afghanistan they immediately demonstrated solidarity with the mujahedeen, but this developed into a general philosophical support for ordinary people everywhere, and a mistrust of governments, regardless of what they were. The religious belief of the Uighurs seemed to me to be profound, but less fanatical than that of some of their brethren in Iran, Afghanistan and Pakistan. The Uighurs are mistrustful of infidels. Many dream of doing the hajj, now that it is permitted, and many families are desperately saving money to send their fathers to Mecca. However, devoted as they are to Islam, few are fully versed in the concepts and practices of the religion, as I noticed when I saw them at prayer, which at times they only seemed to half remember the rite for. Those of them who had actually performed the hajj had returned with a newly acquired taste for radios, watches, and absolutely anything electronic; but these superficial trappings of the West had not altered their own attitudes or affected them with new attitudes. The girl who prepared my room at the guesthouse was greatly amused when I told her about some of our customs. The one she greeted with the most giggles was that of a man and a woman sharing a double bed. I was very touched by the open, innocent laughter of the young Uighur women, and maybe it was a combination of the lack of female companionship and the local women's natural, fresh cheerfulness that almost led me to accept one man's offer of his daughter in marriage – at least, that is what I thought he was offering me. Later on this same man followed me from Keriya to Niya. There I found out that what he was actually offering me was a prostitute.

Such was the generosity of the people of Keriya that my stomach began to groan again – this time because it was too full, for no sooner had I finished a meal in one house than I was bustled to another to eat again. I ate up to five meals a day at my peak. One man waved aside my feeble protestations that I was too full by saying that the food would be easy to eat as his wife had diced the meat and lettuce very fine. For emphasis he mimed the action for me. I crawled home from days like this to face dinner at the guesthouse, which I couldn't refuse either, for fear of offending the well-meaning cook. To give some idea of what I had to contend with, on one occasion he had prepared no less than six different lamb dishes for me: lamb dumplings, lamb with vegetables, lamb on the bone, lamb kebabs, minced lamb, sliced lamb. As if this wasn't enough, they were accompanied by half a dozen further dishes, and the lot was washed down with a sweet wine from the Turfan Oasis. Even when the meal was over, there was no escape, for the wine was followed by Chinese brandy, which was perhaps marginally worse than my yardstick for unspeakable liquor, namely Iranian 'rocket fuel'. One evening was especially bad. Tudi turned up after dinner and decided that we would have a drinking session together. He raised his glass of brandy in a toast. Naturally I followed suit. We both downed our shots in one go – for me at least, this was the only way to drink it – but no sooner were the glasses empty than they were refilled. Tudi waited politely until I was ready for the next toast, and then he raised his glass again . . .

An audience inevitably gathered. I was determined not to be outdone, and male pride coupled with thoughts of *padishah* and country to raise my flagging will. I don't know how many toasts were drunk, but towards the end I seemed to be floating in a miasma of brandy fumes – probably only marginally less poisonous and intoxicating than the stuff itself. As shot after shot was drunk, so the attendant crowd cheered us on, but in due course the cheering blurred into a drone, and sounded as though it came from far away. Across the reeling room I could still see Tudi sitting opposite me. He seemed far away too, though if I reached out I could touch him. The only trouble was, I couldn't trust myself to reach out.

The outcome was a draw because the drink gave out before either of us did.

I was in danger of becoming complacent. For the moment at least I was on good terms with the authorities and there would be no danger to compare with what I had already faced in Afghanistan. I had no desire to move on, but I felt that I had to – my daemon was driving me again, and the call of the uncharted regions ahead of me was becoming stronger with every day that passed. The local officials were even anxious to help me on to my next staging post, the town of Niya, again some 100 kilometres east, and slightly north. The local police wished me a pleasant journey – if that was possible under such weather conditions as we were having. My hosts were embarrassed to ask me for money for my lodgings, which in fact came to only 2 yuan a night. As for the princely meals I had had at the guesthouse, I almost had to force them to accept the money, which was 1 yuan and 15 fen for full board. The whole amount thus came to just under £1 per day at the official rate of exchange. As far as I was concerned there was only one fly in the ointment, and his presence was kindly meant: they had asked Li Shaoming to accompany me as my interpreter. He was so delighted at the prospect of travelling with me that I concealed my annoyance, but once we were on the spartan bus it soon became clear how badly the unhardened traveller suffers on such journeys. Even with the many layers of clothing he had on he was clearly in agony from the cold, and he wrapped now this, now that part of his hunched body in an extremely long scarf he had brought with him, constantly moving his arms and legs, and sitting on his hands. Finally he wrapped his scarf around his head, which must have caused him some humiliation as it is the fashion for Uighur women to do so and Shaoming was a Han Chinese man. To make matters worse, the other passengers laughed at him, but he ignored their mockery. There can be no false pride when it comes to riding in those mobile ice boxes they call buses.

We arrived in Niya later than we had expected, but our official reception committee was still there waiting to meet us, and a huge feast had been prepared in our honour. I came to the conclusion that the Chinese are as keen on cooking as the French, for the chefs took great delight and pride in their creations. After we had eaten, I spoke to some of the local county leaders, who had come along expressly to meet me, which was ironic in view of the fact that I was now well into forbidden territory as far as the authorities in Kashgar were concerned. They had laid on the best room in the guesthouse for me, but I had had enough of luxury for the time being and so the following day I opted, perhaps foolishly, for I did not wish to offend them, for a more humble inn.

The further I travelled from Kashgar, the more primitive the conditions became. The toilets by now were open-air pits full of excrement and covered by boards laid crosswise, along which you had to totter if you wanted to crap, squatting balanced precariously with one foot on each of two planks, your business section poised in between. There is no sense of privacy or shame in performing these natural functions; indeed the toilet was a forum for discussion – used by the locals here rather as the ancient Romans used their baths. However, these delights are an acquired taste, and after only a short time in Niya I decided to press on eastwards. It was better in any case to keep on the move, for woe betide me if fate should catch up with me, and so far I was clearly one step ahead of it – if it was pursuing me at all, for I had no idea how efficient Chinese internal communications were. I did not, however, wish to put to the test the tempting idea that I was too unimportant for them to bother about.

Few vehicles travel east from Niya, but I discovered that there was a twice-weekly bus service on to Charchan. I took leave of Shaoming, who could barely face the journey home, let alone travelling even further on, bought my ticket, and presented myself at the tiny, dilapidated bus station.

Once on the bus, everyone readied themselves for a new ice age. Sheepskin coats were placed on the hard benches so that people could sit cross-legged on them. Then more coats were wrapped around the legs, tucked in and held in position with a third. Tiny babies, travelling with their parents, were tucked in between sheepskin coat and human skin for maximum warmth. Food, in the form of bread, was placed inside the coat too to prevent it from freezing hard. The women wrapped their scarves round their heads in such way that only their eyes could be seen, but here they did it in the interests of warmth, not Islamic modesty. Having thus turned the bus into a comfortable igloo, we left, but we had only reached the centre of town when it broke down. It was to be a 27-hour delay, during which the driver carried out his own repairs in the courtyard of the inn where the bus had come to rest, a Herculean task which occasionally required passengers to assist in manoeuvring the engine block. During the delay everyone showed much concern over my well-being, and, as had often been the case earlier in the journey, I was provided with my own room, though in this case it didn't automatically guarantee any privacy, since everyone wandered from room to room anyway. My travelling companions were also very concerned that I didn't have a sheepskin coat, but I reassured them by showing them my down jacket. They had never seen anything like it, and became fond of feeling and squeezing it. I don't think they really believed that it offered as much protection from cold as I said. On learning that I had no wife, one or two of the men suggested with grins that I should marry, thus solving the problems of celibacy and cold at one stroke. This set the women giggling like mad, because it seemed that the men had already singled one of them out for my bride.

It is a two-day journey from Niya to Charchan, always with the desert to our left and the distant Kunlun Mountains to our right. There was a fire in the bus that had everyone screaming, and caused one young man to jump overboard. There was a stopover at a remote settlement called Andirlangar – a collection of huts into which the sand had swept in drifts. They looked like beach huts, but there the resemblance between this place and the seaside ended. To move from one building to another, you had to lean into the wind, and your feet would sink immediately ankle deep into the soft sand. At night when we stopped the silence was total. People would wander a little way into the desert but they soon came hurrying back to the group, scared by the silence, the isolation. For all that, the desert was frighteningly enticing.

Charchan lacks beauty. I stayed in a cheap guesthouse that was nothing more than a concrete slab among other concrete slabs, and here I searched for a lift. In fact the town was rather like a Wild West frontier town, with simple one-storey buildings describing a main street. It was invaded by sand, and the only transport was the donkey or the bicycle, although long-distance lorries trundled through. Once more I was given a warm welcome, and in the course of my stay there I even played football as a substitute player for the local school. But the days passed, the local authorities became nervous at my continuing presence (to be fair, they did their best to find me onward transport), and it was clearly time to be going. My chance came when a group of lorry drivers offered to take me roughly north-east to Charkhlik.

Before setting out we sat down to a veritable feast – yet one more banquet – in a restaurant whose one room served as workplace, kitchen, and living quarters for the restaurateur and his family. Yet again I found myself downing Chinese brandy, as I had done with Tudi, only the odds were now stacked against me – there were nine drivers and I had to take turns with each of them individually. It wasn't fair.

'*Ganbei* – cheers!' I slurred for the umpteenth time. I tried desperately hard to remain *compos mentis*, but suddenly I found that I was alone at the table – the others had disappeared. My stomach turned over. My bags were already in one of the trucks. They had left without me. I ran out of the restaurant and bumped into one of the drivers, who had come back to collect me. They'd simply waited for me to finish my meal in peace.

I clambered none too steadily aboard the truck, relieved that my stomach is fairly tough. The cab resembled the cockpit of a DC3 – only there wasn't even one square inch of spare space here. It was barely ten in the morning and I was drunk – a pity, as I had hoped to drive the truck. It wasn't until we were headed towards the Kunlun Mountains as they curved north-east that I began to return to my senses. We skirted the foothills of the range before turning away into the sand. The sand obliterated the track until suddenly we, the last truck in the convoy, became bogged down in it. The driver engaged low gear and tried to move forward slowly, but despite all his efforts the drive wheels flew vainly round. Finally we managed to extricate ourselves by using two long wooden poles which were carried

for this very purpose. I think it's beyond doubt that the reason this route remains closed to foreigners is simply that China is concerned about the spartan living conditions here, the lack of transport, and the dangers which might occur on breaking down.

We reached Charkhlik by early evening. The tiny, filthy guest-house was run by a most unsavoury character. I wondered if the neglected state of the inn was due to the amount of time he spent spying on his guests. The first thing this objectionable person did was make it plain that he'd need a bribe from me if I didn't want him to denounce me to the police. Unfortunately for him he'd jumped the gun, for so treacherous was his nature that he'd already called them. This saved me the cost of the bribe (which I wouldn't have paid anyway), but the young policeman who arrived was unsure what to do about me. The lorry drivers assured him that I was a bona fide traveller, but he refused to be calmed, and remained uneasy and agitated. The easiest solution for him was to get me out of town as soon as possible, and unluckily for me the lorry-drivers provided the means of doing so. I say unluckily, not because I especially wanted to stay in Charkhlik, but because I wanted to head east from here to Dunhuang. The drivers were going north.

I explained my problem to the policeman, but he shook his head firmly. As long as I was off his patch, he'd be content. That much was clear.

'Besides,' he added for good measure, 'the road to the east is in bad repair. And no one's going east. Why, there've been people at this inn waiting five days and more for a lift in that direction.'

The thought of five days and more in that noisome hole was a little more than I could stand. In any case, I had no choice. We would all overnight in Charkhlik. The innkeeper spent his evening shadowing me.

But I was nervous, truly nervous, for the first time. I had never heard of the town the drivers were taking me on to, and though they did their best to reassure me, my instincts told me to stay on the alert.

The road north bisects the TaklaMakan and the Lop deserts. The latter is the driest area on the Eurasian landmass. It is a wasteland of shifting sand, where temperatures can reach 50 degrees Celsius, while the relative humidity remains at zero. The desert is lashed by sandstorms up to eighty times a year, and winds attain hurricane-like speeds. Although we didn't encounter anything quite so ferocious, the first part of our route did lie across desert. It gave way to a desiccated forest, where the drivers collected dead wood. During the work we all became covered with dust and sand. Then on again, until finally we reached fertile land – land reclaimed from the desert through a network of canals and sluices which at the time I was there were dry, but which stood ready to channel the waters of the Tarim River, which was fed by snow from the Tian Shan mountain range. Around this fertile land were the great shoulders of the sand dunes, soaring to several hundred feet in height.

I had been too busy to notice Christmas and New Year, but the cold reminded me that we were now into January. One chilly evening our convoy of three lorries arrived at its destination – the small town of Yuli. I got out of the cab of my lorry, stretched, and looked around a little helplessly. .

'You want the hotel?' asked one of the drivers.

'Yes.'

'Over there,' he said, pointing. 'We'll come back tomorrow and see if we can be of any help.'

'Thanks.'

I walked across to the hotel and asked about a room.

'How much do you want to pay?' said the receptionist.

'Um – I don't know.'

'Ten yuan?'

I was taken aback by the amount – about £3. 'Less, much less,' I answered, horrified.

'Five, then?' she asked, challengingly.

'No, less,' I said.

Finally we agreed on three yuan, but I knew that that was still more than the official price. The hotel was a modern one, built on two storeys. It seemed too grand for the town it was in. I should have smelt a rat, but the Chinese name of the town – Yuli – didn't give me any clues.

There was certainly nothing grand about the second-floor corridor, which had been turned into an ice-rink, from the Chinese practice of throwing the used water from your washbowl out of your door. In this climate, it instantly froze. I skated to my room.

Two of my truck drivers returned the next morning to help me get a bus ticket for Korla, a slightly larger town some 50-odd kilometres to the north, on the easternmost point of the Silk Road that skirts the northern edge of the TaklaMakan. But a walk to the bus station was thwarted by the apparently chance arrival in the hotel reception of two policemen. Within minutes, however, the place was swarming with police, and I was in trouble again.

I wasn't too upset at being caught. I had been on a winning streak; I knew that in time they'd catch up with me, and I'd had a good run for my money. I was preparing myself to parry what I expected to be the usual round of questions, when it occurred to me that these police weren't the same kind of rural easy-going types I had encountered in the other towns so far. They were very efficient, and they didn't look at all amused by my presence. Nevertheless I produced some of my documents, but these were waved aside. A lot of telephoning went on, and police came and went with messages. Finally I saw that they were preparing to charge me formally, but as I can't speak Chinese I asked them to translate it into Uighur. It was when I heard the Uighur name for Yuli that the penny finally dropped.

Yuli was Lop Nur – not just any 'closed' city, but the main staging post for the nuclear testing grounds!

If I'd been standing up I think I would have needed a seat. Would they believe it was an innocent mistake – which, for once, it genuinely was? More seriously, how could I explain my presence here in the first place – since I had travelled along a route which the Kashgar authorities had specifically forbidden me to use? However, it appeared that they were not interested in hearing any explanations from me. I was to be sent to Korla for questioning. Their mission seemed to be to remove me from the town as fast as possible. But there was a problem over transport. I was eventually led to a waiting local bus. Were we to travel to Korla by bus, I wondered. My escort gestured that I should board, but when I did so they did not follow. I couldn't understand it – were they now setting me free? But then I saw another policeman running towards us and my heart sank. Fresh orders, no doubt. They'd probably haul me off and imprison me. He ran up breathless and beckoned me. Reluctantly I came to the door of the bus.

'When you get to Korla, you are to report to the police station there,' he said.

This was a relief. For a moment I toyed with the idea of not doing so. I knew that Korla was a busy, modern city, and it might be possible to lose myself there. But as I thought it over on the short journey I decided against it. The risk was too great, and if I was caught, that would certainly put paid to the rest of my journey.

When I reached Korla, however, I had the greatest difficulty in finding the police station. When I eventually did, it was not the imposing building I might have expected but a tiny place sandwiched between tall office blocks. I was amazed at seeing these familiar constructions; I had grown unused to them, not having seen one now for six months or so. I knocked on the door humbly. It was opened by a constable who seemed rather surprised to see me, but who let me in.

'I am Nicholas Danziger,' I told him.

He looked blank, and picked up the telephone. A couple of minutes later he was joined by a superior officer, who gave me a smile of polite enquiry.

'What can we do for you?' he asked.

Clearly neither of these two policemen had the remotest idea of who I was, or where I had come from. I didn't see the point of illuminating them – after all, I had done what the police in Lop Nur had instructed me to do. And I would probably be in enough trouble just by being here – for Korla is another 'closed' city. Even so, I'd far rather take the rap for being here illegally than for being found in a high-security place like Lop Nur, for if they decided that I was a spy in such a place, they'd lock me up and throw away the key. I reverted to my old tricks – documents, protestations of innocence, and so on. The officer remained pleasant.

'You have broken the laws of the People's Republic,' he told me. 'There will be a fine of 100 yuan.'

'But I haven't got that kind of money!' I protested.

He shrugged. 'You must pay. Or we will have to lock you up.'

'How long for?'

He sized me up. 'One week,' he decided.

Relieved, I picked up my bag. 'All right – let's go.'

'Wait! You can't do that! You must pay the fine!'

The argument continued for some time, but in the end I managed to wear the policeman down and we hit upon a compromise: I would be lodged in the best hotel in town, but I would not be allowed to leave my room, and I must depart first thing in the morning. I began to think that to admit to having an unofficial stranger in their towns was more than all these policemen could stand.

I was the only guest at the hotel, which was brand new, and which had been built to accommodate Chinese scientists and, in the future, scientists and geologists from abroad who wish to prospect for oil in the TaklaMakan. It is in anticipation of this activity that roads are being built so busily, and hotels such as the one I was now in are springing up.

The car that had been arranged to take me to the railway station the following morning failed to turn up, so I spent a frustrating day lounging around the hotel, unable to explore the town for fear of falling foul of the law. However I was not bored, for the staff were very friendly and pleasant. Many of them were Mongolians, with high cheekbones, rosy cheeks and round, open faces. They wore tall hats in luminous colours with polka dots, made of some kind of synthetic material that looked like deep-pile carpet.

In the end the police got themselves organised and I was put on a train heading for Urumchi. Korla is the most westerly terminus of the Chinese railway, and the station was packed. Police searched passengers for benzine, which they may not transport. We were crowded together behind barriers and there was an atmosphere of anticipation, as at the start of a race. Loudspeakers announced the departure of the Urumchi train, the barriers were lifted, and the mob surged forward in a frantic scramble for the carriages. Seats were claimed with the delight and vigour usually associated with people who reach the North Pole or scale a peak.

The journey, much of it at night, was fairly comfortable, but I was disappointed at having to miss the spectacular scenery we were passing through. I could just about make out the massive forms of great mountains under the starry sky. The line from Korla to Urumchi goes through nearly thirty tunnels, of which one is the longest in China. Another has an entrance which is 47 metres lower than its exit. The line also crosses 110 bridges. My fellow-passengers' generosity and concern for my welfare were limitless. One family insisted that I dine with them. The dining car was quite a surprise, reflecting not modern utilitarianism, but Edwardian splendour. I felt guilty that the family, unable to afford an additional dinner, shared with me what they would otherwise have eaten between themselves, but there was no question of my chipping in. I was grateful for the food, and for the distractions the other passengers provided, for the journey, which is over a distance of about 400 kilometres, took 23 hours.

URUMCHI – KAFIR CITY

It was early morning when we pulled in to Urumchi, and the temperature in the streets registered minus 30. This is the capital of Xinjiang, and it was the first real town, in the modern, western sense of the word, that I had encountered for a long time. The streets teemed with people; there was a rush-hour; there were traffic-lights (although they were manually operated); there were urban buses; there was noise and there was even, to a certain extent, pollution – though the rarity of private motor cars means that traffic jams are unheard of, and the countryside hadn't been entirely stamped out even in the centre of town, as flocks of goats and sheep mingled with the office workers. The ideas of a poor and backward nation which I had been building up during my travels around the TaklaMakan were shattered at one blow by Urumchi. Now that I had emerged from the rural backwoods, I could see the other side of life in China, and the two sides were a world apart. Dozens of government department stores offered everything for sale from Japanese stereo systems to Suzuki motorbikes. If you could afford it, you could buy yourself a videocassette recorder – though they cost 10,000 yuan – the equivalent of 12½ years' wages for a farmworker.

The very air of the city had a different charge: there was an all-pervasive dynamism about the people, and that was little wonder, given the material incentives which surrounded them. Only the prices inhibited the attraction of all those carrots, but, given hard work and the resultant economic growth, people could imagine earning enough, perhaps one day soon, to be able to afford them. On every side symbols of the new China were shooting up: offices, conference centres, hotels – and the many building sites testified to more to come.

Urumchi is an 'open' city, and here, where there is no excuse for not knowing the regulations, I had little choice in the way of hotels. There are three types: one for the Chinese, one for the Overseas

Chinese, and one for foreigners – the prices rise with each category, and while the Chinese can usually stay in a hotel open to foreigners, the reverse is not possible. Within the hotels there is a two-tier price system – one for Chinese, and one for foreigners. The Chinese pay in Renminbi, the foreigners in FECs – although people like me who are prepared to be politely belligerent can sometimes pay in Renminbi.

The Kunlun Hotel was built in the fifties with the help of the Russians. It retains the style of the grand pre-war hotels, having an enormous marble lobby complete with fitted carpets and columns. I'd elected to stay here in the cheapest way possible – that is, in a dormitory. This dormitory wasn't the sort I'd been used to – stone floors and dozens of pallets – but a small carpeted room with four proper beds. Each floor had its own attendants, who were all charming and efficient. For the first time since I had arrived in China I had the great luxury of running water round the clock, though I have to say that apart from the sheer pleasure of being able to take a shower, I would not by now have missed it. I was glad to be in such a comfortable place, because the prospect of going out exploring the city in the kind of temperatures found outside was grim indeed.

'Why is Urumchi called Kafir city?' I asked someone on my floor.

'Who calls it that?'

'I've heard it called that by Uighurs in all sorts of places – Kashgar, Yarkand, Keriya . . .'

He smiled slightly. 'The Uighurs are Muslims. This city's population is something like 85 per cent Han Chinese. We are unbelievers in their book. That's why.'

'How big is Urumchi?' I asked, because it seemed stupefyingly large to me, but I had lost all sense of proportion about cities, having been out of them for so long.

'About a million people live here.'

The 15 per cent who are not Han Chinese are made up of people from most of the minority groups. Partly because of them, the modernising influence of Urumchi still only goes skin-deep. Old traditions persist, even now, 35 years after 'Liberation'. A government official in Urumchi told me that certain outlying areas are still prone to fall back on the feudal system of local government that existed under the emperors. 'Under the Mao cap there's still a Muslim skullcap.' Similarly, there is still a flourishing market in traditional medicines, which include bile of bear, and market stalls are stocked with medicinal herbs, of which there are a hundred varieties in Xinjiang: asafoetida for flatulence; safflower; fritillary bulbs, and so on. More outlandishly, alongside the bear's bile, you can buy snakeskin, rhino horn, bears' paws – and I saw a peculiar array of dried rodents of some kind.

Big cities have their drawbacks. I fell in with a group of Uighurs from the south who had come up here to seek their fortunes, but who were homesick for the life they had left behind them. I have come to understand the security that only small provincial towns and villages can offer – the closeness of the community there, so claustrophobic for city-dwellers, can be wrapped around you like a protective blanket. These Uighurs found Urumchi impersonal and uncaring. But they could not leave, and they had become bitter. They complained about the worldliness of the Urumchis; they were distressed that women walked around unveiled; they drank too much.

It was in the tiny back-room of a capmaker, hung about with cardboard templates and shapes, that served both as workroom and bedroom, that I first heard whispers of sedition – of a Uighur nation. Nine or ten of us were gathered round the *kang*, which is a kind of brick bed heated by a fire underneath. Apart from myself, and a middle-aged man and a boy who never stopped cutting and stitching the material for the caps, all those present were merchants. They asked me about the bullet-talisman that hung around my neck, that I had been given by Ismail Khan's Jamiat at parting. The word 'partisan' entered the conversation, and lit a small flame in them which turned into a blaze as the conversation progressed. Few Uighurs are aware of the Afghan War, and if they are it is as remote to them as, say, the troubles in El Salvador are to us, but those present on that night understood well the implications of the struggle their Muslim brothers were engaged in. They had personal experience of being at the mercy of superpowers, for did they themselves not know families which had been split up for twenty years because of closed Sino-Soviet borders? What they were aiming for was a multi-party state, to include an Islamic representation. However, I wondered whether any of their talk would ever find form as action, for while they were very good at rhetoric when it came to politics, their rhetoric was even better when it came to business. Only one of them, younger than most of the others, seemed to have really developed political thinking. His name was Parhat, he was clearly a man of great wealth and influence, and his dream was of a crusade against the Chinese.

'I know weapons are freely available in Pakistan,' he confided. 'Now, if only I could organise the transport . . .' He was well versed in Uighur history, and he identified particularly with the recent Uighur hero Ahmet Jon, who had fought successfully against the Kuomintang.

But I heard of him again six months later. He had not left for Pakistan to buy Kalashnikovs and start a revolution after all, but gone south to Shanghai and Canton to extend his business empire.

But if there were tensions between the races in the town in general, there were none at the Dance Academy, where ten nationalities, including Han, worked enthusiastically together. The Academy was housed in the former Soviet consulate – a neo-classical building now stripped bare of everything it had once contained, except for some dreadful furniture. The administrator, Ibrahim Jon, an Uzbek, had been a famous dancer in his day. I noticed that the women did very similar bar exercises to those practised in the west, though their physical characteristics were quite different. These were not the svelte, feline, feather-light dancers of western ballet; by comparison they were stockily, even heavily built, especially those of Turkic origin. But there was at least one notable exception. Dililar Abla, at eighteen, was the troupe's prodigy. Her father was a musician who had taught her to play the *dutar* when she was five – too young even to be able to reach the top of the fingerboard. Her mother was a dancer who had at first opposed Dililar's own dancing ambitions, but who nowadays dances alongside her in the troupe, performing the more sedate folk-dances whilst her daughter pirouettes and soars across the stage. Dililar told me that as a child she had been deeply influenced by Jiang Qing's revolutionary ballet *The Red Detachment of Women* – and she would copy the parade steps of the soldiers. At twelve she was already showing enough talent to be selected to go to Peking to study at the National Minorities Institute. She spent four years there and studied mathematics, Chinese and art theory as well as the dances of the minority groups.

'What do you think of western ballet?' I asked her.

She hesitated slightly. 'I think I was too young to understand much of what I saw of it. I must say I found it very strange – all those women dancing on tiptoe.'

Although most of the company's women bore little resemblance to their western counterparts, some of the men were slightly built.

I was invited to go to a performance by a young Han Chinese and his girlfriend. These two were obviously fashion-conscious city-dwellers, and they generously invited me out to dinner before the show. We went to the trendiest place in town – a restaurant where you ate with knives and forks. It was amusing to see such a vivid example of *autres pays, autres mœurs* – for the young men who ate here might have impressed their girlfriends with the high prices the restaurant charged, but they couldn't have impressed anyone by their handling of the knives and forks – they were as awkward with them as we are with chopsticks.

I think the most vital area of China's entertainments industry is the cinema, now enjoying freedom again after a long time hobbled by the Cultural Revolution. Certainly films reflect every aspect of China's amazingly rich and diverse cultural heritage. Costumes, music, dance, architecture, furniture and calligraphy come together against a backdrop of landscapes that could only be Chinese – the kind you see in seventeenth century watercolours come to life. Films tend to relate historical stories or social commentaries. I sat in an audience which was moved to tears by *Broken Moon* – the story of a widow unable to remarry without the permission of her family. On the other hand, there were the imported films, from which any scenes remotely connected with sex had been cut, which led to some hilarious non-sequiturs, though the Chinese audiences seemed to lap up the stories without question. No doubt the odd jumps in the movies were glossed over by the dubbed Chinese narration. With little television perhaps, the Chinese are a nation of natural cinemagoers.

Although it was pleasant to relax I still had plenty of work to do, for I was engaged in negotiations with the authorities for permission to continue my journey as planned. After many days of talking and

275

waiting, I had still failed to get permission to cross the TaklaMakan, but I would after all be allowed to visit the remote communities in the desert. Then, most unfortunately, just as everything seemed all set, the Xinjiang Autonomous Region's Central Public Security Bureau learnt of my whereabouts. I was duly summoned to a building that had either half fallen down or was only half built. I never discovered which, for I was bustled into an office where the Chief of Police was waiting for me. He was very angry indeed – though anger loses quite a lot of its force when filtered through an interpreter.

'Are you a Pakistani?' he yelled at me as soon as I entered the room.

'No,' I answered, surprised.

'Is your mother Pakistani?'

'No.'

'Is your father Pakistani?'

'No,' I replied, wondering how long this was going to last. But I need not have bothered, for the Chief, almost hidden behind a large counter, left off this line of questioning and seemed instead to be bursting from sheer rage. His cheeks went scarlet.

'Is he angry with me?' I asked the interpreter.

I think the Chief must have understood enough Uighur to sense the meaning of my question for himself, for I thought I saw a tear start from his eye and roll down his cheek. I was grateful for the stoutly-built counter that separated us. He seemed to be approaching a nervous breakdown now, in his heroic attempts to control his fury.

'You have violated the laws of the People's Republic of China!' he spluttered. 'You entered China illegally!' Such a heinous crime was clearly almost beyond his comprehension.

'I had the official blessing of –' I started, but he overrode me, continuing to recite his charge against me in an unsteady voice.

'You travelled illegally to Keriya, Niya, Cherchen, Korla . . .'

'I didn't really travel to them. I was in transit through them. I have been in contact with the authorities at every point on my journey.'

He had to run out of steam sooner or later and it wasn't long before he did – if he'd kept that up he would surely have collapsed. I was lucky not to be arrested, but I spent an anxious week thereafter reporting to the Public Security Bureau every day. They had made me hand over my passport and my travel permit, which I didn't like at all. I quoted their own laws to them, that I was required to carry my travel permit on me at all times, but it didn't cut any ice with them. I was less worried about being separated from my passport, for it has been my experience that people are only too happy to give you your passport back if it helps them get you out of their country.

In the end, a compromise was reached, by which the police chief saved face and washed his hands of me.

'We have given you permission to do many things that other foreigners haven't been allowed to do, even though we aren't too sure who you are. You must be aware that Xinjiang is China's most sensitive area,' they told me, a little uncertainly and even apologetically. They reconfirmed all the travel rights granted in my permit, and they returned my passport to me. Then I had to listen to a little homily of 'dos' and 'don'ts': no hitch-hiking; no more stopovers between here and Peking; no returning to Kashgar or Khotan, and above all no attempt to enter Tibet.

It was odd that they should have mentioned Tibet like that. Perhaps it was telepathy, for during the days I had been waiting for their decision, I had met a Japanese student called Tadashi, and arranged to meet him in Lhasa. We'd even made a little bet on who'd be there first.

Before I set off for the Roof of the World, I intended to visit two more cities in Xinjiang — Kucha and Turfan.

A FLEETING
ENCOUNTER

Kucha is south-west of Urumchi. The road passes through bleak stretches of shingle desert and barren mountains, and it is heavy with traffic; accidents occur all the time. The locals have found a way to alleviate the tedium of travelling on this dismal route – sunflower seeds. The eating of sunflower seeds is arguably China's favourite pastime. From the moment a child can extract the seed from its shell (not performed by hand, but by manipulation of tongue and teeth) to the day when doddering old age makes the action impossible, all Chinese chew sunflower seeds. Removal of the shell is an acquired skill which is performed with great finesse usually in silence and requiring much jaw movement. But once the seed has been extracted, skill is thrown to the winds: the wet, splintered shells are spat out like a shot from a gun. In the confines of a bus, they get everywhere, falling randomly onto your body, and quickly carpeting the floor. Various shards remain stuck to the eater's lips as well. I found it extremely unpleasant to be covered in bits of wet shell, and took to returning the barrage of fire in the direction it came from. It wasn't until I did this, returning shell for shell, as it were, that I brought about a cease-fire. I took to sunflower seed chewing with great pleasure and would recommend it to anyone as a great way to pass the time, and as a distraction from bitter cold.

The mud-and-brick restaurants at which we stopped from time to time were like taverns in the Middle Ages. Each had rickety wooden benches around a large, solid wooden table. The packed mud ground underfoot was always potholed and uneven, so that the stools lurched drunkenly on the floor. You were provided with a bowl, chopsticks, and a small handle-less cup for the tea. Food was always shovelled into the mouth unceremoniously. Uighurs stoop to the bowl (a friend described them very well as 'noodle hoovers'), Han bring the bowl to the mouth. A thermos of tea and a bowl of chillies always stood on the table. These restaurants were run by husband-and-wife teams, assisted by their children. The food was cooked on a primitive stove, made either of mud bricks or adapted from small oildrums, and run on wood or coke. The steam that came from the cooking added humidity to the normally dry air. The place was invariably lit by one bare lightbulb, and once the guests had departed became the family home.

It was on this route that I had a homosexual encounter. I was on my way to the inn where we were staying overnight *en route*, when I became aware that someone was following me. It was a Uighur, and he was very drunk. During the long walk across the darkened transport yard he suddenly rushed up and attempted to grope me in a rather fumbled way. I sidestepped him and he stumbled off into the dark.

I met another character who asked me if I was Pakistani or Afghan.

'I am English,' I told him.

He beamed. 'That is good. We are both foreigners here.' It turned out that his grandfather was an Afghan who had settled in Yarkand. I would have taken him to be a Uighur. However, you couldn't just assume that people who weren't obviously Han Chinese were automatically Uighur. I made this mistake on one occasion and was informed furiously by the man I was talking to that he was no Uighur, but a Kazakh. The Kazakhs have their own language, which, like Uighur, is related to Turkish; their faces are less Mediterranean than the Uighurs, more Mongolian. Most Kazakhs are herdsmen, virtually born in the saddle, and migrate with their flocks from the plains in winter to the mountains in summer. This man was travelling with his two sons. All were dressed alike, and wore astrakhan hats. He was a fierce, proud man, and as his sons stood silent behind him, like the hoods of a gangland boss, he told me rather boastfully of his visits to Russia.

'I live on the border, and I can speak Russian as well as I speak Kazakh. Conditions are better for us in the Soviet Union. Look at these –' and he bared his teeth to show me their gold caps. 'See that. Gold, not silver. I have made a lot of money on border trade.'

'Why are conditions better over there?'

'Better treatment. More opportunities for trade. Sixty thousand Kazakhs fled there in 1962. They are the lucky ones.'

'But aren't things getting better here?'

'There's always talk of it, but I think, for the minorities, only superficially.'

In contrast to the wealthy Kazakh, one of the most forlorn figures I met on that journey to Kucha was a White Russian. He wore tattered and patched trousers, an old, badly weathered, torn and patched coat which hung limp across his shoulders, and split shoes. His gaze was permanently fixed to the ground, and he dragged his feet laboriously, one in front of the other. It seemed that everyone knew him, but even among the tramps in London it would be hard to find a more destitute person, a more lost soul. When he passed in the street of the forgotten little town he lived in, he was ignored – a relic of days no one could remember any more. In the early years of this century, during the Bolshevik Revolution, 250,000 White Russians crossed into China. Over the years most were sent back to Russia, and others emigrated to Australia. But in 1953 a census revealed that there were still 23,000 ethnic Russians in China, and today 1,000 still live in Xinjiang Province.

The morning after my arrival at Kucha an official from the Foreign Affairs Bureau arrived at the hotel I was staying at to tell me that he was putting his Volga at my disposal. Like a child with a new toy, he was dying to show off this brand new saloon, which he had clearly only had a short time.

'What do you think of it?'

'It's splendid.'

'We bartered it with the Russians for sheep.'

'And you're putting it at my disposal?'

'Of course. You are our guest.'

'I couldn't accept such kindness,' I countered, thinking that the loan of the car merely served as an excuse to keep an eye on me.

'Of course,' he then added, 'there would be a financial consideration for its use.'

I smiled politely and told him that it was part of my job to use public transport as much as possible – I would therefore be travelling by bus or cart.

'That will be very difficult for you,' he said with regret. 'If you want to go and visit the Buddhist caves at Kumtura and Kyzil, I'm afraid my Volga is the only possible means of transport.'

I refrained from pointing out the large number of carts in the streets.

Kucha is a town divided into an old city and a new city. Unlike all other Uighur towns, bazaar day is on Friday, not Sunday. The bazaar here is a match for Kashgar's. It takes place in both parts of the city and the various sections of trade are divided up by streets, rather as they would have been in a medieval European town. One street was full of carts laden with firewood. The main street in the new town was given over to carpet-sellers. But the core of the bazaar lies in the old city some way to the south-east and can be reached by bus. The bus is a horse-drawn cart carrying fourteen to sixteen passengers. The first time I went to the old city I made the mistake of getting onto an empty bus: this had the effect of scaring off other passengers, and so my bus simply did not start. I got off and joined another that was almost full and therefore ready to go. We waited our turn to join the busy main thoroughfare that divided the two parts of the city. It is a long straight strip of road bordered on each side by mud-brick houses, and contains a couple of mosques, a few shops and some 'cart parks'. As in any other much-used street there are accidents caused by reckless drivers who have neither the space nor the time to overtake, but who try to anyway. Accidents left passengers sprawled across the road, carts overturned, animals dazed, and a lot of shouting. I couldn't understand at all why some carters felt impelled by this need for speed, because at the other end of the road they had to join the queue of vehicles waiting to return up the road anyway.

The bazaar here was just like Kashgar's, with the same figures and buildings that came straight from a painting by Breughel. It was set by a river, which a few riders and horses were crossing, while pedestrians teetered on slippery stepping stones. Children played in the mud, and horse carts struggled through it. A steady din rose from the market, the cries of the marketeers advertising their wares. A cluster of men gathered round a bird-seller. Everyone was dressed alike, everyone's arms were folded round themselves and tucked under their armpits against the cold. The men's faces reflected the hardness of their lives: carrying expressions that looked unable to convey extremes of delight or misery, but which were frozen into resignation. The endurance of the human spirit. The women, on the other hand, had faces that were full of expression – lively, coquettish, and charming. Most Uighurs are traders by nature and saw a potential purchase in every animal that passed, and a man with livestock to sell could by his very manner of walking convey his intentions. In their search for the right bolt of cloth, the women easily matched the men for sharpness, and I saw one or two very beleaguered-looking clothiers.

As usual, there were delicious foods available from stalls and benches with little portable stoves attached, set up in the mud. I came very close to eating what amounted to a Sunday roast dinner. I hadn't realised how much I'd missed home cooking until I sank my teeth into the local version of Yorkshire pudding – puffed dough with sugar inside. The greatest treat of all, though, was the roast beef kebabs: six huge chunks of meat on each, cooked skewered on old bicycle spokes and sprinkled with herbs, spices and salt. Since they only cost twopence a stick, I could only assume that beef was less popular than lamb.

It was unusual to have the bazaar on a Friday, since that is the sabbath. It was not long before I heard the muezzin's familiar call of the faithful to prayer. A band of children led me to the towering edifice of the Hanacka Jamaa Masdjid. Like a jewel it rose majestically above the houses that surrounded the hill on which it stood. It was an impressive sand-coloured building, with a taller entrance than any I had seen in Xinjiang. With its crenellated, geometric stucco designs, it contained elements of both Arab and Persian influence. This mosque is surprisingly new – it was re-built as late as 1923 – and I should mention that I saw a new mosque being built in Kucha.

When I returned to my hotel there was disappointment in store for me: I would not be allowed to visit the Buddhist caves of Kumtura and Kyzil after all. I begged the Foreign Affairs Bureau to ring Urumchi for me, but there had been no mistake. I needed permission from the Institute for the Preservation of Archaeological Relics, and this I did not have.

I wondered whether this might be in reprisal for the deeds of European, Japanese and American explorers who at the turn of the century had carted off hundreds of murals and artefacts from these caves. I had made friends with some locals who suggested that I by-pass officialdom.

'Make your way out to the caves anyway,' they told me. 'There's a house out there whose owner has a duplicate set of keys to the site. We'll give you an introduction to him.'

I was sorely tempted but for once I lost my nerve, for if I were caught I could hardly explain my actions away as an innocent mistake. In any case, there would be another chance to see Buddhist caves at the complex near the oasis town of Turfan, which I intended to visit next.

The day before I left Kucha, however, there was one more adventure in store for me. It was a strange and all too brief encounter. The girl had first said hello to me in the corridor of the hotel, but when I tried to start a conversation with her, she became shy and ran away. I went to my room and thought no more about it, but an hour or so later there was a knock at the door. As usual I was staying in a four-bed dormitory, but it so happened that the other beds were not occupied just then as the long-distance buses had not yet arrived in town to unload their passengers for the night.

I opened the door and there she stood, her hands in her jacket pocket, her scarf tied round her neck so that her long hair cascaded out from under it. She wasn't the prettiest of Uighur women, but her timid, delicate smile was enough to melt any heart. She must have been in her early twenties, though her face had the freshness of someone even younger.

We still stood there, staring at each other.

'May I come in?' she asked nervously.

'Of course.' I stood back from the door and she entered. I was pleased to have this fairly rare opportunity of talking to a girl, but the questions she asked me were desultory and soon tailed off. I could sense that she was agitated. She asked me to give her the names of various places in English, and then she wrote them down, but her mind was obviously not on what she was doing. Some of her tension began to communicate itself to me and finally I understood what it was: it was sexual excitement. She had been reading the names off a map she was holding as she sat on the bed opposite mine. Now she stood up and approached me, standing close to me, placing the map on my lap, and pointing to somewhere or other on it. In any other situation I would have taken this as a clear pass, but the last thing I wanted to do was misinterpret her actions. She came from a totally different cultural background. I couldn't just grab her, no matter how excited I was becoming, no matter how sure I was that that was what she was hoping I would do. She returned to her seat on the bed opposite and I was relieved that I hadn't made a fool of myself, or, much more importantly, hurt her feelings by any crude gesture. But now my defences were down and I was relaxed. She stood up, dropped everything she was holding, and came across to me again. The speed with which it all happened caught me

unawares. She stared into my eyes, and at the same time seemed to be trying to avoid them. Like a child pretending to be grown-up, she tried desperately hard to be sure of herself as she bent over to kiss me. I felt as I had as a boy during my first stolen embrace behind the school fountain. It was at once exciting and frightening. As I held her in my arms I felt once more the powerful combination of desire, excitement and nervousness that I always felt in a foreign land with a foreign woman, whose psyche would be the subject of unknown taboos. Unable to restrain myself, I allowed myself to be guided by her, to proceed at her speed, as her initial nervous, breathless passion gave way to caresses of great tenderness. For a moment there passed through my mind that she might just conceivably have been a plant sent by the authorities, but I put this down to my naturally suspicious nature and rejected it immediately. They would have nothing to gain by such an action, and besides, the girl was as taken aback by her own actions as I was – she wasn't hurt or upset, but excited and surprised.

There was the sound of footsteps in the corridor outside. New travellers had arrived, and I thought that their presence would surely put an end to our encounter, but when they entered the room they were made to feel most unwelcome, and did not stay. My companion sat with me a while longer, before she, too, left – suddenly and abruptly, like Cinderella. I remained where I was for a time, thinking over what had just happened. It seemed like a dream. Nor could I understand what it had meant for her. She could hardly tell any of her friends about it, because if it became common knowledge she would risk being ostracised. Perhaps she wanted the status of having had a foreign friend just for herself, but all she had asked about me was my first name.

I soon missed her warmth. It wasn't just that most of the experiences I had had on this journey hadn't been shared with anyone; but it made me realise that I had been lonely, and that I had missed having someone to talk to about all that I had seen and done. Not, of course, that I ever lacked for company. Here in Kucha I had used the same restaurant three nights in a row, for example. On each night my fellow-diners had insisted on sending out for bottles of wine. I went there after my encounter with the Uighur girl, and when I told the proprietor that this, sadly, would be the last, since I was taking the bus for Turfan in the morning, his three daughters (all of whose names ended in *gül*, which means flower) prepared a small feast for me. For this they absolutely refused payment. I had to give them something, but all I had was picture postcards of London. I gave them one and wrote a message on the back. They were delighted with the present, but worried that they would not be able to display both sides at once! I declined their offer of a packed lunch for the journey since I was afraid they would refuse payment for that, too. Parting was a sad moment – everybody wanted to shake my hand and wish me luck. Then, as often before and since, I was tempted simply to sit down and stay. But perhaps it is the transitoriness of the encounters one makes on the road that makes them so poignant – they never have time to become familiar or stale.

When I returned to the dormitory, the other three beds were occupied. I turned in, but I slept badly, my head filled with thoughts of the young Uighur girl. She knew that I was about to leave Kucha, but there wouldn't, now, be an opportunity to say goodbye.

I was wrong. An hour before dawn, when it was still dark, the door opened and she entered. I felt awkward as in front of the other men in the room she laid out my clothes and my toothbrush and toothpaste. I washed and dressed. She didn't say much, and I didn't know what to say to her, but she stayed. The other men dressed, desperately using their quilts to cover their bodies from her as they did so. Finally she left, saying that she would come to the bus station to see me off. It was impossible to tell from her face what thoughts were going through her mind.

It was so unusual for there to be anyone to wave goodbye to me when I left a place that I waited for her quite anxiously, searching among the crowds waiting to join the buses as the drivers called out the various destinations one by one – Aksu, Kashgar, Khotan. The masses of baggage were piled onto the roofracks, the passengers pushed and shoved to be first on board, and one by one the buses left on their journeys, until only ours was left. The bus station was all but deserted when the bus to Turfan was finally called. I slowly took my seat, still looking for her. Once aboard I scratched the thick frost from the window pane, but now the only occupants of the yard were our driver and a stray dog. We left, and there was no one to wave goodbye to.

The bus stopped at Yangi for the night on the way to Turfan, and, having nothing better to do with the evening, I took myself to the movies. The film was *Flight 637* – the story of China's heroic attempts to be the first to fly across the Karakoram from Urumchi to Karachi. The audience was Uighur, and neither I nor they could understand the Chinese dialogue. The people sitting round me kept asking me for translations, which of course I was unable to give, but at least I was able to tell them a bit about the various makes of planes and cars, and about the locations. It was the locations that actually caused the problem. For some reason the street scenes of Karachi had been intercut with some stock film of Paris, so that one moment we would be looking at rickshaws vying for space in a hot, dusty street, and the next we'd be looking at hundreds of Renaults darting about under the shadow of Sacré Cœur. The only way I could account for this was that the film makers had run out of enough footage of Karachi and had stuck in the shots of Paris as a makeweight, but my fellow spectators must have thought me mildly insane as I kept switching from continent to continent in my efforts to keep them abreast of the film.

'Where are we now?'

'In Paris.'

'But you just said we were in Karachi.'
'I know, but we're in Paris now.'
'How did we get there?'
'I don't know.'
'I thought you said they don't have rickshaws in Paris.'
'They don't.'
'Well, what's that one doing there?'
'Where? Oh, well, you see, we're back in Karachi . . .'
And so on.

I seemed to be breaking records for low temperatures. The day I arrived in Turfan was the coldest they'd had for years, but at minus 24.5 it wasn't the coldest I'd endured. The roads were sheet ice across which lorries picked and skidded their way; and cyclists took the most horrendous tumbles. The usual posse of animal carts was waiting to pick up arriving bus passengers. I was pleased to be here, for Turfan is an archaeological goldmine. The first monument I saw was the 200-year-old minaret of the Mosque of Imin Khoja. Its cylindrical body terminates in a hemispherical dome, and it is decorated with cleverly designed arrays of bricks which produce a dazzling number of permutations of geometrical shapes, which in turn create dramatic light and shade, since the bricks are set in different planes. One sees similar designs reproduced in modern buildings. My main purpose in coming here, however, was to visit the Buddhist caves of Bezeklik. My request to do so met with the usual surly response from the local official, who was one of those bureaucrats whose attitude is that if something's unusual – like me not being part of a guided tour – then it's out of the question. But rather than give me a plain 'no', he resorted to extravagant lies and excuses – a tendency shared by many of his kind.

'Can I stay in a village near the caves so that it'll be easy to reach them from there?' I asked, initially.

'Impossible, I'm afraid. There's nowhere to stay.' He was plump and oily – the caricature civil servant.

'Could I rent a horse from the local commune, then?'

'They don't have any.' – That was tantamount to saying that China has no tea.

'But I *do* have your permission to visit the caves?'

'They are closed. Besides, there are no buses, and even if there were, the road is up.'

'Well, I could walk.'

'That is quite out of the question.'

I had, of course, heard it all before, and if I hadn't been convinced of the poorness of official communications around the province I might have thought it all part of a concerted plot against me: prevent Nick Danziger from visiting Buddhist caves at all costs!

I left the official and went in search of a horse. On the street a couple of Uighur girls discussed me, giggling. Some men laughed at the way I was dressed. I felt intimidated and rounded on them angrily.

'What did you say?' I said in Uighur, but the effect was not the one I had hoped for – at first they didn't understand, and then they tried to talk to me in Chinese. When they finally understood that I was speaking Uighur they tittered: my accent was that of a southern peasant.

Their attitude riled me. Far from being friendly, the people here regarded me as some kind of amusing specimen – some kind of ramshackle zoo animal. Their faces expressed neither animosity nor warmth, just naked curiosity. Of course, I was now in an area which has been opened up to foreigners, and where they are no longer a rarity. I found a further example of the effect of this when I tried to hire a horse. It was a very far cry from my experience with Imin Tohte in Khotan.

'How much is it to hire a horse for a day?' I asked the stable-owner.

'Twenty yuan.'

'But that's preposterous – that's four times the normal rate!'

He just shrugged, and turned his back on me.

'I'm prepared to go to ten yuan, but it's still robbery.'

He remained unimpressed. 'The Japanese are quite happy to pay twenty,' he snapped, 'and they just want to sit on the horse and have their picture taken.'

I had my work cut out trying to reach these caves. It wasn't just the surly officials and the grasping tradespeople; even the local bus station refused to sell me a ticket. However I sidestepped this problem fairly easily by buying my ticket direct from the driver. But now the weather seemed determined to hold me back. If the previous day had been bitingly cold, at least it had been still. Today there were icy winds which drove a cutting little blizzard before them. The other people in the bus tried to dissuade me from going to the caves. 'It's still quite a walk from where the bus drops you,' they said. I didn't listen to them, but once the bus had dropped me on the side of the road that forks up towards Bezeklik, I wished I had. I was well wrapped up against the cold, but it was not a good feeling to be all alone in such a desolate spot with the wind howling round me and tearing at my clothes. However by now I was quite determined to reach the caves at all costs, so I wrapped my turban yet more firmly around my head, crammed my sheepskin hat down over it (the crude lanolin smell of that hat can still take me back to the east in a moment) and set off. Within a few metres, the track became barely visible, my toes started to go dead, and I didn't know how to protect my hands. Worst of all was the visibility, since I had to keep my eyes squeezed tight against the driving ice and snow, which bit and stung my unprotected skin. Fortunately for me I had only gone a couple of kilometres, often with only the omnipresent telegraph pole to guide me, when I saw a house, and near it someone who had gone to fetch water from a river that ran by it. When he saw me he put down his buckets and waved, bellowing 'Tea!' against the noise of the wind. Despite the short distance I had travelled, the offer was too tempting to refuse. I slid down the steep bank to the house where the young man was waiting. It was warm inside and the bleating of a small child in the next room was music to my ears. I took off several layers of clothing, which had become soaked, and then frozen. It was impossible to take off my turban until it had thawed, though, as ice had fixed it rigidly to my beard.

The young man ushered me through into a smaller, darker, inner room where a woman sat rolling, punching and kneading dough for noodles, with her children at her side: a young boy and a baby girl. The heat from the *kang* on which I was seated slowly rose upward through my body and dried out the worst of the damp, as the tea I was drinking warmed me from the inside. The woman reached into a basket and pulled out a large *nan*, blowing the dust off it and banging it against her hand. I started to relax: I was back among decent people. That handful of sharks in Turfan faded like a bad dream.

Before I headed off again the woman made me promise to come back for lunch.

'I don't know when I'll be back.'

'It doesn't matter. There will be food for you whenever you come.'

Mercifully the weather had abated somewhat when I emerged into the cold. The man told me I had two kilometres to go, the woman, seven. Mountains rose on all sides. To the north there was a slope that extended to the west as far as the eye could see, its ridge shrouded in cloud. I walked along a clifftop, towards a distant caravanserai. As I came up to it I encountered a group of roadworkers with a bulldozer, who were digging a road through the grit and gravel scree. They pointed to a locked gate and told me that the caves were beyond it. I felt dashed at having come all this way to be stymied at the last moment, but one of the workers shouted something through the bars of the gate, and at the same time tried to force it open. Eventually a boy appeared on the other side of it, climbing down the stairs, hewn out of the sheer rock-face, which led to the caves, and he let me in without any more ado.

Sadly, I was only able to visit a handful of the caves, but even this small sample was enough to give me an impression of the extraordinary artistic achievements of this remote culture. There were exquisite murals depicting different nationalities with an almost caricature technique; there were paintings showing thousands of tiny Buddhas seated in the lotus position, each little Buddha drawn with an individual liveliness. But there were signs of man's intolerance here, too, evidenced by the iconoclastic vandalism of the Muslims who came here after the Buddhists had gone, and of man's ruthless acquisitiveness, for statues had been wrenched from their bases, and murals had been cut away from the rock by past generations of explorers and souvenir hunters.

My appetite for Buddhist art was whetted, however, and I determined, *en route* for Tibet, not to waver from my original intention of visiting Dunhuang, and the Caves of a Thousand Buddhas.

On my way back to the road to hitch a lift to Turfan, I stopped off at the house for my promised lunch. Noodles had never tasted better.

THE CAVES OF A
THOUSAND
BUDDHAS

Resolved to reach Lhasa, I decided to board a train to Liuyan, the nearest terminus to Dunhuang and the fabled Caves of the Thousand Buddhas. Threading my way through the deserted quagmire of muddy streets, I made my way to Qiquanhu station ticket office to find it closed. Several other would-be passengers for the onward journey suggested we go to a nearby restaurant. I agreed, and once there took my time savouring the thick, fresh noodles, the aromatic vegetables and the tender lamb. Full of food, I began to daydream about the last two months of what had been a magical journey through Xinjiang. But not for long. I was recalled to reality by the stirring whistle of the steam train, which had suddenly appeared out of nowhere and was waiting at the station. I had to spring up a flight of stairs to reach the platform – there was no time to buy a ticket, even if I'd been able to. Running alongside the train I was horrified to find that most of the carriage doors were locked. Then I saw some of my fellow diners waving to me from the end of the platform, where they'd found an open door. I scurried along to join them and boarded the train totally out of breath and in the nick of time.

If I hadn't known that China was at peace I would have thought that the passengers were being evacuated from a war zone. Hundreds of people were crammed together, almost sitting on top of each other, squatting on the floor or standing in the corridors. The remaining space was packed tight with their bags, boxes, suitcases and quilts. I had arrived too late even to squeeze into the corridor, and had to stand right in the carriage entrance. The guard, when he had struggled through to me, offered to find me a berth for my twelve-hour journey, but I declined. He left me, but returned soon after accompanied by a posse of attendants whose nightmare job it was to battle against the continuous tide of dirt and refuse, which they had somehow to sweep away from under the seats and between the people, as well as keeping the carriages well supplied with hot water for tea – each carriage having its own samovar. These attendants insisted on finding me a seat, but once again I said no, for that would have meant evicting some other unfortunate person who had probably only gained his seat by some cleverly devised stratagem at the train's point of departure.

'But you are our guest,' they persisted.

'I am just a simple traveller,' I replied, wishing that they would realise that being a guest doesn't entail taking precedence over the locals. There was another reason, too: I was already missing Xinjiang, even though I hadn't yet left the province, so I wanted to remain among the Uighurs who were occupying the space around me. Six of them were making the sixteen-day round trip from Kashgar to Shanghai for a four-day stay in China's largest city. They took it in turns to sit on their luggage, and hoped that in a couple of days' time they would all be sitting on hard seats. Like so many Uighurs, they had taken energetically to China's new programme of liberalisation, and had an eye to any and every means of making money. Some of them were shopkeepers, others tradesmen. All were making the trip in order to bypass the middleman and buy their goods direct from suppliers in Shanghai.

I really wondered how they could stand the rigours of such a journey. It was the middle of the night when the train stopped at Kumul. More people got on than got off, and I only put up weak resistance to one of the attendant's offer of his own cubicle whilst he continued his battle against sunflower seed shells, spilt tea, spittle, and a leak from the overhead water tank which threatened to soak my bags, which, for lack of space, I was unable to move. The attendant asked me to wait, and disappeared into the throng, soon to return with a policeman in a green uniform with gold rings on the sleeve, a peaked cap and a large pistol. They asked me to follow them with my bags. Making our way through the carriages was far worse than any army obstacle course, as we hurdled over children, threaded between adults with delicacy – treading as if on eggs for fear of trampling a limb. I was led to the dining car, which I had noticed tended to be the jewel and showpiece of Chinese railways. It was empty save for the kitchen staff and a few train attendants. I was shown to a seat at a table, and there I was able to rest my head on my arms and gratefully snatch a few hours' sleep.

The kitchen came to life before dawn. There was a breakfast of noodles, eggs and cabbage, served in a polystyrene container with two tiny balsa wood chopsticks. It was still dark when we left Xinjiang and entered Gansu Province, but there remained two stations before we reached Liuyuan.

Dawn was just breaking when I left the train, feeling the sort of *angst* which is peculiar to arrival in a new country. I couldn't speak the language and the characters of the Chinese signs were indecipherable to me. Faced with an alien world – challenging and yet daunting, an unknown quantity – I felt alarmingly disjointed. My thoughts turned to Xinjiang for comfort and a sense of security. Even if the province I had just left didn't represent roots for me, at least it carried with it a sense of identity. The feeling I had had in Afghanistan of being a part of their world lay in sharing the suffering and misery of those who had befriended me. In Xinjiang it had lain in being greeted like a long-lost brother.

However, these feelings didn't stop me from trying to hoodwink the ticket collector at the turnstiles (no one on the train had so much as mentioned a ticket) – but my feigned naïveté and innocence cut no ice with him. Deaf and dumb as I was, as far as the language was concerned, it was still impossible for me to pretend that I didn't know that he wanted the train fare. Indeed, this attempt to outsmart the railways not only failed, but backfired, for I was made to pay the more expensive foreigner's fare – the very thing I had been at such pains to avoid. To add insult to injury, they were going to charge me the cost from Turfan – further down the line than Qiquanhu. At this I protested, an action which promptly brought me up against the local authorities.

My luck was obviously on a downhill path, for I now came into contact with one of the few policemen outside Xinjiang who spoke fluent Uighur. He wasn't all that interested in my non-payment of the fare, but cast doubt on the fact that I had travelled from Qiquanhu.

'Even if you did,' he added ruminatively, 'what were you doing in a closed city in the first place?'

'Oh, officer, I only went there in order to catch the train,' I reassured him.

'Why didn't you catch the train from the Turfan station – it's the same distance from Turfan town as Qiquanhu.'

'But it's in the wrong direction.'

'Ah,' he conceded.

After only a little more toing and froing they agreed to let me off with payment of the Qiquanhu to Liuyuan fare. Maybe they just couldn't be bothered to do anything more about me. Let me be someone else's problem, was probably their pragmatic attitude.

The bus ride from Liuyuan to Dunhuang was more comfortable than the ones I'd been used to, and the climate was more temperate – a mere zero degrees Celsius. The surrounding desert, with its deep ochres and umber hues, was softer and less threatening than the landscapes I had passed through hitherto. And Dunhuang, when I arrived there, turned out to be a modern, prosperous city, dominated by a single image: that of a female votive dancer, twirling like a dervish. She appeared everywhere in the town, either as a painting or a sculpture. I was to learn that her original came from the Caves of the Thousand Buddhas.

The time had come to put the few words of Chinese I'd picked up in Xinjiang to use, but I quickly discovered that my pronunciation was hopeless, and that was serious in a language where the slightest change in the inflection of a word can alter its meaning entirely. However, I did manage to find out one thing: the Caves of the Thousand Buddhas were closed – it was out of season. I felt momentarily crushed: it seemed that every obstacle was being placed in my path by Fate to prevent me from seeing any Buddhist caves along the Silk Road. But I was absolutely determined to see these – they were a high point of my entire journey. I decided to seek out the local Foreign Affairs Bureau, if there was one here, and find out what my chances of an out-of-season visit might be. I went to the nearest hotel and asked for the *Waiban*.

At once I plunged into the thorny undergrowth Chinese presents to the untutored foreigner. The young receptionists at the hotel picked up the *wai* of *waiban* as *wei*, which means 'hello'. They smiled politely.

'Meiyou, meiyou,' I said. 'Waiban.' (No, no – the Foreign Affairs Bureau.)

The young women exchanged their smiles for looks of puzzled enquiry.

'Waiban! Waiban!' I tried, more forcefully.

Now they looked alarmed. This time *waiban* had come out as *weixian*, which means 'danger'.

I composed my face, smiled, and tried again. 'Meiyou, meiyou – waiban.'

Now they looked concerned: *weisheng* means 'health'; but *bing* is 'illness'.

'Do you need a doctor?' they asked me.

'Meiyou.'

'Do you have a stomach-ache?' (*Weibing.*)

'Meiyou.'

'*Weizi?*' they asked, pointing to a seat.

I tried to extricate myself from this impossible situation. '*Xiexie*,' I said, meaning 'thank you' – which they promptly mistook for *xie*, which means 'to write'. If only I could have. In the end, however, and with the help of a Chinese-English dictionary which one of the girls fetched, we were able between us to track the right sense down. It was like a game of charades, first isolating the word *wai*, which carries the sense of 'foreign' and 'outside', then the word *ban* as in 'to arrange'. I think we were all pretty triumphant – though exhausted.

'Why didn't you say so in the first place?' the girls asked me.

There are advantages and disadvantages to travelling out of season. On the plus side one isn't surrounded by hordes of tourists. On the other hand, most of the sights are closed. The man at the *waiban* was polite, but sorry that he couldn't help me. The caves were closed and in any case there was no transport there. Equally politely, I persisted, bringing my official letters as always to my aid. He agreed to phone the curator of the caves, which lay some twenty kilometres distant. The result was that I would be allowed to make one visit. The man at the *waiban* would arrange a car to take me.

The Caves of the Thousand Buddhas constitute without any doubt at all one of the world's great wonders. They are in the desert south-west of Dunhuang. Hewn out of the rock they extend across 1½ kilometres and face a green valley. They are a treasure trove of Buddhist art. The oldest caves were dug in AD 366, and over the succeeding thousand years travellers, believing that building a rock temple, chapel or shrine would ensure their safe passage, had a cave hewn out and decorated with the most magnificent murals and sculptures. Pilgrims, merchants and soldiers prayed here before setting out on, and returning from, the Silk Road, asking for deliverance from expected perils ahead or giving thanks for a safe return home.

Four hundred and ninety-two caves have survived, carved into irregular rows and forming what must be the world's most complete collection of Buddhist art. In 1900 Wang Yuan-Lu, a Taoist monk and self-appointed guardian to the Caves, discovered that one of them contained forty to fifty thousand documents belonging to eight different dynasties – everything from holy scriptures to business deeds, pawnshop contracts, records of the cutting of caves as well as works of reference on astronomy, geography, divination, and a variety of other subjects. The scripts were written in Chinese, Tibetan, Sanskrit, Sogdian, Runic-Turki, Uighur, and previously unknown languages of Khotan and Kucha. Amongst this cornucopia was the first known printed book in the world, and rich embroideries and paintings on silk.

The caves are covered in extraordinary murals reflecting both Indian and Chinese styles and depicting all aspects of Buddhism: Gods and spirits, narratives, portraits, illustrations of sutras, historical and religious anecdotes, and ornamental designs. Other murals are secular in nature, illustrating the life and times of the various dynasties and including hunting scenes, costumes, and the world in which the people lived. Each cave is a unique creation, and however small it is contains small, boxlike niches to house the figures of the Buddha. I was filled with awe. Like all great art, this was enlightening, but it carried too for me the fascination of the past, its peoples, its religion and history, and its experience. The deft strokes of the artists were executed everywhere with a palpable love and joy. Among the sculptures was a seated Buddha 33 metres high, and many caves contained painted statues, most made of clay, of Buddhas, Bodhisattvas, Buddhist disciples, Lokparas, and high warriors. Some were executed with extreme attention to detail, the folds of robes clearly showing the influence of the art of ancient Greece. As the style evolved over the years, it was easy to see the progressive refinements, though I cannot say that any one period was greater than another, as each had its own charm. In one place you could see what could only be described as Fauvism – all bright colours and simplified forms; in another the anonymous artist had gone in for *trompe l'œil*: I saw a form of three rabbits chasing each other, but done in such a way that although each rabbit had two ears, the artist had only drawn three ears between them. So coherent and individual was each cave that a cursory visit to all of them would have been a travesty. Instead, I decided to spend as much time as possible going  around half of the forty that are open every year. (The caves are opened in rotation, to allow time for the preservation and restoration of those that are closed.) Even so I was engulfed by what I had seen, and as I travelled back across the desert after my visit I felt something of what the ancient pilgrims who had created the caves must have felt, or those modern Japanese and Tibetan Buddhists must feel who make holy pilgrimage here.

Complications over language never ceased. I was by now trying hard to make onward progress to Golmud but no one in Dunhuang understood the name of my next destination until I finally pointed to the place on a map: it was called *Ga er mu*. In a bid to find a truck that was going there I needed to find out the province's licence plate number, and the city's corresponding number. I set about this by first drawing a truck and then, pointing to its number plate, I drew two dashes and asked 'Qinghai?' But they didn't cotton on and it was only by saying 'Gansu' and writing in *its* number, '25', that I finally made contact. I then asked 'Qinghai?' again. Someone wrote down '26'. Encouraged, I said 'Gaermu?' The same person wrote down '50'.

All I needed to do now was to find a truck whose number plate began '26-50' . . .

There were none at any of the town's lorry parks, and so on my third day in Dunhuang I walked to the end of the town to try my luck at hitching. For three days I tried. It meant rising an hour before dawn each morning in the numbing cold – not something I relished, but it had to be done. On the first two days I met with defeat. It wasn't that no one stopped, it was simply that all the traffic was local. Then on the third day a vehicle stopped and the driver asked me if I wanted to go to Liuyuan. I told him no, but then I noticed that he carried Tibetan number plates and so I told him that my ultimate goal was Lhasa.

He grinned. 'Lhasa? That's OK. We'll be back here from Liuyuan tomorrow; but after that we're going to Lhasa. You can come with us.'

That was fine by me; besides, I really didn't think I could face spending yet another mindless day at the roadside watching the same old tractors crawl by. And so for the third time in as many days I checked back in to my hotel. I was greeted by nervous smiles from the girls in reception. They clearly thought they were housing a demented maniac who liked to amuse himself by checking in and out of hotels all the time. Or maybe they just put it down to general foreigners' eccentricity.

I met up with my lift the next day without difficulty, and introduced myself to Li Jun, the leader of the group. There were two Han Chinese and two Tibetans, and they were travelling in a Toyota Land Cruiser, which is the Rolls Royce of the Chinese roads. I might have welcomed this kind of luxury, but something in their luggage made me nervous. It was something I hadn't seen since Afghanistan – a Chinese-made Kalashnikov, which they produced from its hiding place under the bed in the hotel room where I met up with them. They wore their trousers tucked into their boots, dark glasses, and one wore a leather jacket and another a green People's Liberation Army tunic. If we'd been in Latin America I would have taken them to be some kind of paramilitary outfit. But the gun made me most uneasy of all. Of course I knew that in the old days the route into Tibet had been dangerous, and travellers had been attacked by wild animals and, worse, by Tibetan bandits, but these threats had long since disappeared. However I didn't want to alienate them by asking questions so I let the matter rest. As it was they had agreed to take me into Tibet, which they must have known was highly illegal.

But once we were on our way, climbing gently into the Danghe Nanshan mountain range, I shelved my fears and settled down to enjoy the semi-rugged scenery which seemed so at odds with the warm, smooth sand gathered around the foothills. Like a knife through butter the sharp ridges of rock drove into the sand. We continued to climb, and once over the first mountain pass a huge plain extended in front of us. At its southern end we could make out a smaller chain of mountains. Crossing the plain we reached it, to find a river frozen in its bed, as if a freezing gale had caught it unawares. Even the water cascading over the rocks had frozen, enveloping them in a coat of ice. It looked for all the world as if someone had taken a fibreglass mould of the river, and I half expected to see droplets of spray frozen and suspended in mid-air. The Cruiser sped over the landscape, leaving a huge plume of dust rising in our wake, stopping for nothing but occasionally engulfed in the dust cloud raised by a truck passing in the opposite direction – to emerge from it into another striking scene. As we drove down and across one incline, its opposite wide expanse of open slope would sweep up to meet us – at its crown a ridge of small serrated peaks. At times it seemed as if the Land Cruiser was racing across the mountains of the Moon.

We descended from the mountains into the Qiadem Basin. Its northern half was orange-beige in colour, but its southern half, extending all the way to the Kunlun range, was mauve. At one point my companions stopped the car and got out to show me that if you dug away the desert's surface sand you struck a layer of salt beneath.

Our stops were rare, but on the few occasions that they happened I was left alone with Wangchuk, our Tibetan driver. In those few minutes he had much to say, though because of our common language difficulties our conversation was bordering on the monosyllabic. But he got a lot of information across. He talked of Tibetans exiled in London and India – his own father was an Indian exile.

'What do you think of the Dalai Lama?' he asked me once.

This wasn't an easy question to answer, not only because of my lack of language, but because I simply hadn't considered it. My knowledge of recent Tibetan history was minimal. I knew that since the Chinese communists had 'liberated' the country, there had been Tibetan uprisings against them, which the Chinese had crushed; the Cultural Revolution then attempted to eradicate all traces of Tibetan culture and civilisation.

In answer to Wangchuk's question I gave a tentative thumbs-up, which became more positive as he beamed in response. There was a bond between us. But as the Chinese made their way back to the Land Cruiser Wangchuk indicated that they should learn nothing of our conversation.

Golmud when we reached it turned out to be one enormous transport depot. Hundreds and hundreds of lorries rolled through the streets or were parked in large yards. Goods from all over China passed through here on their way to Tibet. I'd hoped not to stay in Golmud at all, but Li Jun told me that he'd organise both my accommodation and my onward transport to Lhasa. 'Don't worry about a thing,' he told me, but the hotel wanted an exorbitant sum for the overnight stay. Li Jun's response to this was to offer to put me up in his own suite. As I got to know him better I realised what a remarkable man he was: in the privileged position of factory manager in Lhasa, he nevertheless shared everything with his workers. His kindness to me simply ignored the myriad regulations, but it could not halt gossip. Someone must have told the Golmud police that Li Jun had a guest, for they duly arrived. I was told to report to the police station in the morning, and in the meantime was obliged to take a room of my own.

But for once I thoroughly enjoyed my visit to the police station. They had brought in a local schoolteacher to translate for them. There seemed to be no problem about my onward journey. Perhaps Li Jun had squared it with them.

'Will you be travelling to Lhasa by bus or truck?' they enquired politely.

'By car,' I said guardedly.

They were very surprised. 'You have a small car?'

'No. It's the one outside,' I said, pointing to where the Land Cruiser was parked, with Wangchuk in attendance.

Something must have been lost in the translation, for they clearly thought that the Toyota was my own, and Wangchuk my chauffeur. Their faces became wreathed in deferential smiles.

'May I remain in Golmud until tomorrow?' I asked tentatively.

'Of course.'

'Thank you.'

As I took my leave they bowed and shook my hand, finally all coming out onto the porch of the police station to wish me a safe journey. I basked in the reflected glory of the Land Cruiser, quietly thankful that there would be no difficulty in staying in Golmud until Li Jun was ready to continue on to Lhasa.

However I was still suffering from the germ of a doubt about my journey to Tibet. The country had never been on my itinerary proper – but then I had already made several unscheduled side trips. However this detour would be harder to explain to my sponsors, and it was impossible to contact them from here to seek their advice. I had written letters to them whenever possible, but my journey was now several months behind schedule and I was still 1200 kilometres due south of my projected route. It, however, held little charm when compared with Tibet.

By luck very few local officials, even on seeing a map of my journey and itinerary, questioned what I was doing so far off it. As I had come so far, I reasoned, I would be foolish not to take advantage of the opportunity. There was a less frivolous reason too. I felt that if Chinese influence hadn't totally destroyed the Tibetan way of life, foreign tourists might well now do so. Up to now few foreigners had ever been to Tibet, but things are changing fast. Lhasa is now open to all comers, and I dread to think what their influence will be on such a fragile civilisation, which has survived for so long intact precisely by keeping foreigners at bay.

The remoter and more elusive the civilisation, the greater is the desire to visit it, but I wondered if I too would not be contributing to its decline. Would I not, in common with so many tourists, be going to Tibet to marvel at the Tibetans, not as people, but as objects in some kind of living museum? Tibet, too, is suddenly no longer as safe behind her mountains as she has always been until now, because of the aeroplane. That, and the expensive hotel, far out of the reach of locals' purses, reinforce the tourist's cosmetic and distanced view of what he sees as the 'colourful' natives – so long as he can have his air-conditioning, central heating, bar and flush lavatory. The victims of tourism are rarely responsible for the position they find themselves in. In the case of Tibet, the Chinese, now in full command, feel the province they've annexed must pay its own way. And tourism to them seems the most logical means.

There will soon be a 1000-room international hotel in Lhasa. But the number of *chang* stores has increased tenfold, and alcoholism is becoming endemic. A friend of mine who works there has written to me since my return that even old countrywomen coming to Lhasa to sell, demand FECs in return for their increasingly shoddy goods. Perhaps this is the natural course of things. Perhaps Tibetan culture and society, preserved by isolation in its medieval entirety for so long, was bound to crumble on its first contact with the modern world, just as an ancient artefact, preserved for thousands of years in the dry atmosphere of a sealed cave, will disintegrate the minute an archaeologist breaks into the cave and lets in fresh air. Most people are better off than they were under the lamas. But one cannot help wishing that Tibet had been allowed to make its own choice.

But all this still lay ahead of me as I settled down for a second night in Golmud, looking forward to travelling on to Lhasa in style in the Land Cruiser. My considerations weren't just aesthetic, however: the Cruiser had efficient heating, and I'd heard that the previous year several drivers had frozen to death in their trucks, crossing the high passes. In the morning, though, I was in for a rude shock. Golmud was as far as the Toyota was going. The rest of the journey would be made in Daihatsu vans. There were three of them, brand new, but stripped down to basics. They'd just arrived by train from Xinjiang, but no one had sent operation manuals with them. I was able to make myself useful because there was a transfer on one of the doors describing the use of the choke in English. I conveyed as much of this information as I could to Wangchuk, but it didn't stop him from flooding the engine twice. Something else that was completely new to him was the rear-view mirror. Whenever he wanted to see if the other vans were following he would simply turn round in his seat, which, considering the speed at which he drove and the precipitous drops at the side of the road, was a very dangerous manoeuvre.

We'd been joined by four new drivers, two of whom had wives in tow. Everyone had been in a desperate hurry to leave Golmud but last-minute goods were bought consisting of fireworks, a bicycle, buckets and towels. In the end the vans were full and everyone had run out of money. We were quite a little group, and in some cases it was hard to tell the Tibetans and the Chinese apart. This was further complicated by the fact that some of the Tibetans had taken Chinese names.

The journey certainly wasn't for those of a nervous disposition: it wasn't ever fear that a bird might fly into us, but rather that we might fly into a bird – though in fact in this respect Wangchuk was a good driver; he took the wildest evasive action to avoid hitting anything on the road. Tibetans believe in reincarnation and the transmigration of souls: if you kill any living thing, you might just be killing the animal that is presently housing the soul of your late father. Thus deliberate killing is forbidden.

If travelling by day was difficult, travelling by night was worse. When you approached an oncoming vehicle, both sets of lights were switched right off. There was then no telling how close or far apart we were, or the condition of the poor road, except for short bursts of headlight which seemed to be permitted. At the last moment of approach, all lights were switched back full on, flooding and dazzling everyone and everything.

At least on the second day Wangchuk took to using the rear-view mirror. He became so enthusiastic about it that he attached the wing mirrors that had been supplied with the van.

There was no logic in anything we did. We made frequent halts to eat, and when we did so we took our time. But as soon as we had finished there was a mad scramble to move on again and we drove at breakneck speed. And the only time we stopped to rest was at the roadside close to the highest point on the route, the 5,300-metre Tanggula Pass. You could never stop for long in any case, for the bitter cold soon crept into the vehicles, and the radiator water might freeze (anti-freeze being unheard of).

As befitted the Arctic conditions, the scenery was bleak and barren. We started to climb as soon as we had left Golmud. The towering mountains gradually diminished as we reached the plateau. Snow-capped hills surrounded the bleached plain, and the clear blue sky could be touched by an outstretched arm. I took to sharing the daytime driving with Wangchuk. This was just as well for the first time I took over he fell asleep as soon as he reached the passenger seat. I knew that he'd been tired, for no sane person would have kept the windows open as he had – letting in the icy wind that was several degrees below freezing. But as dawn broke on the second day scenery was revealed that made the whole nerve-racking trek worthwhile. The Tibet of my dreams stood before me: remote, wild and mysterious. Yaks were scattered across the plain and up the mountainsides, bedecked in red and red-and-white tassels attached to their ears. Some of them were being driven towards a small market town which we could see ahead of us – Nachu.

Within seconds of our arrival Tibetans had surrounded us, pressing up against the van's windows, hands and faces flattened there by the weight of others behind them trying to get a look.

Their piercing eyes were both soft and threatening.

Their clothes, hats and shoes were made from animal skins, furs and wool. A bulky, knee-length sheepskin coat was the main article of apparel, worn off the shoulder with the loose arm wrapped around the waist, forming a pouch-like overhang which seemed to be concealing a beerpot. The coat was knotted around the waist, and a knife was stuck in the waistband. The hats were of fox fur, and the colourful boots made of wool with a leather sole. The men's hair was quite often worn uncut – a mane wrapped round the head and decorated with ribbons, bones and jewellery. The women's coats were longer, reaching right down to the ground and decorated on the lower half with bands of red and green material. Their hair was worn in pony-tails plaited with brightly coloured threads – red, pink, blue, purple, green and orange. Babies slept wrapped in blankets on their backs. Sometimes the babies were carried by sisters not much bigger than themselves, staggering under their weight. The air was crisp and the sky was bright.

Nachu's architecture was unlike anything I had seen. The typically Tibetan edifices were made of stone and rose at an inwardly-sloping angle. Their solidity reminded me of the buildings of the Incas. The windows also sloped, but they were protected from above by a jutting wooden ledge which was decorated with painted crenellations. The temple was concealed from view by the buildings that surrounded it. The streets were so narrow that our vehicles only just managed to squeeze along them, but we reached the little temple square at last, where worshippers prostrated themselves in the dust and dirt in front of the building. I wondered if I should go in or not, but Wangchuk led the way forward. As my eyes adjusted to the candlelit dimness of the interior I was filled with awe – I was on the edge of discovering a new world once more. And this magnificent, alien treasure house meant even more to me than the Caves had done, for it was alive, now! I smelt the burning rancid butter; I heard the muttered incantations of the lamas and the heart-stopping sound of the temple drum, which stilled the soul, just as the clash of the cymbals freed the spirit. We passed by empty rows of cushions which would normally be occupied by lamas, and I saw that in the empty places their habits lay – just as if their owners had been magically lifted from this world. Uninitiated in their mysteries, I trod carefully in Wangchuk's footsteps, admiring the temple's magnificent murals and its rich *thankas* – free-hanging paintings or embroideries on silk – and bowing my head as I passed its golden Gods. They were unforgiving, their expressions variously sinister, sarcastic, mocking, serene or wise. Offerings of yak butter were poured from thermos flasks. Bowls of money. The spinning of a hand-held prayer wheel. A photograph of the Dalai Lama on the altar in front of his Gods.

The scenery beyond Nachu became even grander, and was never without its sprinkling of yaks. Approaching Lhasa I had a hint of what was to come: the Roof of the World – bleak, barren and yet majestic. A land at one with its religion. We passed pilgrims making their way to the holy city on foot. Alone or in pairs they took three steps forward and then prostrated themselves, before retracing their steps to fetch their cart of belongings and tow it after them. Never have I seen such laborious progress so patiently made. It was an almost inhuman patience. They would take 90 days to reach the city, starting from Golmud – a journey we would make in our vans in about 36 hours.

At last there were only twelve kilometres between us and Lhasa. I had tried to keep my excitement in check, telling myself that the Potala was bound to be a disappointment, but then we rounded a bend and there in the distance it stood astride a hill against the mountains.

I was almost choking with excitement as we passed beneath it on our way to the guesthouse.

PART SIX

Tibet
and Bhutan

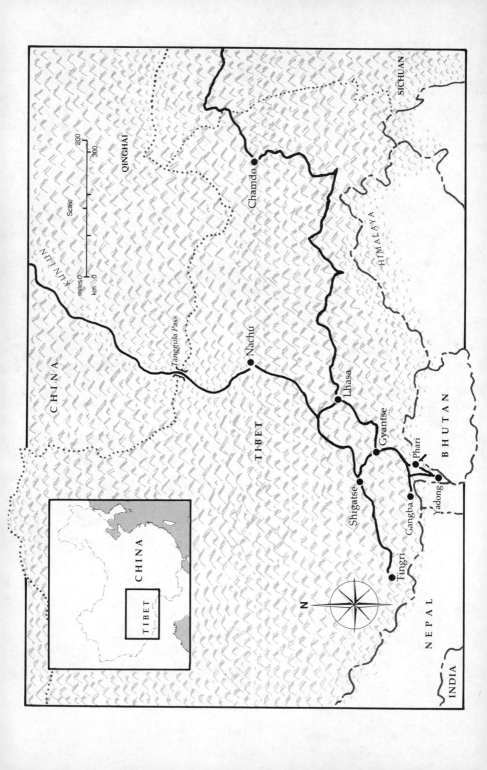

SKY BURIALS

The cold fresh morning ushered in a new world for me. At times like this I felt overwhelmed by so many new impressions, as if on the point of cultural saturation. Hunger however focused my attention on basics and so I sallied forth in search of food. My first practical impression of Lhasa brought me down to earth: it appeared that time had not only stood still here, but had accumulated in the form of countless layers of dirt and grime in the streets. It should not be forgotten that water is rare here, and using it for washing streets would be a luxury indeed. The pace of the city was slow, and the lazy jingling of bicycle bells contributed to an atmosphere of deceptive tranquillity. I made my way through the tumbling labyrinth of crooked, narrow and uneven streets towards the centre of town, stumbling as I did so over a variety of jetsam on the path: chiefly old shoes and excrement. A large number of emaciated dogs also appeared underfoot at every corner. I was following a sound, louder and more urgent than the bicycle bells. Suddenly at the end of an alleyway I was given a hint of what was to come – crossing my path was a long unbroken chain of people, shuffling slowly forward.

Shuffling and alternately prostrating themselves, these were the pilgrims who to acquire merit in the next life were ritually walking around and around Barkhor Street, which encircles Lhasa's central 'cathedral', the Jokhang. People of every age and description were to be found here. I noticed particularly one Golok woman from Changthang, her waist-length hair braided into 108 plaits to reflect the 108 Blessings of the Buddha.

The women from the city itself were disarmingly natural and even coquettish. All of them wore jewellery – here, an anchor-like pendant hanging from a belt; there, a finely worked steel-and-flint pouch encrusted with semi-precious stones. The gaudy jewels offset the raw, fresh exuberance of these women, whose refined but natural good looks I immediately found seductive. I was not alone: in the past the beauty of the women had apparently had such a distracting effect on the men that a former Dalai Lama ordered them to blacken their faces with soot.

Of the outsiders circling the Jokhang, the most striking were the Khampas from the eastern province of Kham. Fierce and arrogant, this warrior race had a presence that would have outfaced even Pathans. Their looks were dishevelled and wild, and their long manes of plaited hair were drawn through large rings of bone and coral and twined around with brightly-coloured cotton bands. Like the women, they too wore jewels and coins in their hair. Without exception they wore knives in richly decorated scabbards which protruded from the coats worn loose over their powerful bodies.

Here as elsewhere on my travels, I noted that hats were a very important article of dress, denoting status and place of origin. Tibetans have a particularly flamboyant range of different headgear, the most luxurious being covered with gold and silver thread embroidery.

Religious objects also formed part of their dress. *Gaus*, or amulet boxes, which were a sort of miniature, portable shrine, hung round the neck over the chest, or down the back and tied to a sash. Many held small prayer wheels, each of which contain the famous mantra: *Om Mani Padme Hum*. Each spin of the wheel sends a blessing to heaven, and thus increases one's credit there. The wheels themselves came in a variety of designs, but they must have been status symbols as well as a means of acquiring merit for some were most richly decorated.

But, to return to the pilgrims on Barkhor Street, theirs was the means by which most merit could be attained. To aid them in their prostrations, they wore leather aprons, knee-pads, and a primitive kind of mitten made of wood and metal to protect the palms of the hands. Some of those making the circuits had found means of speeding up the process. I saw one man, dressed lightly, who took the three steps between each prostration as great bounds, and then, a stone in each hand, threw himself down for the prostration and glided along the ground, the stones acting as skates.

Barkhor Street seemed peopled with characters who might have stepped straight out of a medieval morality play. Men dressed like court jesters, complete with cap and bells; lamas who blew strange trumpets made from human femurs. Each side of the street the pilgrims passed along was lined with beggars and cripples, the destitute and the infirm. People plagued by diseases and poverty of an unimaginable ghastliness held thin arms out from bodies that were no more than bundles of appalling rags and implored alms: 'Guchi, guchi,' they said – please, please. For the more fortunate or the less devout, refreshment was available from chang stalls. Chang is the local barley beer, and Tibetans drink it in vast quantities.

As they all shuffled round and round in the obligatory clockwise direction they passed not only the deprived and the maimed, but souvenir shops, and shops with a religious slant: selling prayer flags, sutras, votive plaques of clay, effigies of the Buddha, and white *khatas*, or shawls, which are exchanged on meeting. Interspersed with the beggars sat lamas, a *drilbu* – bell – in their left hand and a *dorje* – a thunderbolt, one of the attributes of the Buddha – in their right. This is one of the most important objects in Vajrayana Buddhism, especially in exorcism. The trumpet, drum and drilbu all keep evil spirits at bay, but the drilbu shares with the dorje a higher symbolism. The two represent respectively wisdom and faith, female and male.

The circuits made by the pilgrims are called *korlas*. Lhasa has three routes for korlas to be made along. The one around the Jokhang is known as the Middle Walk, also known as 'the country'. The second, outermost korla, with a circuit of four miles, is called the Linkhor, and takes in not just all of Lhasa but also two major hills – that on which the Potala stands, and the Chokpori, or Iron Hill; it is known as 'the continent'. The third walk is around the very centre of the Jokhang and is called the Nangkhor – 'the capital'. At the centre of this most hallowed sanctum stands the revered statue of Jowo Rinpoche, the Precious Lord, Buddha-Sakyamuni, who draws the faithful to him from right across Tibet and beyond, from Gansu, Qinghai, Sichuan and Yunan. Built in AD 652 by King Songsten Gampo, it contains the enormous gold-plated statue, encrusted with endless turquoise and coral, which was brought to Tibet by the king's Chinese wife, the Princess Wen Cheng. It is here that the Dalai Lamas are enthroned – though it is possible that the ancient ceremony will never be seen again.

I entered the forecourt of the Jokhang to see it scattered with the faithful, prostrating themselves. They knelt facing the great columned entrance of the temple, painted bright red but partially hidden by huge white canopies which billowed in the breeze, stitched all over with blue knots symbolising eternity. The broad paving stones of the square were polished smooth by generation upon generation of prostrators, who laid between them and the stone anything from cardboard to leather to rags to make their task more comfortable. I felt the breeze on my face gratefully and listened to the sound of the cardboard rubbing the flagstones as the people prayed. Near me, a knot of children watched in respectful silence, though some of them made halting attempts to ape their parents. Other children lazed among the stray dogs in the sun. You had to pick your way between them to reach the temple.

Before entering the temple the pilgrims pass before a giant prayer wheel and they give it a turn – no devout person passes one anywhere without doing so. The giant drum of this particular wheel is packed with thousands of rolled mantras, so one turn is enough to send many thousands of invocations heavenwards. As in Xinjiang, the foreign non-believer is allowed to enter. This courtesy does not extend to the Han Chinese, though many of them try to do so. I joined a long line of pilgrims waiting to go in. Slowly we moved forwards, passing into the cavernous, dark building one by one, filing past innumerable small votary butter lamps. But the dark walls all but suffocated the light.

Many of the pilgrims had come to Lhasa to buy and sell goods, the pilgrimage being repeated as often as they could afford to make it. They arrived with yaks and their dog – usually a kind of mastiff – and lived in encampments at the edge of the town, from where they made trading forays to the market. The Tibetan diet is very limited, so those with produce to sell would head for the butter market or the meat market – they face each other. Much of the yak butter comes from Qinghai. It travels wrapped in sheeps' stomachs, in which rancid butter will keep for up to two years. This butter, by the way, is more like a cheese; it is certainly quite palatable.

Though all killing is forbidden, there are Tibetans who slaughter (or employ Muslim slaughterers) and eat meat, which is necessary to withstand the wintry cold. They usually eat the meat raw and dry, but fresh meat is also available. The meat market is a pretty gruesome place, the meat laid out in slabs on grimy tables, and the blood from it dripping into puddles on the dirty earth beneath. Under one such table a dog slept; and a baby, held splay-legged by his mother, urinated.

Urination is a very public thing. What I had taken for cattle troughs set into street walls turned out to be pissoirs, though they were rarely used by the Tibetans, who simply urinated against the wall wherever they happened to be. As I have said, the streets were littered with excrement; but the people here don't clean themselves with sand or water as I had seen them do in Afghanistan. At night one's nose was the best guide along the unlit streets. At least the dogs weren't much of a threat. For all their barking all you needed to do was shout at them or fling a stone to get rid of them. But if you were picking up a stone from the street, it was wise to look hard before you touched it to make sure it *was* a stone.

For all the influence of the Chinese, the Tibetans are still in the main devoted to the Dalai Lama. Barkhor Street shops were full of his photograph, framed or unframed, or set into keyrings. These were hand-coloured black and white photos, which the Tibetans were fond of pressing against their foreheads as a token of respect. Another mainstay of life is chang, to which I quickly became addicted, so much so that I found myself irritated when I felt like a drink in the late evening and found all the chang stores closed. I got around this problem by buying a one-litre plastic bottle and filling it at closing time for a modest 17 pence. Enough chang to tide me over until the next morning. The stores were usually next door to one another, and as the quality of the beer varied from stall to stall, it became a pleasant evening pastime to try out different hostelries. Usually, you were invited to try the beer before you bought, having a sample poured into your cupped palm.

Food was in short supply. I saw no fruit at all apart from some very tired dates. The staple Tibetan diet is based on *tsamba* – barley flour ground to a powder. It is mixed with tea and rancid butter to form a dough – when it is ready to be eaten. The process of squeezing and kneading to saturate the flour properly needs care, or the food will crumble like a badly-built sandcastle. Once the art has been mastered, you can vary the flavour by mixing the flour with chang or sugared tea. I once successfully introduced chocolate flavouring. The whole process can be facilitated by the use of a tsamba bag, which is a small chamois-leather pouch which you fill with tea and flour and then wring out again and again until the mix is perfect. It's also useful for storing prepared tsamba to take with you on a journey. Tsamba is eaten so much by Tibetans that they appear to live on little else. For such a monotonous diet they appear well-nourished. Tsamba must contain a generous spread of nutrition. It is sometimes supplemented with raw yak meat. I thought that little could perturb my hardened eating habits, but I was somewhat surprised at the method employed in Tibetan restaurants for carving up the dried meat. 'Carving' is hardly the word, though, for the yak carcass was placed on a tree trunk in the middle of the tables. The *maître d'hôtel* approached it axe in hand, and I half expected him to yell 'Timber!' as he raised it above his head and brought it crashing down with a mighty blow. He then proceeded to hack away for a few minutes, reducing the meat to ever smaller chunks. From time to time a piece would fly off and land on the floor, and sometimes the *maître* would recover it before the dogs ate it. I was presented with a piece retrieved from the floor and wiped on his filthy jacket with a flourish. I dared not refuse his hospitality, and in any case my hunger for meat overcame any queasiness. I blew the dust off my prize and tried to remove as much of the grime as possible. The taste was pleasantly surprising, tasting like beef jerky. I soon took to buying my own raw yak or sheep joint from the market, hacking strips off the bone as the Tibetans did, though my Swiss army knife was a rather more fastidious tool to use for this than the weapons they carried.

Other supplements to the diet included yogurt, a rock-hard white cheese similar to that found in Xinjiang and Afghanistan, barley-corns, and puffed barley.

At night the market trade slowly petered out, but the endless circling of the pilgrims continued unabated. Those not taking part went home to bed, picking their way across the rickety paving stones, stooping through the low entrances to their houses, which gave onto small courtyards piled high with litter, some of which also contained small manual water pumps. The houses themselves were very simple stone and wood structures, the rooms ill-lit, with soot-covered walls. The furniture by contrast was brightly painted, predominantly in red, and the carpets and bedspreads were gaily patterned with dragons and peacocks, flowers and tigers. Nearly every house contained an ornate shrine in one corner of the main room, usually arranged on a showcase cupboard, inside which would be photos and statuettes of the gods, together with a prized photo of the Dalai Lama if the owners were lucky enough to have one.

I had been out of England for nearly a year but my energy was kept alive by the mesmeric effect these people and their religion had on the mind. For all that I was tired, and it was pleasant to laze around sipping chang talking to other foreigners. I hadn't seen many since leaving Europe, and never so many in one place since Istanbul. In having to fit into cultures that were not my own I had not only had to efface my personality, but keep my guard up. Now I was free of those constraints for a time and it was like the loosening of a stiff collar. There were one or two foreigners who even brought their own amusing sense of 'decorum' to their unusual environment – like the two Americans I met who insisted on referring to the Dalai Lama either as 'The Big Cat' or 'Big Daddy'.

The greatest surprise in store for me was when I met up again with my Japanese friend Tadashi. It had taken him sixteen days to reach Lhasa from Kashgar, and so he had beaten me to it by one day. We decided to celebrate our reunion and could think of no better way of doing so than by going to the newly opened Tibetan disco-theque, held in what had once been a Tantric seminary. The place was like a dance hall in a wooden barn, with a stage at one end and illuminated by bare lightbulbs. You paid your entrance fee at a desk and squeezed into the packed room. People were drinking energetically and the floor was strewn with empty bottles. It was like Saturday Night Fever gone mad – the whole town seemed to be letting its hair down, dancing to the thunderous beat of disco muzak imported from India. The Khampas were there in force, stamping their feet, shouting and cooing. They'd obviously taken to disco like ducks to water and the dance floor was a jungle of jumping legs, flailing arms, whirling and thrusting bodies. The Khampas, knives still in their belts, had their own version of punk, and gave as good a version of the pogo as was possible in the rarefied air. They were completely intoxicated, oblivious to their surroundings, and showing a complete lack of respect for anyone else's space. In their state of high euphoria they asked Tadashi and me to dance with them. I noticed that the Tibetan girls who were there were also busy asking foreign girls to dance with them. The revelling went on until the small hours.

One of the symptoms I noticed in myself, being once again among other foreigners, was that I suffered from bouts of verbal diarrhoea when I wanted to impress them. On the other hand, I could also become withdrawn, especially when I encountered people whose behaviour I found irritating or shameful. Then I would be keen to move on, to get away from this circle. But there was still much for me to see here, and every infuriating foreigner was, to be fair, counterbalanced by one who showed genuine interest in Tibet, and respected its people and its customs. Among them was Dave, a warmhearted American language teacher – and a Trotskyist (he insisted on not being called a Trotskyite). In company, his comments on the topic of conversation, whatever it was, would always make everyone else furious. Later, I was to spend two months travelling in his engaging company.

In Muslim lands I had found that reciting the *kalimeh* had done me no harm, and so here I turned to the often repeated *Om Mani Padme Hum* – which means 'O Hail Jewel in the Lotus'. Whether I did this to avoid bad karma or to attract good I cannot say, but what was certain was that I was becoming increasingly superstitious. Before setting out on each leg of my journey that followed, I was possessed by a nagging fear that my luck was going to run out. I never failed to leave a temple without ringing one of the bells at the gate.

The temples are filled with the most menacing images. Yama, Lord of the Dead and King of Religion, is seen in the most terrifying posture. This three-eyed, yak-headed god is depicted with a glowering expression, riding an equally aggressive bull who appears either to be trampling a human being underfoot or sexually mounting it. Yama is a rotund figure, but nonetheless threatening for his portly body. His hair rises like flames, his head bears a diadem of skulls, and round his neck is a garland of human heads. His penis is large and erect. In his outstretched right hand he carries a staff made of bone and mounted with a skull for the chastisement of mankind, and in his left hand he carries a noose. His sister Yami, who for some reason is known as Minister of the Exterior, steps onto the bull to offer her brother a skull cup full of blood. In her free hand she brandishes a trident. By contrast to Yama, she is slender and athletic, an animal skin draped over her back her only clothing. The figures are set against a background of dancing flames and they are painted with such vitality that they seem ready to spring at you out of their grotesque world, and yet Yama is only one of a great and complex pantheon of gods, subject to Buddha but constantly ready to rebel, to wreak havoc on the world and the human race.

Despite the appalling ruin wrought by the Red Guards on the monasteries of Tibet, those that are left present a magical sight to the traveller when glimpsed across the hills. Drepung, the world's largest monastery, rises above a sparse forest through which a winding path gives access to the majestic complex of whitewashed stone buildings, built layer upon layer, with russet roofs and temples with golden canopies, separated by winding, cobbled pathways which meander up the rocky hillside backing onto the mountains beyond. Drepung, whose name literally means 'nice heap', lies four kilometres west of the Potala. It was founded in AD 1416. It was not exempt from the depredations of the Red Guards, but now the Chinese are trying to make good the harm they did in the sixties, and a programme of rebuilding and renovation is under way.

To the north of Lhasa lies Sera, with Drepung and Ganden one of the 'Three Pillars of the State', and built in AD 1419 by followers of Tsongkhapa, the founder of the dominant Gelukpa Buddhist sect, more commonly known as the 'yellow hats'. Like Drepung, its glittering golden canopies and gleaming white stupas shine like jewels, but as you approach the devastation it has suffered becomes plain to see: broken and gutted temples, frescoes ruined by overpainting and graffiti. During that period of insanity most of the temples

317

of Tibet were destroyed, their treasures desecrated or carted off to be sold abroad. The empty buildings were turned over for use as workshops and granaries.

The locals often helped the Red Guards in their work of destruction. However, this cannot be seen simply as a manifestation of ignorant evil. The romantic image Tibet has acquired as a kind of pristine Shangri-La hides a darker past – one in which the country emerges as an unenlightened, feudal theocracy whose very inflexibility contributed to its downfall, just as that of the Incas did hundreds of years earlier. Before the Chinese moved in to 'liberate' Tibet, 5 per cent of Tibetans owned most of the land, while the monasteries owned great estates covering a third of the country, consuming half of Tibet's total revenue and controlling tens of thousands of serfs. Drepung alone had 25,000 serfs, and ruled over 700 minor monasteries. Every family in the land was expected to contribute one son to the monastic order and the lama population of 110,000 accounted for a quarter of the male population. The ruling lords and lamas resisted progress staunchly, and there was virtually no education outside the monasteries. The only wheeled vehicles were the three cars owned by the Dalai Lama. The majority of the population were all but slaves, trapped by poverty and punitive taxation.

Thus they lived cocooned from the world, apart from occasional skirmishes with British colonial forces, until 1947. Tibet, fearing a Chinese invasion then, sent a delegation to Britain and the USA. Both countries refused to recognise her as an independent nation. She had no developed army of her own – indeed the army encountered by Younghusband's expeditionary force only forty years earlier had been one of medieval cavalry. Tibet's policy of isolation was rebounding on her.

In 1950 the Chinese invaded and during the course of the next thirty years Tibetan culture was systematically erased. Only a dozen monasteries out of 2,400 survived; the language was suppressed, and in the best tradition of revolutionary fervour, place and street names were changed: the Dalai Lama's summer palace, Norbulingka, the Jewel Park, predictably became People's Park; street names had to be relearned: Revolution, Liberation, and so on.

For all this cosmetic change, Tibet remained backward, and after thirty years literacy was still half the national average for all of China.

In 1980 the Chinese rulers ordered a complete reversal of the autocratic policies that had suppressed Tibetan religion, language and culture so brutally for so long. Monasteries were once again allowed to recruit youngsters willing to devote themselves to Buddhism. The novices, aged between 7 and 20, must be honest, devoted, and dedicated to the cause of religion, in good health, and unmarried. This last condition also applies to lamas who, having left a monastery for the secular life and a wife, wish subsequently to return. All these rules are old rules, but there is a new one: the postulant novice must also be a 'patriot'. One practical advantage is that these children are assured of an education. The total number of lamas permitted to be recruited is fixed by the government. Thus it is that the sprawling complexes of such monasteries as Drepung and Sera, in reality small towns, are now a mere shadow of their former selves – the atmosphere is hollow, the ambience all but non-existent. At their height, Drepung had 10,000 lamas, and Sera 7,000. Now they have 400 and 300 respectively. They stand as monuments to a time that will never return.

Certain customs remain exclusively and privately Tibetan. Despite the fact that it was the Chinese and not the Tibetans that allowed foreigners into the country, I found myself as a total outsider in the rather odd position of being allowed to watch a ceremony that Tibetans forbade the Chinese to see – that of disposing of their dead. The sky burial is similar to the practice of the Zoroastrians, as the body is given up to be eaten by vultures, the birds benefiting from the body which is useless after the spirit has left it. The rite was expensive at 60 yuan – a price which under the old regime only the wealthy could afford. In those days the poor were simply thrown into the river – a practice which has resulted in most Tibetans refusing to eat fish.

It was a bizarre, stark setting at the foot of a mountain. The burial crew of six men and a boy sat warming themselves round a fire and drinking cups of tea. Near them, like a small promontory, an enormous flat stone projected from the mountainside. It was here that the corpse would be offered to the birds. Disposing of the dead is an hereditary function, handed down in families over centuries. The man in charge wore a white tradesman's coat as a mark of office. The rest were dressed in leather jackets, their dark trousers tucked into black boots. Once the bodies have been brought out from the city the leader of the team must make sure that the vultures are waiting, as the bodies must be entirely eaten. The cold was intense but they set to work before first light, as soon as the body they had to prepare had arrived. They stripped it naked and shaved its head. The corpse was then carved up. First several small incisions were made as part of the ritual process, and then the meat was sliced from the bone. Once this task was done, the boy took the skull and bones and crushed them, mixing them with tsamba as he did so, so that the birds would consume them too. If any part of the dead was left uneaten it was considered a bad omen. Anything that does remain must be buried.

As the sun broke over the horizon, bringing immediate and welcome warmth with it, and throwing deep shadows across the moonscape of the plateau, I imagined myself at some ancient ceremony of the Aztecs or the Mayas. By now the meat had been spread out on the stone and the vultures were circling. But all was not well: few birds settled to eat, and a gang of huge ravens arrived instead, displacing the vultures. The burial crew shooed the ravens away, and then wooed the vultures with enticing cries, lobbing extra morsels into the rounded 'dishes' worn into the stone. Gradually the bolder of the vultures broke from the bunch of forty or fifty who were sitting hunched a short way off, and it wasn't long before the feast had begun in earnest.

The ceremony had been a highly charged one to watch, and it demands the utmost respect from the onlookers. Any uninvited voyeur immediately incurs the wrath of the Tibetans, and on the very day that I was present two foreigners who had been taking photographs from a distance were chased with knives. But, although invited, my position was just as hypocritical, for I had succumbed in true western manner to the voyeuristic attraction of the morbid which affects nearly all of us. The fact that I was a friend, that I had even drunk tea with the crew, didn't alter that. I worried that I had attended a private burial for no other reason than curiosity about what by western standards was a very unusual ceremony.

No matter from what direction you approach the Potala, it always appears untainted by its surroundings – it looks as if it had nothing to do with them, floating there on its mountainside. To its west the Chinese quarter is little more than an industrial estate. To the east a small depression hides much of the city, to give the villages on that side an unobstructed view of their palace. Inside Lhasa itself, you could rarely lose sight of it, hovering above the humdrum activities of the town like the shimmering heat from the surface of the desert.

The present palace was built in the mid seventeenth century by the great Fifth Dalai Lama, and it took thousands of labourers half a century to complete. Standing over a hundred metres up and straddling the cliff face of a hill, it is reached by a series of ascending switchbacks, the steps hidden from view. Its entrance is an enormous double door covered by a vast curtain. Wide stairs lead up from it through a passageway, and here you notice that the outer walls of the palace are several feet thick. The passageway takes you to an open courtyard overlooked by the Dalai Lama's living quarters.

It is a warren of rooms, altars, temples, shrines, halls and passageways, almost like an organism, rather than a building. From everywhere there are magnificent views over Lhasa. The workmanship here is exquisite down to the smallest detail, capitals and corbels revealing wooden sphinxes, lions and a multitude of other real and mythological fauna. Influences are many: here one could detect that of Iran, there that of China. Craftsmen from all Tibet's neighbours had come to work on the Potala in the days of her greatness. Red and gold are the dominant colours.

The rooms are decorated with rich fabrics, tapestries and frescoes, the detail of whose work defies description, the illustrations telling stories of heroes and the gods, or simply representing views of the local landscape, with Lhasa and the Potala in prominent positions.

The light from candles below them illuminates the faces of the golden statues of Buddha in all his forms.

And at the very heart of the palace is its heart indeed – the enormous chamber containing the sarcophagi of the former Dalai Lamas. The gloomy gallery is so high that you can't see the tops of the tallest stupas within it, though each stupa was richly gilded and encrusted with precious stones. The biggest shrines are those of the Fifth and the Thirteenth Dalai Lamas – the former is covered with 300,000 ounces of gold.

Wandering through the Potala was like walking through a time-warp, but amidst all the magnificence of its history, you couldn't help remembering that the religious coffers were being filled by poor peasants who could ill afford to give donations. But the only hope in the lives of the poor was for better luck next time, and the way to achieve that was by subsidising their church.

I was always drawn to the Muslim minority, and this was possibly because Islam had provided a link throughout my journey. I thus found the cultural gap between me and them less than that between me and the Han. Their company provided me with a sense of home. For in contrast to the Tibetans, the Chinese Hui Muslims were always immaculately groomed. They wore sombre blue or brown multi-pocketed Mao suits and a cap to match, though the more stylish among them went for a Borsalino fedora, which gave them the air of thirties gangsters. Their drive for profit was almost pathological. Like their fellow Muslims, the Uighurs, they were natural entrepreneurs, and most of them made a living as traders. They sold their wares from a groundsheet spread out on the street, or hung carpets for sale from the walls. A lucky few even had stalls. Several Huis owned restaurants, which were frequented by Tibetans as well as Muslims, and in this area they seemed to have struck gold. Not that it was easy. They worked tirelessly, and alone – for many of the Huis had left their wives behind to come to Lhasa, and hadn't seen them for years. Those wives who were with them wore chadors. To my surprise, some of the Hui viewed the new liberalisation programme with cynicism:

'They've only introduced these new reforms allowing us to run our own businesses because they can't provide us with jobs,' said one.

The Hui were doing well, and I sat in on a clandestine meeting where they discussed how best to maximise their resources. The meeting might have been going on anywhere in the world. The talk covered an astonishing network of enterprises, from a factory for reconditioning engines in Gansu to chains of stores in most of China's major cities. They were keen to expand further, and clearly had the means to do so, but the problem was how to escape the high taxes they would attract. So they discussed the setting up of shadow companies and cooperatives, and the appointments of figurehead directors, and fund-channelling. I might have heard the same kind of conversation in any City or Zurich boardroom.

Meanwhile I had succumbed to the worst form of traveller's disease: I had reached saturation point but my appetite for yet more impressions remained. But with the desire to go on making new discoveries came a question – would my perception be up to it, or would I be incapable of taking any more on board? This doubt provided a forceful argument against roaming across Tibet, but the lure of setting off once more into the unknown was too much for me. I began to wonder whether I had ever really appreciated England for wouldn't a Tibetan marvel at our hills and moors as I marvelled at his austere mountains?

Giving in to my desire, I promised myself that this would be the last jaunt before I resumed my scheduled route. That promise made, I set about preparing myself mentally and physically for the rigours ahead – for I foresaw further battles of wits with the authorities as well as tussles with the land and the elements. The first job was to secure permission to travel within Tibet. Summoning my remaining energy, I proceeded to do so.

Undaunted by the usual outright refusals, I persisted. Sent from one office to another I was punctilious to a fault, which is very important when dealing with Chinese officials in Tibet. You mustn't call it Tibet, for example, but the Tibetan Autonomous Region of the People's Republic of China. Added to that you have to have the patience of a sage. I found resources of will within me somehow and presented a rocklike front to the officials who broke on it like waves. My letters came in handy as always, and provided the officials with the excuse they needed to get me off their backs and grant me permission. The promotion of greater understanding between our peoples, the letter said, and what a good idea that was. No one could possibly disagree with it. And on the letterhead there was even a picture of Winston Churchill.

'But this letter comes direct from your Prime Minister,' gasped the official who read it.

Who was I to disillusion him? They issued me with a permit which amused me: its number is 00001.

But if I was soon to travel around Tibet before starting off on the long road to Peking I would have to obtain money. I had come into China with £200, and half of that I had already spent. In fact, the way things turned out, the hundred I had left would have sufficed to reach Peking three months later – and there would still have been change out of it. But at the time that didn't seem likely, frugal as I was, and I didn't like the idea of running out completely, so I approached the Lhasa branch of the Bank of China and asked them if they would forward my cheque to Peking, so that in due course I might pick up some cash.

'I'm sorry, but that won't be possible,' said the clerk.

'Why not?'

'Because it'll take a week.'

'All right. Then I'll wait.'

'That's not possible,' repeated the clerk. But he was disconcerted.

'Why not?' I said again, reasonably.

'You'll have to wait two weeks,' he decided, doubtfully.

'Fine, I'll wait two weeks.'

'That won't be possible, either . . .'

We had agreed to six weeks before I realised that a new tactic was called for. I suggested sending the cheque air mail, and when that failed to register, I stretched out my arms, made a spluttering noise as the aeroplane's engines connected, and then flew around the clerks' desks. They were greatly taken by this – all except the assistant manager who was afraid of being run over.

Finally they took pity on me.

Despite my dishevelled appearance I was invited to several grand occasions, and even banquets, thanks to my friend the factory manager Li Jun. I must have become something of a local celebrity, for I found myself a kind of social linch-pin, introducing the assistant bank manager to members of the Public Security Bureau, and factory managers to members of the Foreign Affairs Bureau. They exchanged visiting cards when they met – a novelty in China.

During one week of banquets any doubts I had that China was an egalitarian society were swiftly confirmed. The élite were swept along in chauffeur-driven cars to feast themselves on delicacies specially flown in from China proper. At one dinner, there was a floor show during which a Han female dancer performed the Snake Dance – an erotic piece involving her slithering, spiralling and entwining herself round her male companion. There were games, too, prizes and a disco. It would have been easy to forget the harsh poverty outside the restaurant's windows.

There was very little contact in general between what I can only describe as the colonial Han Chinese and the Tibetan 'natives', whom the Chinese regarded as dirty, but exceptionally there had been the occasional intermarriage. Through Li Jun I met one such couple, a Tibetan singer and his Chinese wife at a New Year feast. It was a meal of meals, featuring such delicacies as dog meat, which was tender and quite delicious, pig's trotters, and the famous 100-year-old eggs, which in fact are only 20 days old, pickled in lime and packed in clay. Other dishes included duck, served to be eaten complete with its head, neck and even its webbed feet. We washed down the lot with beer and Mao Tai, a sorghum-based liquor that took one's breath away.

We ushered in the Year of the Ox with toasts drowned by the noise of fireworks, which were supplied in vast quantities. The effect their noise had on me was interesting: for they terrifyingly recalled the bombardment of Herat. At times they seemed no less dangerous than the Russian bullets, as rockets whirled crazily off course and crackers whizzed underfoot.

In the two and a half weeks I'd spent in Lhasa, living among other foreigners in comparative luxury, and attending an endless social round of banquets of the type I've described, I had undergone a metamorphosis. I was no longer as keen as I had been to forsake the soft life for the hardships of the road once more. But just when my resolve was faltering, my American friend Dave offered to go with me. The idea of a companion after so long alone was attractive, and besides Dave offered a fresh set of eyes to see with, and someone to share experiences with. Not only that, he was an excellent linguist and a brilliant conversationalist – truck drivers would be begging to offer us lifts in exchange for the pleasure of our company.

During my negotiations with the officials for my travel permits, I had chosen the Chumbi Valley as my destination, for it was far enough away, between Bhutan and Sikkim, to offer opportunities for numerous detours and stopovers *en route*. It might even be possible to visit Phari, the world's highest town. But Dave, who knew me quite well already, made it clear that if I tried to get across the border into Bhutan he would not be accompanying me there.

LAMAS AND
MORE LAMAS

Gyantse, once an important commercial and religious centre south-west of Lhasa, is now a rather sleepy medieval town. Beneath the monastery's walls women knelt by a pond pummelling wool with sticks, the steady kettledrum beat not deterring the horses which came to drink the water. The horses and the housewives ignored one another.

The monastery itself, Palkhor, screamed rape, but the world ignored its cries. Its temples had been gutted, the wood of its beams, columns and struts made into a funeral pyre, its frescoes blackened by the flames of the Cultural Revolution, and its possessions looted and dispersed. Revolutionary slogans had been daubed on the walls that were still standing, though their message was lost on the locals, who couldn't read Chinese. From the ruins, the Tibetans had salvaged what building materials they could, along with the timber that had not burned – for wood is much valued in this treeless land. Pilgrims still come here to pass the magnificent *kumbum* (a stupa with attached chapels). This multi-tiered wedding cake of a stupa with its dozens of chambers inexplicably escaped total ruin, and its golden dome has no rival in all Tibet.

The monastery still has a small population of lamas, and those who were not engaged in the daily rituals in the shrines were busy hand-printing prayer-flags, a job which consisted of taking wooden blocks, stretching canvas over them, and applying pressure to transfer the ink from block to material. These flags have the same sort of function as candles in our church: as the flags ripple and decay in the wind, so the prayers on them are sent to the heavens. The temples were also home to some impressive butter sculptures, the first I had seen. These huge pieces are generally carved for festivals. Hand-coloured, they are not as ephemeral as they sound, for the butter has the consistency of rubber and the look of cheese – such a sculpture can last for many years, if not forever. Often they are circular, reflecting the mandala, or wheel of life.

There was a new hospital in town, but this, which ought to have been a showpiece, looked like a chunk of vandalised housing estate. In the last stages of collapse from neglect, it was all but deserted, host only to wind, dust, and playing children; a dream that had foundered. Signs above doors proclaimed: 'Western Medicine', 'Chinese Medicine', and 'Tibetan Medicine'. I had gone there to be examined for a bout of 'flu. It had been so rare for me to feel ill on this journey that any sign of malaise sent me into a panic. My main fear now was that I might have contracted meningitis, which is endemic in Tibet. But the hospital no longer provided diagnosis or treatment. Instead I was directed to a grey group of barracks-like buildings. If the hospital had been grim, this was worse. The surgery was a room piled high with unpacked cartons, gas cylinders, and a blackboard with some scribbled writing on it. The floor was uneven, but the furniture was so heavy that it stood firm. A young army doctor wearing a white coat and mask was alone on duty. In front of a group of curious onlookers he questioned me from across a long bench table before giving me an examination. Finally he told me that I was in no danger of meningitis, TB or altitude sickness. Having thus given me a clean bill of health, as far as he was concerned, he gave me some tablets for a sore throat and earache. There was no charge for his services as medical treatment is free in Tibet.

Dave and I continued on our way, staying at a caravanserai the colour of pus, and sleeping there on beds which looked as if they'd just been vacated by fourteen amorous yaks. The sheets were unspeakably soiled, but not half so much as the mattress underneath. The 'hotel's' penthouse lavatory added a new dimension to architecture. From the roof, you descended into the pit by way of a ladder. Once there, it was so dark at night that you couldn't tell if members of the opposite sex were already installed until it was too late – but then it was equally impossible to tell if you were correctly positioned over one of the six small holes which you were supposed to aim down into the void.

The place had added colour in the form of the manager, a demented drunk who derived immeasurable pleasure from tormenting us, waking us in the middle of the night to check our papers, and one moment telling us to bolt ourselves into the room lest we be attacked, the next instructing us to leave the door open at all times. He was never sober, but he must have had the semblance of a memory, for when we returned to his inn two weeks later he had the temerity to reprimand us for not having made the beds properly when we'd left. What beds, we felt tempted to ask him, but to our amazement when we got to our room we found clean, hitherto unused sheets. I could only assume that over the years what he'd saved on soap he'd spent on new bed linen. This time before leaving we straightened our sheets, rolled our quilts up to the head of the bed, and placed the pillow on top for his inspection and approval.

When I reached Phari, on a plain that lay beneath the hills separating China from Bhutan, I asked a herdsman if the yaks observed the national boundaries.

'Aren't you worried about your animals drifting across into Bhutan?' I asked.

He shrugged his shoulders, unworried. 'Some of them do go backwards and forwards,' he said.

'So you lose them.'

'No, we don't,' he replied with a grin. 'If anything, it seems that the yaks prefer living under socialism in China than under a monarchy in Bhutan.'

Most people probably know what a yak looks like: it's a domesticated beast somewhere between a buffalo and a cow. So centrally important is this animal to the Tibetans that they have several words which apply to it (just as the Eskimos have 45 words for snow). The word 'yak' means the male of the species. The female is called a *dri*, and a *dzo* is an animal that is a cross between a yak and a cow, and can thus live at lower altitudes than the high ones yaks are happiest at. Many yaks were carefully groomed, and some sport headdresses – usually red, but sometimes white or grey. They also occasionally wear earrings; two wooden splints; and stylish haircuts – the most attractive being a crewcut on top, but long under the chin. This all-purpose animal provides milk (and butter, cheese and yogurt), meat, wool and transport – and its bones, and especially its horns, are used for house construction and ornamentation. The yak's backbone, properly crushed and mixed with gold dust, is traditionally prescribed to Tibetan women as a contraceptive ('but it doesn't always work,' I was told. 'Anyway, the backbone of a mule does just as well.'). The dung is dried and provides fuel and insulation. The yak is used as a plough animal, and it can even be raced during festivals.

It was inevitable that the lure of Bhutan should prove too much for us. The wall of mountains that separates it from China barely hints at the magnificence beyond them. Dave, who earlier had fainted from lack of oxygen at the high altitudes we were travelling, couldn't refuse the short day-trip over the border. When we reached the pass, high up, a stupendous sight spread out before our eyes: the sub-continental plate crashing into the Asian landmass resulted in towering, glistening white peaks and great chasms of valleys. Mount Jomo Lhari, the 'Celestial Mountain of the Goddess', lay to our left. One of Tibet's tallest mountains (in a country of high peaks), it seemed close enough to touch. We gave it the nickname of 'Mount Yak Tooth' because it resembled one of the large number of yaks' molars that lay scattered around Phari. So plentiful were they that we considered a modest business venture – turning them into necklaces. Wildlife here was so unaffected by man's intrusion that deer grazed within yards of us and inquisitive eagles hovered close. It was like sitting on Olympus, commanding views over hundreds of square miles, overlooking a battalion of peaks – the clouds doing battle with the summits, seeming to suffocate them, but never quite succeeding as they drifted across the tops, always leaving the bases naked.

On our onward journey far above the treeline we only had cause for alarm once, when Dave thought he saw a couple of border guards. Instantly we dived for cover and lay trembling behind some boulders, scarcely daring to draw breath as we heard footsteps coming closer. Just as we were about to give ourselves up, praying that we wouldn't stop a hail of bullets, we saw that our pursuers were two yaks.

We came to a deserted stone house, with some flattened ground near it where nomads' tents had once stood. We were weary. My assurances to Dave that we would reach the capital, Thimpu, within two days' walking, failed to impress him. He doubted if we would make it. Frontier regulations are strict. Any Tibetans wishing to visit relatives in Bhutan must first travel to Lhasa or Shigatse to get permission, and then they have to travel via Nepal and India. Thus do politics and officialdom make a mockery of kinship and geographical proximity.

We didn't meet any Bhutanese in Bhutan. However as we left Bhutan we met a group of them huddled together on the Tibetan side of the border. They hailed us from a path below our own. Poorly dressed, with walking sticks and large bundles on their backs, they were waiting for nightfall. We had been warned that the Bhutanese border guards might shoot on sight, and this information must have been true, for the smugglers were anxious for any news we might have on the movements of frontier patrols. The oldest member of the group, a man in his early twenties, spoke diffidently in faltering English and kept on referring to us collectively as 'Sir'. We passed the time of day with them peacefully, and then went our separate ways.

Curiously in this small corner of Tibet there were many Bhutanese smugglers. They trade between Bhutan, India, Sikkim and Nepal, but they still appeared as elusive as the gophers. If they caught sight of me, they promptly vanished into the nearest doorway. The doors were adorned over the lintel with horns, and covered with cloth pelmets which billowed in the wind. Like so many mountain people they are sparely built, but they have the strength of an ibex. The standard dress is a coat, not unlike a dressing gown in appearance, formed of check lines. From a bulge in the material in the waist a knife protrudes. The coats hang low over tight trousers, and over these they sometimes wear an extra pair of socks with an Argyll design. Their hats are Russian-style, with earflaps joined together and a pompom on the top of the head. On the front of these hats they wear a proud badge depicting their king. Their haircuts, almost without exception, were sixties Beatles. For trade they bartered conventional trousers, though they never wore such garments themselves, for Chinese plimsolls and trinkets. I was unable to acquire one of their badges but I did swap Chinese money for Bhutanese currency. This is extraordinarily colourful, and features dragons and conch-shells, thunderbolts and *kinnaras* – a beast which is half bird and half human. I didn't know what I gave for what, for nobody knew the rate of exchange – if one existed. However the transaction brought an immediate posse up to me.

'Change money?'

It was early March 1985 when we were travelling past Phari to Yadong, at Tibet's southernmost tip. We entered the Chumbi Valley, and there we got a taste of the semi-tropical monsoon weather that was prevailing at the time – in other words, a dense blanket of rain. Here, the atmosphere was Alpine: there were streams, pastures, water mills – and food was plentiful: yakburgers with cabbage became our staple. The houses, of stone and wood, were like Swiss chalets, with carved balustrades and balconies. The standard of living here was obviously high. There was a postman who did his rounds on horseback. We found a public showerbath where for 5 *Mao* (about 10p) we could chop wood to heat the water siphoned from a pond beneath a waterfall.

In the Chumbi Valley, the sky was so far above the valley floor that no vultures descended. Thus it was that there were no sky burials; the dead were put into the earth.

But there was a serpent in this green and pleasant Eden. Here, Tibetan culture had been mercilessly crushed. The world of the people had been turned upside down. The landscape was littered with ruins, and we could have drawn up a catalogue of destruction as we passed village after village, each with its temples and forts laid waste: Phari, Gangba, Tingri . . . and the ancient fortified monastery of Shigatse, where in huge Chinese characters along one wall had been written the message, 'SMASH REVISIONISM'.

Recriminations over the destruction were plentiful, but odd:

'This was done by a landlord,' said one peasant, pointing out to me what was probably the work of the Red Guards.

'The British came with their planes and bombed here,' said another, even more fancifully, pointing to havoc wreaked by the same intemperate hands. I looked where his hand indicated – towards a fort reduced to spires where vultures perched. Elsewhere, a Chinese official blamed the vandalism of twenty years ago on the Nepalese. Another spoke of British Imperialism.

The authorities were certainly not at all happy about our presence in the region and it was only after a long discussion that I was allowed to take photographs – but even then only of the temple. By now I had acquired a 'minder' – the so-called Head of the Religious Affairs Bureau. It turned out that he didn't even know that there were different religious sects in Tibet. He became nervous when I asked someone to move out of the frame of my photo – obviously worried that thereby I'd get in some of the mountains in the background. I found this arrangement unsatisfactory in general, and I demanded that I be allowed to photograph wherever I pleased. It took them two days, but then I was issued with a new set of regulations: I would be allowed to photograph whatever I wanted, but I was not to photograph the temple – which was OK by me, as I had already taken lots of photos of it in compliance with their earlier ruling.

Fate caught up with us in the form of two Public Security Bureau officials, who travelled the 500 kilometres from Lhasa to Yadong to have a chat. The upshot of this was that Dave, who had no permit, was to be fined, and we were both to return to Lhasa forthwith – though I was granted permission to stop at Shigatse on the way. But I was not in the mood to return to Lhasa, and Dave wasn't about to pay any fine. He was, however, made to write a piece of 'self-criticism' about his irresponsible behaviour as a guest worker in China. He complied, but in it he dwelt lengthily on semantics, and added for good measure a perceptive statement about his understanding of Chinese policy-making, past and present. It might not have been self-criticism, strictly speaking, but its clever argument absolved him of any breach of the law. It went way above the heads of the officials, though.

Two days later we left Yadong, taking the 'wrong' road out of town – the one which headed away from Lhasa. No one supervised our departure. Perhaps, again, the officials felt they had discharged their duty and were only too pleased to be rid of us. In any case, I've never believed in taking the same route twice, if there was an alternative to hand. We disappeared from all official view for the next month, and even when later they caught up with us and charged us with travelling to closed areas they never found out that we had used a road which they'd described as a 'military throughway'.

On this journey through the byways of Tibet I began to question the new Chinese attitude towards their minority races – and the

Tibetans had become part of what might be called Colonial Greater China. Tibetan society had already been irreversibly changed. In many villages the prayer flag had been replaced by the red flag, and on the walls were written the great slogans of Mao's brave new world: 'Dig tunnels deep – store grain everywhere'; 'Grow more wheat'. At least on an individual level there was still a sense of humour – I smiled when I saw the following daub on the wall of a latrine: 'Shitting comrades – please aim accurately.'

Religion no longer played any kind of prominent role in this province that nestles between Sikkim and Bhutan – although few villages were without an enormous prayer flag at their gates, and most doors had the symbols of the sun and moon painted on them – if not an actual wheel of fortune.

On my travels in this unvisited region, I was to disappoint some and frighten many.

'You don't speak Tibetan,' one villager told me disapprovingly.

'I'm afraid that's true.'

'But you were educated at a western university.'

'Yes.' It was barely a lie. After all, I had an MA from the Chelsea School of Art.

'But you don't speak Tibetan.'

'No.'

'Very odd.'

'Why?'

'Well, doesn't everyone who's educated at a western university learn all the languages of the world?'

Somewhere else, a man rushed up to me in great excitement. He looked at my long hair and beard in amazement.

'Can I help?' I said.

'You're English, you say!'

'I am.'

'I have seen an English film.'

'Yes.'

'You cannot be English.'

'Why not?'

'Because they all have short hair and are clean-shaven!'

This was a new one for me – for until now, my hair and beard had given me an aura of respectability. I looked faintly like Karl

Marx. Thus it was that Uighurs and most Tibetans alike had assumed that all leading British officials looked like me, long hair and beards for them reflecting the apogee of respectability. I wondered what twenty- or thirty-year-old movie my suspicious friend had seen.

Films were certainly awaited with eager anticipation. When the films arrived in a village, everyone brought their chairs out of their houses and into the square, or stood around, or sat on the bonnet of a truck. The screen (where I saw a film) was an enormous white cloth hung from a balcony in a school playground.

Tibetans were aware of being Tibetan.

'What do I look like?' one asked me.

'Well . . .' I hesitated, unsure of what kind of answer he wanted. At times it was simply impossible to differentiate between Tibetans and Han Chinese.

'Tibetan but maybe a little Chinese,' said Dave diplomatically.

He seemed unhappy. 'Tibetan or Chinese?'

'Well . . . maybe Tibetan.'

'Positive?'

'Ehrm . . . yes. If you like.'

He still seemed in need of reassurance, but his next question was surprising: 'Are you sure I don't look English?'

This time we had no doubt. 'Absolutely not.'

'Sure?'

'Positive.'

'Absolutely?'

'Totally.'

'It's very important, you see.' But he seemed relieved already.

'Why?'

He looked apologetic. 'Well, my mother was living in Lhasa about nine months before I was born and there was this Englishman . . .'

We all laughed. 'You've had a lucky escape,' Dave joked, pointing to his own huge nose. 'After all, you wouldn't have wanted to end up with a nose like this.'

In another village a local earned the strong disapproval of an official who happened to overhear him ask us if we were staying with our embassies in Lhasa – thus presupposing that Lhasa was still the capital of a state independent of China.

Our diet on this side trip was limited. Normally, I would happily eat dry raw yak meat, but on one occasion I hesitated. In fact, my stomach turned, for I was offered some really ancient meat covered with a patina of dust and grime. It looked as if it had been festering in a cupboard for years.

'How old might this be?' I asked tactfully, as one enquiring about the vintage of a wine.

The question pleased the Tibetan. '1983,' he said proudly.

'1983?!' Horrified.

'November.' A true connoisseur.

There was no answer to that. I ate it. I must admit that it tasted just like what it was – vintage, raw yak meat. Dried. I felt that it was even a good year, and a good month.

More often than not food was scarce, and we came to rely on our skin pouches to mix tsamba in. We grew adept at mixing the right amounts of tea and flour, and the dough eggs we lived on we found surprisingly nutritious and even tasty. But food wasn't the only thing that was scarce. There wasn't a lot of accommodation either. If we arrived at a village, we were totally dependent on the kindness of the villagers, for we had nothing to barter. Many at first mistook us for the local travelling salesmen, who go from village to village with their wares, but we encountered great generosity, once the misapprehension had been overcome. We had to repay this somehow and once when we stayed with a family for four days and they refused payment, Dave gave them our supply of butter – something they could ill afford. The butter was welcome to them, as they were very poor, but they smeared the teacups' rims with it generously, as custom requires.

Climbing one valley wall, we came across some hot springs. We were bashful about bathing in them in front of the village women, but the men pointed out with a grin that the ladies had seen all that sort of stuff before. I had noticed that in Lhasa the general view foreigners held of Tibetans was that they were filthy. But in the capital there is little water available for the luxury of washing as the land is frozen hard for most of the year, whereas here, where water is plentiful, Tibetans are as clean as most westerners, and cleaner than many I've known.

If my appearance was one of respectability for most, it nevertheless frightened babies into tears (most Tibetans are beardless or, like Mongolians, have sparse facial hair). Children were curious but cautious. When I extended my hand in friendship they were puzzled at first, but once one nervously took the initiative and shook my hand, the action gave rise to general merriment – so much so that sometimes the handshaking became a game: who could shake my hand hardest and longest. To cement the new friendship, I would do my Charlie Chaplin impersonations for them. Or I'd be an angry old man and pull faces. Some of the children took to us so much that they insisted on accompanying us on excursions. Four delightful such companions were Mimo, Mima, Putsch and Auto, who waited for us to appear every morning that we stayed in their village. Leading us, they showed us shortcuts that we'd never have found by ourselves. And if it sometimes involved walking through the middle of military barracks, the soldiers never seemed to mind.

Handshaking was one thing, but in some areas older traditions persisted. As a token of respect you have to stick your tongue out in greeting. I never quite got used to this.

Gangba, known for its grazing lands, was the centre of vast tracts where yaks and sheep huddled together against the arctic winds. As darkness fell, you could hear the wild, cascading, whooping calls of the shepherds as they gathered in their flocks, sometimes hurrying the beasts along by firing a stone against their flanks from a slingshot, and herding them into pens made of stone in the bosom of the mountains. They slept near them in small tents barely large enough even for one person. The enormous rolling hills that edged the plain yielded square blocks of peat, cut out of the landscape with geometric precision, to be dried and soaked, and then dried again for use as fuel.

I encountered a man here who insisted that I take what he called his English money – in fact, it was some Chinese Foreign Exchange Certificates.

'But this is legal tender here,' I told him. 'You could get twice its face value if you took it to Lhasa and exchanged it.'

337

He was unconvinced. 'I can't use English money,' he said.

Here, polyandry still existed, with a woman married to several brothers to avoid any division of inherited land. Few of the houses in this region had more than one bedroom, but I was told that the brother currently in bed with the wife left his boots outside the door as a sign that they were not to be disturbed.

Wild, and poorer than anywhere else Dave and I had travelled to, it seemed odd to us that a Sichuanese Tibetan lama should have chosen this lonely and remote spot to hold a blessing ceremony – a *chorga*. He didn't seem to be a very holy man. He looked like a smalltime Latin American generalissimo, with his closecropped black hair and his dark glasses, which he never took off, even after sunset. He was fat, youngish, and wore a green nylon western shirt with grey worsted trousers under his monk's robes. He was surrounded by a retinue of adoring men and women, who, we learned, had left their own villages to accompany him on his travels in the region, doing all his work for him – loading and unloading his truck, cooking and washing for him, and so on. He wouldn't give blessings unless the gifts given him in return were substantial enough – those who couldn't afford the high standards he set had to go without the *khata* – the white scarf he conferred as a sign of being blessed. I had been taking photos with my Olympus, but he put a stop to this after I'd refused to take one of him with my Polaroid. The lama sat crosslegged on a podium of large, hard, thick cushions. The whole village had dressed in their best clothes but the audience was larger than one village could muster, and he boasted to us that some of the people had walked miles across the mountains just to see him. Unlike the thin and even ascetic-looking lamas I had seen hitherto, he looked like a man who enjoyed the good life. Two female attendants saw to it that he never went without his chang or his tea, and his male entourage kept the excited crowd in order, often roughly manhandling individuals into place. He sat surrounded with donations, while in front of him the locals had formed a semi-circle; in the space between exuberant dancing took place.

I was appalled at the way the suppliants for a blessing were relieved of their offerings. Money and goods were rudely snatched from them, and the line was shoved forward at a grotesque speed. By way of a blessing, the lama laid a perfunctory hand on the villager's forehead and knotted the strip of white cotton around the person's neck. One woman complained of losing her eyesight. He blew into her eyes.

This was not a one-day event. We noted that he had taken up residence in the house of the truck-driver (who doubtless considered it a great honour), and there he held court. Far from feeling any kindness towards those he blessed, he treated them with undisguised contempt.

'The food these people eat is disgusting,' he told us. 'We in Sichuan are more civilised – we have a great variety of food.' This didn't prevent him from consuming vast quantities of what he was offered here.

'We in Sichuan are more hygienic than these urchins,' he said; however this didn't stop him from leering at his women attendants. One day, doubtless in an effort to impress us westerners, he asked in an offhand way, as one would when enquiring after an intimate mutual acquaintance, 'By the way, how is President Nixon?'

After two days of blessings and fleecing, the lama was ready to move on. His truck was piled high with his booty. There was a coffer full of cash and several artefacts which must have been of high value, including an ornate skull cup. The lama offered us a lift, which was at least generous of him, as the truck was so full that he had to leave several sacks of loot behind. Also on the truck were his female attendants and half a dozen porters. Our departure from the village was a bit of a farce, as we were accompanied by villagers running alongside and waving their goodbyes – but no sooner had we drawn away from them than the truck broke down.

Finally we were on our way again, and after stopping for a picnic of tsamba and antelope, we parted company with the lama.

'If ever you're in Ganze, come and visit me in my temple,' he said grandly.

He had claimed to be the high priest of Sichuan, and yet he gave me the truck driver's address to forward the picnic photo to. Frankly, there was so little of the true lama about this man that we had already decided that he was a confidence trickster, and that he was probably constantly on the move, ripping off gullible peasants in the remoter provinces.

Later, much later, in Ganze, I checked up on our lama. Needless to say, no one had ever heard of him.

Shigatse is Tibet's second largest city, and it counts among its population a number of Muslims. But unlike Lhasa's Muslims, these people consider themselves Tibetan – although they are in fact of Kashmiri descent. Their customs are identical to those of other Tibetans, although they do not drink chang as it is alcoholic. They speak several languages – Tibetan, Chinese, Urdu and Koranic Arabic. We made friends with two of them, Haida Yadullah and Abdul Rahman, who showed us their mosque – a small, simple temple with the inscription *masdjid* above its entrance. They had temporarily lost their Imam, and Friday prayers for the time being had become a democratic evangelical service with each man reading from his own Koran. At the end of the service sweets were handed round, a custom which they claimed was traditional among Kashmiris. Their community was small and even beleaguered – there are only ten families left here.

Haida and Abdul lodged at the mosque, and in return they had to look after its upkeep. This hadn't prevented them from also establishing a small noodle-making business. They also lodged a Muslim from Qinghai, who was trying to make money selling plastic jugs. But as they lay in huge piles around the outside of the building, he had obviously not found fame and fortune yet.

I wondered how they had fared under the Cultural Revolution.

'We were in the unusual position of being a minority within a minority,' they told us. 'The mosque was closed for a few years, but not damaged; and as for us, they left us alone.' However, they told me a sad story of a book they'd had, a history of the world written in Arabic, about the size of a small table, which they'd buried to save it from desecration by the Red Guards. Unfortunately, no one could remember where it was buried now.

'Are there any Uighurs here?' I asked.

'Yes. There are two who arrived here after fifty-nine. They work on a commune. We don't speak to them – they are communists.'

We approached the Shigatse Public Security Bureau in some trepidation, but not only were they delighted to see us, they gave us permission to travel to Sakya and Tingri, from which we hoped for a view of Everest from the north. They even thanked Dave for acting as my interpreter, and the only condition they imposed was that we should complete our trip within a week, and then return to Shigatse to surrender our travel permits.

Delighted, we accepted – hardly daring to hope that communication concerning us between Shigatse and Lhasa had broken down completely. On our return to Lhasa, however, we would be in for a rude awakening.

In our search for a view of Everest we travelled south to Dinngye. In fact, we had been advised against taking this route, and the howling winds were only a prelude to the treacherous conditions we were to meet. We were hitching lifts, and the truck we were travelling on that day slowed to pick up three more travellers – a pair of lamas from Qinghai and a layman who was their disciple. They were journeying in search of a *poussa* (a living god), and they were headed straight towards the Himalayas. I feared for their safety, because they were dressed in the barest rags, and had no supplies at all to equip them for their journey. The truck driver overcharged them for their lift, which made them angry, but you could see that they were already sapped of all their strength, and the only thing that kept them going was their religious conviction. When the time came for them to leave the truck, you could also see that they did so reluctantly. Tempted as ever by the challenge of new things, for a moment I thought of joining them, but I am not really one for suicide missions, and I fear that that is what theirs was.

We travelled on, through a landscape whose contours resembled those of an enormous ear laid flat. But we were cheated of a view of Everest by low cloud. However, returning by the way we had come, we did get a brief, unobstructed view of the mountain which here is called Jomolangma – 'Goddess Mother of the World' – rising majestically at the end of a valley stretching away at right angles to the road. We were passing through barren desert country, the curves of whose dunes were so soft and voluptuous I wanted to run my hands over them. A river ran through the centre of this wasteland – which lay 2½ miles above sea-level. Now, we struck out westwards towards Tingri. On the road we passed the traffic of Tibet: mendicants shuffling from village to village, some with the aid of a staff-like walking stick, others with a donkey cart; pedlars and lamas; and a farmer with a horsedrawn cart on which a lame yak rode, its statuesque head rising above the other luggage aboard.

We arrived at a bridge at one end of which a hovel housed some local militia whose job it was to guard the crossing. For two *yuan* a night they were only too happy to let the hovel to us. There were eight soldiers, all of them hopelessly and disgustingly drunk. One even said 'I'm going to be sick,' as he plied himself with more chang. They rolled about, or wrestled each other in an unfocused sort of way. Sharing this place with these hoodlums was an elderly couple, dressed in rags, who lived in a corner with a wretched dog. Clearly the militia enjoyed the kudos of their status, but I doubt if they could actually have fought for the bridge, even sober, if the need had arisen, and certainly the little village nearby would have been glad to see the back of them.

Corruption existed at an astonishing level. The army made fat side-profits by bootlegging, and the police supplemented their income by fining truck drivers. Even some of the monasteries were not above trying to swindle people. We had firsthand experience of this when on our return to Shigatse we visited Tashilhunpo, one of Tibet's largest monasteries and once home of the Panchen Lama – the second holiest man in the country. On our first attempt to visit, the officials charged us for a guided tour, and then refused to allow us in. We demanded either a refund or a receipt against a return visit when we might perhaps be allowed to visit the temples they had promised to show us. The receipt was grudgingly issued, but we weren't optimistic about its value, and so I decided to enlist the aid of the Foreign Affairs Bureau, leaving Dave at the monastery to look after our bags. No sooner had I gone than the monks set about Dave and beat him up, so that when I returned I found him dazed and bruised, although – as a pacifist – he had refused to put up any resistance. A small crowd that had rallied round had been similarly treated by the lamas.

The police agreed to take action, but the lamas refused point blank to cooperate or to appear before the authorities, and we discovered that the secular authorities have no jurisdiction inside the monasteries. Eventually, we wrung an apology out of the head lama, but there remained the question of the money we'd paid for our tour of the temples, plus compensation for the damage Dave had sustained to his clothes and belongings during his beating. When this was put to the head lama, he promptly retracted his apology and laid the blame for the entire incident squarely on us. Surprisingly, perhaps, the locals were all behind us. 'Why didn't you fight back?' they asked Dave. It seemed an odd question, in view of the fact that there had been several lamas, all large, strong and young. They wore leather jackets and army boots, and each carried a wicked-looking knife. For good measure, we were told, they were karate experts, too.

The authorities by now were begging us to forget the whole incident. They seemed to despair of ever getting any satisfaction out of the lamas. I countered this by saying that if we didn't see some action I would write an article describing how the People's Republic of China seemed to be powerless against one cell of Tibetan Buddhists. Finally, after five days of complicated and at times vitriolic parleying, Dave received some compensation from the monastery, and we renegotiated our guided tour – paying the full admission price to the entire complex, which turned out to be well worth it. The greatest surprise of all was a treasure trove of objects hidden in a dark temple beneath inches of dust – a veritable Aladdin's cave. There were face masks, elaborately carved, hats with great wooden sculptures on their crowns, tridents, swords, statues and conch trumpets with silver mouths and silver inlay work along their sides. Most magnificent of all were the thankas stored in crates. Two lamas unfurled the scrolls – in this case of cotton or linen mounted on brocade. In Tibet the thanka developed out of mural painting in the seventh century, and then flourished between the fourteenth and nineteenth. The themes are mainly religious, but other subjects they cover include lives of famous people, historical tales in quasi-strip-cartoon format, the sciences, herblore, astronomy, medicine and the calendar. The thankas we saw here, dating from the eighteenth and nineteenth centuries, were especially beautiful for their bold use of colour and finesse of line. They dealt with powerful subjects – terrifying images of gods and demons picked out in gold on black backgrounds.

We both felt it had been worth the struggle to see them.

THE PILGRIMS'
WAY

Six weeks after leaving Lhasa, we returned to the Tibetan capital to find a different city – one which rang to the sound of chisels hammering at granite blocks, while the air was laden with the dust of demolished buildings. The pace of development had taken on its own momentum and thousands of workers and technicians had been brought in from Peking, Shanghai, Tianjin and many other cities and provinces. Old buildings had been torn down and there were now empty plots, prepared to make space for no less than 22 major projects – hotels, a stadium, a hospital, and cultural, educational and tourist facilities. The 1300-year-old city now covers 25 square kilometres – eight times the size it was in 1951. Its population is 110,000 – treble what it was in the same year.

I thought I'd been moving quickly, but events had certainly overtaken me. A new government directive allowing locals to leave their work units and go freelance had resulted in a spate of entrepreneurial enterprises. There were new restaurants, shops and video parlours, whose deafening pop music was designed to attract the passer-by. On the other hand the Saturday-night disco had been closed because a Khampa had, in a drunken stupor, stabbed someone to death on the dance floor. To counter this, the Khampas now strolled around the streets proudly playing and displaying their latest acquisition – the ghetto-blaster.

My Muslim friends hadn't been left behind – their businesses had expanded too. One had moved his restaurant into larger premises which also provided more luxury for his customers. Another had embarked on a new venture – another restaurant, for which he was renting premises four times the size of his original trading house from a Tibetan landlord. This landlord was a member of the Tibetan nobility, to whom, like so many of his peers, much of the property confiscated under the Cultural Revolution had been returned. My friend's new restaurant had turned out to be so successful that he was, he told me, all but bewildered. It was packed every hour it was open, and he had trouble keeping food supplies to it flowing. He'd already sent for friends in Gansu and Qinghai to help him run it. In fact his success had attracted the attention of the press and the media, with journalists begging him for interviews, but he preferred to keep a low profile, fearful lest a swing in policy might take from him all that he had gained. Material success hadn't robbed my friends of their hospitality, either: I practically had to fight to be allowed to pay for a meal. But it made a pleasant change from the frugal diet I'd been used to on the road, where I had always been hungry.

Despite all this burgeoning capitalist success in the capital, Tibet is still burdened by an undeveloped economy. The province was subsidised by the Chinese state to the tune of 7500 million yuan in the years between 1952 and 1983. But during the course of this time the entire economy of Tibet has declined and become more and more reliant on state subsidies, and statistics show that the increase in Tibet's industrial and agricultural output is entirely attributable to them. The problem is that the state's money has not been used to develop local commodity production. There is also the question of abuse at an individual level. The Han truck driver who drove us back to Lhasa was dealing privately in firewood, on the sale of which he made the equivalent of six months' salary in one day – and that at his work unit's expense. He had done this by haggling over his purchase price with the Tibetans who sold him the wood – over amounts which represented pennies to him, but a small fortune to them. Truck drivers could also make large amounts of money by carrying passengers, but that never stopped them from saving costs wherever possible – turning off their engines to cruise downhill, running their trucks on bald tyres, and sleeping in their cabs.

There were social problems too. Not only were there great discrepancies between the rich and the poor, but the old were at odds with the young, who did not know the destitution of pre-Chinese administration days. One older man who had consistently refused to move from a blue-collar job to a white-collar job sighed as he overheard a young man speak of his desire to own a hotel for foreigners. 'Young people have such high aspirations,' he said.

Those who had experienced the founding of the People's Republic were frightened by the false economies that lead to dangerous practices, everything geared to making money. This, they argued, was resulting in a fundamental change of attitude among the people – one in which money was becoming the primal driving force, in turn leading to the collapse of a system that they had fought hard to win, and to an end of traditional values. On the other hand, I found that even the young educated Tibetans whom the Chinese have had ample time to indoctrinate showed little sign of losing their religious conviction. Dave and I made friends with Lobsang, a second-year student at Lhasa's College of Higher Education, and proficient in three languages. He was happy to show us round Lhasa and proudly pointed out the large houses that once belonged to the nobility. These have now been restored to their former glory, but house several families instead of just one. He was also anxious for us to visit his own digs. His small room was reached by a very steep ladder-stairway which led from a courtyard. This environment spoke of poor students' quarters throughout the world, but it was significant  that in Lobsang's digs a large part of the room had been turned over to a carefully constructed, boxed-in shrine, completed with a window which presented a religious scene. When you opened the doors of the altar, fairy lights surrounding it came on. Lobsang spent what little spare money he had not on records, magazines or western clothes, but on reproductions of thankas, sutras, or votive plaques.

Another friend I made was Zhang, a Han Chinese who, having emerged from the turmoil of the Cultural Revolution, had embarked on a career as a painter. During the 'Ten Years', his father had been shot, two female relations committed suicide, and his mother had been subjected to a humiliating torture in which the victim is forced to walk with head bent low and arms outstretched backwards and upwards through a gauntlet of abuse and blows. Zhang himself was sent to work in the countryside in Shandong Province, where his portraits of Mao won him recognition. When the universities were reopened he was sent to art school. His interest in religious art had led him to Tibet, but his passion for the nation and all things Tibetan was a blind love.

'Tibetan culture is the best, and indeed the Tibetans are the only Chinese minority with any culture to speak of,' he would say – but he was unaware of the dozens of other Chinese minority cultures.

His paintings reflected his passionate affinity with his adopted home. In them, he had truly caught the wonder and the horror that is Tibet's – they were dark, realist paintings, depicting the one room of a herdsman's house with a woman nursing a baby engulfed in its mother's thick sheepskin *chuba*. The paint was alive; the earthen colours soft and tactile – one could feel and smell the confined spaces, the charcoaled walls, the uncured sheepskin, the wool of the mother's coat. The candlelight's flicker lent a touch of homeliness to the scene, its light catching the woman's soft breast and careworn forehead with an intensity that made me think of Caravaggio.

Zhang used a totally different style for his religious paintings: in one, a guru, that most powerful figure in Tibetan society, seemed to be escaping from an inferno – but the inferno was also his robe. In all his work, the artist had captured the paradoxes of Tibet. But in spite of this, he wanted to venture abroad. And like the vast majority of the people I'd met in the undeveloped world, he wanted to go to the USA. He wouldn't even consider the possibility that France or Italy might have more to offer him in the way of religious art. He was convinced that on reaching the USA he would be able to make his fortune – free of the constraint of only being able to sell official art through government channels. He also lived under the delusion that American agents would charge a far smaller commission when handling his work.

I met other young people caught in the trap of backwater living. Song, a committed member of the Communist Party, and his colleague spent dead time during office hours reading books and learning English and Japanese – not for their own amusement, but to make them more useful servants of the state. However, they were instructed to stop. Song had then asked his boss what he was meant to do with the time – stare at the walls? Yes, his boss had answered, and Song, a man of principle, wanted to resign. In his letter of resignation, he had outlined a plan of how to run the work unit more efficiently, thereby saving funds. In these plans he had excised his own job, so selfless was he. A graduate and a qualified technician, he had reasoned that his job was superfluous to the requirements of his work unit. His action was brave, if not foolhardy, for job prospects in China are not great, even for someone of his education. And the job he was giving up carried with it a salary of 150 yuan, a paid-for flight home once a year, and what by Chinese standards amounted to very spacious accommodation.

But despite the frustrations, the spirit of the young here was indomitable. One of the greatest sights I saw, and one which filled me with awe and a sense of humility, was that of a student studying in the street under the halo of a street-lamp for want of other light to read by at night. This I encountered in many towns across China.

Dave and I had hoped to stay for four days in Lhasa but once again we were in trouble with the police – charged, not surprisingly, with travelling to closed areas. Dave was to be fined for not returning to Lhasa immediately as he had been required to, and I was asked to leave Lhasa forthwith. We countered with the fact that the authorities in Shigatse had given us travel permits; but we'd returned them, and Shigatse denied all knowledge of them. Fortunately the authorities in one town, Tingri, had stamped our passports, but this *imprimatur* had no effect on the Lhasa police decision. Dave even had his passport confiscated. I pointed doggedly to the Tingri stamp in mine.

'Doesn't this prove us innocent?' I asked.

'Yes,' agreed the officer I was talking to, indulgently.

'Then what about waiving the fine?'

'Impossible. And you must leave the country.'

'But if we're innocent of travelling illegally after all –'

'It's not just a question of that – you have a bad attitude!'

We took our case to the Foreign Affairs Bureau, who showed great sympathy but were unable to affect the police decision. There was worse in store: for every day the fine remained unpaid, it would be doubled. Dave threatened to go on hunger strike and I, feeling much to blame for his predicament, agreed to join him.

'Don't do it,' warned the people at the Foreign Affairs Bureau. 'In any case, the police will happily let you starve to death – regulations are regulations.'

But the regulations seemed to be made up on the spot. As for bad attitude, the police, alone in the population, seemed lazy and parasitical. Meanwhile, our predicament grew grimmer with every day that passed. The Foreign Affairs Bureau gave up on us, offering to give us plane tickets out of Tibet but refusing to have anything more to do with us. It was as I had feared: I'd pushed too hard. Now I was faced with the terrible possibility that I might not be able to achieve my ambition to complete the journey from London to Peking by land. To have overcome so many difficulties, and to have got so close, was infuriating. I had put my entire project in jeopardy because of my undisciplined pursuit of new discoveries.

'Why don't you make a run for it?' said Dave. In fact, I'd already considered it, but I wasn't about to desert my friend now. His fine now stood at 800 yuan. We had to find a solution quickly.

I had forgotten that the bank had sent my cheque to Peking, and it came as a welcome surprise to find that extra funds were now waiting for me. I was down to £20, but the extra £70 that had arrived would enable me to travel for another two or three months. I offered to pay Dave's fine, but Dave refused – and in any case it was clear by now that the police were bored with us and simply wanted us off their hands without any loss of face. After some bargaining the fine was reduced to a mere 20 yuan, and once it had been paid Dave had his documents returned to him. My only aim now was to get away from the authorities as fast as possible, so that I would not be forced onto a plane bound for Peking. We decided that Dave should stay in Lhasa while I explored the possibilities of an escape route we could both use.

While all this had been going on, we were allowed a certain freedom of movement. We'd moved to a Muslim hotel, a basic place with dormitories of wooden benches for beds, but what it lacked in facilities it gained in ambience. In the evenings the Buddhist guests prayed, and in the mornings the Muslims. However, we didn't stay long here, for it was impossible to ignore the generous offers of a room from the staff of the Snowland Hotel. Besides, our funds were running low and the Snowland was cheap. Once we'd moved, we were thrust into an atmosphere that was far removed from the monastery-like one of the Muslim hotel. At the Snowland, chang flowed freely, the guests rolled about drunk and grappled and groped the female staff as often as they could. All this, I hasten to add, in the friendliest and most sociable manner possible.

The socialising at the Snowland would usually begin in the early afternoon with a game of *sho*, a game of dice not unlike craps which Tibetans go wild about. Little shells were used as chips, and the faces of the players reflected the full gamut of human emotion. The game went on until no one could muster the energy any more to hurl the dice out of the shaker to the requisite accompaniment of loud shouting. Then and only then would the hotel guests turn in for the night, as two or three beds were placed together across the room and everybody, men and women together, settled down in a huddle.

Spending time in Lhasa while we sorted out our problems with the police, I had ample time to observe the behaviour of tourists in the town. It was a depressing occupation. One foreigner I observed, who professed a love of everything Tibetan, was quite content to intrude upon their lives; yet when he was surrounded by a group of innocent children who had come to stare at him, felt free to hit them because it was an invasion of privacy.

The Tibetans who were aware of what was happening to them accepted it with a grim fatalism, like a brave man who's been told that he's dying.

Once Dave's fine had been paid, I decided not to waste a moment before checking out a route out of Lhasa and across Tibet to China proper. But we had a shock when we returned to the hotel after our final visit to the police station. For there, in our dormitory, the other guests had been replaced by none other than six policemen. Surely they couldn't have divined our plans? I had hoped to set off before dawn, but now there was nothing to do but settle down for the night and await events.

Events, however, turned out to be rather bizarre. Before turning in, one of the policemen asked the room in general if anyone wanted to leave for a final pee. When there was no answer, he dragged his bed across the door and lay down on it. To prevent our exit, obviously. I approached his bed. Nothing ventured, nothing won, I thought.

'Excuse me.'

'Yes?' Quite affably.

'I'm thinking of going out quite early in the morning, and I don't want to disturb you . . .'

'That's OK, just wake me up.'

I went back to my bed feeling happy but bemused. If he was prepared to let me out, why had he dragged his bed across the door in the first place? I rose before five o'clock, dressed, woke the policeman, and asked him if I might leave now please. Without getting up, or really waking up much, he indicated that I should shift the bed away from the door. I did so, and closed the door quietly behind me, still pondering the significance of all this strange behaviour. I made my way through the filthy streets, trying to avoid the ugly dogs and not to tread in the excrement. I crossed Barkhor Street, where the eternal pilgrims were shuffling round in the dark, and made my way towards what would be the first obstacle – the Lhasa Bridge, which was guarded. However, I found it easy to slip across unnoticed since the sentries were fast asleep in their boxes. Now I was free to hitch a lift, and soon a Chinese truck driver stopped for me.

Without Dave to translate, conversation was stilted, but I knew that the driver was giving me the usual story about a hard life and poor wages – a story which you hear the world over. I barely listened, occasionally interjecting a polite 'shima' (you don't say), or, if it seemed that he was asking for my agreement, 'dui-dui-dui' (yes).

My exploration turned out to be successful. Having said goodbye to the driver, I climbed the steepest and most direct path to my goal – Ganden. Built in 1409, this was the most holy of the Gelukpa monasteries. Little remains of it today, though it is still a popular place of pilgrimage. Renovation work is going on, and when the small community of lamas gave me a warm welcome I offered to paint a small statue for them. They only had primary colours, and the hairs of the brush were so clogged that I had to lob the paint on and then rub it into place. If the statues were small enough, they were passed along a human conveyor belt, each lama applying one particular colour to the right parts.

Towards the end of the day, I made my way back to Lhasa. Once again I crossed the bridge without difficulty. I returned to the hotel having established that we would be able to get out of town unchallenged as long as we were over the Lhasa Bridge before daybreak.

But what of the police and their strange behaviour? When I returned to the hotel they were gone, and Dave was out somewhere. I asked one of the maids if she knew what'd been happening.

She giggled. 'They had a thief with them, in custody.'

'Where've they gone now?'

'After him. He escaped early in the morning – the policeman who'd put his bed across the door didn't bother to move it back after you'd gone out. He just fell asleep again. So the thief simply walked out too.'

Dave rejoined me and we bought supplies of chocolate powder to mix with our tsamba on the journey. One of the maids gave us a large bag of tsamba, and another plaited red ribbon into my hair for good luck. That night I barely slept. The plan was to rush across closed areas to Chengdu, which I hoped to reach in seven to ten days' time, though it was 2,400 unpredictable kilometres away and the chances of getting caught were high.

Retracing the route I had taken on my reconnaissance trip to Ganden, we crossed the Lhasa Bridge without difficulty and to our delight noticed a long line of trucks parked on the far side of it, along the south bank of the river. We approached it cautiously, for the lorries bore military licence plates. Encouraged by the fact that they had civilian drivers, we asked one of them for a lift as far as Ganden. That way, we reasoned, if we were stopped at a checkpoint, we could always say that we were merely taking a day trip to the monastery. On the other hand the likelihood of being stopped was remote, for military trucks are almost never checked, and these were Jiefangs, through whose minute windows guards were unlikely to see us *da bize* ('Big Noses', as foreigners are known to the Chinese; the Tibetans call us 'Round Eyes').

The drive was nothing short of purgatory as the lorry bounced and rattled along the unmetalled road like a demented bucking bronco. Every bump and pothole sent us flying towards the hard metal roof of the cabin, against which we frequently crashed our heads. It was like being in a speedboat driven too fast in rough seas. The driver had cushioned himself with his large sheepskin Russian-style military overcoat. His eyes scanned the road ahead constantly for fresh obstacles – swerving wildly whenever he saw one and

clinging to the steering wheel for support. The trucks were not
equipped with radios, and so out of boredom on the long journeys
the drivers had taken to chain smoking. They saw their trucks as an
extension of their own bodies, or so it seemed, as their ears were
constantly attuned to the slightest variation in the engine's hum and
at any alteration which gave rise to concern, they would stop and set
to tinkering under the bonnet.

Once we were well away from the military garrisons that surround
Lhasa we asked our driver if, instead of simply going as far as Ganden
we could accompany him to his destination, some two days away.
At first he agreed, but later he became nervous and it was clear that
he regretted his offer. He pulled up twice to consult his fellow drivers
in our convoy of eight trucks – first in a village, which was the surest
way of attracting attention to us since we became the centre of
attraction for a fascinated crowd. The second time was on a deserted
stretch of road, where for a moment it looked as if we might be
abandoned, but fortunately the other drivers mocked ours for his
cowardice. Shortly afterwards, however, the truck broke down, and
as we were in a hurry to put as much distance as possible between
us and Lhasa in the shortest possible time, we had to desert our driver
though he was clearly relieved that we were parting company.

The next two lifts introduced us to the glorious scenery that was
to be the hallmark of this section of the journey. The windswept
mountains and tablelands leading to the passes, the descents along
winding paths that clung to the outcrops of rocky mountainsides,
through gullies surrounded by trees, and valleys with gushing
streams. We crossed churning rivers bordered by lush vegetation,
and travelled through forests that exploded in a riot of greens sparked
off by pink blossom. And behind and above us all the time were
the great mountains, towering brown snowladen rocks – chocolate
sundaes topped with cream.

We were dropped at a small settlement where the sight of a Toyota
Land Cruiser – usually the mark of officials – brought our hearts to
our mouths. We took refuge in a teahouse until it had gone, and
then we were out on the road again. The next truck to stop for us
was, oddly, from the same work unit as that which had given us our
first lift. We pulled into Bayi at 3 am the next morning, and from
there tried to hitch a lift with a small convoy of homeward-bound

pilgrims, but their drivers refused to take us. On our way we came across a building site, and put up for the rest of the night in one of the unfinished rooms, using loose timbers to barricade ourselves in from the scavenger dogs, yaks, and other four-footed souls with whom we were sharing the place.

We were off again at dawn, gritting our teeth against the biting frost. It was a shame to be so pressed. Had we not been, we might have found time to spend with the Mengba and the Louba – local forest-dwelling tribes of the region. Instead, we were confronted by a vast cultivated plain where horses and yaks roamed in a landscape that might have come from the brush of the young Turner, with trees and bushes by Constable. These fertile fields were fed by the tentacular tributaries of the meandering Nyang Qu River – itself a tributary of the mighty Brahmaputra.

However, we were soon trundling uphill again – zigzagging through a forest with trees a hundred feet high. As we broke through the treeline the engine strained for lack of oxygen. In the clear air across the naked terrain the pass we were crossing at 4720 metres gave us a view over a sea of towering pristine glacial peaks. Then came the descent – through treacherous melting snow and slush, over crumbling bridges, round hairpin bends. Below us, there was a valley of verdant pastures and swift streams. In the fields, we could see knots of livestock in pens, while above the sun poured its energy down on us. Here there was little to disturb the tranquillity, apart from a handful of rummaging pigs, and the occasional army convoy – with which we took care to avoid too close contact.

Truckloads of pilgrims returning home also stopped to eat at the wayside restaurants. One such contained 31 Sichuanese Tibetans. Their driver, Wong, a flamboyant, jovial man, invited us to join him, his wife and a friend for breakfast at one of the restaurants. Over breakfast, he offered to take us all the way to Sichuan. I could hardly believe our luck. I had always wanted to travel on a pilgrims' truck and now we had a ride on one to the relative security of Sichuan. What was more, it appeared that Wong was as anxious to avoid the police as we were, since he was already carrying more passengers than he legally should. He told us that we'd only be travelling into towns at night. This suited us fine.

With scant regard for the wishes of his passengers, Wong arbitrarily decided on the right moment to leave. He stood up abruptly, leaving most of the food he'd ordered untouched, which I found extraordinary until Dave, who had lived a long time here and who knew the people well, explained to me that the gesture was intended to impress upon others the degree of Wong's personal wealth. The back of the truck had been converted into a travelling shrine, adorned with prayer flags hoisted on bamboo poles which were festooned with amulets, kettles, pots, bags of tsamba and hats. To the front of the truck, the pilgrims sat perched on crates of empty beer bottles which Wong had collected in Tibet in the hope of supplementing his income back home by selling them to a bottling plant in Sichuan. The rest of them sat on sacks of their produce and their belongings. What couldn't be stored beneath us had been tied to the roof of the cabin, the bags acting as a windbreak. They'd collected precious firewood *en route*, and what couldn't be carried between the body and the chassis was strapped to the sides and the back.

Wong had already started the engine and moved off before the tight jigsaw puzzle of the passengers' seating arrangement (now made even tighter by our arrival) had been completed. Those left in the hamlet stared in astonishment at the bulging human mass on the lorry, so we must have been pretty jammed even by Tibetan standards. We were prevented from falling out by ropes tied to iron uprights that fitted into the sides of the truck. For lack of space, some of us found it easier to face outwards and dangle our legs over the side.

Stops were frequent and not always voluntary. In the course of the first afternoon alone we had four punctures. Lao Er (the name means Old Number Two and refers to the second son) – Wong's friend, Dave and I all did our best to help repair the tyres. Wong himself applied melted rubber plasters to the split inner tubes. The rest of our group foraged for firewood.

We drove through yet more idyllic scenery, which was matched by the exhilarating, festive atmosphere on board. As the pilgrims sang out their '*Om Mani Padme Hum*', the lorry twisted through deep gorges, past trees clinging to near-vertical slopes, waterfalls, sheer rock pinnacles, and a small jewel of a lake – an emerald thrown amongst the browns and greys. When darkness descended, though, the cold crept into the truck and invaded bones already aching from the cramped conditions. Above, the mountains rose and blocked out the stars, and the stony silence they imposed was only punctuated by the deep murmur of invocations to Buddha, and by the truck's patiently-straining engine.

When we stopped for the night, we slept with the Tibetans, whilst Wong, his wife and Lao Er went to a hotel – of the dormitory type. The rest of us camped where we could. On the first night this was in a marketplace, on the concrete floor. Everything was working out far better than we could have hoped, for the mass of pilgrims provided perfect camouflage.

We awoke to find one of the pilgrims – a newlywed who was travelling home with his bride – clowning about on top of another truck. He was parodying the two Round Eyes – Dave and me – turning out his empty pockets to show how poor we were – how we had to sleep outside and eat tsamba like anyone else. To judge by their laughter, the other pilgrims were enjoying every moment of his entertainment. Yet it was all without malice, and there was no real resentment at our having joined their group, even though it made cramped conditions even more so, and if we'd been discovered they might have been in trouble with the police. Certainly the bridegroom's takeoff was accurate. We had very little money – an inn at 30p a night would have stretched us. But even if we could have afforded hotels, we couldn't have used them, for fear of drawing attention to ourselves.

To add to our destitution we were robbed one night. In the early hours we were awoken by rustling noises. The thief was already off with one of our bags. We scrambled out of our sleeping bags and gave chase, though we could hardly make out the figure scampering across the road ahead.

'It's a dog!' I said as my eyes became accustomed to the dark.

'No, it's not,' said Dave. 'It's a pig!'

The pig ran away with a plastic sack full of tsamba.

Wong had insisted on early starts because of his fear of police checks, but his enthusiasm for them soon waned, and most of the rest of us found it exhausting to have to make do with only a couple of hours' sleep a night. Wong himself could hardly be woken at all – on one occasion both his wife and Lao Er spent an hour trying to do so. The pilgrims teased him about this, jumping into the spare beds in a dormitory where he was sleeping and mimicking his deep slumber. But they had a second motivation: they enjoyed the sensation of soft beds and sheets. However, once Wong was dressed, and had made up his mind to get started, there was no stopping him.

'Zou ba! (We're off!)' he would shout, and the pilgrims, who might be in the act of brewing tea in their huge, black iron pots, would have to abandon the entire operation and leap aboard.

Dave felt increasingly bad about our imposing ourselves on the Tibetans, and he found the bumpy drives, wedged in so that he couldn't move, almost unbearably uncomfortable – so much so that he was all for leaving Wong to look for another lift. I didn't like imposing either, but my main concern now had to be travelling to Peking in the way that I had set myself, and I was not about to abandon the huge advantage I had gained through Wong. We couldn't pay for the ride and we couldn't explain our predicament for lack of language, so the only way we could endear ourselves to the Tibetans was through our behaviour. I let people take lots of pictures with my camera, and they did so with delight, though curiously they insisted on holding it at an angle of 45 degrees. Some of the pilgrims shied away from it altogether, burying themselves in their coats or blankets when it was pointed at them. As the days passed and they became more and more used to us, so their behaviour became increasingly unbridled. One woman found the hairs on my hand especially loathsome, probably because Tibetans have little body hair and I am very hirsute. This woman was often exchanging blows with the bridegroom, but just as often she would mollycoddle him – as much as the bride did, and would even cuddle up under the newlyweds' blanket with them. When I was seated next to her, the men nearby would torment her by grabbing my arm and forcing my hand towards her face. She countered by hitting me with all her force. Battles aboard were a daily occurrence, with no holds barred and no punches pulled because of a person's sex. In our complicated mini-society, there were pacts, broken treaties, declarations of war, ceasefires and alliances. There were even neutrals, like the peaceful middle-aged man who sat near me. He had long hair and a straggly beard, and was almost always at prayer. His personality was so gentle and reserved that he wasn't drawn even when he had water thrown all over him. Apart from the physical fights, there were song contests, each competitor trying to outdo the other. The groom excelled at these, his ad lib lyrics meeting with roars of approval from the others. Our energy waxed and waned with the sun, and when it was at its peak we were a real roaring crew. The pilgrims called encouragement to the people we passed on the road, but the greatest shouts of all were reserved for pilgrims on their way to Lhasa on foot, doing their prostrations patiently hundreds of kilometres from their goal. Hardly a day passed without our encountering groups of them.

I was reminded of being on a coach full of football supporters of the winning team. No opportunity was missed of decorating the truck with flowers, blossoms, twigs and branches, which were attached to the bumpers, radiator and side-mirrors as well as all over the luggage. They also overloaded the truck with firewood, and although Wong could bully them about most things, he was unable to make them budge when it came to throwing off their firewood. Despite the deep discomfort (sometimes I simply couldn't get off the truck when it stopped, so seized had my muscles become), there was, I thought, no better way to travel than this, open to the elements. Above all, I had people to share the experience with, for at least some of the pilgrims were by now beginning to warm to us. When our progress was impeded, we all worked together – collecting stones once to form a pathway for the truck out of a snowdrift: each of us gathering rocks according to our own size and strength. Once we found our way along a mountain road blocked by a landslide that had occurred ten minutes before our arrival. The avalanche was still going on ahead, and it was a spectacular sight to see huge boulders come tumbling down, bouncing off the remains of the road, leapfrogging the river below it, or crashing into the water with an almighty thud and whoosh! This was one obstacle we couldn't clear ourselves, but a crew of sixty-odd Han engineers and labourers was on hand and they worked for thirteen hours to fashion a piste over the debris while we watched, drinking endless cups of tea. We were on our way again by eight in the evening, all of us walking past the smashed section of road while Wong guided the lorry over the scree. It dipped and lurched like a ship in heavy seas. We clambered aboard, and Wong then tried to make up for lost time by driving through part of the night. The silence was total. I wondered what views I was missing.

Settlements were few and far between. Some could only be reached by winding paths. So remote were they that to reach them at all must have been disheartening, even to those who lived in them, so inhospitable was the terrain through which one would have to pass. Changes of landscape on either side of the road were frequent and no valley was the same as another, though each was magnificent. There were narrow corridors hung with a massive framework of brown, craggy mountains. There were naked rockfaces with the occasional ledge dotted with trees where a settlement would huddle close to an escarpment. Temperatures would vary wildly from valley floor to mountain pass, and one side of a valley might be cloaked in the darkness of deep shadow while the other was fully exposed to the bright sunlight. Despite the rich greens of the few plants that had found refuge on ledges, the overall impression was of the greyness of the mountains, whose sheer flanks were only scarred by the pencil-line tracks leading to distant villages. But the splendour was everywhere, and I realised that in Tibet everything tends skywards.

We had been travelling with the pilgrims for four days. On the dawn of the fifth, we reached the upper reaches of the Mekong River. Here, the wrinkled folds of the bosomy mountains were cut in green terraces – the farms of remote settlements built out of the bauxite-coloured earth, accessible only by raft or by suspension bridges swung giddily across the piercing blue water of the river. We entered Chamdo, Tibet's third city, which stood on a promontory at the confluence of two rivers that formed the headwaters of the Mekong. Wong dropped us at the gates of the town. It was a dirty, modern, semi-industrial place.

'We'll meet up on the other side of town in an hour and a half,' he told us.

We wandered into Chamdo with the pilgrims in search of tsamba. Little by little our group dispersed until there were only six of us left together: Dave and I, and a man with a limp, and three of our most boisterous women, whose enormous coats hid their large frames and plump haunches. The man was an interesting type. As jolly as the rest of them, he rarely joined in the daily fighting on board the lorry, preferring to spend his time praying, his eyes hidden by large sunglasses. But our companions soon deserted us, for we were attracting unbelieving stares wherever we went. Unable to find any tsamba, we climbed a small hill to the temple that stood above the town. It had been devastated during the Cultural Revolution, but now it was in the process of renovation, and we met a nun mixing concrete. She invited us inside one of the restored buildings, its hall packed with lamas reciting mantras. Outside, their boots were piled up – exactly as they would have been outside a mosque, save for the fact that here all the boots were identical. Suddenly we noticed the time and rushed to our rendezvous point with the truck, fearful that Wong would have left us behind; but we found him in a nearby restaurant, about to tuck into a meal.

One more day and we would reach China. It wasn't far on the map, but there was still another climb ahead of us. The scenery continued to amaze, ascending from climax to climax. Eagles peered at us from tawny crags above; below, sheer drops fell into dark forests. We came to the Drichu, the Gold Dust River that in time becomes the Yangtze. It forms a boundary between Tibet and Sichuan. But any feelings of elation at having arrived at a new frontier were dashed when Wong drew up at a bridge which had a military emplacement at its farther end.

'There will be an inspection here,' he announced.

'What shall we do?'

'There are plenty of blankets and coats. Hide under them.'

This part of Sichuan was closed to foreigners. I could only hope that if they caught us, they would deal with us here, rather than send us back to Lhasa. After such a run of luck, that would have been too much to bear.

For the first time on the truck there was complete silence. Everyone was visibly worried as we crossed the bridge but at the far end Wong didn't slow up – he accelerated. Clearly they were just waving us on. A huge sigh of relief went up from all the passengers.

It had taken us a bare week to reach Sichuan from Lhasa. After five months of travel in her remote provinces, I had at last arrived in China proper. The scene that greeted my eyes was an idyllic one: a beautiful valley bisected by a small river with grazing animals, and mountains in the shape of *tormas*, specially prepared conical cakes offered on temple shrines. Little had changed from Tibet except for the houses which were painted purple here. The houses had windows with wide frames painted in primary colours and were faintly reminiscent of paintings by Mondrian.

My first impression of Dege was of the much higher standard of living this town boasted than its Tibetan counterparts. Apart from this, and a few pagoda-roofs, Dege could have been a Tibetan town – its pattern and architecture were the same. It was built on a hill, and at its centre stood a colossal fort-like temple, with big cracks down its massive walls. The pilgrims immediately made for this temple in order to circle it. Around the base of the wall were sculpted stones depicting snakes and toads.

This temple had the usual quota of fearsome images of gods, but it also housed a large printing works. The Tibetans were made to pay an entrance fee, in addition to which they purchased bottles of ink, which they would donate to the printers. Whether this ink had been produced by the monks in the traditional manner, using soot obtained by burning yak dung, I couldn't tell. We were first shown to a series of dark and dusty interconnecting rooms which housed over 210,000 carved wooden printing blocks piled from floor to ceiling in pigeonholes. Each block measured about 24" x 8". The curvilinear characters had all been carved into them by hand.

I immediately incurred the wrath of one of the pilgrims by failing to bow to these holy blocks in the approved manner, which was to press one's forehead against a random selection of them. From then on I knocked my head against a block every so often. We emerged from the storeroom into a sunny inner courtyard. Blinking in the light, I saw that it was occupied by about a hundred young men, busily printing the holy scriptures. There were no machines, and the only noise was the clatter of blocks being printed by hand at a furious pace. The men worked in pairs sitting opposite each other on stools with a block positioned between them. One inked the block with a sponge, then the other would slap a piece of paper onto it. The paper was rubbed up and down once, and then the paper handler would strip it off with one hand as he laid down the next sheet with the other. The freshly printed strips of paper were gathered and hung out to dry wherever space permitted. The loose pages are not bound but enclosed between two wooden covers which are then kept wrapped in linen or silk. One codex, the Kahgyur, runs to 108 volumes, each consisting of about 1,000 pages. Judging by a large bin of misprints the standard of printing must have been very high, as the misprints looked unblemished to me. On a gallery running round the courtyard, and protected from the sun by a wooden canopy, more young men sat in a row either side of a long dugout tree which served as a trough and in it they scrubbed the used blocks clean. Our pilgrims devoutly drank some of the inkstained water and dabbed some on their heads. They donated their ink to the printers, and refilled their empty bottles with the inky water – one more holy relic to take home. They were in a triumphant mood, holding their bottles of murky holy water aloft before stowing them in bags. Those who had too much generously shared what they had with those who had none.

Not far from Dege we dropped two of the pilgrims, including a softspoken middle-aged man who had sat next to me for most of the journey. The departure of the other man here surprised me, for I thought he must be leaving his wife behind – so close had he and this particular woman seemed on the truck. I realised that a lot of apparent intimacy in the form of cuddling is due to the necessity of keeping warm – as well as being an indication of pure, joyous friendship. The families of these two men came out to meet the truck, accompanied by yaks to carry the men's belongings home. We were all invited in for tea. Wong never needed any prompting to accept tea from the Tibetans. This was untypical, for the Chinese share the Tibetan etiquette that dictates that any offer should be courteously declined at least twice before one allows oneself to be pressed into accepting. Wong on the other hand even asked for extra helpings of rancid butter in his tea – which he was given. Contrary to what the fake lama we had met back in Gangba had told us, the Tibetans here did eat raw yak meat, and Wong wasn't averse to claiming his share, which pleased the Tibetans because it showed that he didn't consider himself above them. On the other hand, his greed offended them, as did his habit of discarding chunks of meat he considered not good enough to eat – meat which they could have done with. Wong chucked it on the floor for the dogs.

Wong ignored their hurt and even angry expressions. He even seemed to enjoy baiting them. He held a lecture by the truck, squatting on a nearby rock.

'People who keep kowtowing to gods, their hearts are no good,' he told the pilgrims gathered around him. 'In fact, your Buddhism is no different from our Buddhism.'

The pilgrims were silent.

'Do you know what,' continued Wong, impervious to the atmosphere he was creating, 'you lot are no better than yaks.'

Silence.

'Yes, just like yaks – you're always fucking.'

Silence. Even, oddly, diffidence. They might have been embarrassed for him now.

'No,' continued Wong thoughtfully, 'you're worse than yaks. They only fuck when they're on heat. You fuck all year round.'

To this day I don't know what made so many truck drivers, even halfway decent ones like Wong, into such pettish little bullies. Wong couldn't bear to be ignored. The Tibetans ignored him. Failing to get a rise out of them made him wild. He sprang up.

'Zou ba!' he yelled, and then a small grin arrived on his lips as he watched them scatter to collect their belongings and get aboard before he drove off.

There followed an endless climb. Three more passes, each at 4,000 metres, had to be crossed before we reached Chengdu. High up we had to stop as three trucks ahead of us were trapped in the ice and snow. It was biting cold and the weather began to close in. Everyone huddled together under a mass of coats and blankets, but as the cold inexorably began to penetrate our protective layers, so everyone's face became taut. One woman whose pinched face and upturned eyes gave her a pained expression at the best of times seemed to be in real agony now, for she was transfixed by the cold, and the only thing she did to protect herself against it was to draw a scarf over her face. It had begun to sleet, and the icy rain cut one's skin like a cruel electric shock. A middle-aged woman next to me, whose serene face with its constantly parted lips gazed at the world from under the rim of a fox-fur hat, now curled closer to me for warmth. I insisted that she take my gloves. Ahead of us, the bogged-down trucks inched forward, only to stick in another rut, but every time we were able to move forward, prayers were offered that we would be able to continue to do so. On one side of the lorry was a drop into nothingness – a vortex of swirling snow and cloud. At long last we inched to a space wide enough to pass the beleaguered trucks. And on the other side of the pass the weather miraculously cleared. In the middle distance, a tiny turquoise lake nestled in a valley.

'Were you scared?' I asked my neighbour.

'That is why I was praying.'

We arrived at Manigang before dusk. Now only a short way from Ganze, the dropping-off point for most of the pilgrims, Wong decided to torture them by delaying his decision as to whether to continue on to Ganze after dinner that night or not. In the end he decided not to and the angry pilgrims were forced to sleep rough for yet another night on the damp ground with the drizzle falling. The journey was beginning to wear everyone down. Someone in the kitchen at the local restaurant made a wisecrack at the expense of Mrs Wong. She screamed in outrage and Wong rushed to the kitchen to beat the offender up. They had to be separated forcibly.

'The bastard doesn't know better, he's from Qinghai,' simmered Wong afterwards.

Dave's brooding worsened too. Added to the burden of guilt at having imposed ourselves on the Tibetans was his irritation at Wong's treatment of them. Nor could he begin to interest Wong or Lao Er in a discussion about Marxist dialectics. Added to these frustrations, too, was anxiety about his future. He spoke much of the need to settle down. A teaching post was being held open for him in Shandong Province. But I knew that there was more to it than all of this. I was to blame. Dave's Chinese was fluent, mine non-existent. I had constantly pestered him for translations and used him as my interpreter, and Dave was never the easiest or most compliant of people. I made his position as intermediary worse because I could not pick up Chinese as I had done Persian and Uighur. Nor could

I relate its inflection to the speaker's mood, frequently mistakenly interpreting the harsh tones of Chinese for actual anger, and unable to detect a change of mood or an interrogative note.

Despite these pressures, I was sad that the journey would soon be over. Only six of the pilgrims would continue on from Ganze. Ganze itself was a compact, bustling market town crowned by a temple that looked down onto ugly concrete buildings surrounded by wooden Tibetan ones. We pulled into the central truck and bus depot where the majority of the pilgrims left us, taking their huge sacks of belongings with them. We were comfortable at last, and could stretch out, but the lorry felt empty and desolate. My feelings were mixed. I felt rewarded to have shared their journey with them, and to have experienced the highs and lows of their religious intoxication, but I still felt that I had been an uninvited guest. And I was parting with something forever that no photo could ever catch or retain: their warmth, their gregariousness, freshness and exuberance. Things our civilisation has lost. And for what would I use photographs? To whet other foreigners' appetites for travel? To encourage them to intrude on these people's lives, as I had done? My greatest moral and ethical dilemma is that, in communicating my own sensations and experiences, am I not encouraging tourism – thereby precipitating the downfall of peoples I love?

My heart ached as the truck pulled out of the bus station and the pilgrims waved us goodbye. They had become my family.

PART SEVEN

The Heart of China

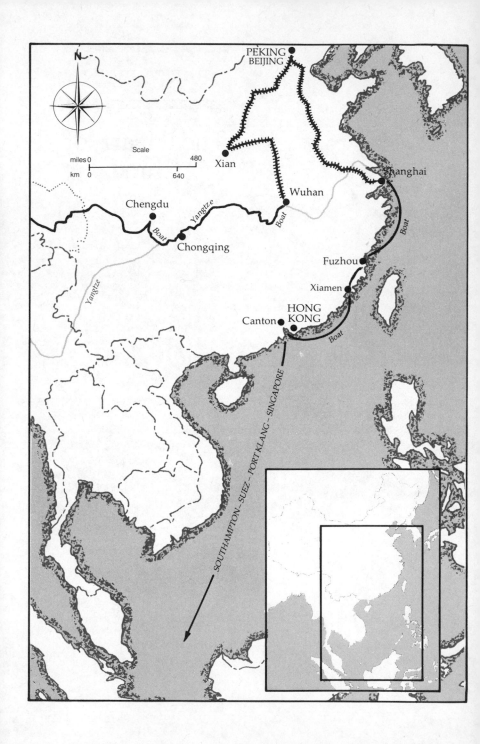

YANGTZE RIVER
TRIP

One pass further on and we had lost all trace of Tibet. The further east we travelled, the greater was the increase in the standard of living, and the cheaper the cost of living became. I could have my canteen filled with hot water for 1 fen (0.3p), and as much tea as I could drink for 1 mao (3p). But in these borderlands there were still signs of peoples other than the Han. A woman with a thick cloth folded on her head held in place by her plaits may have belonged to the Yi. And at Kanding where we bathed in hot springs there were clusters of beautiful women dressed in long blue robes, with broad turbans wrapped round their heads. The mode of dress was almost identical to that of the Afghans, but these women were Qiang.

And now I was coming to those densely populated areas inhabited by the Han. Towns where svelte peasant women, carrying not an inch of fat, but with every muscle fine-tuned like a thoroughbred horse's, had exchanged the hoe of the farm labourer for the wheel-barrow of the construction worker. I thought I had sensed the rebirth of a nation in Urumchi, and yet passing through the city of Ya'an I was amazed at the endless rows of department stores, the number and variety of products on sale. And this was a minor town, not a provincial capital. Outside the towns, I was aware of another fundamental change, for the vast open tracts of Tibet and Xinjiang were exchanged here for neat parcels of fertile farmland. People were everywhere. In an hour of travelling I passed more people than I'd seen in the whole of Tibet. Men, women and children worked alongside each other. I saw a group knee-deep in mud, pulling at the reins of a stranded buffalo. It was clear to see that the strength of China lies in its sheer man- and muscle-power. Farming is done with virtually no machinery. A peasant waters his land by staggering under the weight of a yoke of buckets, and the new incentives of the government encourage him to work even harder, because nowadays once they have met the state crop quotas they are free to sell the surplus on the open market. This has led to a new burst of wealth which has expressed itself in a forest of new buildings and TV antennae. Roads built for oxcarts now trembled under the wheels of juggernauts, which weaved their way among the cyclists and barrows like elephants among antelope. At the teashops in the villages, the old men sat smoking longstemmed pipes and playing cards or Chinese chess. Or just sat passively staring at the furiously passing trucks, which disturbed the tranquillity of the villages with blaring horns and roaring engines, but which scarcely raised an individual eyebrow. People played billiards by the roadside on tables with blankets stretched over them for baize. On every wall, posters and hoardings loudly encouraged birth control:

MAMA HAD ONLY ONE FOR ME AND MY COUNTRY.
ONE CHILD – THREE MOUTHS.

In a country where the population is increasing by 12 million a year (the same number as all the inhabitants of Australia), Sichuan, as the most populous province, has become a prime target for family planning campaigns; it already contains more than 100 million people. By the year 2000, the Chinese government hopes that the total population will have stabilised at around 1.2 billion. Family planning, which is an efficient service and provides free contraception and abortion, coupled with penalties for families with more than one child, has led to a slackening in the rate of population increase. But there is a darker side. Traditionally, male children are preferred, and there have been cases of parents killing an unwanted female baby so that they will be free to try for a male one. To counter this, nine out of ten population control posters depict attractive-looking little girls.

Wong's home town was Wenjiang, some sixty kilometres from Chengdu. He insisted that we stay the night and the following day there.

'But Wenjiang's closed to foreigners,' we said.

'Never mind,' said Wong, sending Lao Er off to find us a 'safe house'. Within an hour he returned to escort us to a little inn, always making sure that we walked in the shadow of the buildings. But it was inevitable that news of our arrival should spread, and sure enough at half past midnight two policemen turned up on our doorstep. But as had so often happened, concern that we were in a closed city gave way to anxiety that as foreigners and therefore guests we should be properly treated. This attitude stemmed not only from traditional Chinese hospitality, but also from a desire not to appear 'backward' and from a belief that all westerners lived lives of unexampled luxury. Thus their first concern was that we should transfer to the best hotel in town. We liked our inn, which was simple but immaculate, and turned their suggestion down. This baffled them.

'You must move to the hotel.'

'But we don't want to.'

'If you move to the hotel, your illegal presence here will be overlooked.'

'But we're helping a small business by staying here,' said Dave cleverly. 'I thought it was government policy to help small businesses at the moment.'

This left them speechless for a moment, but then they gave in, saying that we could stay two nights. But that wasn't the end of the matter, for they returned later to question us in more detail, no doubt having received instructions to do so from their superiors:

What route did you take to get here?

Why have you come to Wenjiang?

Who brought you here?

We tried to be as helpful as possible. We told them that we had travelled by truck by way of Nying Qu, Bomi and Chamdo, that it had taken nine days and that we were simply *en route* for Chengdu.

'What is the name of your truck driver?'

'Which one?' we asked.

'The one who brought you here.'

'Lao Er,' we said.

'That means Old Number Two in Chinese. We want to know his name.'

Of course we knew what Lao Er meant, but we could honestly also say that that was the only name we had for him.

The police decided that it would be simplest to leave us in peace.

It wasn't 5.30 am and yet the street outside our inn in Wenjiang, Wong's home town some 60 kilometres from Chengdu, was bustling with activity. Dozens of street stalls and small eateries open to the road offered a cornucopia of breakfast dishes: *youtiao* (deep-fried, twisted doughsticks), *zhagao* (fried, glutinous riceflour cakes with a sweet filling), and *doufu* (beancurd).

After breakfast, which we took at a variety of different stalls, we made our way over to Wong's work unit, a transport depot which included a residential concrete block for the workers. Wong and his wife had first been allocated a small room on the third floor and then a year after their marriage had been given an extra room across a communal corridor. One of the rooms now served as their bedroom, while the other was their kitchen-cum-sitting room.

Many of the vehicles belonging to Wong's work unit were left idle for lack of orders. The workers were free to find their own business to make up for the lack of work, and so Wong contracted one of the trucks to Tibetans making the pilgrimage to Lhasa. Money had been an essential ingredient in Wong's marriage. The simple ceremony alone had cost him 2,000 yuan, the sum needed to buy the obligatory 'forty-eight legs' of furniture (bed, table, chairs and so on).

'Wouldn't it've been simpler and cheaper to build a table with forty-eight legs?' joked Dave.

'Be even cheaper to live like the Afghans – on the floor,' I added. But it turned out that the forty-eight legs of furniture weren't all that was necessary for a marriage to take place. A bride will often also require 'the four things that go round' – a washing machine, a tape recorder, an electric fan and a bicycle, before she will consent to marry. And these were only half of the 'eight must-haves', which change with the standard of living. A colour TV is now necessary, not just a black-and-white one. A radio-cassette player is better than a mere radio, and a motorbike is better than a bicycle. If it *has* to be a bicycle, then it must be one of the four famous makes. The Chinese seem to be obsessed with status symbols. A Japanese motorbike is high on the list. As foreign cigarettes cost about ten times as much as local ones, smoking them brings you a lot of kudos.

On our second day in Wenjiang, Wong, his wife and Lao Er started to prepare a feast. They had heard that all foreigners drink coffee, and as it is an expensive luxury in China Dave quickly bought some, fearful that they might go to even greater expense. With deceptive ease they produced a magnificent farewell dinner. The only thing I couldn't quite get used to was spitting out the bones and gristle onto Wong's uncarpeted living-room floor. But it was the accepted practice, and to have placed them on the edge of the table or back in one's bowl would have been considered the height of bad manners.

The following day we said our goodbyes and caught the bus to Chengdu. I fell asleep during the journey, but awoke with a start in my first Chinese metropolis. Streets teemed with cyclists, and pedestrians skeetered about, unused as yet to the furore of modern traffic; drab monolithic buildings lined the streets. There were broad avenues meant to impress, and little lanes filled with dingy dwellings, though no lane was without its food stall, shoe and bicycle repair shops and engravers.

At the centre of the city there is a towering statue of Mao, his arm outstretched. Is he telling the Chinese people to march bravely forward? Perhaps nowadays he's beckoning a welcome to the West, or telling the Russians to keep off. Or both. Despite all the reforms the old guard still maintain a very visible presence. There are posters of Marx, Engels, Lenin, Stalin and Mao everywhere. They are always arranged in that order, with the full beard of Marx first and the downy cheeks of Mao last, as if to express the proposition: their Marxism is in inverse proportion to their facial growth.

The small amount of advanced technology China possesses is in ironic contrast to the simple technology on which her society still largely relies. Thus you see huge Isuzu lorries hopelessly stuck in a traffic jam behind a donkey cart loaded with nightsoil collected from the communal toilets. And the communal toilets themselves reflect a part of life that is essentially Chinese: they are more than just loos; they are a place to read the paper, have a chat or even a political argument.

The streets of the city were full of notices – explicit, gory black-and-white photographs of accidents to remind people of the dangers of not putting safety first, for example – though the government takes no steps to introduce safety measures on the factory floor. It's not all that uncommon for a worker to lose a hand as a result of having to work on machinery with no safety guards. There were even more sombre notices – advertising public executions. The convicted are made to kneel, and are shot in the back of the head.

The venue for their trials is often the local sports stadium. The crimes are not only murder and rape, but economic sabotage (that is, the embezzlement of state funds), and even petty crimes – repeated theft, possession of cannabis, and hooliganism. There are no accurate figures available of how many have been executed since the government's anti-crime drive began in November 1983, but an often-quoted figure arrived at by foreign journalists put the toll at 10,000 in the first year since the campaign began. The campaign is directed against those who 'steal, deceive, kill and burn; against hooligans, and those who beat, smash and loot; against bad elements who seriously violate social order', and it has the approval of the general populace. One Chinese said to me, 'Sure, I agree with the executions – there are enough of us as it is, we don't need the bad ones.'

Outside a temple's main gates old women sold banned tabloids. Labelled 'yellow' – synonymous with pornographic, or superstitious, or sensationalist – by the state, these papers sold like hot cakes. They were simple magazines of intrigue, romance, war, crime, detection, secret societies, spies and UFOs. Man's common heritage!

Although by now we had reached the area of China where foreigners are allowed, and had no further need to dissimulate, we continued to sleep in the open, I with my sleeping bag as a pillow, and wrapped in my patou. It was by now the late spring of 1985 and mild enough to do so in the lowlands without discomfort. We chose riverbanks, market squares, or the forecourts of ticket halls as our 'hotels', and on waking at about 5.30 in the morning we would always be surrounded by dozens of astonished locals. Dressing in front of their unwavering stares made me feel as much like a Martian as I will ever do. The reason we didn't stay in hotels was simple: we couldn't afford to. In the open cities, foreigners must without question stay in the hotels specially for them, and they cost at least three times the rate locals would be expected to pay. But there was more to it than this. It was a desire to avoid tourist ghettos. The tourist hotels were designed to try and cocoon foreigners from the real China – and to present to them only that facet of China that the Chinese wanted seen. I wasn't prepared to have my movements hampered by artificially imposed barriers, and I wanted to break the myth that all foreigners were a breed apart. But entering a small local restaurant could cause near-panic among the staff, and they were further thrown off balance by Dave's fluent Chinese. They nevertheless automatically offered us the best (and most expensive) items on the menu – and couldn't understand it when we didn't necessarily want them.

Mixing as much as we could with the people of the towns brought many rewards. There was the time we bumped into a young Vietnamese on a bus. He had come to Chengdu to study at a Catholic Seminary, one of six in China to be opened since 1982. And if Dave had the misfortune to be bitten by a rat one night as we slept, this too was a reflection of life in China, for the rat population there had reached frightening proportions – there are three times as many rats in the People's Republic as humans. Several cities have put a price on rats' heads to stem the tide, and entrepreneurs have set up a variety of money-spinning rat enterprises – an idea sponsored by the *Economic Daily*. Ideas include rats as a delicate *hors d'œuvre*, the application of rats in medicine (Heaven knows how), and – most reasonable of all, I think – ratskin quilts.

Dave and I had expected to part company in Chengdu, but the Yangtze River was tantalisingly close so that it was impossible to resist going there. Even though its upper reaches were closed to foreigners, we hoped to be able to travel by boat not only from Leshan to Chongqing, but on through the open sections down to Wuhan in Hubei Province. We boarded a coach for Leshan. Although reserved for ticket holders only, would-be travellers besieged it every time it stopped, even at traffic lights, and the lone driver was all but powerless against their determined assault, having nothing but the doorhandle to wedge shut against them. Once on the open road, however, we began to envy those who had failed to get aboard, because the driver took to overtaking at high speed on blind corners.

Leshan's streets were full of promenading Chinese tourists, unflustered by the light rain, dawdling at stalls selling local delicacies, which included delicious small crabs fried in batter and eaten whole. Dave's initial efforts to find us a room in a Chinese hotel proved unfruitful, but in the end persistence paid off. With his fast talking,

375

and possibly with the additional help of one of my letters, written in Chinese on Chelsea School of Art letterhead, we obtained a self-contained apartment at the Guesthouse of Students of the Fine Arts. This was a really pleasant and serene place. What made it even nicer was the sound of people practising the violin.

The following day I was mistaken for Yasser Arafat. The PLO leader was visiting China at the time, and his photo was in all the newspapers. I still dressed in my Afghan clothes, simply because they were so utterly practical, and with my beard and turban I attracted lots of double-takes. My only worry in being taken for an Arab, was that if I behaved badly the Chinese would with unwitting unfairness think that this was Arab behaviour and blame them for my mistakes.

We tried in vain to buy a boat ticket from Leshan to Chongqing. There was even a sign in English on the kiosk: NO FOREIGNERS. I appealed to the Public Security Bureau, brandishing my official letters, but they were intractable. We decided not to persist, but to catch a bus down to the first closed town where the boat called. There, we argued, they'd probably be unaware of the regulations governing foreigners' travel, and we'd buy our boat tickets with ease. Things were not to be that simple. We drove down to Wutongqiao, about 30 kilometres away, but the locals were suspicious of us from the start, and one elderly official, whose job it was to keep tramps and vagrants on the move, pursued us beyond the edge of town. He did explain to us that it was illegal to sleep rough, but that we could have accommodation for as little as two mao. However we wanted to avoid registering because that would bring the police down on our heads. We headed further out of town, and finally the old official dropped back. When night fell, Dave made the six-kilometre trip back into town to the boat-ticket office. He returned several hours later to say that the office was closed, but that he'd discovered that the boat left at five in the morning. He was exhausted, but we had to pick up our bags and return to town again, avoiding people as far as possible, which is a near-impossibility in China. I was frightened to see how grossly overpopulated even a minor city like this could be. Towns and cities are badly overstretched too by shortages. While I was waiting for Dave to return, an elderly woman was being rushed to medical attention by six young men who carried her on an improvised stretcher. Even for the peasants within reach of a doctor, treatment has not been free since the dissolution of the commune. It seemed more like Tory Britain than Communist China.

We found a place to sleep on the river bank near where the boats were moored, but almost immediately a policeman came and shone his torch at us.

'Papers?'

We stressed that we were in transit and would be leaving first thing. He seemed to be in two minds about what to do with us, but finally he simply bade us good night and went on his way.

The next morning we had no trouble at all in purchasing a couple of tickets for the boat, and soon we were on our way, as the modern two-decker cut through the tranquil waters. The landscape we travelled through might have been created by Monet, if he had ever chosen to paint a dawn scene of a broad river dotted with sampans.

At our first stop peasants were waiting by the quayside with their produce beside them in neat piles. They carried everything aboard on bamboo poles, including hemispherical baskets packed with live geese destined for the markets downstream. Unfortunately our stop was not the brief one that was scheduled, owing to the arrival – yet again – of the police. The usual rigmarole followed, but once again we were allowed to travel on. After the police had gone, the crew were apologetic, and I wondered if they had given the authorities the tip-off by radio: indeed, no one else could have done. But at least our little run-in had broken the ice between us and the Chinese on board – passengers and crew alike.

As night fell we carried on, navigating between illuminated buoys. When finally we berthed, Dave and I settled down to sleep on deck while fellow passengers disembarked to check into the local guesthouse.

Chongqing loomed ahead of us like a citadel, perched on a mountaintop. It was the middle of the following afternoon, and the

377

air was hot and humid. We docked next to a gravel bank where groups of men in T-shirts and shorts waited to carry passengers' luggage up the steep steps to one of China's biggest cities, with six million inhabitants. Our stay here would be long or short depending on the availability of onward boat tickets.

It was a thriving place, with crowded streets, overloaded buses and a vast number of pedlars and open stalls everywhere. Oddly, there were a number of Art Deco buildings which were refreshing to the eye after all the concrete architecture I had seen in towns up to now. But despite the variety of these buildings, the city was a place limited in scope. Wandering into the packed streets that night, we saw immediately how the older and younger generations of Chinese were drifting apart. The old were packed into teahouses which spilled onto the street, where they chatted and played cards or chess. The young had exchanged their Mao suits for jeans, and T-shirts with the usual slogans; some of the girls had donned bright dresses, wore lipstick, and even draped themselves over their boyfriends. Most wandered aimlessly about. Theirs was a life destined for the world of disco music. Gone would be the street operas of tradition that are for the moment still being played – but only to audiences over 40 years old. I watched one such opera, which was being given in front of the shop-cum-home of a family who had engaged the troupe to perform as a memorial to a deceased relative, a man who'd been a keen fan of the art. The artists wore exquisite robes and highly stylised make-up, and sang in voices that were deep and broad one moment, shrill and piercing the next. The family invited us to sit behind the players, and gave us tea and a snack. I found the performance captivating, and even with no knowledge of the language I could follow the gist of the tales it told – tales of romance, intrigue, corruption and justice (just like those in the banned 'yellow' magazines) – with marvellous caricatures of corrupt mandarins, dictators and wicked merchants.

We had thought of sleeping in one of the town parks, but they were too full of courting couples and roving policemen. Instead we found a quiet street near a marketplace. By day it was full of trade; by night an alfresco hotel for peasants, who slept slouched against their produce. Dave found an empty butcher's table to doss down on, while I settled on a stretch of pavement.

At first light most of the peasants were already up and unpacking their goods. We followed a procession of mainly elderly people and found that they were on their way to one of the parks, which by dawn were filled with people doing callisthenics and shadow-boxing *(taijiquan)*, the movements slow, deliberate and graceful. One or two old men were rotating large steel balls in their hands – an exercise said to stimulate the vital flow of *qi* (energy) and to counteract arthritis.

For ourselves, we took part in another kind of exercise – queuing at the maritime ticket office. The previous night had seen the vast hall turn into a camping ground with passengers stretched out on the benches and the floor. There were seven classes on the boat to Wuhan from which we chose upper fifth (for an extra *yuan* – 25p – a night this entitled us to a berth). We queued for two hours.

We joined the boat the night before sailing. Our dormitory was like a submarine's – it consisted of 108 beds (anything to do with Buddhism again, I wondered?) arranged in bunks on three levels that allowed just enough room to turn over in. Each bunk had a reed mat for a mattress. On the plus side there was boiling hot drinking water (for tea) freely available, and hot showers, which were bliss. These were going to be the three most comfortable nights in many months of travel, and I could barely contain my excitement at the thought of the famous Yangtze gorges we would pass through on our route.

The downriver cruise was also a time to unwind. We progressed at a leisurely pace the first day, passing through a gentle landscape dotted with pagodas and temples – points of peace in a land where you sometimes felt engulfed by the sheer weight of numbers. But on the second morning I was startled out of sleep by the sound of the boat's cantankerous horn. I thought maybe it was fire drill, but passengers were keenly scrambling up on deck and one said to me excitedly, 'The gorges!' Still sleepy, I picked my way over lower-fifth-class passengers, who slept on the floor and for whom the gorges clearly held no charms. Once on deck, I joined a line at the rail and listened unwillingly to a high-pitched female voice over the scratchy PA system, telling us all about the gorges. No one paid much attention to her. The main thing was to be photographed, with a loved one or a friend, with the gorges as a backdrop. One group even wanted me in their snapshot. I felt like a cardboard cutout at a seaside resort.

Beyond the frenzy on board, the deep gorges were indeed something to get excited about – they described a poetic world of mist softly shrouding perpendicular cliffs, and the river waters, channelled more narrowly, drove us through at a brisk pace. The river itself wound and twisted here. On the banks you could see little villages nestling on terraces in between the gorges, whose soaring heights seemed to block our path at every turn – but it was as if a god had cleft the rock for us with an axe as we were carried through the dark valleys on shoals of rapid water. This was precisely the kind of scenery that is so familiar to us from the works of Chinese landscape artists.

By the end of the second day we had reached the natural barrier of the Nanjin Pass. Here, the damp and dense mountains with their shaggy carpet of trees gave way to the flat plains of Hubei. There was an interlude as we made our way through the locks of the Gezhouba Dam, an enormous project designed to harness the electrical energy potential of the Yangtze, and then on into a country of flat, uninterrupted surfaces – blue sky, green plain, and yellow hedges of wheat. The river waters here were brown, torpid, and silt-laden. The blame for this was laid, as are so many of China's ills, at the doors of the Cultural Revolution and the Gang of Four, who had ordered the felling of the trees that had once lined the river and protected it from the results of soil erosion. Rarely was anything divorced from politics in China.

Dave and I had always been keen to visit historical sites, but our energies now seemed to be drained. Besides, the time had come now for us to go our separate ways. Perhaps I had had an easier time of it than Dave, for I hadn't had the job of interpreter, and also I found it easier to ignore the great political divide that separated us. We both had roots in the petty bourgeoisie, but all similarities ended there. I do not tend to define experiences in political terms. And of course we disagreed violently over Afghanistan, since Dave supported the Soviet invasion. In fact, it was rare for us to find common ground, though when we did it was worth all the altercations, for Dave had taken China to his heart and could offer fascinating glimpses into its recent history.

All our differences were forgotten as we ate our last meal together. It was taken informally, at one of the open stalls. The restaurateur had set up his barrow, a table and some stools among a collection of empty crates at the side of a busy road. We couldn't have eaten better. After a time, we even forgot about the roar of traffic right next to our ears.

Despite a failure to get a further extension to my visa, I would travel north to Xian, my last stop before Peking. Dave used my student card to buy me a 'hard seat' on the overnight train there. We said goodbye at the station. He would be leaving later by boat, bound for Jinan and the job he hoped to pick up in Shandong Province. Much later, I learned that the job had fallen through. In the end he returned to Wuhan to teach English there.

FRIENDS ALONG
THE WAY TO
PEKING

Xian, called Chang'an in ancient times, was one of China's former capitals, spanning a period of eleven dynasties. Its golden age was during the Tang dynasty of AD 619–907 when it became the largest city in the world. During this period the arts and commerce flourished, and the city became a cosmopolitan centre with foreigners arriving from all over the world bringing with them their exotic customs, products, music, dance and religions. Apart from Buddhism, which was the most popular religion, Chang'an could boast a variety of others: Zoroastrians, Manichaeans, Nestorians and Muslims all had their own centres of worship.

My first temptation was to seek out the small Uighur community where I could make myself better understood, but instead I took a bus to the university where I had heard that rooms could sometimes be had for a small fee. *En route* I met Jacques, not a Frenchman but a Chinese student who was studying French and who consequently had adopted a French name. He invited me to the tiny room which he shared with five other students. Their accommodation was very basic. They slept on bunk beds, their only furniture was a table, and they had one electric ring to cook on. The communal washrooms only had cold water. None of this prevented them from having a mastery of French that was quite astonishing. They all spoke it without a trace of accent and perfectly fluently – it was difficult to see what there was left for them to study – though I noticed that Pierre and Alphonse were particularly well versed in French cultural history. In addition to this, they could tell me everything about France today, from the cost of a stamp to the price of a loaf. Jacques offered to move out so that I could use his bed for the night, but I declined the offer and slept concertina'd on their table.

I didn't want to run the risk of causing them any trouble either, so the next morning I left for the foreign students' halls of residence at the university. The foreign students were all Arab or African, mainly from the Sudan and the Yemen. They were all studying 'roads and bridges' and architecture. I wondered what the Chinese had to offer on these subjects, but I soon realised that what these students needed was not sophisticated western expertise but the kind of intermediate building technology in which China excels. Most of the students viewed their stay here as a prison sentence. Few had the opportunity of returning home for visits during their five-year stay. In addition to this, they often found themselves the object of racist comment, and in Shanghai they had even been subjected to violence, because, they told me, they had played their music too loudly. Their grants, while they covered essentials, were not generous, and there was no money left over for any of life's luxuries or to spend on travel within China. And relationships with Chinese women (all the foreign students from Arab nations are male) have only recently been permitted by the authorities, and even then the foreigners are restricted somewhat quaintly to one girlfriend. Whether that means at a time or for the duration I do not know. Such friendships are in any case rare.

'They don't understand love,' one African student complained to me of Chinese women.

'Some of them ask for ten yuan before they'll go to bed with you,' another said. 'And that's after you've been going steady for months!'

Both partners were often fearful of repercussions, and intricate plans had to be laid to enable a local girl to visit a foreign student, whose hall of residence would in any case be out of bounds to her. It wasn't too difficult to pull the wool over the caretaker's eyes and whisk a girl past him, but the consequences if you were caught could be serious. I heard of one Yemeni who was found to be dating three girls at once. He was deported. However, I later learned that he had also threatened the caretaker with a knife.

Although almost all the foreign students spoke either French or English in addition to their mother tongue, they used Chinese as their lingua franca. It was odd to see Claude, a French-speaking Madagascan, talking Chinese with Mubarak, an English-speaking Sudanese. It was odder still to play in the foreigners' football team – which was almost entirely Sudanese. The match started in the late afternoon once the stifling heat of the day had passed. I played on the wing, wearing my faded 'You Can't Ban a Chelsea Fan' T-shirt. Despite the fact that they could all speak English, my team-mates shouted instructions to me in Chinese. But later they told me that the Chinese suffered from what I'd thought to be an English social disease – football hooliganism. They spoke of matches abandoned because of fans invading the pitch and attacking not only each other but the players and referee as well.

My visa was now dangerously close to expiry. I went along to the Public Security Bureau with Claude's girlfriend, a Canadian who taught English to Chinese students. We told the police that we wanted permission to climb Hua Shan, one of China's sacred mountains. For that we'd need a travel permit.

'You'll need a letter from your work unit testifying that you are foreign experts working at the university for that,' said the unusually helpful policeman.

'Well, I'm quite happy to ask for one,' replied Kathy, 'but my work unit is fed up with having to issue letters like that every time I ask for a travel permit.'

'I take your point,' said the policeman. But he wasn't totally convinced. 'Let's see your passports.'

We handed them over. Kathy's passport and mine looked much the same, decorated with a confusing and colourful crowd of stamps. It was a hot summer's day, and the policeman clearly didn't want to make trouble for himself. He gave the passports a brief inspection and issued us with the requested travel permit. We thanked him profusely and headed for the exit.

'Oh, I forgot,' I said with feigned absentmindedness. 'I need an extension to my visa.' I hoped that he wouldn't see my exit visa but I had a ready-made excuse in case he did. When he didn't remark on it I filled out another form and he duly franked a further extension on a virgin page in my passport. As we left, another foreigner who had been patiently waiting his turn moved forward.

'I've come for permission to climb Hua Shan,' said the brash young American backpacker.

'I'm sorry, that's not possible,' said the same policeman.

'But . . . !' cried the crestfallen tourist.

'It's closed to foreigners.'

'But you just . . .'
'It's only open to foreign experts.'

I now had ample time to explore the city, and I did so on a borrowed bicycle. Cycling is a fraught experience here – nearly everybody is on two wheels, and experts are merciless to amateurs. Collisions are frequent but serious injury is rare, as riders are adept at jumping off in time. At night, however, the danger is increased tenfold, as cyclists are forbidden to use lights. I can't think why, unless it's another attempt to keep the population down. In the dark you can either be dismounted by a hidden pothole, or flattened by a truck.

I took my bicycle in search of the mosque. I asked an old man in the Hui neighbourhood the way to it.

'Are you a Muslim?' he returned.

'No, I'm sorry.'

'Do you have religion?'

'No.'

'You ought to have religion,' he said, wagging a finger at me severely. 'Do your parents have religion?'

'No,' I said again, apologetically.

'They too should have religion! You must tell them this!'

Despite his severity he did show me the way to the mosque, and I subsequently returned several times to study it. I always went out of my way to say hello to the old man, too, for it turned out that he had the most beautiful granddaughter, but without his religious convictions. She was of slightly bigger build than her Han sisters, though she had the same rich, flowing black hair. Her piercing blue eyes were those of a Middle Eastern woman. Her grandfather, whose name was Ma, persisted in admonishing me about my lack of religious belief. What was nice about him was that he simply encouraged me to believe in something – not necessarily in Islam.

Religion confuses the majority of educated Chinese, the vast majority of whom are atheists, but that didn't deter Anne, an American teacher at the university and a born-again Christian, from proselytising. Her fragile physique made her look like a medieval saint.

'You believe in God?' the puzzled students would ask her.

'Yes.'

'But you can't – you have an MA!'

Xian is a place to enjoy the brilliance of Chinese art. Its cultural history goes back to the neolithic site of Banpo. Here, the Chinese discern what Marx describes as primitive communism. A notice there informs you that members of the same tribe lived and worked together on an equal footing and were buried in the same communal pit. However in the same village there is a rich burial site. The  anthropologists explain it away dubiously by telling you that the girl buried there was obviously a person of 'high standing'. The glory of Xian, and what has recently made it so famous, is the huge grave complex of the Emperor Qin Shi Huang, the founder of the Qin dynasty and the builder of the Great Wall. Here you can see the army of terra-cotta soldiers, with their horses and armour. Each soldier has an individual expression, and much has been written of this, but one should perhaps add that the statues are the result of one of the world's first assembly lines, for the parts that go to make up a whole soldier have been produced wholesale and then interchanged for the sake of variety. Nevertheless the artists – or craftsmen – who produced this stupendous piece of work must go down as some of the greatest in history. In a pit near the soldiers now on display others lie, waiting to be excavated, their limbs still grappling with the mud that has held them for so long.

As my time in Xian was now drawing to a close, I returned to Ma to say goodbye to him.

'If you believe in God He will bring you a beautiful wife,' Ma told me. I immediately thought of his granddaughter, who had left work early to come and say goodbye to me. I can't remember what I said to her – I had mixed feelings about becoming too friendly with a Chinese woman. For her, I would be a kind of illusion, a man from a never-never land to the west; and I feared for her should she ever be seduced by some smooth-talking tourist with fewer scruples than

I have. For there is no such thing as a holiday romance for a Chinese girl. Once their virginity is gone, so have their hopes of a husband. Although I was fully aware of the circumstances, I was to confront them again in Peking – my next and what I thought would be my final stop – in a far more insistent way than I had here with Ma's granddaughter.

As I left for the station, she whispered to me, 'I won't say goodbye.'

Sometimes I wonder what I am doing back in England. But perhaps it is as well to recognise that dreams can only ever be dreams.

I had come well prepared – that's to say I had learnt my lines in Chinese and now as I waited my turn at the railway ticket office queue I rehearsed them in my mind: 'Good day. One hard seat on today's train number 36 to Peking.' It was a long wait, and we inched forward a footstep at a time. Tempers were fraying as the patient passengers were jostled every now and again by latecomers trying to jump the queue by joining a friend. Now only one man was left in front of me. I felt supremely confident, as one must do on such occasions, and there was no reason to think that my fake identity cards would betray me at this late stage in the game. I stepped forward, placing my head at the level of the pigeonhole so as to be in full view of the clerk. I said my piece, pushing my fake student card through the grille – the card was necessary to obtain the Chinese fare, rather than the higher one – almost double – normally charged to foreigners. Everything seemed to be going well, but then the clerk asked me something. I hadn't been prepared for that and of course I didn't understand a word. She repeated her question. Panic set in as I became aware of the impatient queue behind me, but all I could do was repeat my one sentence, however lamely. Luckily the clerk was considerate and spoke to me again, more slowly. I forced myself to calm down and listen.

'Train number 36 will be leaving one half hour late,' she told me carefully.

Relief swept over me. '*Mei guanxi* – no matter,' I replied. She gave me a wry smile as I took my ticket and headed for the platforms.

It's worth arriving in Peking by train just for the railway station. Built in the fifties, it is a horrendous hybrid of modern and traditional

Chinese architecture. It is enough to make a mere human being feel very small indeed, but not far from the station I felt positively ant-like, for I had reached Chang'an Avenue – a vast road that cuts right across Peking, and which was wide enough to land a jumbo jet on. I had arrived here the morning after a riot that had shaken and shocked the nation, but in spite of this everything seemed normal. Roads intersected the Avenue at right angles, and red and white hurdles demarcated lanes for bicycles from cars and trucks. Islands between the two channels so formed held teeming masses of people waiting to board the numerous elongated buses, that resembled giant caterpillars. Busy and aggressive, this was a capital city in a state of change. My first impression was that its inhabitants were the least friendly I'd encountered yet. But one had to take into account that whilst the locals were crammed into mean apartment blocks, spacious hotels along the lines of those in the big western cities had grown up for foreigners. Meanwhile, outside in the *hutongs*, Peking's side streets, families lived behind faceless walls, in flats clustered around courtyards. This was a ramshackle but picturesque world enlivened by plants: hung from eaves, in windowboxes, or climbing up concrete walls in hopeful arabesques which explored every fissure, every crag. Here and there would be a bird singing in a little cage. But a shadow is looming. The *hutongs* are being bulldozed to make way for nondescript high-rises, built to Chinese specifications, and in my view instant slums on a par with those built in places like Chicago and Liverpool twenty-odd years ago.

From that kind of background, the Chinese see foreigners receiving special food, special cigarettes, spending more money than they themselves will earn in a lifetime. Their own diet is simple, and some foods are rationed. In a luxury hotel, a foreigner may spend the equivalent of two weeks' wages for the average Chinese on one ice cream. No wonder there is resentment.

I came into contact with diplomats and journalists who formed part of the expatriate community. They all lead a peculiar life in foreigners' compounds which look like ghettos – tall blocks which are constantly being vandalised – though not by the Chinese, who are forbidden entry (there are special units of the army on duty at the gates of the compounds) but by the bored children of the expats themselves. Many of the Third World diplomats here are all but forgotten by their mother countries, often languishing for years. I came across one or two who'd had their electricity cut as their governments hadn't forwarded sufficient funds to pay the bills.

I had work to do here, though I longed to rest. Since leaving Ismail Khan nearly a year ago I had been anxious to talk to the Chinese government about the situation in Afghanistan. Their role in the struggle against the Russian army of occupation is an important one. Now, in Peking, a letter was waiting for me from Jamila. She had posted it in Haiti six months before. It outlined the worsening situation in Afghanistan as she had left it, and spurred me to action. I asked the British Embassy if they would help me contact the appropriate people in the government, and they raised no objection. It was my naïve ambition simply to be a disinterested emissary, whose work might be of benefit to everyone. My first contact was with a Mr Zheng, on the European desk at the Ministry of Foreign Affairs. He listened to me courteously and then said, 'We will contact you at your embassy.'

I had to explain that I had nothing to do with the embassy, and was seeing him only on my own cognisance. That, unfortunately, sparked off a long period of suspicion during which I had to convince the Chinese that I wasn't either eccentric or a British spy. I couldn't give them the phone number of the British couple I was staying with, as I didn't want to risk compromising my hosts, and that only increased their suspicions. Telephone contact was, however, of necessity frequent. I had to phone the Chinese every time.

Eventually I met a Chinese diplomat called Lin who I was led to understand had regular contacts with all the sides involved in the Afghan conflict. My appointment was for 9.30 in the morning, and, knowing the vagaries of Peking transport by now, I left extra early.

I was greeted by Mr Lin who met me at the gates of the Ministry of Foreign Affairs. He conducted me into the building where another official joined us and escorted us down a corridor lined with cheap porcelain spittoons, which double as wastepaper baskets, to a large reception room. We took seats in deep armchairs with lace antimacassars and spittoons nestling next to them on the floor. Mr Lin spoke first.

'You have been sent by the British government, I think.'

'No, that is a misconception. I have already explained that I represent no one. My interest in the Afghan situation is personal.'

'Not sent by the British?' He frowned, puzzled.

'Absolutely not.' I handed him one of the visiting cards the Churchill Trust provides for its Fellows. 'I'm an independent traveller.'

Mr Lin appeared even more confused, though he volunteered the information that he'd once been posted to Kabul. I gave him a brief outline of my journey and its purposes, but he remained unconvinced. I persisted, and I would like to think that my disinterested approach succeeded in winning him round. He produced a note-pad and began to write in it as we talked. Initially he gave me no more than the standard response: relations between China and the USSR can only improve if three conditions are fulfilled – one of which is the withdrawal of Soviet troops from Afghanistan. The Chinese naturally do not wish the Russians either to become too powerful or to surround them any further. They want to reestablish their common border with Afghanistan, which provides a useful corridor in a volatile area.

Our discussion lasted all morning, but later I would meet other senior officials and a Chinese vice-premier who knew exactly who I was and voiced his displeasure at my having entered China illegally. But he was confused about my journey. 'Did you travel through Afghanistan with a tour group?' he asked through an interpreter. Throughout all these discussions what emerged most importantly for me was the fact that a better understanding of the entire situation could only be had by travelling to Soviet Central Asia and making contact with the people and the way of life there. Could I manage that on my return journey to Britain, I wondered.

In the intervals between meetings, I explored Peking. It was at its best in the early morning and the evening. The day begins with communal exercises taken in the parks and streets, and they are a wonderful sight to behold. During the day, the parks were filled with the sound of singers practising Chinese operatic arias – the Chinese love to sing. They also like breeding birds, and it's not unusual to see bird fanciers taking their pets for a 'walk' in their cages; some of them hung the cages from the branches of trees while they rested. The birdsong in the parks was as rich and varied as that of the humans. But it wasn't so long ago that there had been a campaign to exterminate birds, deemed a threat to crops. They had been literally driven from the earth, not allowed to land, so that they died of exhaustion in their millions. But then it was discovered that without the birds there was nothing to stop the insects from multiplying, and the insects were a far worse threat to the crops than the birds had ever been. So another campaign was started: all the grass had to be pulled up to get rid of the insects.

The mainstay of transport is the bicycle. Even the Army on duty outside the embassies changes guard on bicycles. However, there are also plenty of buses, and I enjoyed riding on them. I used bus 110 and tram 106 with all the regularity of a commuter. Queuing is non-existent. Even before a bus has stopped, would-be passengers are running alongside it, pushing and shoving to get the most advantageous position in front of the hydraulic doors. Getting on and off is like fighting your way through a frantic and overmanned rugby scrum, and the driver spends a lot of time trying to shut the doors, which usually wedge on a knot of struggling passengers caught going in and out of them. The conductress will try to help him, getting up from her little desk by the doors to throw her weight against them, but she can't stop frantic commuters from trying to haul themselves aboard over the bodies stuck in them. Inside, of course, the old expression about being squashed together like sardines simply doesn't describe the press adequately. Finally the conductress berates those jammed in the door and they grudgingly give up and get off – otherwise the bus will never leave. A few make one last attempt to get aboard, though. At last we move off, but already the battle to disembark at the next stop has started. Correct positioning of oneself on the bus from the start is vital, but unfortunately everyone knows it, and I suspect that people quite often miss their stops because they simply don't make it to the doors in time. You can't see where you are by looking out of the windows, for they are darkened by other passengers' bodies pressed against them. I tried counting the number of stops, and only slipped up a couple of times. Luckily the conductress announces the names of the stops, her accent carrying the rolled 'r' drawl that is typical of Peking. I listen carefully. Eventually I am carried out at the right stop with the human tide that is fortunately leaving the bus with me.

———

I had to face the fact that my efforts to influence the Chinese authorities as an independent intermediary on behalf of Ismail Khan could go no further, but I knew that I had done my best. In my efforts to achieve a greater understanding of the overall Afghan problem, I had submitted a request to the Soviet Embassy to travel home via Soviet Central Asia, but this had been so firmly turned down that even I realised that it would be futile to persist. Besides, my energies were not at quite the same high point as they had been at the beginning of my journey almost fifteen months previously. I decided for the moment to profit from what I could learn about Peking. I had, after all, arrived at my destination. In one sense, my mission was complete.

There was always plenty to do and see, and I found that I had recovered my appetite for new cultural experiences. Some of the most impressive sights lie outside Peking, such as the timeworn sections of the Great Wall which cut across the countryside whatever the terrain, like a snake undulating after its quarry. I delighted in the old Forbidden City, where there is a marvellous collection of scroll paintings that tell historical and mythical stories in the manner of strip cartoons. I visited the sprawling residence of the Chinese emperors, with its vast quarters for concubines and eunuchs. Its magnificent wooden pavilions, with delicate roofs built entirely of beams interlocking so precisely that they do not need nails to keep them in place, rival those of the splendid Temple of Heaven in the south of the city. Much of China's cultural heritage was destroyed during the Cultural Revolution. I could understand why the Red Guards had done what they did, but at the same time remained appalled that they could have so little national pride as to smash so much great Chinese art.

Now, much of what was destroyed in the sixties is being restored. The enthusiasm for restoration is in certain cases unbridled. Liuli-chang, the one-kilometre-long cultural market in Peking, is a victim of over-enthusiastic restoration. Garish repainting has reduced the street to something merely bright and gaudy. All that was needed was careful varnishing and some subtle colour to define the original wooden structure of the roofs and balconies. That said, there is definitely a penchant for bright colours among the Chinese. Even on hot days you might see men in the street with their trousers rolled up to reveal orange, vermilion or pink long johns underneath.

I often travelled to one of the free trade markets to buy goods from individual tradesmen, families, or cooperatives. The prices were so ridiculously low that at first I thought I'd put the decimal point in the wrong place – and like a fool found myself bargaining over cauliflower at about 4p a pound. Even so I paid very close attention to the market rate as I didn't want to give the impression that 'big noses' were necessarily a soft touch. I wasn't very good at this since I never had the right change and I couldn't understand the primitive scales that were used for measuring out the goods, though I always made a big show of scrutinising them. Sometimes I came off well. One man offered me a watermelon, and as I didn't really want it I said I'd pay him half what he asked. To my surprise he accepted immediately. I couldn't decide whether he'd thought it was worth it just to get a good look at a foreigner, or whether he'd simply got his own maths confused.

Few foreigners used the local markets. They used the Friendship Stores. These were out of bounds to most Chinese, though paradoxically they were stocked with nothing but the best Chinese goods, together with imported products. Here, tourists eagerly snapped up all manner of local handicrafts, carpets and silks. Then there were the bookshops, some of which were out of bounds to foreigners, because on sale inside were pirated editions of technical and engineering works, dictionaries, medical tracts, and so on, all reproduced in their original language, be it in French, German, Russian or English, but sold for a quarter of their original cost. I was all for this pirating: why should the West have a monopoly on education or advanced technical knowledge?

I had made friends with some of the diplomats. Two of them had organised a Pimm's party on Beihai Lake, north of the Forbidden City. What had been intended as a quiet drinks party on four-man pedalos turned out to be a regular water battle, with ice cubes as cannon balls and even boarding parties. Ice cubes took on a new role – as instruments of torture, as they were slipped down necks and into cleavages. The whole fracas was accompanied by a lot of yelling, screaming and giggling as chancellors, consuls and First and Second secretaries clambered from pedalo to pedalo, trying to capture each other's supplies of Pimm's. Some of the little boats had an advantage: one was commanded by a naval attaché, for example. My own crew was fairly useless: two Third secretaries and a Wren who shrieked a lot. I led them on a boarding party, but they left me stranded, and I fell into the lake with a splash. Although the party hadn't been billed as fancy dress, some of the guests had decided to wear the odd bit of eccentric clothing. One man was wearing an old leather aviator's cap, while another was dressed as a gladiator. To add further colour to the proceedings, alliances were made between nations. In this way the Italians exchanged a French diplomat they had taken as a prisoner-of-war for a glamorous girl who seemed quite happy with the new arrangement. But no matter how many diplomatic arrangements were made, somehow the battle retained its chaotic nature and in the end everyone was soaked to the skin.

It was hard to tell what the Chinese spectators by the lakeside made of our antics. Toddlers with their parents clapped enthusiastically, though their fathers seemed disconcerted by the anguished cries of the participants. But if they were reserved, it was easy to understand why. When the pop group WHAM! gave a concert in Peking, some of the foreigners present started to dance. The Chinese members of the audience who did so too were promptly arrested.

Some time after the Battle of Lake Beihai, I received an invitation from the British Embassy to the QBP. This was one of the highlights of the expat social calendar but at the time I had no idea what the QBP was. The civil servants use acronyms all the time, and although on the days leading up to the QBP the embassy was a hive of unnatural activity, I couldn't break the code. I thought I might be a party to some secret goings-on, for only those with the right security clearance were allowed to attend the meeting in the first-floor office of the embassy. Clearly whatever it was was far too secret for minutes or notes to be taken, and questions flew across the table at such speed that I soon lost track of who was saying what. I am in fact a signatory to the Official Secrets Act, but I don't think that what I am about to reveal will compromise the security of the United Kingdom:

'Have you alerted the PSB about vehicles and security?' one dapper young man wanted to know.

'Yes, but we'll need extra staff from the DSB.'

'Has anyone notified the MFA?'

'The VC is in the PSA van on his way to the MFA via the PSB in the hope of obtaining the full cooperation of the DSB.'

'Who's in charge of deployment?'

'H of C,' someone rejoined. 'Though of course HMA must ultimately have a free hand.'

An aide nodded sagely at this. 'The Ambo is being kept in touch by his PA,' he added.

'I've just had this scrambled cipher message from FO in London,' someone else said. 'Apparently, FED have stipulated that the DA and the NA must be in uniform.'

Cries of disbelief. 'Are you *sure*?'

'FO regulations.'

'Are we expecting anyone from UKMIS?'

'Only Rambo knows that.'

This must be a military operation, I thought, becoming worried. Why on earth did they want me to be in on it? I looked around nervously at the serious faces.

'Rambo?' asked one of the secretaries, who I knew was dating an American marine.

'Has anyone *asked* Rambo?' a thin man wanted to know, anxiously.

'No,' someone snapped curtly.

'Why not?' Agitated.

'He's uncontactable at the present time. He's in the Wendy house.'

After a lot more of this the meeting broke up, and as I was leaving I plucked up the courage to approach one of the Third secretaries.

'Harold —'

'Yes, Nick?'

'Can I ask you something?'

'Of course. Fire away.'

'Do you think I really ought to come to the QBP?'

'Of course you must come.'

'Only I was a little worried about whether I'd be in breach of security, or something. It all sounds pretty top-level.'

'Oh, it is. We don't take the Queen's Birthday Party lightly, you know.'

But it was probably just as well that ordinary Chinese weren't invited. The sight of all those drunks staggering around, their jackets sagging under the weight of stolen bottles, might have been too much for them.

At night Peking takes on a completely different look. The Xi Dan market is a hive of activity, with shoppers browsing amongst the many outdoor restaurant stalls. On the corner of Xi Dan and Chang'an is Democracy Wall. For two years, 1979 and 1980, the government, as one of the 'Four Freedoms', permitted the posting here of 'big character posters', but this right was revoked in 1982 and the wall is now a showcase for quasi-modern Chinese products.

As everyone turns in for the night, only the melon sellers are left in the street, slouched against their huge mounds of watermelons or nestling in hammocks slung between trees. Some sleep on their carts, and a few have even brought a bed along with them. Peking is not a late-night city and once the melon sellers are asleep the only noise to disturb the nocturnal peace is the clatter of hoofs as horse-drawn carts make their way through town.

During this time in Peking my energies had been restored. I felt relaxed, and now the prospect of more adventures beckoned me. I considered a visit to Mongolia, or, even better, travelling south across China into Burma, *en route* for Mandalay. I submitted my request for a visa to the Burmese Embassy, which they diffidently promised to consider. However, it would mean extending my Chinese visa yet again. I had begun to lose track of just how many extensions I had already prised out of the Public Security Bureau, and in any case I knew that the hardest people of all to dupe would be the country's central PSB in Peking. I waited until the day my visa ran out. My chances of obtaining a new visa didn't look too hopeful in the light of information provided by two foreigners, a couple who had explained to me the obduracy they had faced from the Bureau when trying to have their tandem licensed. The Bureau refused to grant a licence because regulations state that 'a bicycle is only allowed to carry a single person'. So it was with great foreboding that I went to the PSB's office.

I went through french doors into a high-ceilinged room that looked as if it belonged in a provincial villa. But the elegant surroundings couldn't disguise the room's bureaucratic function. The décor was suitably drab, and a long desk separated applicants from officials who wore expressions of permanent distrust.

I was first in line. The young policewoman on duty took one look at my passport and declared: 'You have overstayed by three months, and what's more two months ago you were given an exit visa to make sure you left at the beginning of May. It's now the middle of June.'

'But –' I began. She interrupted me with a stern gesture.

'Worst of all, you have obtained three further extensions by deception.'

'But –'

'You must therefore leave the People's Republic of China tomorrow morning, on the first available flight.'

My heart sank. 'You mean you're deporting me?'

'No,' she said. I couldn't quite see why she said that, but it was my signal to go onto the offensive.

'Where's my airline ticket?' I asked humbly.

'I beg your pardon?'

Now I summoned up lots of charm, but it wasn't rated very highly by this young woman. Nevertheless I gave it a go: 'Of course, if you want me to leave the country, you will be providing me with an airline ticket.' I knew from many past experiences, latterly in Lhasa, that it was only after lengthy negotiations, and in an exasperated bid to get rid of me at all costs, that I'd be offered a plane ticket.

The policewoman looked dumbfounded. I outlined my journey, explaining its purpose, hoping for a stay of execution, but she was still unimpressed. She called for reinforcements in the form of her superior, who seemed amazed that I should actually want to spend so long in China. His conclusion, however, was abrupt: 'You have stayed long enough. You must leave tomorrow.'

'But I have unfinished work here.'

'You can finish it today.'

I became petulant: 'Who are you to tell me how soon I can finish my work?'

Of course I didn't say that because I have no regard for authority; but it seems to me that one should always question it.

They looked at each other, sighed, and agreed to let me have an extra day. First round to me. I had become horribly experienced in these bargaining sessions with officials. Within a short time, one day had become three, and three became a week. I stuck out for a month. Without that, I knew I'd never obtain another full month's extension thereafter if I wanted to stay on even longer. Three extensions were unheard of. I had had five – but who would question the granting of a seventh if the sixth had been confirmed by Peking? But the police officers baulked.

'What are the consequences if my passport isn't in order?' I asked, changing tack.

'You won't be able to leave the country.'

I seized on that, for technically my passport *wasn't* in order, but it cut no ice with them. A week later, thanks to a BBC correspondent with whom I was staying, I was granted a two-week extension through the Ministry of Foreign Affairs, but I wasn't satisfied. I held out for the month I wanted. To this end I solicited the help of Pei, a Chinese journalist whose paper wanted to run a story on my journey. I agreed to that, but in return asked that the paper sponsor my extension. I didn't like resorting to such methods, but I was desperate to stay in China. I was given the extension.

The most extraordinary coincidence was that Pei was a former schoolfellow of my policewoman. 'That's Chen!' he exclaimed when I described her to him. They hadn't seen each other in seven years.

When the article appeared in the paper, it carried a photo of me shaking hands with the Imam of Peking. 'Nick Danziger,' explained the caption, 'is the one on the right.' I was still wearing my Afghan clothes.

I had reached Peking for under £1,000, and I had already tried to have the rest of what was left of my Fellowship forwarded to the Bank of China in Peking. The clerks were always frantically busy converting sums of money with extreme dexterity on their wooden abacuses. I had argued over the exorbitant commission they imposed.

'We have no choice – all foreigners have to pay it,' they explained apologetically.

I found a sympathetic ear. One of the young bank clerks. But there was nothing she could do to help.

'I'm only a small potato,' she said.

'Well, if that's so, may I please speak to a big potato?'

She giggled and summoned one.

'I'm sorry, Mr Danziger,' said the big potato. 'Regulations . . .'

However, on the day the newspaper article was published, I became a big potato myself. My commission charge was duly reduced. But there was still some red tape to cut through.

'Can I open an account?'

'How long will you be staying in China?' asked the big potato affably. One big potato to another.

'A month.'

'Oh dear. You have to stay at least six to be able to open an account.'

'I see.' Well, if they wanted me to stay six months, there was nothing to stop me saying that that was my intention. I opened my account. I still have it, and I believe it is accruing interest at the rate of threepence a year.

During my frequent visits to the bank I had struck up a bantering relationship with the pretty young clerk. Very cautiously, I invited her to lunch with me, suggesting that a middlesized potato come too, as a kind of intermediary-cum-chaperon. She seemed to agree, but when I arrived to pick her up, she was totally caught out. She hadn't taken me seriously. Not only are foreigners beyond the scope of Chinese girls, but big potatoes and small potatoes didn't mix either.

Yu Shengli had no such reserve. She was in her early twenties and taught English at one of the art schools. I met her because she'd been instructed to show me round the Peking Institute of Arts and Crafts. Nothing was too much for Yu, who showed me not only the Institute but also the central art school and several art exhibitions. She introduced me to a number of artists. In the art schools, the busts of Marx and Mao have been put in the basement, but the students, in their new-found freedom, find their inspiration not in traditional or even pre-revolutionary Chinese art, but in such movements as Photorealism and Impressionism. Only a very few were painting non-figuratively.

Art has a great role to play in the promotion of understanding between people, but it can also confuse. There was an exhibition of fashion designs by Yves St Laurent at the China Art Gallery. It left the Chinese who saw it bewildered and envious. Yu herself was not alone in seeking some explanation of the extravagant designs, as alien to the Chinese as abstract modern art might have been to a Victorian critic. The Chinese were still just emerging from the period of drab Mao suits, and new materials and designs here were dictated by the need for economy. Small wonder that they were amazed at the yards of expensive fabrics St Laurent used. Not only that, but the plunging necklines of some of the 'creations' were deeply offensive to Chinese sensibility.

Yu lacked the introspective timidity that afflicted so many of the Chinese women I had met.

'Is it true that all foreigners are spies?' she asked me seriously.

She attributed her forwardness and confidence to growing up in Inner Mongolia. Her father, a professor of physics, and her mother had been banished there during the Cultural Revolution and made to work the land. Often they were forced to leave their daughter at home alone, and in their absence Yu was looked after by neighbours. As the Cultural Revolution abated, her parents gave refuge to another of its victims, a one-time English teacher. Yu had learnt her English from him, but it wasn't long before she realised the limitations of Mongolia, and left for Peking.

She told me all this barely pausing for breath. 'My parents worry about me,' she went on, 'but I'm not afraid of anything.' She looked at me. I suspected that she was just telling me that to allay her fears. 'A Singapore businessman fell in love with me and proposed – but can you imagine anything worse than being married to a business-man?' What Yu wanted was to become an artist, whatever it took, and for her Peking was like Paris must have been once – a centre of artistic discourse, rich in ideas and ideals. Sometimes she seemed to have the frivolous whimsy of a debutante, but she was not from a rich or vacuous background, and there was an underlying seriousness to her which became more apparent as one came to know her. Like most Chinese she was keen, if not desperate, to travel. Unlike most she had managed a visit to Shanghai, where she'd spent five hours. 'Too crowded,' was her verdict on that city. She had also lived as a

recluse on one of China's holiest mountains with a nun for a week
– 'Wonderful!'

Her unabashed exuberance was contagious, but also exhausting. I
was grateful to have a rest from her. Then one day she caught me
on one of my rare moments at home.

'Nick? It's Yu Shengli,' she said as soon as I'd answered the phone.
'Can I come and see you?'

I hadn't been avoiding her, but she wanted to spend all her free
moments travelling around Peking with me, eager to learn all she
could from me. Selfishly, I knew that her presence cramped my style
and restricted my freedom of movement, but I didn't have the heart
to say no.

'Would you like to come over to the apartment?'

'Yes please.'

'OK.'

'Terrific. I'll be there in half an hour.'

She knew where I lived, but that wasn't surprising. There were
only three foreigners' compounds to choose from. My hosts lived in
San Li Tun. I was alone in the flat, and wondered for a moment if
it had been wise of me to invite Yu up. Forty minutes later the phone
rang again. I could tell from her voice that she was on the verge of
tears.

'I won't be coming.'

'Why not?'

Then it hit me. She wasn't allowed into the compound alone – she
was Chinese. I could easily imagine the hurt she was feeling.

'Come back. I'll wait for you at the gate.'

As usual she was carrying a sheaf of art journals and cuttings. I
knew she was dying to see the inside of a foreigners' flat but I wasn't
prepared for her reaction to this comfortable but by no means
grandiose apartment. Her eyes grew wide. The living room was
large, sure, but her own room would have fitted into it four times –
and that room was *all* her flat – kitchen, bedroom and sitting room.
She only partly regained her composure, and sat on the sofa. The
ticklish atmosphere of a first date had entered the room, and I didn't
like it. She took off her glasses, and her eyes were unsure what to
look at. She twisted in her best dress – a simple red one which by
European standards would have been the most ordinary of working

clothes. I noticed that she wasn't wearing the knee-high nylon socks she usually had on, in common with most Chinese women. I remembered that I'd told her they made women's legs look ugly.

Her hands began to fidget, and I could tell by her nervous laugh that she hadn't come here to discuss art, but to cross a new frontier. So strong was the urge to do so that it had made her swallow her pride when the guards at the gate had turned her away and she had come back. Something stabbed at my heart, for Yu was so terribly vulnerable, and Chinese women of her age are far less worldly than their European sisters. At the same time I desired her. I had to remind myself firmly what Chinese social *mores* were when it came to unmarried girls who were no longer virgins. And I knew that Yu was not one of the few Chinese women who have experienced the pleasures of the flesh outside wedlock.

As soon as she realised that I didn't want her, she took it personally, like a very young girl. It was hopeless to explain why, so we went for a walk.

But Yu wasn't a girl to give up easily, and maybe she has it in her to beat the system. She hasn't written to me, but I have had news of her – the last was that she had set her sights on another English artist.

I had reached an impasse at the Burmese Embassy. It was a question of time, they told me, but my patience was running out, and so were my reserves – of money as well as energy. I couldn't hang around forever on the off-chance. Of course, a clandestine border crossing would have been possible, but as I had reached my primary objective it seemed foolish to risk all that I had achieved – and possibly the loss of my material – through one more venture. But as one idea was shelved, so another one arose: if I couldn't get home overland, why not by sea? Flying was out of the question, for I had only £200 left, and in any case flying is boring. No, I would travel to Shanghai by train, and from there I'd try to find steerage on a ship bound for England. I decided to put the idea into action immediately. People responded to it. One British businessman suggested, with more trust than I would have accorded myself, that I go to Hong Kong and stay with his fiancée until I could pick up a ship. 'Plenty sail from there,' he said.

My plans remained loose. I'd go to Shanghai, and visit one or two coastal towns, as well as Canton. In both the main cities I'd try and stay with the Uighur communities. From Canton I'd cross to Hong Kong, and from there I'd sail to England via Suez. It was an attractive idea.

Quickly I made my arrangements and soon all was ready for my onward journey. My only regret was that there was no time to take up an invitation to dinner which came unexpectedly from a diplomat at the Afghan Embassy. I would have loved to meet and talk properly to an official on the other side of the war from Ismail Khan, but neither he nor I could manage a date in the time that remained to me in Peking.

Friends drove me to the station on the day I left for Shanghai. They were bemused that I'd chosen a hard seat. But it was good to be back in one, and on the move again. Besides, there was even room on the floor of the compartment to stretch out and sleep. My fellow passengers were astonished that I was travelling so humbly. I explained that not all Englishmen were rich, and that we even had quite a high level of unemployment.

'Unemployment? In Britain?' they echoed in sheer disbelief.

REACHING HONG KONG

Shanghai. City of a hundred film sets. A New York of the East with tenement buildings built in the twenties, thirties, and forties. Art Deco theatres and cinemas standing as a reminder of what had been, in China's pre-revolutionary past. It is a network of teeming streets and unceasing traffic, a maze of lanes festooned with washing, men and children sitting on the pavements, as if guarding their property on the most packed of beaches. The peasant traders somnolently recline under their wide straw hats, which are their only protection from the heat of the fierce sun. The unsteady silence of alleys broken by the tiny clatter of crickets, sold in miniature wicker cages by sad-eyed old men. But nevertheless Shanghai of old was reemerging. Boutiques blared out the sound of disco music, and some of the owners even owned banned paintings. At night, tea-houses came alive to the sound of live bands.

 There was the building called the Great World, once a prodigious brothel where human flesh was traded with as much insouciance as you might trade whisky and cigarettes. Now it has been transformed: it has a new name: The Workers' Cultural Palace. A wedding cake of an amusement house for the proletariat, with distorting mirrors, electronic games, dodgems, a cinema, videos, theatres, operas, and acrobatics.

Soon after my arrival in Shanghai I gravitated, as I had done so often before, towards the Uighur community. Here there was a difference from the expatriate Uighurs I'd met before. They all looked the part of 1920s gangsters – right down to the peaked cap, baggy tapered trousers, patent black winkle-pickers and string vest. All that was missing was gaudy braces. But there was a desperation amongst these toughs that I hadn't found in the community in Peking. According to some of them their lapse into pimping, prostitution and drugs was due to the difficulty of earning a living in this exciting, brutal city.

And the Uighurs weren't the only ones. One city-dweller told me frankly, 'Everyone wants to earn money, and it doesn't matter how.' There was something very sinister and disturbing about being approached by young Chinese women dressed in ordinary clothes, white bobby socks and sandals. No fishnets and minis here for the prostitutes. They were the picture of innocence offering themselves for ten to twenty yuan, corrupted by economic pressures brought about by the portrayal of the new obtainable wealth. Selling their bodies for about a fiver a time would bring them within range of undreamt-of luxuries.

I spent my first evening in Shanghai drinking at the Seamen's Mission which was housed in the old Russian consulate. The Polish and German seamen were huddled around the wooden panelled bar room. The atmosphere was leaden, for the women the sailors had picked up hadn't yet mastered the art of adroit arousal: they were as wooden as Dutch dolls. When the bar closed I grabbed my sheet and belongings, and, unable to gain illegal entry to a Uighur-run hotel, went for a walk along the Bund. This splendid promenade runs along the Huangpu River. It is to the Bund that lovers come to walk hand-in-hand; where Chinese visitors and sailors come to marvel at the river traffic, with its small barges and junks that bobble dangerously around the bows of large, modern ocean-going ships; and to have their photos taken, standing in front of the towering stone and marble edifices built along the front by the merchant princes of yesteryear.

It wasn't easy to find a quiet spot to doss down for the night, away from staring eyes and gently embracing lovers. I retraced my steps across Waibaidu Bridge over Suzhou Creek to find shelter by a loading bay where I settled down and wrapped myself in my sheet.

Just after midday on my second day in Shanghai I bumped into a Reuters' correspondent whom I'd met in Peking, in the lobby of the Peace Hotel. This is one of the most famous (and expensive) in all China, and I had simply gone there to use the cloakroom facilities. Anthony asked me where I was staying. I demurred, but he persisted, and it wasn't long before he guessed that I was leading the life of a tramp. Most generously, he asked the reception clerk if I could use the second bed in his room. There was no objection, and not even an extra charge, and so I spent the next two nights luxuriously, even eating in the hotel's penthouse restaurant, where Noël Coward had once sat, enjoying its fabulous views of the river.

Socially, my life began to pick up. I was wined and dined by some of Shanghai's expatriate community at the most élite restaurants – colonial villas restored to their former magnificence and only patronised by foreigners and *gaoji gambu* (high party officials).

Canton is Mecca for all those Chinese who wish to buy the latest imported goods. In the suffocating heat, you are assailed everywhere by the smell of food and rubbish. The pavements are choked with pedestrians and the streets roar to the sound of motorbikes and ring to the sound of bicycles. 'Cool' in Canton is driving around on a motorbike. The police, unwilling to be outdone by these wide boys, pull them up and fine them on the most trivial of charges.

It is said of the Cantonese and their food, 'If it has four legs and it isn't a chair, if it swims underwater and it isn't a submarine, if it flies and it isn't a plane, the Cantonese will eat it.' Streetside stalls prove this with a vengeance. Huge pots of boiled snails are on offer, with lots of restaurants giving prominence to baskets full of frogs and snakes, all destined for the cooker, and ready to be killed, skinned and prepared before one's eyes. I was offered cat as an exotic delicacy.

The British might once have held China in the thrall of an opium-dependent economy. Now, the country seemed to be in a grip of a different kind: the fuel is money. Motorcycles, TVs, videos. Far be it for me to deny anyone such things. I only wish everyone could have them. But underneath all this materialistic scrabbling the very fabric of society is rotting. The fundamental values of the Chinese Revolution are being bent out of shape. The good of those times is almost forgotten, the best glossed over in a tidal wave of consumerism. Gunboat diplomacy is a thing of the past, yet the real reins of power remain in the hands of the developed nations.

On my last nights in China I dreamt of all the Public Security officers I had duped. They were waiting for me as I left the country. In their hands was a list of all the violations I had committed. To them I was just another member of the western countries who saw China as a place of unlimited exploitation: if only we can sell one unit for every Chinese per year . . .

Honda, Levi-Strauss, and Coca Cola are the vanguard of this philosophy.

For myself, I was weary. Confronted by countless scenes of political repression, senseless civil war, revolution, pollution, exploitation, overpopulation and hunger, I longed to return to my art. More than ever I believed that art in its vast variety of forms offers the possibility of transcending the morass which threatens to engulf us. But it is a paradox that amongst all the suffering and misery, the journey had above all restored my faith in humanity, with its countless expressions of friendship crossing so many boundaries.

I longed to work again, to use my hands, and this longing was aggravated by spending my first night in Canton at the art school guesthouse. There is nothing like the bare beams and tall ceilings of a studio to set my mind in full motion. But there were still battles that had to be fought, no matter how much I longed for a studio of my own to retreat to. Meanwhile, ironically again, the Cantonese art students dreamt of making a fortune from their acquired skill – rather than using inspiration and talent to comment on humanity. But they had nothing more than very basic possessions. I had a comfortable home to return to. I cannot judge them too harshly.

I was depressed. My journey was coming to an end. I must not dawdle. I must find a ship. Sea travel, with its timelessness and slow pace, attracted me more and more.

Nothing could have prepared me for the gap that separates Hong Kong from China. Stepping ashore after the short journey was, of course, to enter a totally different world – another planet, even, for here you find, instead of not enough, too much. The island is a concrete jungle dedicated to Mammon, its workers cocooned from the elements in high-rise blocks. Neon blots out the difference between day and night. Even the plants in the overdesigned foyers flourish in recycled air. And outside on the streets the cocoon is preserved. The average pedestrian hears no sound but that fed him by his Walkman. Hundreds of feet above the heads of the men in the street the captains of industry pay homage to the new moralities of success, high performance and optimum returns. Satellite dishes keep the financial centres of the world linked in a continuous twenty-four-hour communion. The slaves of the imperative are highly rewarded, but what is the reward? What you'd expect: Rolls Royces and Ferraris – though they live on an island with not one kilometre of motorway and only a dozen miles of road from end to end – and seeking enjoyment in the cardboard sex of the brothels of Manila hundreds of miles to the south.

Night bathes the island in an ocean of light, from the streets below to the office blocks and planes above. Flashing, nervous, multicoloured lights. The bezazz of nothing. I went up a block. Third floor: ethnic Japanese restaurant; second floor: ethnic Indian.

In such blocks live the green-eyed, grey-suited international financiers and their minions. Brilliant young comets who equate Having with Happiness, Better with More. But China waits on the doorstep, and the seconds are ticking away. Indeed, in the slums that fester below the luxury apartments, where families live in cardboard boxes, one wonders why the Chinese Revolution has taken so long to arrive. But the poor have come to worship at the shrine too. And their reward is copies: copies of what they long for; copies of Armani clothes, Rolex watches, Cartier lighters. And – irony of ironies – Pakistani businessmen in western suits admire *my* clothes – which are precisely the clothes their grandfathers wore every day. West apes east apes west.

News of my travels had reached Hong Kong before my arrival. It was as if I had been sent as a court jester. Some of the most powerful far eastern corporations entertained me royally. The invited guests would initially squirm at my appearance – my eccentricities, my long hair, and my bizarre dress. Fortunately, these could be overlooked in the light of what I had achieved, and (more important to them, perhaps) my good manners. I regaled them with tales of my travels, and although the circumstances weren't perhaps the most appropriate I also tried to break down some of the ignorance, prejudice and bigotry that I encountered and that plague all of us. I knew that for most of them I was nothing more than a performing monkey, but I suppose I had the last laugh, for I had used the name of one of my hosts – a multinational – when claiming to be an executive of the company months earlier in an attempt to get a visa into China from Pakistan.

Much of my time in Hong Kong I spent in Stanley, a small village on the opposite side of the island – away from the skyscrapers. There I lived in Lucy's flat – Lucy being the fiancée of my contact in Peking. I was so bemused by the amount of what was on offer in the supermarkets that I hung around in them like a zombie, mouth agape, and Lucy had to drag me away. I stood mesmerised in front of the shelves of meat and fruit coated in synthetic freshness by the cleverly concealed fluorescent strips of pink light. Rows and rows of shelves stocked with a dazzling array of products. Standing before rakcs of wine I read the labels, each name conjuring up a mistress; full-bodied, sweet and fruity, delicate. How I imagined their fragrance as they tickled my throat. To my horror one day I found myself wandering around the supermarket stuffing my purchases unconsciously into the pockets of my Afghan wasitcoat! Prices were crazy: the price of a paperback would have paid for a week's board in China; the money for a cauliflower would have bought three meals in Pakistan.

Talking of money, mine had finally run out. I was paid handsomely for the briefest of lectures to a group of managing directors, though, and I'd hoped that through it I might have made contact with someone who'd help me to a passage home, but it was not to be. I didn't want to involve myself with the press and the media too much, but now in desperation I published an article with one journal called 'In the Footsteps of Marco Polo', in a bid to find a shipping company willing to take me home. Again, I had no luck. I was driven to contacting the Churchill Trust for more funds. I even had to call them reverse-charge. The ebullient Director-General, Sir Richard Vickers, chatted away for so long that I wondered if his secretary had failed to tell him that he was paying for the call. There was no problem about another advance, and he left me with a cheery 'Best of luck! See you soon?' His question was well justified, since it had taken me seventeen months so far to fulfil a three-month bursary.

I had to return home. And yet I seemed to be pipped at the last post. I couldn't hitch a lift from anyone. Finally I decided to take direct action. I found out the names of the managing directors of the shipping agencies. Once outside the office of the first one I phoned him to make sure he was at his desk. But of course I didn't have an appointment. I entered the office block and found my way to the correct floor. I was guided across a vast open-plan office by two pretty secretaries – it was still so odd to see Chinese women wearing make-up – to a pair of doors in a corner, in front of which was a desk where another secretary sat. She was very pretty too.

'Mr Ho's office, please,' I said, wondering which door was his.

'Have you an appointment?'

'Not exactly . . .'

'Well –'

'I'd like to see him if he's free. Or is he in a meeting? On the phone, maybe?'

She was confused by my diatribe. I edged past her and aimed for one of the doors.

'Mr Ho? Please forgive me, I won't take a moment of your time . . .'

The secretary was right behind me but she was too late to stop me. At least I'd chosen the right door.

'It's all right,' Mr Ho told her.

He gave me two minutes. I told him all about my journey and about my plight. He agreed to help me, but told me that it was no longer possible for a traveller to work his passage – nor do modern cargo ships accept fare-paying passengers. I had no money, and all I could offer was the small recompense of a mention for the shipping company in any book that I might write.

'I'll do what I can,' said Mr Ho.

A week later he phoned me at Lucy's.

'I think they've taken the bait,' he told me excitedly.

'Who?'

'OCL.'

I knew who OCL were, because every morning I scanned the shipping pages of the *South China Morning Post*. Overseas Containers Ltd was a British registered company. The latest copy of the paper told me that it had two ships under way: MV *Liverpool Bay* was leaving soon for Singapore and Port Klang *en route* to Southampton – the ship wasn't due to arrive in Hong Kong for

410

another three days. But the *Kowloon Bay* was leaving on 17 August. She was a massive container ship, and OCL were willing to take me home on her.

COMING HOME

The hardest part of the journey had begun. I had to put everything I had seen and felt into words. It was to take me almost as long to achieve this task as the journey itself. Worst of all was the fear that I might harm someone in the process. That nightmare had begun soon after my return home, with the news that the head of the Sino-Pakistan Trade Mission had been sacked because he had unwittingly helped me. One of my main tasks would have to be to protect the identities of those who had helped me. Added to that, I wanted to paint with words – and I wanted to paint a Caravaggio: every apple its pitted, rotting or fresh skin depicted in minute detail. I had kept a journal throughout most of my travels, and now it was half a million words long – woefully inadequate words for a book, but enough to jog my memory. The book had to be factual, too, and I didn't want to play too central a role in it myself. But my agent and my publisher wanted to know my feelings about my experiences. I wondered who could possibly be interested in them, but in time I realised that I could only write about what I had done in the light of why I had done it, which immediately made it personal. It had been a journey with a public intent – to show that frontiers should not separate peoples. But it was also, inevitably, a journey of private self-discovery.

On board the *Kowloon Bay*, I led a cloistered life to begin with, bringing the untidy mass of my journals up-to-date and into some kind of order. My isolation was partly forced on me, for the British crew viewed my appearance with suspicion and even disdain. To be fair to them, I did look like a tramp, and I don't blame them for wondering what on earth they'd taken on board. But as news of my adventures filtered through to them, the officers overcame their prejudices.

'Is it true that you've just walked from London to Peking?' one of them finally asked me. He was almost friendly.

My appearance wasn't the only thing that was against me. Rumours abounded on the ship, and they centred on me, as the only stranger aboard. What's more, as a guest of the company, I'd been given the owner's cabin, which was less of a cabin than a private suite, with a double bedroom, a living room and a bathroom. There was even a phone in each room. The ship was very luxurious for a crew of 32.

'Are you related to Kerry St Johnston?' asked the cabin steward.

'No, Martin,' I answered. 'I've never heard of him.'

'I don't clean the rooms of supernumeraries,' he pointed out, aggressively.

'OK. I don't see why you should, anyway. Tell me where to find a mop and a duster, and I'll do it myself.'

This took him completely off guard. 'Oh,' he said.

'Who is Kerry St Johnston?' I asked.

'I was told you were related to him,' said Martin lamely. He went on to explain that there was a rumour going around on board that I was the chairman's cousin. Now he found that I wasn't he became much friendlier – he simply hadn't wanted to be conned into cleaning my cabin, he explained. In the end we split the 'housework' between us. I was grateful for this incident, because it served to break the ice between the crew and me.

'You're all right,' one of them said to me later. 'We had one director's son on another ship. Right toffee-nosed bastard, he was. So we tarred and feathered him and tied him to the mast aft.'

Our first port of call was Singapore. Modern container ships are so streamlined in their operations that they rarely stop over for more than 24 hours, and so the crew had to cram its pleasures into a very tight schedule. We were whisked to Bugis Street where large rats juggled in and out of sewers and drain pipes, and the skyscrapers loomed overhead. Bugis Street is given over to the traditional shore-time activities of sailors – booze and women – but with a twist: the best pair of legs on the block belonged to Sally East – who was not only originally from Fulham, but who had also been a man. She had long legs, long dark hair, small proud breasts, and a dress no longer than a shirt. But there were real girls too – if real is the right word. One sent me a message scrawled on a bit of cigarette packet: 'Hi darling! Kiss my ass.' And noticing my Arab appearance another crooned,

'Al Hamid, fuckie-fuckie?' The crew thought this was great. We all drank too much beer. Melissa, the girl nestling on my lap with the tip of her tongue in my ear, drew unspeakable scenes. The girls made you believe they lusted after you with the passion of someone who had emerged from a convent, starved of carnal pleasures after years of abstinence.

The ship left to sail on through the dazzling blue waters east of Sumatra and on south of Sri Lanka across the Indian Ocean, and so through the Gulf of Aden and the Red Sea to Suez. In the danger zone of the Red Sea I learnt from one of the officers that the *Kowloon Bay* was built in such a way that she could be sealed hermetically to prevent contamination by nuclear fallout in the wake of an atomic war.

We waited at the mouth of the canal to join a convoy of ships passing through it at dawn. In the meantime we locked up our personal belongings against the invasion of hawkers, local boatmen and security guards who boarded us for the night. Most corrupt and inept of all these, however, were the pilots, each of whom demanded a 'tip' of a bottle of Scotch and two hundred cigarettes, however short their tour of duty was with us – one stayed exactly 2 minutes and 55 seconds. As for doing their job properly, we'd have been better off without them:

'Course 323,' one pilot ordered the helmsman.

'323 it is,' he acknowledged.

There was a pause. The canal is busy, and concentration must be intense if accidents are to be avoided.

'323,' said the pilot.

'We're already steering 323,' said the helmsman, confused.

'324!' retorted the pilot, like a teacher rebuking a child who's spoken out of turn. But the most alarming incident came just as we were leaving the canal. The Swedish car carrier in front of us, the first in our convoy of thirteen, came to a halt. Our pilot didn't know what to do.

'My God, this is dangerous!' he burbled. Then he said, 'Reduce speed to a minimum.'

We all looked at each other. Did he mean 'Slow Ahead', 'Stop Engines', or what?

We were still heading steadily towards the stern of the Swedish ship.

'Steer to port,' quavered the pilot.

Captain Railton, forever the quiet but cool, authoritative master, issued the order: 'Stop all engines.'

'Stop all engines,' came the echoed confirmation from the engine room.

Despite the efforts of the pilots, we reached the Mediterranean safely. For the first time in eighteen months I felt that I was close to reaching home.

On my return to England I led a monastic existence, working non-stop on this book except for two short breaks. Penniless, I returned to my parents' home to live, although I felt something of a burden to them. However I found my return home was as unsettling as travelling, as the apparent security of the English countryside contrasted vividly with the 'flood' of memories of the journey which pass before my eyes as I write. Although my convictions remain intact, I find myself caught between two worlds: I have become a stranger to my previous world but at the same time remain an outsider in those countries which I journeyed through.

I spent a lot of time with my former girlfriend Noo. I was restless, and discontented, but I took comfort in Noo's company. She is one of the few people who can understand my predicament, perhaps because she has shared one journey with me, and because her experiences of life are similar to my own. For others, I must sometimes make life difficult. It's hard for me to sit down to Sunday lunch, at table, with the place settings neatly laid. And now, even more than in the past, I find it hard to join in the agreeable small-talk of dinner table conversation. But I am lucky in my surroundings. My parents live deep in the Wiltshire countryside and my bedroom overlooks rolling hills. Here, I swim, I walk, and I write.

There are the occasional unnerving moments. The first sound of a helicopter or a jet causes my heart to miss a beat. The thumping sound of rotor blades brings all the horrors of Afghanistan flooding back. I think the greatest shock was going out jogging at dawn once. Again an image was stirred by the sound of a jet overhead. Half of

Britain was asleep, and yet in Hauze Kerbas everyone would be out in the dirt road waiting, waiting for the first bombing raid.

The journey brought me many friends, and still now, a year and more since my return, I correspond with many of them. I receive news from mujahedeen, they are waiting for a copy of the book; and the last I heard of Ismail Khan, several hundred of his mujahedeen remain besieged in Hauze Kerbas surrounded by 20,000 Afghan government and Soviet soldiers.

Perhaps that is not my battle any more. I want to return to painting; I want to discuss work with art students; and I want to explore the great possibilities that I have become aware of in writing. There is a part of me that would like to try acting; and there is certainly a part of me that would like to travel again. The vast world is forever calling.

Why have I said all this? Probably just to set the record straight. I have yet to feel any sense of accomplishment. The most important thing for me is the knowledge that I have tried my best, and attempted to stick to my principles and retain my integrity. What I brought back, and what I want to communicate, is the greatest reward travel can give you: understanding. I got home shortly after there had been severe riots in Birmingham. But the rioters had much in common with many of the people I had met in the Third World. People with a stake in society, with property, don't riot. It is those who have nothing that do, and they do so not out of envy, or irresponsibility, but out of frustration. Revolution is born of a poverty which does not allow the sharing of material wealth. My journey has taught me that there can be misery and deprivation in the most beautiful of settings. I hope that now I can see beyond what is picturesque to deeper understanding. And my journey has taught me something else: that we are all the same under the skin, and under the sun.

Sadly, even the superficial differences between us that make travel worthwhile are disappearing in the face of western cultural domination. I won my Fellowship to follow ancient trade routes. The rich variety and colour of life along those routes continues – but only just. And it will go under forever unless the nations of the east can compete on equal terms not only in trade, but in ideas. Why should they think that what comes from the west is automatically best? Why should they ape us rather than be true to their own values?

I arrived in Southampton on 10 September 1985, dressed in my Afghan clothes. The crew of the *Kowloon Bay* had told me that I'd find things difficult dressed as I was, but I hadn't taken them seriously. They'd ordered a taxi to take me from the dock to the station. The cabbie neglected to put his meter on, until I asked him to in a broad cockney accent which made him jump. Then he was all apologies.

The train journey wasn't a problem. In fact, it was even comfortable, because although my carriage was crowded I was left alone with four empty seats around me – and it wasn't as if I hadn't made full use of my bathroom aboard the *Kowloon Bay*. In London, however, things really began to tighten up. Not one taxi stopped for me, so that in the end I was obliged to go to my stepfather's place of work and get him to flag one down.

'Why won't anyone stop for me?' I asked the cabbie as soon as we'd set off.

'Can't be too careful these days, mate.'

'Would you have stopped for me if I'd been alone?'

'Yes, but then I recognise your costume. I was in Afghanistan in the sixties. Got any smoke?' It was a question I was asked many times.

I suppose I ought to have abandoned my Afghan clothes, but I found wearing them in London most educational. Everywhere I went I was either shunned or regarded with undisguised suspicion. But the biggest shock came on my second day back. I was walking down an empty John Islip Street in Westminster when suddenly I heard the sound of a van approaching me from behind. I knew it was a van because I used to drive one and the engine has an unmistakable sound. It slowed slightly as it drew level with me. A red Post Office van. The man in the passenger seat was sliding his door open. He was looking at me. The look wasn't friendly.

'You fucking nignog,' he yelled. Then the van sped off.

I was home.

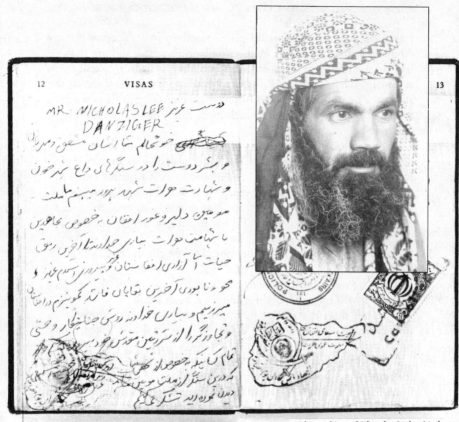

Photo of Ismail Khan by Stefan Lindgren

Translation of Ismail Khan's note in Nick Danziger's passport

My dear friend, Mr Nicholas Lee Danziger,

I am glad to see you, a warm-hearted, kindly and humanitarian person in the fiery trenches of the City of Blood and Martyrdom, Herat, breeding-ground of martyrs. We, the nation of the courageous and proud Afghan Faithful [i.e. Muslims], in particular the brave Holy Warriors of Herat, with God's help will fight to the last breath until the liberation of our beloved Afghanistan, the victory of our beloved Islam and the elimination and destruction of the last corrupt remnants of Communism in Afghanistan; and, with God's help, we will expel the criminal and savage Russian aggressors from our sacred land. We thank all those people, and especially yourself, who have visited the Nation of the Faithful in this battlefield.

Index

INDEX

Afghanistan 24–5, 34, 71, 100, 119, 389
  Afghan greetings 153
  Afghan 'tummy' 157, 161, 162–3, 166, 171–2
  'Afghani novalgin' powder 157
  army defectors 132–3
  author's attempt to gain Chinese help for 389–90
  bandits 140
  contempt for Russians 138
  deaths in Soviet-Afghan war 101
  demographic make-up 103, 114
  disappointment with West 138
  dress 115, 116, 131
  French medical teams 25, 193
  generosity of nomads 150
  government militia 139
  guerrillas' weapons 129–30
  Halq (People's) party 139
  Harakat resistance groups 139, 164, 165, 169, 170
  Hesbi resistance groups 81, 95, 139, 160, 165, 166
  Jabhe resistance group 175, 176
  Jamiat-i-Islami resistance group 81, 82, 95, 100, 101, 103, 104, 107, 108, 131, 139, 160, 164, 166, 169, 185
  KHAD secret police 132, 133
  'komiteh' groups 128, 129, 131, 133, 135, 136, 140, 152, 160, 163
  life with guerrillas 136–8
  mujahedeen 103–4, 108n, 109, 110, 111, 117, 119, 123, 128, 129, 136–40 *passim*, 144–7 *passim*, 149, 151–64 *passim*, 169, 170, 171, 174–7 *passim*, 185, 186, 198
  pancake-like bread 164, 165
  Parcham (Red Flag) party 139
  prayers 137, 162, 178
  refugees from 101
  Shindand Soviet base 22, 132
  Soviet air strikes 126–7, 128–9, 134–5, 142, 151, 168–9, 171
  Soviet carpet bombing 131
  Soviet tanks 144, 179
  Soviet use of Afghan vanguard 140
  Symorgh jeeps 170, 171, 172, 176
  travelling with guerrillas 123, 144–5, 156–81

turbans 111
Western satisfaction at Soviet entanglement in 198
Aide Médicale 25
Aksu, China 241, 253
Aleppo, Syria 36–8
  citadel 37
  night life 37–8
Ali, Imam 78, 80
Al Paihissar, Afghanistan 158, 159
Anamur, Turkey 31
Ani, Turkey 41
Antiochus I, King of Commagene: funerary sanctuary 32
Assad, Pres., of Syria 36
Ataturk, Kemal 30
Aziz, Dr 102, 103, 116

Batura Glacier, Pakistan 210
BBC Persian Service 112, 138
BBC Urdu Service 208
Bezeklik, China: Buddhist caves 287–90 *passim*
Bhutan 330, 331
  smugglers 331
Brahmaputra River 355
Buddha-Sakyamuni 7, 311, 317
  statue in Lhasa 311–12
Buddhism 311, 316–17, 364
  Gelukpa sect 317
  Kahgyur codex 363
  mantra 310, 316, 356
Bulgaria 27
  trucking concerns in Iran 59

Camels 253–6 *passim*
Canton, 406–7
Cappadocia 32–4
  extinct volcanoes 33
  troglodyte dwellings 33–4
Central America 2
  Mayan civilisation 1
Chaman, Pakistan 181, 185
Chamdo, Tibet 360–1
Charchan, China 263, 264
Charkhlik, China 264, 265–6
Chashma Azizan, Afghanistan 157, 158
Chengdu, China 373–4, 375
  Mao's statue 373

Nick Danziger was born in 1958 of an American father and an English mother. After schooldays in Switzerland he went to Chelsea Art School, later becoming a visiting lecturer at art schools and universities and holding one-man exhibitions of his work in London and New York. He has travelled extensively in South and Central America, and in 1982 was awarded a Winston Churchill Memorial Trust Fellowship to follow ancient trade-routes. (He set off in 1984.) He is a Fellow of the Royal Geographical Society.